VOLUME FIFTY FIVE

ADVANCES IN CHILD DEVELOPMENT AND BEHAVIOR

Studying the Perception-Action System as a Model System for Understanding Development

ADVANCES IN CHILD DEVELOPMENT AND BEHAVIOR

Series Editor

JANETTE B. BENSON
Department of Psychology,
University of Denver,
Denver, CO, United States

VOLUME FIFTY FIVE

ADVANCES IN CHILD DEVELOPMENT AND BEHAVIOR

Studying the Perception-Action System as a Model System for Understanding Development

Edited by

JODIE M. PLUMERT

Department of Psychological and Brain Sciences
The University of Iowa
Iowa City, IA, United States

ELSEVIER

ACADEMIC PRESS

An imprint of Elsevier

Academic Press is an imprint of Elsevier
125 London Wall, London EC2Y 5AS, United Kingdom
525 B Street, Suite 1650, San Diego, CA 92101, United States
50 Hampshire Street, 5th Floor, Cambridge, MA 02139, United States
The Boulevard, Langford Lane, Kidlington, Oxford OX5 1GB, United Kingdom

First edition 2018

ISBN: 978-0-12-814763-4
ISSN: 0065-2407

Publisher: Zoe Kruze
Acquisition Editor: Sam Mahfoudh
Editorial Project Manager: Andrea Gallego Ortiz
Production Project Manager: Vignesh Tamil
Cover Designer: Christain J. Bilbow

Typeset by TNQ Technologies

CONTENTS

CONTRIBUTORS

Jane E. Clark
Department of Kinesiology, University of Maryland, College Park, MD, United States

Matthew Clark
Department of Psychology, The University of Tennessee, Knoxville, TN, United States

John P. Connell
Department of Psychology, The University of Tennessee, Knoxville, TN, United States

Daniela Corbetta
Department of Psychology, The University of Tennessee, Knoxville, TN, United States

Abigail DiMercurio
Department of Psychology, The University of Tennessee, Knoxville, TN, United States

Nicholas E. Fears
Department of Psychology, Tulane University, New Orleans, LA, United States

Matthew J. Jiang
Department of Psychology, University of Wisconsin, Madison, WI, United States

Wendy P. Jung
Department of Psychology, Tulane University, New Orleans, LA, United States

Joseph K. Kearney
Department of Computer Science, The University of Iowa, Iowa City, IA, United States

Jeffrey J. Lockman
Department of Psychology, Tulane University, New Orleans, LA, United States

Karl M. Newell
Department of Kinesiology, University of Georgia, Athens, GA, United States

Jodie M. Plumert
Department of Psychological and Brain Sciences, The University of Iowa, Iowa City, IA, United States

Kerstin Rosander
Department of Psychology, Uppsala University, Uppsala, Sweden

Karl S. Rosengren
Department of Psychology, University of Wisconsin, Madison, WI, United States

Peter M. Vishton
Department of Psychological Sciences, College of William & Mary, Williamsburg, VA, United States

Claes von Hofsten
Department of Psychology, Uppsala University, Uppsala, Sweden

Michael G. Wade
School of Kinesiology, University of Minnesota, Minneapolis, MN, United States

Jill Whitall
Department of Physical Therapy & Rehabilitation Science, University of Maryland, Baltimore, MD, United States; University of Southampton, Southampton, United Kingdom

Rebecca F. Wiener
Department of Psychology, The University of Tennessee, Knoxville, TN, United States

PREFACE

Perceiving and acting are part of a unified system that forms the basis for adaptive (and sometimes nonadaptive) functioning in the world. Yet these two parts of the developing perception–action system are often studied separately. A key question for the field is understanding how parts of the system work together as infants and children interact with the physical and social world. My original intent when I accepted the invitation to guest edit this volume was to move in this direction by showcasing research on the development of the perception–action system. As I started reading the chapters, however, it became clear that the authors were bringing together perception, action, and *cognition* to better understand developmental change. For example, Peter Vishton asks why infants seem to know different things about the world when presented with looking versus reaching tasks, and Matthew Jiang and Karl Rosengren consider how young children's cognitive development influences their learning of what the environment affords for action. By broadening the scope of the developing perception–action system to include cognition, the authors in this volume have provided a richer understanding of how perceiving, acting, and thinking work together in both typical and atypical development. Below, I briefly overview each chapter and highlight how the work presented on the developing perception–action–cognition system serves as a model for understanding development more broadly.

The chapter by Daniela Corbetta, Abigail DiMercurio, Rebecca Wiener, John Connell, and Matthew Clark focuses on how repeated cycles of perception and action lead to the development of new skills in infancy. Along with several other authors in this volume, Corbetta and colleagues begin by noting the reciprocal relations between perception and action – perception informs action and action informs perception. Such perception–action loops provide the foundation for the learning of new skills through the embedded processes of exploration (trying out different actions) and selection (reproducing actions that work). Over time, skills become more finely tuned to goals as infants use action to generate perceptual feedback and use feedback to guide further action. They illustrate these perception–action loops in the context of how infants learn to reach for objects, discover the properties of objects, learn to use tools effectively, and acquire names for objects. At a deeper level, this work serves as a model for understanding the active role young organisms play in generating and using feedback from their own actions to guide learning about the world.

The chapter by Jeffrey Lockman, Nicholas Fears, and Wendy Jung looks at the problem of how young children learn to fit objects into apertures. Object fitting underlies many of our interactions with everyday objects and tools, from inserting keys into locks to lacing up shoes. The chapter begins with an interesting historical overview of the roles that object fitting and form boards played in the education and assessment of young children. These endeavors largely focused on what children could do at a given age (e.g., how many shapes or which shapes children could fit into matching apertures). Far less attention has been paid to how children of different ages approach the problem of fitting objects into apertures. Lockman and his colleagues take a process-based approach to understanding the development of object fitting, first discussing how the development of object fitting is built from advances in shape perception, physical knowledge, and motor behavior, and then how young children learn to use action to coordinate multiple reference frames (i.e., rotating and translating the object so that the object and aperture reference frames align correctly). A key component of this reference frame coordination process is figuring out how to gain prospective control over the object fitting action. Lockman and his colleagues illustrate how understanding the development of object fitting requires thinking about how all components of the system work together in the moment. As such, this work is a beautiful example of the integration of the perception–action–cognition system in real time.

The chapter by Claes von Hofsten and Kerstin Rosander broadly considers the role of the developing sensorimotor system in extracting knowledge about the world, with a specific focus on how infants gain prospective control over their actions. They begin by discussing the origins of perception, action, and cognition in early infancy and then proceed to discuss why predictive control is important in each domain. As they note, a key problem faced by all developing organisms is coordinating behavior with on-going events without lagging behind. Given a highly dynamic world in which events happen prior to sensory feedback, infants must learn to anticipate what is going to happen next and use this information to guide their actions. von Hoftsten and Rosander illustrate how predictive control develops as infants begin to interact with objects, from visually tracking and manually intercepting moving objects to fitting objects into apertures. For example, by 8 weeks of age, infants exhibit smooth pursuit in their eye movements when visually tracking a moving object. By 18 weeks of age, infants direct their reaches ahead of the interception point when attempting to catch a moving object. Both of these behaviors require the system to operate in a proactive rather than reactive manner. von Hofsten and Rosander end their chapter by discussing the importance of exploration for learning about the physical world and for learning about self- and other-produced actions. Such learning feeds into the perception–action–cognition system, making it possible for infants to plan their actions to meet their goals. By examining predictive control in the context of the developing sensorimotor system, von Hofsten and Rosander provide a model for understanding why predictive control is critical in all domains of functioning.

The chapter by Peter Vishton considers why studies of infant looking and reaching often produce divergent results about infant perception and cognition. The most typical pattern is to find more adult-like perception and cognition in studies of looking compared to reaching. Other studies indicate that looking and reaching behaviors follow different courses of development, rather than reaching behavior simply lagging behind looking behavior. To understand this phenomenon, Vishton reviews his own work on adult reaching, which shows opposite patterns of responding to visual illusions when people choose which of two disks is larger by making a verbal versus a grasping response. Even though they were viewing the same disks, preparing to reach for the disks changed how people perceived them. Vishton proposes that infants also attend to different information when looking and reaching, resulting in different "answers" to the problems presented to them. For example, infants respond to shape and color information specifying an object boundary in a reaching task, whereas they respond to motion information specifying an object boundary in a looking task. This way of thinking about looking and reaching studies challenges the notion that these behaviors are simply "measures" of infant knowledge. Rather, looking and reaching actions are part of complex systems that have their own neural substrates and environmental constraints. A general consequence of this view is that knowledge is not a static representation in the head, but the outcome of an emergent process that brings together many aspects of perceptual, cognitive, and motor functioning.

The chapter by Matthew Jiang and Karl Rosengren focuses on the errors that infants and children (and adults) sometimes make when acting on objects. For example, infants sometimes attempt to grasp objects in highly realistic photos and young children sometimes try to fit themselves into miniature replicas of objects. Under certain task demands, even adults will mistakenly try to pick up an object in a photo. Jiang and Rosengren argue that these errors result from a failure to inhibit an action plan that is activated by a conceptual representation of an object or event. Typically, such action plans are highly associated with that object or event. Less well-developed inhibitory control in young children make such errors more likely than in older children and adults. Individual differences in inhibitory control may make some children more susceptible to action errors as well. More generally, Jiang and Rosengren argue that behavior is multiply determined, arising in the moment out of an interaction of environmental, individual, and task constraints. However, the child's intended action serves to organize the behavior in the moment. For example, without the goal of sitting, the child would not make the error of attempting to sit in a miniature chair. Although such errors are rare, they require explanation for a full accounting of the development of the perception–action system. This chapter beautifully illustrates how children's action errors reveal the ways in which conceptual understanding of the world is woven into the perception–action system.

The chapter written by Jodie Plumert (me) and Joseph Kearney summarizes our program of research on how children and adults perceive and act on dynamic affordances, or possibilities for action that change over time. Our goal is to bridge the divide between basic and applied research by using road crossing as a model system for studying how children's ability to perceive and act on dynamic affordances undergoes change with age and experience. The basic task is for participants to cross virtual roads with continuous traffic either on foot or on a bicycle. This work has consistently shown that children often choose the same size gaps as adults, but time for their entry into those gaps less tightly than adults. As a result, children typically end up with less time to spare than adults when they clear the path of the vehicles. Improvement in movement timing occurs gradually over development, indicating the perception–action system undergoes continuous change well into adolescence. A key part of this development is gaining prospective control over movement—the pedestrian or bicyclist must anticipate the arrival of the car so as not to enter the roadway too soon or too late. As in other areas of development (e.g., face perception, word recognition), this kind of gradual developmental change appears critical for the fine-tuning of the system. More generally, this work underscores the fact that even perceptual–motor skills take a surprisingly long time to develop.

The chapter by Karl Newell and Michael Wade considers how the development of perceptual–motor skills is tied to changes in body scale that occur with physical growth. The central idea is that the timescale of physical growth is related to the timescale of skill acquisition via the mechanical constraints imposed by changes in body scale. For example, changes in the limb length lead to changes in the moment of inertia (i.e., resistance to acceleration in movement). Muscle strength also increases as limbs grow, although strength lags behind increases in height and weight. The developing perceptual–motor system must continually adapt to these changing mechanical constraints on movement, which often occur at different rates for different limb segments. Such changes are particularly notable during the growth spurts in infancy and adolescence and pose even greater challenges for children who are overweight. Newell and Wade also consider another perspective on body scaling—how children learn to scale their actions to opportunities for action present in the environment (i.e., affordances). The ecological approach to perception and action emphasizes the fit between the organism and the environment. For example, young children's grip configurations are dependent on the ratio of body scale (hand length) to object size, and infants vary their grip depending on whether the goal is to mouth the object or shift its base of location. Newell and Wade conclude their chapter by discussing the idea of scaling the size of playground and sports equipment to children's size and skill as a means of enhancing learning and safety. Underlying the rich array of research presented in this chapter is the key concept of actions emerging from relations involving the body, the environment, and the task.

The chapter by Jill Whitall and Jane Clark uses a perception–action framework to understand both typical and atypical motor development. Although there is a long history of studying movement independent of perception, Whitall and Clark view perception and action as reciprocally related parts of a system. The challenge for this system is to control a multisegmented body to achieve desired goals in an ever-changing environment. They illustrate the utility of this approach for understanding motor development by describing their program of research on the development of postural control, rhythmic interlimb coordination, and goal-directed reaching and drawing. Their research strategy is to perturb the perceptual system by removing or enhancing a source of information and then to measure the effects of this change on the motor system. They study both typically developing children and children with Developmental Coordination Disorder (DCD), along with adults. Children with DCD are both late in developing motor skills and exhibit motor difficulties that interfere with daily life. Onset of motor difficulties occurs early in development and cannot be explained by other factors such as intellectual delay or visual impairment. In an elegant series of experiments, Whitall and Clark show that typically developing children often respond to perturbations differently at different ages, and that children with DCD often respond to perturbations differently than their typically developing counterparts. By studying how the developing system adjusts motor actions in response to degraded or enhanced perceptual information, this program of research provides important insights into the mapping between perception and action and points to possible interventions when perceptual–motor development goes awry.

I want to end my comments by acknowledging the profound impact of Herbert L. Pick, Jr. on the research reported and ideas expressed in this volume. Most if not all of the contributors to this volume were influenced by Herb Pick in some way, either as his students or colleagues. I remember telling Herb about the driving simulation research at the University of Iowa on one of his visits to Iowa. He suggested that I should look into getting a bicycling simulator, which led me directly to my long-time computer science collaborator, Joe Kearney. Unbeknownst to me at the time, Joe had done his undergraduate honors thesis with Herb at the University of Minnesota, so it's no surprise that he enthusiastically agreed to collaborate on the bicycling simulator project. Thanks to Herb, we embarked on a long and productive line of research on using virtual environments to study child pedestrian and cyclist road crossing, much of which is reported in our chapter. I am sure other contributors to this volume have their own stories to tell about how a conversation with Herb sparked a great research idea. We will always be indebted to him for his openness to new ideas and love of research.

Jodie M. Plumert

CHAPTER ONE

How Perception and Action Fosters Exploration and Selection in Infant Skill Acquisition

Daniela Corbetta[1], Abigail DiMercurio, Rebecca F. Wiener, John P. Connell and Matthew Clark
Department of Psychology, The University of Tennessee, Knoxville, TN, United States
[1]Corresponding author: E-mail: dcorbett@utk.edu

Contents

Abstract

In this chapter, we discuss how perception and action are intimately linked to the processes of exploration and selection. Exploration, which we define as trying several variations of the behavior, and selection, which involves attempting to reproduce the behaviors that work, are essential for learning about the environment, discovering the properties of objects, and for acquiring skills in relation to goals. Exploration and selection happen in the moment and over time as behaviors are repeated, hence leading to their fine-tuning to the goal. We illustrate this time-dependent developmental process using several examples from infants reaching for objects, to discovering object properties, to learning about the functionality of tool use, and

Advances in Child Development and Behavior, Volume 55
ISSN 0065-2407
https://doi.org/10.1016/bs.acdb.2018.04.001

even to word learning. As we present those examples, we introduce a more detailed perception–action loop to illustrate those moment-to-moment behaviors and show how they contribute to the acquisition of perceptual, motor, and cognitive skills in infancy.

1. INTRODUCTION

Interacting with our environment is essential to our everyday life. Perception and action play a major role in those daily exchanges. While perception informs our actions, actions also inform our perception. These two vital components of our everyday activities interact continuously, moment-by-moment, as we carry on a conversation, work on our computer, drive our car, cook dinner, and so on. In fact, perceiving and acting are so deeply ingrained in our every moment that in most daily tasks they unfold seamlessly as a natural, well-coordinated, and coherent process. In many day-to-day activities, fluent exchanges between perception and action occur in familiar environments with well-practiced tasks, where uncertainty about the action outcome is minimal. In those situations, we are familiar with the parameters of the task, we know the environment, we know what to look for, we know how to act, and in most cases, we know how to respond to potential unpredictable events. For those daily, highly practiced skills, our mind and our body are usually in tune with the intended goal of the task.

Such an in-tune process between the intended goal and perceiving and acting, however, is not always perfect, particularly in the case of learning a new task. Novice learners may not pick the relevant perceptual cues to achieve a goal; they may not be familiar with all the properties of the task context or object being manipulated; and they may have to figure out how to use their limbs and body in the specific context to achieve the intended goal. The aim of this chapter is to address these learning issues in relation to the processes of perception and action in the acquisition of skills. We focus on early development because infants are constantly facing new behavioral challenges, as they interact with their environment. Indeed, infants display one of the fastest rates of behavioral growth. In the first 2 years of life alone, they generate more new forms of behavior than at any other time in development. With such rapid development, adapting, updating, and revising skills moment-by-moment to tune them to new emerging goals is critical, particularly as new experiences and body changes accumulate at a fast rate.

In this chapter, we discuss how perception and action and the embedded processes of exploration (trying different variations of the behavior) and selection (reproducing what works) play a primary role in this rapid transition in skills. Perception and action not only are essential to ensure the flow of exchanges between an actor and its environment, but also provide the fundamental mechanism by which the discovery and formation of new behaviors occur. Via repeated cycles of perception and action, new skills form, existing behaviors are updated and refined, and the diversification of behavior unfolds as skills are applied to an increasing number of situations. We argue that this repeating cycle of perception and action and the processes of exploration and selection embedded within provide meaningful experiences to create valuable and effective interactions within the environment, which ultimately will lead to tuning our interactions more closely to our intended goals. Perception and action and exploration and selection are important for the discovery of one's own action capabilities, for the discovery of actions' outcomes on the physical world, and for the provision of unique learning opportunities not only for acquiring knowledge about the world, but also for learning how to better act within it in the moment. This process involves a constant mapping between perception and action, in relation to the features of the environment and the goal to be attained.

Many influential developmental psychologists (Gibson, 1988, 2000, 2003; Piaget, 1936/1952; Thelen, 1990, 2000) have already emphasized the critical role of perception and action for development and learning. We do not pretend to reinvent the wheel. Our contribution to this topic, however, will be to build on what our predecessors have proposed to illustrate at a deeper level, how the microstructure and time dynamics of the perception—action loop can help us better understand the moment-by-moment process of infant learning. In this chapter, we argue that acquiring new skills is about tuning perception and action in relation to the goal of the task. This involves discovering the properties of the objects via perception and action (i.e., vision, touch, hearing, proprioception), and it is about learning the properties of our own actions and their outcome to regulate the movement successfully and meet the requirements of the intended goal. In the following sections, we begin by discussing how perception can initially provide important foundations for identifying basic regularities in the world; next, however, we stress the importance of action for learning and development. We illustrate our approach using a number of examples from our research. Specifically, we demonstrate via work performed in our laboratory how perception and action and exploration and selection contribute to object and action discovery in the contexts of object manipulation, tool use, and even word learning.

2. PERCEPTION: A VALUABLE TOOL FOR EXTRACTING REGULARITIES FROM THE SURROUNDING WORLD

Newborns come into the world with limited experience about their bodies. They also have extremely limited knowledge about all the "things" and people that fill their environments. At birth, newborns have some level of sensorimotor experience that has been acquired in the womb. The senses of taste, smell, hearing, touch, and even vision provide the newborns with the basic perceptual means needed to ensure their immediate connections with the world. However, how these initial sensory experiences and connections with the world contribute to the creation of "meaning" of the world is a long process that is deeply embedded in the child's history of perception and action (Gibson, 1991; Piaget, 1936/1952; Thelen, 2000; Thelen & Smith, 1994).

Infant research has made huge strides toward understanding the development of infant perception, particularly visual perception. For example, we know that from birth, infants respond to overt features of a scene (i.e., high light contrasts, salience, motion) (Johnson, 2011; Slater, 1995, 1998). Within a few months, they begin to scan their environment (Bronson, 1990) and learn to control their head and eye movements to track objects in space (Aslin, 1981). They also assemble elements of a scene to form complete representations of objects (Johnson, 2004; Johnson, Davidow, Hall-Haro, & Frank, 2008), and they learn to detect objects' inner and global features (Colombo, 2001). Furthermore, they differentiate object features (e.g., Cohen & Younger, 1984), perceive object distance (Slater, Mattock, & Brown, 1990), and even integrate figure and ground to identify objects and their location in space based on background depth cues (Guan & Corbetta, 2012; Yonas, Elieff, & Arterberry, 2002).

Explanations used to account for those increasing visual capacities have emphasized both the rapid maturation of the visual system (i.e., Bronson, 1974; Colombo, 2001; Johnson, 1990), as well as infants' exceptional ability to learn from their visual experience and detect regularities within their environment (Bulf, Johnson, & Valenza, 2011; Haith, Hazan, & Goodman, 1988). Changes in perceptual cues, the number of elements on a scene, and prior looking history have all been shown to dictate where infants look and how they allocate visual attention (Bogartz, Shinskey, & Schilling, 2000; Kidd, Piantadosi, & Aslin, 2012; Schöner & Thelen, 2006). Statistical learning has emerged as a domain-general learning mechanism for identifying and extracting information from the complex world (Saffran & Thiessen, 2007). Statistical learning focuses on the ability of young perceivers to discover the underlying regularities (or high transitional probabilities) that combine a defined subset of elements within a complex visual or auditory scene. Statistical learning has been extensively applied not only to language acquisition (i.e., Hay, Pelucchi, Estes, & Saffran, 2011; Lany & Saffran, 2010; Saffran, Aslin, & Newport, 1996) but also to the context of infant visual perception (Bulf et al., 2011) and action observation (Monroy, Gerson, & Hunnius, 2017).

However, detecting perceptual regularities may not suffice to help infants fully understand the complex world within which they live. Performing actions while perceiving the environment (as opposed to only perceiving the environment) is critical for fully understanding the physical and social world, figuring out how it works, identifying relevant cues for action, and interacting effectively with others. Directing visual attention and selecting specific elements of a scene are crucial skills in most daily situations for guiding actions, for understanding "what is out there," or even simply for developing visual preferences that might influence personal choices or future decisions. Performing actions in turn helps fine-tune visual attention allocation. Indeed, learning how to pick up critical information goes beyond detecting visual regularities in the environment. Learning how to act in the world is part of a larger multifaceted process than simply learning from our senses (Johnson, 2010). Some inborn propensities of newborns may help identify particular objects of a scene that are critical for survival (e.g., a face), but understanding what is out there involves a series of experience-dependent processes contributing, among other things, to infants' growing ability to situate themselves in their surroundings. These processes, although multiple and varied, are all likely contributors of infants' growing understanding of the visual and physical world. Johnson (2010), in line with prior influential researchers (Gibson, 1988; Piaget, 1936/1952; Thelen, 2000), explains that infants learn about the visual world not only through association and assembly but also, importantly, via sensorimotor exploration.

Although researchers agree that learning about the world involves experience-dependent mechanisms and direct exposure to the world, much remains to be known about how infants actively engage in their explorations of their surroundings, how they come to attend to particular elements of a scene as opposed to others in the absence of perceptual saliency, and how they form "a meaning of the world" from such a time-dependent process. We know that repeated exposure and problem solving capabilities are important for learning, for the brain to form new and strong connections, for shaping neural maps, and for creating long-lasting memories (i.e., Edelman, 1987; Sporns & Tononi, 1994). Many studies also rely on stimulus repetition to assess learning, but they often focus more on the outcome than the time process leading to the observed outcome. Here we are particularly interested in the time process that takes place during exploration and selection in the perception–action loop. Similar to Amso and Johnson (2006), we see learning by selection as essential for shaping infants' discovery and understanding of the physical world, but we also consider how learning about the value or significance of particular actions during this process is essential to guiding learning. Thus, in this chapter, we examine the time-dependent changes occurring in perception and action, and we discuss how added "values" to the perception–action loop can shape visual attention, sensorimotor exploration, and action selection in the moment.

3. EXPLORATION AND SELECTION IN THE DEVELOPMENT OF INFANT PERCEPTION AND ACTION

One assumption of the process of learning is that infants and individuals, in general, make sense of their surroundings because their experiences and encounters with the world can become valuable or can acquire particular significance for the observer and actor (Barto, 2002; Barto & Mahadevan, 2003; Edelman, 1987). Encounters that become valuable can in turn shape future sensorimotor explorations and actions on the world and thereby contribute to the selection and formation of new patterns of interaction. Thus, visuomotor explorations and selections are embedded in the immediate, moment-by-moment history of the looking and acting behavior, but they are also stimulated by the presence or discovery of valuable/significant motivators that can act as intrinsic (or extrinsic) reinforcers on the organism's actions. In the context of visual perception, an element being discovered in a scene may acquire increasing value or significance for the observer, thus triggering more future looks and greater visual attention to that particular "more valuable" element, while others are progressively ignored. Here we do not refer to saliency maps or other external physical characteristics of the scene (e.g., size, brightness, and patterned contrasts) that are known to drive and attract visual attention. We specifically aim to focus on the particular intrinsic value that some objects or elements of a scene may acquire for a specific individual as he/she explores the visual world. Such value may arise because some elements of the scene may provide some endogenous reward or pleasant outcome to the observer (e.g., preferring to look at a particular image or face or directing attention to a particular flower in a botanical garden because they resonate with the observer's own preferences), but value may also arise and be dictated by a specific goal as some elements of the scene can acquire special relevance for solving a particular task.

The same reasoning can be applied to patterns of action that can lead to desired, interesting, or even sometimes unexpected outcomes. The intrinsic rewards generated by those outcomes may not only stimulate the actor to attempt to reproduce such outcomes but also contribute to refining the perception—action loop and allow for the formation of a memory of what works and what does not work.

The processes of exploration and selection, in the context of forming intrinsic values, are not novel to the developmental field, as they have been applied to infant motor skill acquisition (Angulo-Kinzler, 2001; Bojczyk & Corbetta, 2004; Corbetta & Snapp-Childs, 2009; Goldfield, Kay, & Warren, 1993; Thelen & Corbetta, 1994; Williams & Corbetta, 2016). An essential idea brought about by those studies is that before the skill emerges, infants have no knowledge of what they can do with their bodies, and they have no knowledge of what is out there to be discovered, nor do they have clues of what they should be attending perceptually. As they move their limbs around, presumably without a specific goal or direction in mind, they may come across a novel or interesting event (e.g., hitting a toy by chance while flailing their arm around or triggering an overhead mobile while randomly kicking with their legs). Those unplanned events may provide an unexpected but interesting outcome, offering novelty and potential value to the organism. This may spark the infant's attention in new ways and trigger a change in behavior geared toward seeking to reproduce the novel event. Generally, when this occurs, infants' initial attempts to reproduce the event are performed under conditions of uncertainty. They have no idea how to make it happen again; they do not know how to control their limbs; and they do not know which aspects of the task are relevant to generating the event. All of these aspects have to be discovered. Despite initially acting under uncertainty, studies reported astonishing learning curves following the occurrence of that first unexpected event. For example, Angulo-Kinzler (2001) found that 3-month-old infants quickly learned to identify the exact flexion at which they needed to maintain their leg to keep the mobile active. Bojczyk and Corbetta (2004) found that by the age of 8–9 months, infants learned to coordinate their arms efficiently to open a lid and keep it open for the other hand to retrieve a concealed object, a skill that typically has been described to emerge toward the end of the first year (Bruner, 1970; Diamond, 1991; Fagard, 1994). What drives such rapid task-oriented development? We suggest that such dramatic learning is linked to two embedded temporal processes: (1) the infants' intrinsic drive to explore novelty and act on the world (i.e., curiosity) and (2) the formation (through exploration) of potentially valuable, meaningful, and rewarding action outcomes. Outcomes, in turn, can drive exploration by providing positive, reinforcing values, and thus sustain future attempts seeking to reproduce the desired outcome. However, outcomes can also create a negative or penalizing value, especially when an action fails to generate an interesting outcome, or when the action becomes too familiar to maintain curiosity. Thus, values (positive and negative) associated with the outcome can act as constraints onto the active organization of future actions and exploratory behavior, thereby allowing the increased selection of meaningful actions and the decreased selection of useless actions that fail to generate the valuable outcome.

In the following sections, we illustrate these theoretical ideas in the context of learning to reach, discovering objects' properties, tool use, and word learning.

4. EXPLORATION AND SELECTION IN THE CONTEXT OF LEARNING TO REACH

Infants begin to reach for objects around 3–5 months of age. How they come to direct their hand toward a seen object and make contact with it in the first place is still somewhat unclear. Piaget and several researchers after him contended that the emergence of reaching was primarily occurring under the guidance of vision (Bushnell, 1985; Lasky, 1977; McDonnell, 1975; Piaget, 1936/1952; White, Castle, & Held, 1964), but others have not been able to verify this claim (Clifton, Muir, Ashmead, & Clarkson, 1993; von Hofsten, 1979; see also Corbetta, Wiener, Thurman, & McMahon, 2018 for a recent review). We know that when infants approach the age of reach onset, they intensify their look at the object target, but they direct little or no attention at their hands (Corbetta, Wiener, & Thurman, 2018). We also know that, at that age, when objects come within the infants' reaching space and the infants are looking at them, they typically begin moving their arms actively, although not necessarily in the direction of the objects (Thelen et al., 1993). It is possible that the first encounter of the hand touching the object occurs by chance, as infants flail their arms around while simultaneously staring at the object. Infants also may not have a clear goal in mind at that stage, as purposefully reaching for a desired target has never happened before. However, one crucial outcome of this first hand–object contact, even if it occurred by chance, is that it will create a valuable event, one that will set a goal aimed at repeating this action. Clearly, one casual hand contact with a seen target will not provide an immediate solution to the infant about how to make it happen again, but the haptic feedback provided by the hand touching the object will trigger a new sequence of actions, aimed at reproducing this interesting event. The reinforcing value of the first casual contact will entail the production of new reaching attempts and the exploration of new movement patterns in the direction of the target. As repeated attempts to reach for the target succeed in time, new contacts will contribute to further reinforce the successful response and increase the likelihood that this particular response will be reproduced in future attempts whereas unsuccessful attempts will be more likely ignored (Berthier, Rosenstein, & Barto, 2005; Schlesinger et al., 2001, 2000; Sporns & Edelman, 1993; Williams, Corbetta, & Cobb, 2015). This repeated process of trying to succeed by exploring a range of varied movement patterns will eventually lead to the selection of more effective patterns that work and to the abandonment of the patterns that do not work (Thelen & Corbetta, 1994). Thus, this process of repeated exploration and selection within this perception–action loop can impact the emergence and reproducibility of new behaviors, such as reaching, and can contribute to the fine-tuning of future new attempts.

In recent work, we have examined how modifying the action outcome, or the action "value," would affect reach onset and its subsequent development (Williams & Corbetta, 2016). We modified the "value" of the action by manipulating the consequence of the action on the object contacted. Young infants unable to reach for objects when they entered the study were distributed in three 16-day intervention groups. In a contingent group condition, the target object was mounted on a spring. Thus, in that condition, if infants happened to make contact with the target, they would see the object moving and sounding in response. This visual–auditory event provided an added value to the successful hand-object contact. In a continuous (noncontingent) group condition, the object was mounted on a small motor such that it would move back and forth and sound independently from the infant action. This provided a visually interesting event that could help trigger attempts to reach for it, but successful contacts with the object would not necessarily provide an additional value to the action because the motion of the object was not contingent on the infant action. A third group of infants, the control group, did not receive any particular intervention. Infants in this group were tested on day 1 and day 16 only for comparison purposes.

Comparisons of object contact performance across the three groups on day 16 revealed that the contingent group significantly outperformed the continuous and control groups (Williams & Corbetta, 2016). Not only did the contingent group grow to contact the object significantly more than the other two groups over the 16-day intervention, but target contacts were also performed proportionately more while visually attending the target compared with the continuous group. Thus, even though the continuous group had a visually dynamic event to look at (the object moved back and forth and sounded continuously), this did not suffice to reinforce the perception–action loop that led to increased reaching. Exploration and selection and the tuning of perception and action as a function of the intended goal (i.e., contacting the object) occurred at a much faster rate in the contingent group where an added action value was provided.

5. OBJECT MANIPULATION: A MORE DETAILED PERCEPTION–ACTION LOOP

Infants are not able to grasp objects right from the onset of reaching. Thus, the primary goal of early reaching attempts as we described above is to make contact with the target. Within a few weeks, however, infants figure out how to orient their hand at contact to begin grasping the object (von Hofsten & Lindhagen, 1979). This new ability marks another important developmental transition that corresponds to the beginning of object manipulation. Objects that were only touched before can now be held, brought to the mouth, banged, thrown, moved around, etc. These manipulations of the objects offer new opportunities for exploring novel actions and their effects on objects. These actions, in turn, contribute to the discovery of objects' many physical features. For example, lifting the objects will provide information about their weight, shaking the object can reveal a sounding bell inside, banging the object may also provide interesting feedback depending on the surface on which it is banged. Banging an object on a hard surface may provide some crisp, interesting feedback that may offer some rewarding value and entice more banging, whereas the same banging on the surface of a crib mattress may only provide a dampened sound that may not be so motivating. During those manipulations, where perception and action are fluently cycling and exchanging information, exploration and selection are fully at work. Some actions (e.g., banging on a hard surface) may be more likely to end up being selected and reproduced based on their interesting effect, whereas others (e.g., banging on the crib mattress) may be weeded out for the lack of producing a valuable outcome.

Thus, the emergence of grasping in the infant movement repertoire opens the path toward more complex interactions with the world, and importantly, grasping adds a new layer to the perception–action loop. Fig. 1A displays the classic perception–action loop the way it is typically depicted. In prior work (Corbetta & Snapp-Childs, 2009), we proposed a more detailed action–perception loop (Fig. 1B) illustrating the different steps from perceiving to manipulating objects where perception and action interact in several ways during the infant–object interaction. Fig. 1B

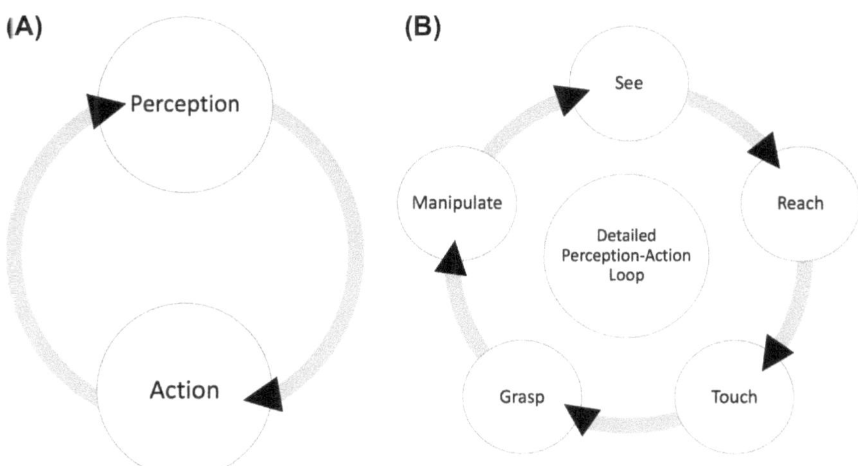

Figure 1 The classic perception–action loop (A); a more detailed perception–action loop (B) representing each step that is performed from reaching to grasping and manipulating an object.

illustrates this detailed perception—action loop in the context of reaching. Visual information is generally considered the first step in planning a goal-directed action, but when the hand contacts and grabs the object, new haptic/proprioceptive information is also obtained that is relevant to how the hand and fingers will be used to grasp the object. In adults, we know that the reach and grasp are closely related to how the actor intends to use the object once in hand (Crajé, Lukos, Ansuini, Gordon, & Santello, 2011; Marteniuk, MacKenzie, Jeannerod, Athenes, & Dugas, 1987). For infants, however, who are still learning to reach and grasp, these moment-by-moment experiences involving seeing, reaching, touching, grasping, and manipulating all constitute critical sensorimotor experiences that are providing opportunities for learning about their own actions on the object and the object itself. In a prior study (Corbetta & Snapp-Childs, 2009), we found that every step of this repeated, detailed perception—action loop played an important role in helping refine and select appropriate actions to meet the intended goal and increase the fit between the actor and the environment. However, we found that not all the pieces of this perception—action loop came together at the same time in development.

If we trace the development of infant reaching and grasping over time, we find that these responses are quite undifferentiated initially. Infants tend to use a synergic palmar grasp to grab objects at first (Halverson, 1931), and they also tend to use two-handed responses for reaching regardless of the object size (Corbetta, Thelen, & Johnson, 2000; Fagard & Jacquet, 1996; Gesell & Ames, 1947). Reaching and grasping, however, progressively change over the first year of life as infants interact with a variety of objects. They increasingly use one hand for reaching for smaller objects and two hands for larger objects (Corbetta et al., 2000; Fagard & Jacquet, 1996); they learn to anticipate hand orientation and preshape it during the reach to match objects' orientation and their physical properties (von Hofsten & Fazel-Zandy, 1984; Lockman, Ashmead, & Bushnell, 1984; Schum, Jovanovic, & Schwarzer, 2011; Witherington, 2005); and they develop increasingly differentiated finger activity for manipulating objects (e.g., grabbing a pellet differently from a baby rattle).

This process of arm/hand differentiation clearly occurs slowly over several months as infants reach and grasp for objects over many repeated trials. However, in our study (Corbetta & Snapp-Childs, 2009), we wanted to investigate the moment-to-moment of this transition and assess whether and when infants could take advantage of the information gathered during their manipulation of objects to plan and modulate a reaching response on subsequent trials. We examined the repeated reaching and grasping responses of 6- to 9-month-old infants enticed to reach for large or small objects depending on their initial preferred reaching patterns. If they tended to reach more bimanually, they were offered small objects to see if they would switch to unimanual responses after a few trials of handling the small object with one hand. If they tended to reach in a more unimanual manner, they were presented with large objects requiring two hands to be held to see if they would switch to bimanual reaching after a few trials. They were also presented with large pompons made of yarn that looked like they would require two hands to be grasped but were actually easily graspable with one hand. We introduced this condition to assess whether infants would rely on their grasping and haptic experience to revisit their reaching response on the next trial. Our overall goal was to study whether infants could make inferences for future actions based on their prior history of reaching and manipulation of these objects.

We know that adults typically only need one trial to make those reaching decisions. For example, if adults reach for and grab a large box by its handles with two hands at first and discover when lifting it that the box is empty and light, they may aim for the box the next time around by grabbing it by one handle only. At what age and after how many trials would infants begin to display response adaptation based on inferences drawn from prior perception–action interactions?

In this study (Corbetta & Snapp-Childs, 2009), infants 6-to-9 months old were exposed to 10 consecutive reaching trials within conditions using repeated presentations of objects similar in size and texture. This was done to build a history of reaches and grasps and assess to what extent infants of different ages would switch their response over the repeated trials. We found that at 6 months, infants did not really modify their systemic reaching and grasping responses. If younger infants were predominantly reaching and grasping with two hands at the beginning of the study, they continued to reach and grasp with two hands for the objects trial after trial, even though they were repeatedly presented with small objects or pompons and despite experiencing holding these objects with one hand after having grasped them. Switches in reaching response showing an adaptation to object size and texture began to occur around 8 months of age, but only the older infants revealed more consistent switching in their reaching patterns.

Responses were different for the grasp, however. From 7 months of age, infants were able to modify their grasp based on haptic information following the moment of contact. However, this response only seemed to have a lasting impact on the holding and manipulation that immediately followed the grasp. Such a response adaptation did not really carry over to the reaching response of the subsequent trials until infants were 9 months old. The only object exploration that had an impact on subsequent infant—object interactions were in relation to object mouthing. Mouthing the object is a frequent response in the age range tested; however, response adaptions depended on the object condition. Infants continued to bring the small solid objects to the mouth for further exploration, but they quickly learned to quit mouthing the large solid objects and the pompons after one trial. Thus, for mouthing, exploration and selection occurred extremely fast, while for reaching, selection did not occur until infants were much older. We concluded that perception and action imposed loose constraints on the reach; that is, preferred biases in reaching (i.e., two-handed tendencies) would continue to dominate reaching behavior regardless of the object's physical characteristics because the object could always be attained. In contrast, for grasping and manipulation, the constraints were tighter because holding and handling the object necessarily required appropriate one- or two-handed grasping responses. As for mouthing, a tighter mouth—object fit was also required to allow oral exploration.

6. OTHER VARIATIONS OF THE PERCEPTION—ACTION LOOP

Recently, we have continued investigating how the perception—action loop and processes of exploration and selection affect infants' exchanges with their environment. In particular, we have begun examining how perception and action influence the discovery of object features, modulate tool use learning, and even promote the learning of word labels. To gain greater insights into how infants explore objects and their environment visually, we added eye-tracking to these studies so that we could capture more accurately where they directed their gaze prior and after object interaction. The idea was to assess whether visual patterns of object exploration would change after manual interaction with objects and if the subsequent patterns of visual exploration of the same object would become predictive of subsequent actions on the object. Here, we present preliminary analyses of three ongoing projects as a means to illustrate different ways in which the more detailed perception–action loop can help capture the nature of the interactions between child and environment.

6.1 Discovering Objects' Features via Manipulation

Wiener (2018) aimed at investigating how competing perceptual properties of two objects would influence 11-month-old infants' perceptual motor exploration of those objects. Infants were presented with a set of two same-shaped objects that differed in color. One object had visual details on top of the solid color (black polka dots) to make it more visually interesting but was empty inside (we will refer to this object as the unfilled/detailed object). The other object was filled with rice or beans as to make it more interesting to manipulate but was visually plain, although of a different solid color from the unfilled/detailed object (we will refer to this object as the filled/plain object). This filled/plain object would produce an auditory–tactile effect if manipulated. Both objects were presented at the same time on a black surface and background and were first held out of reach for 5 s to capture infants' visual exploration and selection of the objects via eye-tracking. Then, the objects were moved toward the infants so that they could reach for and manipulate them for up to 30–40 s. Finally, the objects were removed and placed back on the tray for a new trial. This procedure was repeated up to nine trials following a first baseline trial, where the infants looked at the objects but were not allowed to reach for them.

Wiener (2018) investigated the time-dependent pattern sequence from visual to manual exploration according to the five dependent variables depicted in the detailed perception–action loop displayed in Fig. 2. She measured the following variables: which object was fixated first (first fixation); which object was looked at most based on accumulated looking to each object (most look); which object was contacted first during reaching (first contact); which object was contacted most across the trial based on accumulated contact (most contact); and which object was shaken in the air or banged on the presentation tray the most (most shaking and banging). For the analysis presented in Fig. 2, she looked at to what extent each step of the perception–action sequence was linked to the next step in the sequence. So, for example, Wiener examined if the first look on the unfilled/detailed object matched or was predictive of the most look on that object, and she assessed if the most look at that object matched or was also predictive of the first hand contact with that object when within reach, and so on.

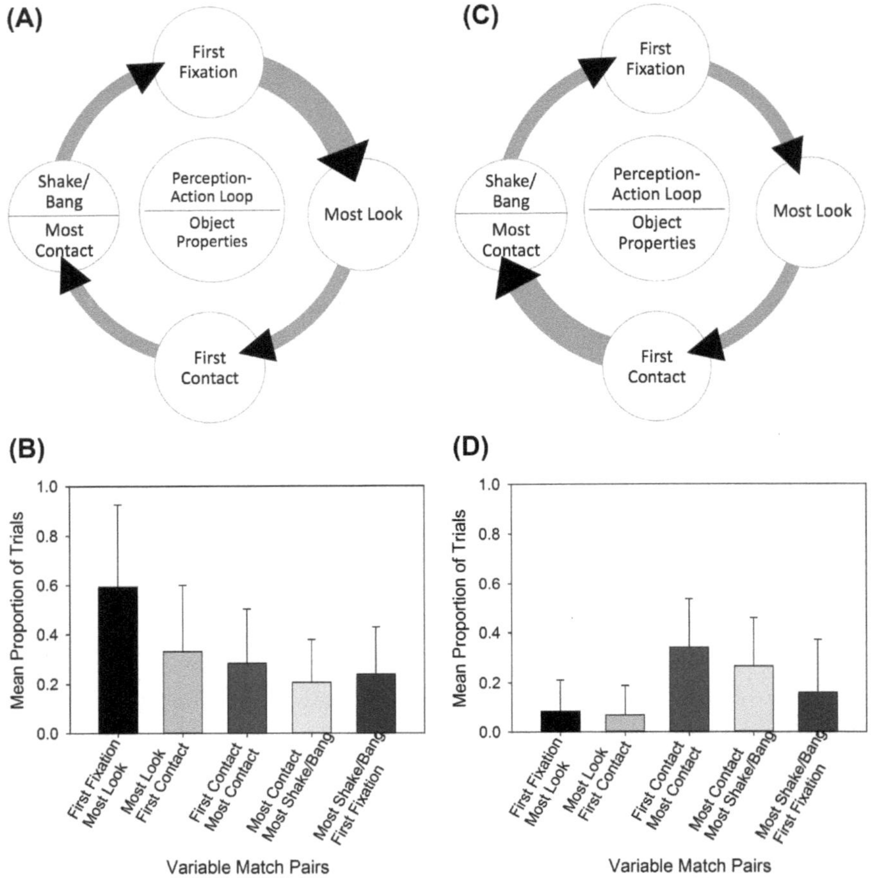

Figure 2 Perception–action loops related to the exploration of objects with different visual and auditory-tactile properties. On the left, the object explored was covered with polka dots on its surface, making it visually more interesting (A–B). The loop diagram (A) and bar graph (B) show that when exploring this object, infants' first fixation and most look variables were more strongly related than the reach and manipulations variables. On the right, the object was visually plain but was filled with rice or beans making it more interesting to manipulate (C–D). The loop diagram (C) and bar graph (D) show that for this object, first contact was more highly related to most contact than to any of the other variables.

The bar graphs in Fig. 2 report the mean proportion of trials, where a response selection matched the subsequent response selection at each step of the perception–action loop. Fig. 2A reports these data for the unfilled/detailed object, and Fig. 2B reports them for the filled/plain object. These graphs show that for the unfilled/detailed object, the match proportion was highest for the looking variables (first fixation and most look), while for the filled/plain object, the match proportion was highest for the reach and manipulation variables (first contact and most contact). These findings indicate that the infants were responsive to the perceptual properties of the objects in that they explored them quite differently. The polka dots on the one object attracted more looking and more matches between first look and most look to that object than any other sequence pairs involving object manipulations. In contrast, the auditory–tactile property of the filled/plain object, once discovered through object manipulation, attracted more object manipulation and more object banging after first object contact than any of the other sequence pairs that involved looking patterns. This result can be tied to the property values that drive exploration and selection in the perception–action loop. A visually interesting pattern on an object can drive visual exploration and visual selection of that object over another visually plain object, while an interesting manipulatory consequence of an object will drive the manual exploration and manual selection of that object over an empty object that is providing no interesting consequences when banged or shaken.

6.2 Perception and Action in the Context of Tool Use

The perception–action loop is also useful for understanding the ontogeny of tool use during infancy (Lockman, 2000). Infants can explore a tool and its effects during manipulation, and they can select the actions that are more rewarding. Research paradigms have also used demonstrations to assess which cues infants rely on to learn how to use the tool (Rat-Fisher, O'Reagan, & Fagard, 2012; Somogyi et al., 2015). In our laboratory, we have begun using a detailed perception–action loop to perform a moment-to-moment microgenetic analysis of how tool use demonstrations can affect tool use learning. Using eye-tracking, we measured where on the tool infants directed their gaze before demonstration and manipulation, and then we observed how they manipulated the tool as a function of prior looking and demonstration. More importantly, and as in the object manipulation study described above, we were interested in capturing changes in looking, reaching, and manipulating the tool as perception and action cycled through repeated trials of tool use demonstration.

The tool use task we have started to study is a drumming task. Drumming is a behavior that infants begin to perform in the second half of the first year and continues to develop in the second year of life (Kahrs, Jung, & Lockman, 2013). We know from a prior study that 9-month-old infants look mostly at the sphere of a drumstick-shaped object and also reach more often for the sphere as well (Corbetta, Thurman, Wiener, Guan, & Williams, 2014). In that study, however, there was no demonstration of the functionality or tool-like characteristics of the object. When demonstration is introduced, other studies with older infants have found that infants are more likely to benefit from the demonstration if they can infer the intent of the demonstrator (Esseily, Rat-Fisher, O'Regan, & Fagard, 2013; Fagard, Rat-Fischer, Esseily, Somogyi, & O'Regan, 2016). Furthermore, Kahrs et al. (2013) have shown that infants are able to identify targeted goals during demonstrations more readily when they are allowed to perform the task, even when the tool is not identical to the one demonstrated.

In our tool use study, we wanted to determine whether infants change their perception of a toollike object—in this case a drumstick—after they are introduced to its functionality. We wanted to assess whether repeated demonstrations, thereby creating expectations of how the demonstrator intends using the tool, would impact infants' subsequent looking behavior and tool use manipulation. Here we present just a few trials from one infant as an illustration (see Fig. 3A–D). The first trial is designed to capture infant baseline looking, reaching, and manipulation of the tool before the functionality of the tool is introduced. The procedure goes as follows. The infant is first presented with the drumsticklike object to look at, and after a few seconds, the object is moved forward to allow the infant to manually explore it. On subsequent trials, the infant looks at the same object again, and after a few seconds, an experimenter grabs the handle of the tool and strikes the plate surface on which the tool rests a few times before setting the tool back in place. Finally, the drumstick is moved into the infant's reaching space for exploration and manipulation. During the looking and demonstration phases of the cycle, eye-tracking is recorded to establish where the infant directs his or her gaze on the object (the head or the handle), and during the manipulation phase, we code where the infant holds the object (head or handle) and whether he or she performs drumming attempts.

Fig. 3 presents a baseline and three consecutive trials for one infant. Over these few trials, this infant increasingly directed gaze toward the handle following demonstration and performed some strike attempts but only following demonstration trials. There was no striking behavior observed in the baseline trials when functionality had not been demonstrated. In these figures, each bubble corresponds to a distinct step of the perception–action loop and is coded gray if the looking or manipulation behavior is directed

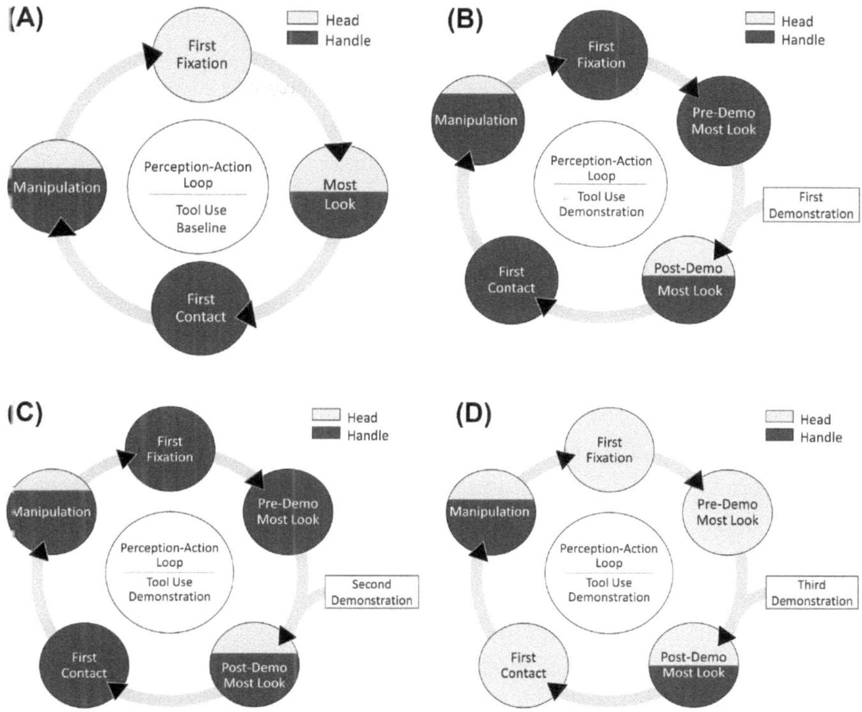

Figure 3 Perception–action loop sequence revealing the looking, reaching, and manipulation of the head or handle of a drumstick-like tool by one infant. Baseline trial, no demonstration (A); demonstration of the functionality of the drumstick by an experimenter and infant's responses (B–D).

toward the head and black if the looking or manipulation behavior is directed toward the handle. The first Fig. 3A corresponds to the baseline behaviors before demonstration introduction. This infant looked first at the head of the drumstick and then visually explored head and handle roughly equally. Baseline first contact and manipulation were mostly directed toward the handle. We observed no attempts to strike the surface with the object during baseline.

On the next cycle (Fig. 3B), the infant's manipulation of the handle during baseline seems to have carried over to the attention focus on the following trial, as the first look and most look at the object on that second trial and before the introduction of tool use demonstration are now both directed 100% at the handle. After the first demo, however, looking behavior is again split between head and handle but is followed by a first contact and manipulation of the tool at the handle, and the first strikes attempts are performed. On this second trial, this infant performed one successful strike and four failed attempts.

On trial 3 (Fig. 3C), the same sequence of behavior is observed, but this time after the second demo, the infant produced 8 successful strikes and 11 strike attempts. By trial 4 (Fig. 3D), the infant shifted his visual focus on the head again, which prevailed through much of the cycle (i.e., a reach to the head) and resulted in no strike attempts. Similar to the object manipulation example presented above, we found that for this infant, a first look at one area of the object often led to a most look in that same area and a first touch at one given area often led to more contact to or more handling of the object at this same area.

We analyzed the looking behavior during demonstrations, and we found that looking was mainly directed toward the strike area over the arc of the strike. There was little to no looking at the handle of the drumstick or even the hand of the experimenter during demonstration, despite the infant displaying high manipulation of the handle of the drumstick on the trials presented. This suggests that this infant may have focused more on the outcome of the action (the rewarding aspect of the action) than the action itself for imitating the behavior. Selection of the drumming action that provides the most feedback is likely to evolve as the infant explores the effects of his action with the tool on the plate and discovers the weight properties of the tool in conjunction with its action.

This is just one example of one infant over a few trials. Nonetheless, it illustrates that tool use demonstration can have an impact on revealing the functionality of an object and can potentially help unravel the mechanism enticing a child to attempt to reproduce the interesting outcome. The moment-to-moment cycle of looking and acting can provide a deeper understanding of the time dynamics involved in tool use learning. The visuomotor exploration and selection incurring within the perception–action cycle may drive these changes.

6.3 Perception and Action in the Context of Word Learning

The process of exploration and selection of objects within the perception–action cycle can also be linked to word learning in infancy and early childhood. A small body of research has shown a well-established relationship between the onset of motor skills and vocabulary size such that individuals who have begun to walk show greater receptive vocabulary size than their same age but not-yet-walking peers (Walle & Campos, 2014). This relationship exists cross culturally (He, Walle, & Campos, 2015) and persists independently of the language environment experienced by the infants (Walle & Warlaumont, 2015). One of the crucial shifts that occurs as infants acquire new motor skills is that they can explore a greater amount of their environment. The emergence of locomotion in particular seems to have wide ramifications on infants' ability to learn about their environment (Campos et al., 2000). We have shown in our laboratory that as infants increase their self-produced mobility over time, they also increase their interactions with a greater number of objects (Thurman & Corbetta, 2017). It could be that sensorimotor interactions with the environment constitute an essential mediator for novel word learning and could offer a potential explanation for the reported relationship between the onset of motor skills and increases in vocabulary.

Research has also shown that in seminaturalistic play tasks infants demonstrate a significant increase in novel word learning when they physically manipulate objects (Yu & Smith, 2012). The timing at which the novel label and novel object are paired appears to be the mediator promoting word learning. Infants more readily learn the novel label—object pairing if the label is provided by the parent while the infant is holding and looking at the object at the same time (Pereira, Smith, & Yu, 2014). In these studies, infants learn the novel object labels in an environment containing several other novel objects they could select. Word learning is associated with embodied attention because the selected object is actively manipulated and physically dominates a larger proportion of the infant's visual field, creating an optimal moment for novel word learning (Yu & Smith, 2012).

In our laboratory, we have begun assessing this embodied process of word learning using our detailed perception—action loop as a reference to structure and control for different word learning conditions. Particularly, we wanted to assess how the active sensorimotor exploration and selection of objects, while infants are looking and physically interacting with the objects, relate to early word learning. In this ongoing project, older infants (18—22 months of age) are presented with three novel objects, each paired with a novel word label. Each of the three objects is paired with its corresponding label at different specific timings within the perception—action loop and varies with the type of visuomotor exploration the child can perform (see Fig. 4A—C). In a *look only* condition (Fig. 4A), one object is presented out of reach, and the infant hears the novel word labels while viewing the object first standing still on a surface and then being rotated by an experimenter. In this condition, the infant never interacts physically

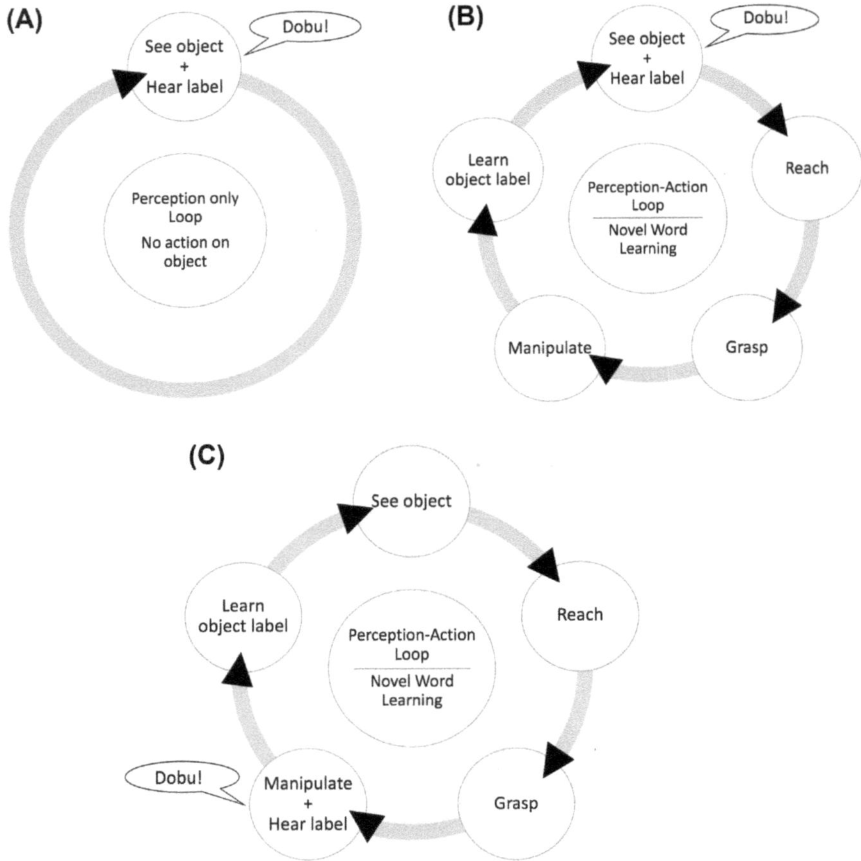

Figure 4 Perception–action loops representing the three conditions of the word learning task. The novel object and label are presented only visually (A). The infants were not given the opportunity to manipulate the object. The novel object and label are paired during visual presentation and before the infant is given the opportunity to manipulate the object (B). The novel object and label are paired during object manipulation (C).

with the object. In another condition (*out-of-sync* condition, Fig. 4B), the object is also presented first out of reach and the infant hears the label while looking at it as in the *look only* condition; however, after the presentation, the object is moved into the infant's reaching space to allow for manual exploration. In this condition, the timing of the novel word label occurs only during the object viewing phase but not during manual exploration, making the word label presentation asynchronous with visuomotor exploration. In the third condition (*in-sync* condition, Fig. 4C), the object is also presented first visually; however, now the novel word label is provided later in the sequence, when the object has been moved into the infant reaching space and the infant is actively manipulating and viewing the object while in its hands. Thus, in this condition, the word label is heard in synchrony with object manipulation (embodied attention).

Three other novel objects were also presented, each in one of the three timing conditions described above, but for these objects, infants received no distinctive word label when an experimenter referred to them; they simply heard "look at this one." Twelve test trials were performed after the infants had received four exposures of each object with its unique timing and word label in a random order. During test, objects that received a novel word label (target object) were always flanked by one object that did not receive a specific label (distractor object). Infants heard the novel word label matching the target object, and we used eye-tracking to determine to which object infants directed their gaze to the most. We inferred that infants had learned the novel object–label pairing if they looked longer at the target object compared with the distractor object.

Fig. 5 presents preliminary data from two participants as an illustration. In the look only condition, we found that the two infants directed a greater proportion of looks at the distractor object than the target object. This suggests that these infants may not have learned the target word label

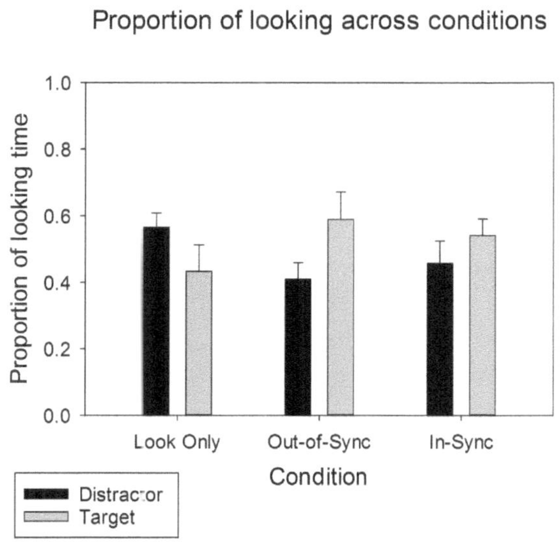

Figure 5 Proportion of looking time (and standard deviation) the two infants directed toward the distractor versus target object by condition.

in these looking only trials. In the two other conditions, in which the infants could manually explore the objects, both infants showed greater proportions of look durations toward the target objects than the distractor objects during test trials. These preliminary results generally support the embodied attention hypothesis (Pereira et al., 2014; Yu & Smith, 2012), although it is not clear at this very early stage of the study whether one condition (out-of-sync or in-sync) offers greater benefits for word learning than the other condition. However, these data seem to support the notion that manual exploration of physical objects can lead to increased novel word learning, underscoring the idea that infants are active agents in their environment, and their interactions with their environment relate to gains in cognitive skills, such as associating novel word learning to novel objects. We can see this through the detailed perception—action loop in which repeated reaching for and manipulating of an object as opposed to simply viewing it may promote and strengthen word learning.

7. CONCLUSIONS

In this chapter, we argued that acquiring new skills is about tuning perception and action in relation to the goal of the task. This tuning process involves discovering the properties of our actions to regulate our movements successfully as a function of the goal to be attained. It also mediates the learning and discovery of the properties of the objects being manipulated. Such discovery is intimately related to the time-dependent processes of exploration and selection that are embedded in the perception—action loop. Action exploration corresponds to trying different movement patterns or trying different ways of manipulating objects, which ultimately will provide information about the action outcome and properties of the object being manipulated. Action selection relates more specifically to the process resulting from the value received from the child environment—specific interaction. Actions that worked, or provided interesting and novel effects, or were closer to attaining the intended goal are reinforced and more likely to be reproduced on subsequent attempts, while actions that did not work are selected out and less likely to be attempted again.

We illustrated how explorations (visual, haptic, and motor) are tied to several steps of a more detailed perception—action loop, where each step can inform the next step in the loop and feedback to the next perception—action cycle. Each repeated cycle offers a moment-to-moment dynamic exchange between the child and the situation at hand, which provides direct information about the various parameters of the child's action, its effects on the environment, and thereby promotes learning. We illustrated how such a perception—action loop and exploration and selection can be applied to the emergence of new skills such as infant reaching, the fine-tuning of reaching in later months, the discovery of object properties via observation and manipulation, the discovery of object functionality in tool use, and even word learning. We discussed how tasks constraints can have a different impact on the rate of behavioral change observed over time, and we discussed the importance of action for development and learning as opposed to simple observation. Together, we hope these examples will inspire other researchers to study developmental change using similar microgenetic approaches. From our perspective, every moment matters for change and every moment contributes to the history of change, thus providing deeper insights into the processes of perceptual, motor, and cognitive skills acquisition in development.

REFERENCES

Amso, D., & Johnson, S. P. (2006). Learning by selection: Visual search and object perception in young infants. *Developmental Psychology, 42*, 1236—1245.

Angulo-Kinzler, R. (2001). Exploration and selection of intralimb coordination patterns in three-month-old infants. *Journal of Motor Behavior, 33*, 363—376.

Aslin, R. N. (1981). Development of smooth pursuit in human infants. In D. F. Fisher, R. A. Monty, & J. E. Senders (Eds.), *Eye movements: Cognition and visual perception* (pp. 31—51). Hillsdale, NJ: Erlbaum.

Barto, A. G. (2002). Reinforcement learning in motor control. In M. Arbib (Ed.), *Handbook of brain theory and neural networks* (2nd ed., pp. 968—972). Cambridge, MA: MIT Press.

Barto, A. G., & Mahadevan, S. (2003). Recent advances in hierarchical reinforcement learning. In *Discrete event dynamic systems: Theory and applications (DISC)* (pp. 42—77). Kluwer Academic Press.

Berthier, N. E., Rosenstein, M. T., & Barto, A. G. (2005). Approximate optimal control as a model for motor learning. *Psychological Review, 112*(2), 329—346.

Bogartz, R. S., Shinskey, J. L., & Schilling, T. H. (2000). Object permanence in 5-and-a-half-month-old infants? *Infancy, 1*, 403—428.

Bojczyk, K. E., & Corbetta, D. (2004). Object retrieval in the 1st year of life: Learning effects of task exposure and box transparency. *Developmental Psychology, 40*, 54—66.

Bronson, G. W. (1974). The postnatal growth of visual capacity. *Child Development, 45*, 873—890.

Bronson, G. W. (1990). Changes in infants' visual scanning across the 2- to 14-week age period. *Journal of Experimental Child Psychology, 49*, 101—125.

Bruner, J. S. (1970). The growth and structure of skill. In K. Connolly (Ed.), *Mechanisms of motor skill development* (pp. 63—94). New York: Academic Press.

Bulf, H., Johnson, S. P., & Valenza, E. (2011). Visual statistical learning in the newborn infant. *Cognition, 121*, 127—132.

Bushnell, E. W. (1985). The decline of visually guided reaching during infancy. *Infant Behavior and Development, 8*(2), 139–155.
Campos, J. J., Anderson, D. I., Barbu-Roth, M. A., Hubbard, E. M., Hertenstein, M. J., & Witherington, D. (2000). Travel broadens the mind. *Infancy, 1*(2), 149–219.
Clifton, R. K., Muir, D. W., Ashmead, D. H., & Clarkson, M. G. (1993). Is visually guided reaching in early infancy a myth? *Child Development, 64*, 1099–1110.
Cohen, L. B., & Younger, B. A. (1984). Infant perception of angular relations. *Infant Behavior and Development, 7*, 37–47.
Colombo. (2001). The development of visual attention in infancy. *Annual Review of Psychology, 52*, 337–367.
Corbetta, D., & Snapp-Childs, W. (2009). Seeing and touching: The role of sensory-motor experience on the development of infant reaching. *Infant Behavior and Development, 32*, 44–58.
Corbetta, D., Thelen, E., & Johnson, K. (2000). Motor constraints on the development of perception-action matching in infant reaching. *Infant Behavior & Development, 23*, 351–374.
Corbetta, D., Thurman, S. L., Wiener, R. F., Guan, Y., & Williams, J. L. (2014). Mapping the feel of the arm with the sight of the object: On the embodied origins of infant reaching. *Frontiers in Psychology, 5*, 18.
Corbetta, D., Wiener, R. F., & Thurman, S. L. (2018). Learning to reach in infancy. In D. Corbetta, & M. Santello (Eds.), *Reach-to-grasp behavior: Brain, behavior, and modelling across the life span*. Routledge: Taylor & Francis (in press).
Corbetta, D., Wiener, R. F., Thurman, S. L., & McMahon, E. (2018). The embodied origins of infant reaching: implications for the emergence of eye-hand coordination. *Kinesiology Review, 7*, 10–17. https://doi.org/10.1123/kr.2017-0052.
Crajé, C., Lukos, J. R., Ansuini, C., Gordon, A. M., & Santello, M. (2011). The effects of task and content on digit placement on a bottle. *Experimental Brain Research, 212*(1), 119–124. https://doi.org/10.1007/s00221-011-2704-1.
Diamond, A. (1991). Neuropsychological insights into the meaning of object concept development. In S. Carey, & R. Gelman (Eds.), *Biology and knowledge: Structural constraints on development* (pp. 37–80). Hillsdale, NJ: Erlbaum.
Edelman, G. M. (1987). *Neural darwinism: The theory of neuronal group selection*. New York: Basic Books, Inc.
Esseily, R., Rat-Fisher, L., O'Regan, J. K., & Fagard, J. (2013). Understanding the experimenter's intention imporves 16-month-olds' observational learning of the use of a novel tool. *Cognitive Development, 28*, 1–9.
Fagard, J. (1994). Manual strategies and interlimb coordination during reaching, grasping, and manipulating throughout the first year of life. In S. Swinnen, H. Heuer, J. Massion, & P. Casaer (Eds.), *Interlimb coordination: Neural, dynamical, and cognitive constraints* (pp. 439–460). San Diego, CA: Academic Press.
Fagard, J., & Jacquet, A. Y. (1996). Changes in reaching and grasping objects of different sizes between 7 and 13 months of age. *British Journal of Developmental Psychology, 14*, 65–78.
Fagard, J., Rat-Fischer, L., Esseily, R., Somogyi, E., & O'Regan, J. K. (2016). What does it take for an infant to learn how to use a tool by observation? *Frontiers in Psychology, 7*, 267.
Gesell, A., & Ames, L. B. (1947). The development of handedness. *Journal of Genetic Psychology, 70*, 155–175.
Gibson, E. J. (1988). Exploratory behavior in the development of perceiving, acting and the acquiring knowledge. In M. R. Rosenzweig, & L. W. Porter (Eds.), *Annual review of psychology*. Palo Alto, CA: Annual Review, Inc.

Gibson, E. J. (1991). *Learning, development, and conceptual change: An odyssey in learning and perception*. Cambridge, MA: The MIT Press.
Gibson, E. J. (2000). Perceptual learning in development: Some basic concepts. *Ecological Psychology, 1*(4), 295–302. https://doi.org/10.1207/S15326969ECO1204_04.
Gibson, E. J. (2003). The world is so full of a number of things: On specification and perceptual learning. *Ecological Psychology, 15*(4), 283–287. https://doi.org/10.1207/s15326969eco1504_3.
Goldfield, E. C., Kay, B. A., & Warren, W. H. (1993). Infant bouncing: The assembly and tuning of action systems. *Child Development, 64*, 1128–1142.
Guan, Y., & Corbetta, D. (2012). What *grasps* and *holds* 8-month-old infants' looking attention? The effects of object size and depth cues. *Child Development Research.* , 439618. https://doi.org/10.1155/2012/439618, 10 pages.
Haith, M. M., Hazan, C., & Goodman, G. S. (1988). Expectation and anticipation of dynamic visual events by 3.5-month-old babies. *Child Development, 59*, 467–479.
Halverson, H. M. (1931). An experimental study of prehension in infants by means of systematic cinema records. *Genetic Psychology Monographs, 10*, 107–283.
Hay, J. F., Pelucchi, B., Estes, K. G., & Saffran, J. R. (2011). Linking sounds to meanings: Infant statistical learning in a natural language. *Cognitive Psychology, 63*, 93–106.
He, M., Walle, E. A., & Campos, J. J. (2015). A cross-national investigation of the relationship between infant walking and language development. *Infancy, 20*(3), 283–305. https://doi.org/10.1111/infa.12071.
von Hofsten, C. (1979). Development of visually guided reaching: The approach phase. *Journal of Human Movement Studies, 5*, 160–178.
von Hofsten, C., & Fazel-Zandy, S. (1984). Development of visually guided hand orientation in reaching. *Journal of Experimental Child Psychology, 38*(2), 208–219. https://doi.org/10.1016/0022-0965(84)90122-X.
von Hofsten, C., & Lindhagen, K. (1979). Observations on the development of reaching for moving objects. *Journal of Experimental Child Psychology, 28*(1), 158–173. https://doi.org/10.1016/0022-0965(79)90109-7.
Johnson, M. H. (1990). Cortical maturation and the development of visual attention in early infancy. *Journal of Cognitive Neuroscience, 2*, 81–95.
Johnson, S. P. (2004). Development of perceptual completion in infancy. *Psychological Science, 15*, 769–775.
Johnson, S. P. (2010). How infants learn about the visual world. *Cognitive Science, 34*, 1158–1184.
Johnson, S. P. (2011). Development of visual perception. *WIREs Cognitive Science, 2*, 515–528. https://doi.org/10.1002/wsc.128.
Johnson, S. P., Davidow, J., Hall-Haro, C., & Frank, M. C. (2008). Development of perceptual completion originates in information acquisition. *Developmental Psychology, 44*, 1214–1224.
Kahrs, B. A., Jung, W. P., & Lockman, J. J. (2013). Motor origins of tool use. *Child Development, 84*(3), 810–816. https://doi.org/10.1111/cdev.12000.
Kidd, C., Piantadosi, S. T., & Aslin, R. N. (2012). The goldilocks effect: Human infants allocate attention to visual sequences that are neither too simple nor too complex. *PLoS One, 7*, e36399. https://doi.org/10.1371/journal.pone.0036399.
Lany, J., & Saffran, J. R. (2010). From statistics to meaning: Infants' acquisition of lexical categories. *Psychological Science, 21*, 284–291.
Lasky, R. E. (1977). The effect of visual feedback of the hand on the reaching and retrieval behavior of young infants. *Child Development, 48*, 112–117.
Lockman, J. J. (2000). A perception–action perspective on tool use development. *Child development, 71*(1), 137–144.

Lockman, J. J., Ashmead, D. H., & Bushnell, E. W. (1984). The development of anticipatory hand orientation during infancy. *Journal of Experimental Child Psychology, 37*(1), 176–186. pii:0022-0965(84)90065-1.

Marteniuk, R. G., MacKenzie, C. L., Jeannerod, M., Athenes, S., & Dugas, C. (1987). Contraints on human arm movement trajectories. *Canadian Journal of Psychology, 41*(3), 365–378.

McDonnell, P. M. (1975). The development of visually guided reaching. *Perception and Psychophysics, 18*(3), 181–185.

Monroy, C. D., Gerson, S. A., & Hunnius, S. (2017). Toddler's action prediction: Statistical learning of a continuous action sequence. *Journal of Experimental Child Psychology, 157*, 14–28.

Pereira, A. F., Smith, L. B., & Yu, C. (2014). A bottom-up view of toddler word learning. *Psychonomic Bulletin & Review, 21*(1), 178–185.

Piaget, J. (1936/1952). *The origins of intelligence in children [La naissance de l'intelligence chez l'enfant]* (M. Cook, Trans.). New York: Basic Books.

Rat-Fisher, L., O'Reagan, J. K., & Fagard, J. (2012). The emergence of tool use during the second year of life. *Journal of Experimental Child Psychology, 113*, 440–446.

Saffran, J., Aslin, R. N., & Newport, E. L. (1996). Statistical learning by 8-month-old infants. *Science, 274*, 1926–1928.

Saffran, J. R., & Thiessen, E. D. (2007). Domain-general learning capacities. In E. Hoff, & M. Shatz (Eds.), *Blackwell handbook of language development*. Oxford, UK: Blackwell Publishing Ltd.

Schlesinger, M., & Parisi, D. (2001). Multimodal control of reaching-simulating the role of tactile feedback. *IEEE Transactions on Evolutionary Computation, 5*(2), 122–128. https://doi.org/10.1109/4235.918433.

Schlesinger, M., Parisi, D., & Langer, J. (2000). Learning to reach by constraining the movement search space. *Developmental Science, 3*(1), 67–80. https://doi.org/10.1111/1467-7687.00101.

Schöner, G., & Thelen, E. (2006). Using dynamic field theory to rethink infant habituation. *Psychological Review, 113*, 273–299.

Schum, N., Jovanovic, B., & Schwarzer, G. (2011). Ten- and twelve-month-olds' visual anticipation of orientation and size during grasping. *Journal of Experimental Child Psychology, 109*(2), 218–231. https://doi.org/10.1016/j.jecp.2011.01.007. pii:S0022-0965(11)00018-X.

Slater, A. (1995). Visual perception and memory at birth. In C. Rovee-Collier, & L. P. Lipsitt (Eds.), *Advances in infancy research* (pp. 107–162). Norwood, NJ: Ablex.

Slater, A. (1998). *Perceptual development: Visual, auditory, and speech perception*. London: Psychology Press.

Slater, A., Mattock, A., & Brown, E. (1990). Size constancy at birth: Newborn infants' response to retinal and real size. *Journal of Experimental Child Psychology, 49*, 314–322.

Somogyi, E., Ara, C., Gianni, E., Rat-Fisher, L., Fattori, P., O'Reagan, J. K., et al. (2015). The roles of observation and manipulation in learning to use a tool. *Cognitive Development, 35*, 186–200.

Sporns, O., & Edelman, G. M. (1993). Solving Bernstein's problem: A proposal for the development of coordinated movement by selection. *Child Development, 64*, 960–981.

Sporns, O., & Tononi, G. (1994). *Selectionism and the brain*. London: Academic Press.

Thelen, E. (1990). Coupling perception and action in the development of skill: A dynamic approach. In H. Bloch, & B. I. Bertenthal (Eds.), *Sensory-motor organizations and development in infancy and early childhood* (pp. 39–56). New York, NY: Kluwer Academic/Plenum Publishers.

Thelen, E. (2000). Grounded in the world: Developmental origins of the embodied mind. *Infancy, 1*(1), 3–28. https://doi.org/10.1207/S15327078IN0101_02.

Thelen, E., & Corbetta, D. (1994). Exploration and selection in the early acquisition of skills. *International Review of Neurobiology, 37*, 75–102.
Thelen, E., Corbetta, D., Kamm, K., Spencer, J. P., Schneider, K., & Zernicke, R. F. (1993). The transition to reaching: Mapping intention and intrinsic dynamics. *Child Development, 64*(4), 1058–1098. https://doi.org/10.2307/1131327.
Thelen, E., & Smith, L. B. (1994). *A dynamic systems approach to the development of cognition and action*. Cambridge, MA: The MIT Press.
Thurman, S. L., & Corbetta, D. (2017). Spatial exploration and changes in infant-mother dyads around transitions in infant locomotion. *Developmental Psychology, 53*(7), 1207–1221. https://doi.org/10.1037/dev0000328.
Walle, E. A., & Campos, J. J. (2014). Infant language development is related to the acquisition of walking. *Developmental Psychology, 50*(2), 336.
Walle, E., & Warlaumont, A. S. (2015). Infant locomotion, the language environment, and language development: A home observation study. In *Presented at the CogSci*.
White, B. L., Castle, P., & Held, R. (1964). Observations on the development of visually directed reaching. *Child Development, 35*, 349–364.
Wiener, R. F. (2018). *Perceptual-motor exploration and selection of objects in 11-month-old infants* (Dissertation). Knoxville: University of Tennessee.
Williams, J. L., & Corbetta, D. (2016). Assessing the impact of movement consequences on the development of early reaching in infancy. *Frontiers in Psychology*, 7, 15.
Williams, J. L., Corbetta, D., & Cobb, L. (2015). How perception, action, functional value, and context can shape the development of infant reaching. *Movement and Sport Sciences/ Science et Motricité, 89*, 5–15.
Witherington, D. C. (2005). The development of prospective grasping control between 5 and 7 months: A longitudinal study. *Infancy*, 7(2), 143–161.
Yonas, A., Elieff, C. A., & Arterberry, M. E. (2002). Emergence of sensitivity to pictorial depth cues: Charting development in individual infants. *Infant Behavior and Development, 22*, 495–514.
Yu, C., & Smith, L. B. (2012). Embodied attention and word learning by toddlers. *Cognition, 125*(2), 244–262.

CHAPTER TWO

The Development of Object Fitting: The Dynamics of Spatial Coordination

Jeffrey J. Lockman[1], Nicholas E. Fears and Wendy P. Jung
Department of Psychology, Tulane University, New Orleans, LA, United States
[1]Corresponding author: E-mail: lockman@tulane.edu

Contents

Advances in Child Development and Behavior, Volume 55
ISSN 0065-2407
https://doi.org/10.1016/bs.acdb.2018.05.001

Abstract

Fitting objects into apertures is an adaptive skill that is incorporated into the design of many tools. We match or align shapes with openings when we insert keys into locks, when we put lids atop containers, or when we align a screwdriver with the groove of a screw. Traditionally, the development of object fitting has focused on children's abilities to successfully complete shape sorter tasks (e.g., square peg through square hole). By measuring children's success in these tasks, investigators have determined that there is substantial development during the second year, but little research has addressed the processes children employ to solve object fitting challenges during this time period. Here, we provide a process based account of object fitting, which emphasizes how children coordinate information about spatial structure with action. We suggest that a process-based approach can illuminate the real-time dynamics of perceiving, acting, and thinking.

1. INTRODUCTION

Animals, across several species, are able to match and fit objects into apertures. To paraphrase Cole Porter, children do it (Meyer, 1940; Örnkloo & von Hofsten, 2007; Shutts, Örnkloo, von Hofsten, Keen, & Spelke, 2009); chimpanzees and capuchin monkeys do it (la Cour, Stone, Hopkins, Menzel, & Fragaszy, 2014; Fragaszy, Stone, Scott, & Menzel, 2011); even cockatoos in some labs do it (Habl & Auersperg, 2017). This ability is highly adaptive. Fitting objects into apertures enables animals to solve problems and, in some cases, use objects as tools. Human children manifest this skill when they correctly place objects into a shape sorter but so too do nonhuman primates and birds when they select or manufacture appropriately shaped sticks to probe for prey or retrieve a lure (Bluff, Troscianko, Weir, Kacelnik, & Rutz, 2010; Chappell & Kacelnik, 2002; van Lawick-Goodall, 1968; Suzuki, 1966; Weir & Kacelnik, 2006; Weir, Chappell, & Kacelnik, 2002).

Object fitting, then, may be a foundational skill that is not unique to humans but, nevertheless, has been incorporated into the design and usage requirements of human artifacts throughout ancient and modern history (MacGregor, 2011). For instance, we match or align shapes with openings when we dress, when we insert keys into locks, when we put lids atop containers, or when we align a screwdriver with the groove of a screw. Furthermore, molding and casting, which allowed the rapid replication, transmission, and escalation of human technology within and across cultures (Ashton, 1951), are fundamentally object fitting processes.

In his classic book on the psychology of everyday things, Norman (1988) argued that good object design follows from the physical characteristics and capabilities of the user, just as modernist architects argued that "form ever follows function" (Sullivan, 1896). To this dictum, we add form also follows cognitive function. That is, the implementation requirements of many artifacts designed by humans exploit our available cognitive, perception, and action skills. In the case of object fitting, our ability to relate positive to negative space by fitting objects into apertures has been incorporated into many aspects of human technology. Studying the ontogenesis of object fitting can thus illuminate how spatial action involving relations between objects and apertures enables us to engage as well as produce our artifact culture.

1.1 Object Fitting and Education

Object fitting is important for other developmental reasons. In cultures with formal educational systems, object fitting is considered to be part of the suite of cognitive and motor skills that contributes to school readiness in young children. Common developmental assessments of adaptive behavior and early intelligence include tasks in which children must perform shape matching or fitting (Bayley, 1969; Dearborn, Anderson, & Christiansen, 1916; Newell, 1931; Sylvester, 1913). Furthermore, during early childhood, the ability to match and fit shapes is thought not only to help build spatial competence but also to pave the way for the acquisition of later mathematical knowledge (Kim, Duran, Cameron, & Grissmer, 2018; Mix & Cheng, 2012; Verdine, Golinkoff, Hirsh-Pasek, & Newcombe, 2017; Verdine et al., 2014). For instance, research has shown that children's spatial and mathematical performance at 5 years of age is predicted by their performance on object assembly tasks, some of which required object fitting, at 3 years of age (Verdine et al., 2017). In a related vein, kindergarten and first-grade children showed improvements in spatial and mathematical performance after they were given almost daily experience over several months with object assembly tasks, some of which required object fitting (Kim et al., 2018).

Yet even before 3 years of age, during the course of everyday activity, children try to fit objects into apertures. During exploration, play, and tasks of daily living, infants and young children often attempt or are helped by caregivers to fit objects into openings. This ability not only provides a foundation for spatial and mathematical achievement in the early elementary school years (see above) but can also offer clues into spatial understanding, action planning, and the associated neural systems that underlie these abilities before 3 years of age.

1.2 Object Fitting as Process

In much of the research on object fitting in young children, investigators have relied on outcome scores. That is, the ability to fit different types of shapes into apertures has often been treated as a set of developmental milestones, with researchers documenting at what ages children match shapes of varying geometrical complexity into corresponding holes. Likewise, popular developmental assessments often include object fitting in developmental scales that are used to index normative adaptive behavior (Bayley, 1969; Gesell & Thompson, 1934). In these assessments, children are typically given a summary score derived from the number of shapes or which shapes they can fit into corresponding apertures.

Critically, however, the summary or outcome score approach based on the number of right or wrong responses does not inform us about the "how" of object fitting: the process by which children of different ages attempt to fit an object into aperture, regardless of their success or failure to do so. In addition, even if young children pass the object fitting items on these scales, the process by which they accomplish object fitting might still undergo significant developmental change. Summary scores based on overall success would not reflect such change.

A similar emphasis on outcome to the exclusion of process is also evident in lab-based research on object fitting in children. Researchers have tended to focus on which shapes, typically based on geometry and/or size, children attempt to fit into apertures (Örnkloo & von Hofsten, 2007; Örnkloo & von Hofsten, 2009; Shutts et al., 2009), rather than the process by which children do so. Although some studies have moved away from summary scores and asked whether children prealign objects before inserting them into apertures (Örnkloo & von Hofsten, 2007; Street, James, Jones, & Smith, 2011), even here the process by which children achieve prealignment has largely been ignored.

In the present review, we argue that there is much to be gained by using a process-oriented approach to understand the development of object fitting in young children. We highlight how a focus on process can illuminate how the development of object fitting involves the coordination of perceptual, motor, and cognitive skills. The review has three main goals. First, we place research on object fitting in historical context. We suggest that the assessment and summary score approach that characterized the majority of research on object fitting in much of the first half of the 20th century hindered progress in understanding the development of this ability in young children. With studies focusing on how many shapes or which shapes children could fit into matching apertures by a certain age, research on object fitting ultimately stalled. There was little to address once these normative questions had been answered. Note that a similar situation occurred in the literature on the development of locomotion, where a normative approach that emphasized motor milestones to the exclusion of process hindered understanding of developmental change (Adolph, 1997; Thelen, 1989). As we hope to show, more recent efforts to investigate the "how" of object fitting have opened up new avenues of inquiry regarding developmental change in the process, planning, and neural systems that underlie these changes.

Second, we consider the cognitive, motor, and perceptual precursors that give rise to object fitting. Object fitting is a composite skill, built from advances in shape perception, physical knowledge (e.g., containment), and motor behavior. We discuss how the development of object fitting represents an integration of behavior across these different domains.

In the final section, we consider how a process-oriented approach to object fitting can lead to new insights into how this foundational skill develops. We view object fitting as a problem of coordinating multiple spatial frames of reference, both within an object and between the object and aperture. Technological advances in recording and analyzing motion at high speed have provided new ways of capturing this spatial coordination process and, more broadly, how spatial thinking can be revealed in children's actions. We conclude by considering how a focus on process can inform educational and intervention efforts to promote spatial ability and STEM learning in children.

2. OBJECT FITTING IN HISTORICAL PERSPECTIVE

Object fitting or form board problems have long been incorporated into assessment inventories and educational curricula for young children. These types of tasks were included in some of the first developmental scales of intellectual development (Gesell & Thompson, 1934). In fact, by as early as 1916, there was already a burgeoning literature on different kinds of form board tests to warrant a review of this area (Dearborn et al., 1916).

The use of object fitting or form board tasks to assess intellectual function in children persisted for at least two important reasons. First, these measures place few verbal demands on participants. They can be administered by using simple instructions and/or demonstration. Thus these tasks are suitable for testing children across a broad developmental range, regardless of children's language ability or whether children are developing typically or atypically. Second, children find object fitting tasks highly engaging. They delight in putting objects into apertures, and they enjoy doing so over and over again. Consequently, these tasks can be employed repeatedly with the same child, enabling more accurate assessments of developmental level and psychometric evaluation of test—retest reliability.

2.1 Form Board Task Origins and Early Childhood Education

The origins of form board tasks as tools for assessment and education can be traced to the work of Dr. Jean Marc Gaspard Itard in the famous case of Victor, the Wild Boy of Aveyron (1801/1962). To minimize verbal demands, Itard used form board problems to educate Victor, who had a profound language deficit. Itard constructed form board problems from simple cardboard cutouts, which Victor had to match on the basis of color and then form. Itard's longer term goal was to replace the shapes with letters of the alphabet to promote literacy development in Victor. Although this goal ultimately failed, one can already see how object fitting at this time was viewed as a foundation for later educational achievement, an idea that continues to be prevalent in the early childhood education field.

In the mid-1800s, Edward Seguin (1866), a physician and former student of Dr. Itard, published his "physiological method" for treating and educating children with mental disabilities. In this volume, Seguin adapted some of Itard's methods for educating Victor. Seguin proposed that children with mental disabilities could benefit from extensive training in motor and sensory activities. An essential part of this training involved practice with form board tasks.

Up to the end of the 19th century, form board tasks were primarily used by physicians to assess cognitive abilities of children with mental impairments. However, in the early 1900s the use of form board tasks began to be incorporated into the emerging field of early childhood education. Perhaps stemming from her medical background as a pediatrician, Dr. Maria Montessori initially came across the work of Itard and Seguin while searching through the medical literature for information about treatment of children with mental disabilities. She argued that the treatment of mental deficiency was largely a pedagogical issue, not a medical one, and built on Seguin's work in developing the Montessori Method (1912) to educate children with mental disabilities. She modeled much of her didactic learning materials after the ones used by Itard and Seguin. Subsequently, she had the insight to apply this method to the education of typically developing children. As recounted by Montessori, "It was pure chance that brought this new idea to my mind" (1912, p. 42).

In 1907, Montessori opened the first Casa dei Bambini (The Children's House) in Rome, Italy, which served typically developing children from 2 through 5 years of age. Montessori's didactic materials included wooden cylinders that differed in diameter and height and which could be inserted into a wooden box with holes of increasing diameters and heights. In addition, there were multiple trays of geometric wooden insets that differed in size and/or shape (see Fig. 1). Montessori's approach differed from Itard and Seguin by explicitly incorporating the tactile sense in her method. She capitalized on children's interest to touch things and proposed

Figure 1 Maria Montessori using the geometric insets with a young girl around 1910. *Photo credit: Maria Montessori Archives held at Association Montessori Internationale, Amsterdam, www.montessori-ami.org.*

that if they had not learned to recognize a figure by looking at it, they could learn through touching and following the contours of each shape (1912).

Montessori believed that object fitting tasks promoted mathematical concepts, the development of fine motor skills, and scientific thinking, themes that are echoed in contemporary work on the relation between object assembly tasks and subsequent STEM learning (Verdine et al., 2017). For instance, she maintained that object fitting reinforces math concepts, such as shape names and size relations, and fine motor skills that are important for handwriting. At the heart of Montessori's approach is the importance of active experimentation and the learning process. According to Montessori in her volume, *Dr. Montessori's Own Handbook* (1914), children experiment with objects and forms when attempting to insert objects into holes. She states, "The educative process is based on this: that the control of the error lies in the material itself, and the child has concrete evidence of it (p. 71) ... Hence a series of 'experiments,' of 'attempts' which end in victory" (p. 94).

While Montessori was developing her early childhood education approach, object fitting tasks became more widely employed as a nonverbal instrument to assess individuals' intellectual abilities. The form board used by Seguin was developed into the first commercially available nonverbal test by Goddard and then standardized by Sylvester (1913). Form boards were also commonly used at Ellis Island (Knox, 1914) to assess mental abilities of newly arrived immigrants. At this time, much of the research literature on form boards focused on issues of standardization (Atkins, 1931; Dearborn et al., 1916; Newell, 1931; Sylvester, 1913; Young, 1916), especially in terms of the administration and scoring of these tasks.

In subsequent work, Gesell and Thompson (1934) incorporated form board tasks into their scales of normative development. In these scales, form board tasks were used to help chart typical development in children, including infants under 1 year of age. Although infants under 1 year of age do not routinely solve such tasks, Gesell was interested in describing how infants explored the shapes and form board apparatus in an effort to catalog the natural progression of different types of manual behavior.

2.2 Form Board Tasks and Spatial Cognition

Gesell and Thompson's (1934) use of form board tasks was part of their broader effort to understand normative development and neuromaturation in children. Building on this goal, Meyer (1940) began to directly link object fitting to children's developing conception of space. In some ways, Meyer's 1940 work at Gesell's Clinic of Child Development at Yale University serves as the transition (along with Piaget and Inhelder's *The Child's Conception of Space*, 1948/1956) to more contemporary work on object fitting, with its focus on how developmental changes in spatial cognition underlie changes in object fitting. Meyer (1940) included object fitting in a battery of tasks to examine developmental changes in spatial understanding in children from 18 months to 5.5 years of age. Although sample sizes were small at some age levels (e.g., 18 months, N = 3; 24 months, N = 9; 30 months, N = 6; 36 months, N = 11; and 42 months, N = 6), Meyer classified children's object fitting behavior into three stages, which largely correspond to observations reported in more recent investigations of object fitting (e.g., see Örnkloo & von Hofsten, 2007; Shutts, et al., 2009). In the first stage, children (all 18-month-olds and some 24-month-olds) failed to insert an object (a rectangular block) into a corresponding opening. In the second stage (mainly at 24 months, but also at 30 months), performance was variable, with children aligning the block with the opening on only some trials. Finally, in the third stage (36 months and beyond), children consistently aligned the block with the opening and succeeded on the task. When more complex shapes or misalignment problems were presented, however, it was not until near 5 years of age that children consistently solved these fitting tasks. Notably, Meyer related her findings to Piaget's then available work on sensorimotor development (*The Origins of Intelligence in Children,* 1936; *The Construction of Reality in the Child,* 1937) and his proposals about spatial understanding in the infancy period.

In sum, research on object fitting peaked during roughly the first third of the 20th century and was primarily concerned with object fitting as an index of mental status. Research focused on the construction of form board tasks and the psychometric properties of various versions of such tasks (Dearborn et al., 1916) and documented developmental norms associated with object fitting (Gesell & Thompson, 1934). In addition, object fitting activities were incorporated into emerging early childhood education programs (Montessori, 1912), consistent with its conceptualization as an indicator of mental growth.

Ultimately, though, research on object fitting stalled. Meyer's (1940) work on object fitting linked performance on these tasks to children's emerging conception of space, but this idea took some time to take hold.

The publication of Piaget and Inhelder's volume "*The Child's Conception of Space* (1948/1956)" would provide later researchers with ways to think about shape in terms of different kinds of geometric relations (topological, projective, Euclidean), although Piaget and Inhelder did not report direct investigations of object fitting in this volume. Nevertheless, new interest in object fitting has emerged in recent decades due to a combination of factors. One factor stems directly from Meyer's and Piaget and Inhelder's foundational work, linking object fitting or shape understanding to more general ideas about the child's conception of space. Another factor, following in part from Piaget's infancy work, stems from a resurgence of interest in infants' perceptual and physical knowledge (Arterberry & Kellman, 2016; Baillargeon, Spelke, & Wasserman, 1985), and how such physical knowledge may set the stage for later spatial advances. Still another reason for renewed interest in object fitting can be traced to neuroscience research that has used object fitting as a behavioral system to study potential dissociations between the neural pathways that serve perception and action (Dilks, Hoffman, & Landau, 2008; Milner & Goodale, 1995). Finally, harkening back to the ideas of Maria Montessori and perhaps an example of work coming back full circle, new studies have been showing how experience with object fitting and related object assembly tasks during the preschool years paves the way for mathematical and scientific thinking in the early elementary school years (Verdine et al., 2017).

3. NEURAL BASES OF FITTING

Although the study of object fitting was originally conducted by investigators in the fields of assessment and education (see Section 2.1), more recent research on object fitting has also been influenced by the neuroscience literature of the late 20th century. In 1982, Ungerleider and Mishkin proposed a model of two independent visual systems comprised of dorsal and ventral streams (Ungerleider & Mishkin, 1982). This model was adapted and further developed by Goodale and Milner (1992). Goodale and Milner's model of two independent visual systems, a vision for perception system (ventral stream) and a vision for action system (dorsal stream), was largely founded on work with a visual form agnosia patient, D.F., with extensive damage to her ventral stream (James, Culham, Humphrey, Milner, & Goodale, 2003). Milner and Goodale's work with D.F. demonstrated a neurological dissociation by examining her ability to align a card with a slot perceptually and her ability to fit or "post" a card into a slot (Goodale, Milner, Jakobson, & Carey, 1991; Milner & Goodale, 1995). Although D.F. struggled to align the card to the slot perceptually, D.F. was readily capable of fitting the card into the slot, suggesting that there are two independent systems that use the visual information necessary to perform these tasks (Goodale et al., 1991).

In the developmental literature, a similar approach has been employed to study Williams Syndrome (WS), a rare genetic developmental disorder that is characterized by severe visuospatial impairments but relatively spared language fluency and high sociability (Dilks et al., 2008; Nardini, Atkinson, Braddick, & Burgess, 2008). Dilks et al. adapted the "posting task" developed by Milner and Goodale to measure fitting in WS children (8–17 years of age) and WS adults as well as typically developing 3-, 4-, and 6-year-old children. The findings from this study indicate that WS children and WS adults show similar fitting abilities compared with 3- to 4-year-old typically developing children but show significant deficits in fitting abilities compared with 6-year-old typically developing children. Dilks et al. posited that this pattern may be due to the protracted development of the dorsal stream, making it more vulnerable to disruption.

Recent work with typically developing children, however, has found that the neural circuitry for visually guided action appears to be adult-like by 5 years of age. James and Kersey (2018) demonstrated that children between 4 and 8 years of age activated similar brain regions (i.e., regions of the intraparietal sulcus) compared with adults when "posting" cards and when reaching for objects. Interestingly, when moving beyond an analysis of the dorsal stream, James and Kersey (2018) found that children showed significant activation in the middle cerebellum. They hypothesized that the middle cerebellum helps children monitor the execution of motor acts. More generally, these findings suggest that coordination across multiple brain regions, such as the intraparietal sulcus and middle cerebellum, underlies visually guided action systems. Whole-brain analyses such as these could further our understanding of the neural circuitry involved in the development of particular perception–action systems, including object fitting, during childhood.

These new approaches to understanding neural connectivity within the brain have challenged claims that the two visual systems develop independently of one another (Byrge, Sporns, & Smith, 2014). Consistent with this perspective, behavioral research has demonstrated that perception and action actively develop together. For instance, children reach for and act on objects which change the views of those objects; how children view objects then informs their developing perceptual systems (Libertus & Needham, 2010; Libertus, Joh, & Needham, 2015; Soska, Adolph, & Johnson, 2010). In turn, the perceptual systems then bias how children act on and hold objects (James, Jones, Swain, Pereira, & Smith, 2014; Pereira, James, Jones, & Smith, 2010). This dynamical perspective on the development of perceiving and acting on objects has begun to guide investigations into the development of object fitting (Smith, Street, Jones, & James, 2014). For instance, the way in which 18- to 30-month-old children orient objects for viewing may influence how they align an object with an opening. Questions around object fitting are no longer constrained to which visual system plays a role in this task but rather how the visual and motor systems develop and function together to enable successful object fitting.

In the following sections, we adopt a developmental perspective and ask, "What are the perception–action building blocks of object fitting?" We first consider developmental changes in the perception of objects, with a focus on those properties or dimensions of objects that are especially relevant for understanding the development of object fitting—namely the perception of object unity, shape, spatial relations between objects, and apertures. Subsequently, we discuss manual action on objects and focus on how infants relate their actions to an object's size, orientation, and/or shape. We then consider the problem of object fitting in detail. We use a process-based approach to understand how children relate the biomechanical properties of the manual system to an object's spatial structure to accomplish fitting. We conclude by discussing how a process-based approach can further inform our understanding of object fitting and spatial ability more generally.

4. PERCEPTION–ACTION FOUNDATIONS OF OBJECT FITTING

4.1 Object Perception

Object fitting is inherently a relational task. Individuals need to relate an object to an aperture, based on the size and/or geometry of the object and aperture. But this seemingly straightforward task presupposes some basic concepts regarding what constitutes and individuates one object from another. To differentiate between objects, infants must learn what movement patterns define a unitary object (Johnson & Aslin, 1995;

Kellman & Spelke, 1983). Similarly, infants need to recognize the physical characteristics (i.e., object boundary cues) that define the presence of single or multiple objects (Kaufman & Needham, 2010). Collectively, these abilities enable infants to differentiate whether a single or multiple objects are present and establish a foundation for relating objects together and eventually object fitting.

Infants learn how the pattern of movement of an object defines object unity in the first few months after birth (Johnson & Hannon, 2015). Four-month-old infants who were shown a box with two visible rod pieces moving in synchrony behind the box looked longer when the box was removed and the rod was depicted as two separate objects rather than a single object, suggesting that they had perceived the original rod as a single unitary object (Kellman & Spelke, 1983). Further investigation indicated that infants as young as 2 months of age would look longer at the separate rods if the occluder contained openings or was shorter, again suggesting that infants had perceived the original rod as a unitary object (Johnson & Aslin, 1995). Taken together, these findings indicate that young infants quickly begin to rely on the movement patterns of objects for the perception of object unity (Johnson, 2004). In the context of object fitting, sensitivity to movement cues would reinforce the perception of object unity, which would be important for predicting how segments of a rigid object should move in tandem as the object is inserted into an opening.

Besides movement information, infants as young as 4 months of age also begin to use visual cues about object boundaries to differentiate the presence of one versus multiple objects (Kaufman & Needham, 2010; Needham, 2016). Infants are more likely to perceive adjoining objects as separate when salient object boundary cues (i.e., a seam between objects) are present compared with when those cues are absent. With regard to object fitting, this ability will help children understand where one object ends and another begins, thus providing them with information about the boundaries of the object that needs to be inserted into an opening.

4.2 Shape Perception

Beyond the perception of object unity, object fitting also requires individuals to detect at least one axis or plane of correspondence between a solid shape and an aperture. In the canonical form of object fitting, that correspondence involves a match between the outer contours of the solid object and the inner contours of the aperture. In addition, individuals must detect the relative sizes of the object and aperture. For objects to be inserted into apertures, the object must be smaller than the corresponding aperture, even allowing for a snug fit. Detection of these potential relations or correspondences typically occurs in the context of dynamic activity. Because planar views of the object and aperture might not be simultaneously available or change as an object is moved through space or individuals shift their positions, individuals need to perceive that the form of the object and of the aperture remain constant despite different and dynamically changing views during object fitting. The same is true for the relative sizes of the object and aperture. At the least, this requires individuals to possess some kinds of shape and size constancy. When do these abilities develop?

Notably, research with newborns indicates that some aspects of shape and size constancy are already present at birth. With respect to shape constancy, newborns generalize habituation on the basis of the constant or real shape of a rectangle or a trapezoid, rather than the projective shapes of these objects (Slater & Morison, 1985). With respect to size constancy, newborn infants look preferentially to a novel cube based on the actual rather than projective size of the cube observed during a familiarization period (Slater, Mattock, & Brown, 1990). Taken together, these findings suggest that newborns already evidence some basic perceptual constancies that will enable them to register the stable shape and size of an object across different views of the same object.

These perceptual capacities are fundamental building blocks of object fitting, where children need to recognize that the shapes of the object and aperture remain invariant despite dynamically changing views of each as they try to relate the two. At the same time, it should be noted that relying on the overall constancy of an object's shape and size may lead to problems when attempting to insert a shape into an aperture. Not all orientations of the same object license object fitting. Some errors in object alignment with respect to an aperture may reflect an overreliance on shape and size constancy. This overreliance may come at the expense of recognizing that orienting the same object differently may have consequences for object fitting. We come back to this possibility when we consider young children's attempts to fit objects into apertures in greater detail.

Other important aspects of shape perception that are relevant for object fitting emerge during the first few months after birth. By 4 months of age, infants are able to register the three-dimensional form of an object from sequences of different continuous transformations of that object (either a triangular or L-shaped object) rotating in depth (Kellman, 1984). The early ability to recognize the overall three-dimensional form of an object from limited or partial views of an object presumably contributes to the later development of object fitting skill. In the Kellman (1984) study, infants were initially habituated to different sequences of either a triangular or L-shaped object rotating in depth. When subsequently shown each of these objects undergoing movement around a new axis of rotation, infants dishabituated to the novel object but generalized habituation to the familiar object—although they had not previously observed these particular rotation sequences.

In research on the related problem of perceiving the three-dimensionality of an object from partial views of that object, infants near the middle of the first year show evidence of recognizing objects as enclosed solids from limited viewpoint information. For example, by 6 months, infants register that a wedge-like object should be a solid enclosed surface from limited views of the object (Soska & Johnson, 2008). The age at which this three-dimensional object completion ability first appears, however, varies with both the richness of the perceptual information that specifies three-dimensionality and the complexity of the form that infants see (Vrins, Hunnius, & van Lier, 2011). With richer perceptual information that specifies three-dimensionality, 4.5-month-old infants show evidence of three-dimensional form completion (Vrins et al., 2011). With more complex forms (i.e., a multisegmented L-shaped object), it is not until 6 months that males and not until 9 months that females show evidence of three-dimensional object completion (Soska & Johnson, 2013).

Collectively, this work suggests that infants are able to register that objects are solid and enclosed from limited or partial views of their surface areas. It should be pointed out, however, that the results of these three-dimensional form perception studies are ambiguous with reference to what infants expect these solid forms to look like geometrically. In these studies, conclusions are necessarily derived from comparisons with a control condition that uses an object with a different shape (e.g., a triangular vs. L-shaped object; Kellman, 1984; Soska & Johnson, 2013; a convex vs. concave wedge-like shape; Soska & Johnson, 2008; Vrins et al., 2011). The studies do not offer comparisons with a range of different shaped objects. Thus the studies do not establish whether infants perceptually register the *particular* form of an object from continuous transformations but partial views of that object rotating in depth (Kellman, 1984) or perceptually complete the volume of a form with a *particular* shape (Soska & Johnson, 2008; Vrins et al., 2011). Instead, the studies establish only whether infants evidence these abilities for one shape in comparison to another one used in a given experiment. Additional research is needed to understand how these types of three-dimensional form perception abilities develop when shapes that are more similar geometrically are compared. Such work would help bridge the literatures on early form perception and later object fitting, where children often need to process objects with respect to their geometric structure.

4.3 Perception of Spatial Relations Between Objects

In work on infants' perception of object unity, the tasks that have been employed also require infants, at least implicitly, to register information about between-object relations—namely, the relation between the rod and occluder. In other research, investigators have specifically looked at infants' understanding of between-object relations, such as containment. Recognition of the physical conditions under which an object can fit into an opening or another object is another prerequisite for object fitting. When do infants begin to recognize that one object may fit into another? This issue has been addressed in research on infants' perception of the physical conditions under which containment is possible. By 2.5 months of age, infants recognize that a container must be open for an object to be inserted into it. They look longer at impossible events in which an object is inserted into a container through a closed lid (Hespos & Baillargeon, 2001). Subsequently, infants begin to show sensitivity how the relation between the size (width, length, and height) of the object and opening constrains the possibility of containment. By 4 months of age, infants show sensitivity to how the width of an object in relation to the width of an opening affords containment (Wang, Baillargeon, & Brueckner, 2004), but it is not until 7.5 months of age that infants show sensitivity to how the height of an object in relation to the height of a container affords containment (Hespos & Baillargeon, 2006; Wang, 2011). Thus, in the second half year, infants are able to recognize whether an object's size in relation to a container's dimensions affords containment. These studies provide important information about infants' recognition of the necessary conditions for containment and by extension object fitting, but they leave open the question of whether infants recognize the conditions that allow an exact fit of an object into the opening of a container based on the geometric properties (i.e., shape) of each. In addition, as will be discussed later, the fact that infants can recognize the perceptual conditions under which containment is possible does not guarantee that they will be able to use action to exploit these relational possibilities.

Further refinement in understanding containment and differentiating this spatial category from other spatial categories continues to develop through the first 2 years (Casasola, 2018). Although 6-month-old infants can discriminate between the spatial categories of containment and support (e.g., one object stacked on another object; Casasola, Cohen, & Chiarello, 2003), 8-month-old infants have difficulty in discriminating the spatial category of containment from occlusion (one object behind another; Rigney & Wang, 2015). By 11 months of age, however, infants show evidence of discriminating between the spatial categories of containment and occlusion. To account for this differential developmental pattern across containment, occlusion, and support, Rigney and Wang (2015) suggest that at 8 months of age, infants may be discriminating spatial categories via perceptual differences, but by 11 months of age, infants are beginning to discriminate spatial categories using more abstract representations. Given the timing of this developmental change, infants' knowledge of the spatial categories of the relations between objects may be influenced by their developing competencies in reaching, grasping, and manipulating objects. Support for the potential role of action in helping to refine spatial category understanding comes from other research on 18-month-old infants understanding of tight fit relations (see Casasola, Bhwagat, & Burke, 2009).

4.4 Aperture Perception

As noted, object fitting is a relational achievement, requiring the individual to relate the shape of an object to that of a hole. Holes, however, present a paradox for the perceiver. Holes are not material objects, yet they are perceived by adults as having geometric properties, including shape (Bertamini & Casati, 2015; Bertamini & Croucher, 2003; Palmer, 1999), and as discrete entities, which can be counted even by 3-year-old children (Giralt & Bloom, 2000).

Although most research relevant to the developmental foundations of object fitting concerns how young children perceive the shape of an object (see Section 4.2), less research has focused on how young children begin to perceive the shape of a hole. Nevertheless, there is reason to believe that perceiving the shape of a hole may be more demanding than perceiving the shape of an object. Despite some evidence indicating that adults can remember the shapes of holes and the shapes of objects (Nelson, Theirman, & Palmer, 2009), other work suggests that adults do not process the shape of a hole without also processing the shape of the object "owning" the hole (Bertamini & Casati, 2015; Bertamini & Croucher, 2003). Consistent with this latter idea, adults show an advantage in perceiving the shape of a hole when the shape of the object surrounding the hole and that of the hole are congruent (Bertamini & Helmy, 2012).

How are these findings on the perception of the shape of holes relevant for understanding the development of object fitting? We highlight two ways. As noted, the findings in the adult literature suggest that the perception of the shape of a hole involves processing the hole's shape in relation to the shape of the surround in which the hole is embedded. In the literature on the development of object fitting, however, this relation has not received much theoretical or empirical attention. Instead, developmental investigators have focused primarily on the relation between the shape of the object to be fitted and that of the hole. We suggest that systematic variation of the shape of the background surface in which the hole is embedded (in addition to the geometric relation between the object and hole) may yield new insights into how aperture shape is perceived and, in turn, how a relational act like object fitting unfolds.

Second, explicit consideration of how children begin to perceive the shape of holes also directs developmental investigators to consider a different class of fitting problems. To our knowledge, virtually all research to date on the development of object fitting has focused on the problem of relating positive space (the object) to negative space (the hole). The reverse problem of fitting negative space to positive space as would occur when fitting an object with an interior hole onto an object (think inserting a paper towel roll into a holder, a cap on a bottle, or even the Tower of Hanoi task) has received little consideration in the spatial cognition literature. Investigation of how children fit negative space (holes) onto positive space in combination with the typical problem of how children fit positive space into negative space would broaden understanding of the development of object fitting.

Although there has been little research on how young children perceive the shape or geometric properties of holes, there is work suggesting that infants are able to register information that specifies the presence of an aperture. Three- to five-month-old infants react defensively by blinking to an approaching object but not to an object with a large aperture embedded in it (Schmuckler & Li, 1998). This differential pattern of responding suggests that infants perceived the approaching solid object to specify collision but the object with the hole in it to specify unobstructed passage.

Related developments associated with the perception of the convexity/concavity of surfaces, which would be important for supporting object fitting, occur in subsequent months. By 7 months of age, infants use the pictorial depth cue of shading to distinguish between two-dimensional spherical surfaces that appear convex or concave: They attempt to reach more to the former than the latter display under monocular conditions, when conflicting binocular information for the flatness of the displays is not available (Granrud, Yonas, & Opland, 1985). In addition, by 6 months, under some viewing conditions, infants reach to different areas of convex and concave objects, suggesting that they are able to perceive what convexity or concavity affords for graspability (Corrow, Mathison, Granrud, & Yonas, 2014). Collectively, studies on the perception of apertures and convexity/concavity suggest that by or soon after the first half year, infants are becoming sensitive to perceptual information that specifies the existence of a hole or a depression in a surface—information that is critical for targeting where on a surface an object may be inserted during object fitting.

Despite early sensitivity to perceptual information for the presence of an aperture or the convexity/concavity of a surface, sensitivity to the geometric properties of holes or apertures appears to develop gradually. Evidence for this developmental conclusion comes from work on how infants and young children attempt to relate their bodies to gaps or openings in surfaces. Infants in the second half year evidence greater sensitivity to the size of a gap that is safe to cross when they are sitting and reaching than when they are prone and crawling (Adolph, 2000). Other work suggests that even in the early preschool years, young children sometimes make dramatic scale errors when judging the relation between the size of their bodies and that of an opening or gap. For instance, 18- to 30-month-old children will sometimes try to fit into small toy cars, despite large differences in size between the two (DeLoache, Uttal, & Rosengren, 2004). Still in other work, 18- to 26-month-old infants make errors when choosing between a wide enough but low opening to crawl through versus a tall enough but too narrow opening to walk through (Brownell, Zerwas, & Ramani, 2007). It should be noted, however, that these errors may not always reflect perceptual insensitivity but instead stem from toddlers' indifference to the penalties associated with mistakes in these situations (Franchak & Adolph, 2012).

Fitting the body through an opening, of course, entails a different set of demands than fitting an object in an opening. For one thing, the scale is different. For another, the goal can vary. In many object fitting tasks, the goal is to achieve a tight fit between object and hole. In so-called body fitting tasks, however, the goal is typically unobstructed and safe passage through the hole or opening. Effecting a tight fit might result in entrapment (e.g., see Franchak & Adolph, 2012). Yet it remains an open question as to whether the development of sensitivity to size and shape information for body fitting and object fitting constitutes domain general or specific achievements. Work demonstrating that sensitivity to perceptual information in one action mode may not generalize immediately to other action modes or tasks (Adolph, 1997, 2000; Lockman, 1984) suggests that children may learn about size and shape constraints for body and object fitting separately.

5. ACTING ON OBJECT SIZE, ORIENTATION, AND SHAPE

Object fitting requires not only the accurate perception of size, orientation, and shape with respect to both object and aperture, but the ability to act adaptively on this information by grasping the object based on its spatial structure and then transporting and aligning the object with respect to the aperture. In the following section, we consider the development of the initial part of this sequence—namely, how do infants relate their grasps to the shape and size of an object?

The biomechanical properties of the manual system enable individuals to tailor their arm and hand movements to the spatial properties of objects. Individuals can rotate their forearms almost 180 degrees, which allows for pronation or supination of the palm. This range of movement, in turn, allows individuals to align the hand with the orientation of an object, a segment of an object, or even a preferred axis of an object—all of which facilitates ease of use. Likewise, the combination of an opposable thumb and the ability to fractionate movement of the fingers enables individuals to adjust the type and size of their grips according to the size of an object. Furthermore, by coordinating these biomechanical properties with visual information about the object before contact, individuals can boost the efficiency and performance of the entire perception–action system. Developmental researchers have asked when do infants begin to show these types of prospective adjustments when they reach for objects? Here we focus on the dimensions of size, orientation, and shape, the dimensions most relevant for understanding the foundations of object fitting.

5.1 Object Size

When reaching for an object, prospective manual adjustments for object size can occur in a number of ways. One type of adjustment involves reaching with one or two hands. When small objects are presented, a unimanual reach may be more appropriate than a bimanual one, but when large objects are presented, a bimanual reach might be the better choice. In addition, prospective manual adjustments for size might occur at the level of the hand. Grips involving the opening and closing of the index in relation to the thumb (i.e., the pincer grasp) might be better suited for very small objects; grips involving the opening and closing of all the fingers of the hand in relation to the thumb might be more fitting for larger objects (e.g., a palmar grasp). Of course, motor development will constrain when infants can exhibit some of these adjustments or strategies.

Earlier research on infant visuomotor coordination for object size suggested that even before infants had developed the ability to reach, they produced different kinds of arm movements to objects that varied in size. In a longitudinal study of prereaching behaviors in infants, Bruner and Koslowski (1972) reported that large objects evoked swiping and small objects evoked bimanual fingering at midline. Whether these differential reactions indicate visuomotor sensitivity to object size is, however, uncertain (Lockman & Ashmead, 1983). One might argue that unimanual arm movements are more appropriate for small objects, whereas bimanual arm movements would be more appropriate for larger ones (Fagard, 2000). In addition, infants at this age may not have found the smaller object very interesting and instead resorted to midline fingering. In fact, subsequent work suggests that when reaching, infants first begin to make prospective manual adjustments based on visual information about object size by the middle or latter part of the second half year. These prospective adjustments may entail unimanual versus bimanual reaches, grip type, and/or grip size (Berthier & Carrico, 2010; Corbetta, Thelen, & Johnson, 2000; Fagard & Jacquet, 1996; von Hofsten & Rönnqvist, 1988).

The findings that infants in the second half year adjust their arm and hand movements to an object's size during reaching suggests a degree of prospective control and, from a spatial standpoint, the use of a body-centered frame of reference (Lockman & Ashmead, 1983). Infants are relating a part of the body to a spatial feature (i.e., size or extent) of an object. Yet these findings raise a puzzle when object fitting is considered. Although infants relate their grasps to object size during reaching, children in the second year still have difficulty relating object size to opening size during fitting, often misjudging whether an object is small enough to fit into an opening (Shutts et al., 2009). Similar asynchronies in performance arise when we consider the object feature of orientation.

5.2 Orientation

A similar type of developmental progression is evident for the object feature of orientation. During the second half year, infants begin to prospectively use pronation and supination movements of the forearm to align their hands with the orientation of an object. In these studies, infants are typically presented horizontal or vertical rods. The results of these investigations suggest that during the second half year, infants show progressive improvements in their ability to prospectively align their hands with the orientation of the rod (Lockman, Ashmead, & Bushnell, 1984; McCarty, Clifton, Ashmead, Lee, & Goubet, 2001; Wentworth, Benson, & Haith, 2000; Witherington, 2005), although one study reports that infants already evidence this ability by 5 months of age (von Hofsten & Fazel-Zandy, 1984). In studies showing progressive improvement in anticipatory hand alignment during the second half year, it is important to note that the limitation does not stem from motor factors alone. In the Lockman et al. (1984) study, 5-month-old infants demonstrated the ability to pronate and supinate the forearm, resulting in the hand being oriented horizontally or vertically. These 5-month-old infants, however, did not prospectively relate these movements to the object's orientation, suggesting that they did not coordinate vision with action.

Research on visuomotor sensitivity to object orientation raises two important issues for understanding the development of object fitting. First, in most studies on anticipatory hand alignment for orientation, investigators presented infants with rods that were oriented horizontally or vertically. An exception is the Wentworth et al. (2000) study in which diagonal rods were also used. In that study, only the oldest age group, 11-month-old infants, showed different patterns of anticipatory hand alignment for horizontal and diagonal rods. In short, before the end of the first year, infants show prospective alignments for an object's orientation, regardless of whether that object is oriented horizontally, vertically, or diagonally within a plane. Second, and consistent with the work on anticipatory adjustments for object size, although infants can align their hands with the orientation of an object, they show a marked delay in aligning a handheld object with an opening in fitting tasks. In a comparable task in which young children were prompted to fit a rod into a horizontally or vertically oriented slot embedded in a table, it was found that it was not until near 2 years of age that children prospectively aligned the handheld rod before it contacted the slot (Jung, Kahrs, & Lockman, 2015). Thus as is the case for the dimension of size, using vision to align the hand with respect to an object appears to develop earlier than the comparable requirement of using vision to align an object with respect to an opening. We consider this developmental asynchrony in more detail when we examine work on the development of object fitting (see Section 7.1).

5.3 Size and Orientation

In most research on whether infants show anticipatory adjustments for size or orientation when reaching, investigators have considered sensitivity to each of these object features independently of one another. In daily life, however, these object dimensions naturally combine. Individuals typically need to make anticipatory adjustments to size and orientation simultaneously as they reach for different kinds of objects. The increased demands of processing two object dimensions simultaneously and making anticipatory adjustments for them during reaching might present challenges for infants, however. Consistent with this idea, Schwarzer et al. report that between 10 and 12 months, infants show improvement in their ability to show simultaneous adjustments for size and orientation of an object when reaching (Ransburg, Reiser, Munzert, Jovanovic, & Schwarzer, 2017; Schum, Jovanovic, & Schwarzer, 2011). It will be almost another year, however, before infants consistently use information about object size and orientation to align and/or fit handheld objects into apertures (see Section 6.4).

5.4 Shape

Shape is a geometric property that refers to the spatial organization of the outer contour of an object. Shape, however, can comprise a combination of several different object dimensions (size, orientation, angle, etc.), so it is often difficult to isolate shape from other dimensions. Reaching studies suggest that infants show anticipatory manual adjustments for some aspects of shape during the second half year, but not to other aspects of shape until after this period (Barrett & Needham, 2008). In this connection, one variable along which the spatial structure of shape may vary is symmetry. By 11 months of age, infants show greater separation of the hands when initially contacting an asymmetrical object as compared to a symmetrical one, suggesting that they are attempting to increase grip stability (Barrett & Needham, 2008). By 18 months of age, young children begin to evidence sensitivity to the more abstract spatial property of an object's axis of elongation. They become increasingly more likely to grip and hold an object so that the longest axis of the object is either parallel or perpendicular to the line of sight (Pereira et al., 2010).

Collectively, these findings suggest that by the middle of the second year, infants can integrate vision and manual action. They use visual information about different object features—size, orientation, shape, etc.—as they reach for objects and adjust their manual actions accordingly even before they physically contact the object. Such prospective control will help infants use objects effectively and efficiently and help set the stage for object fitting.

6. FITTING

6.1 Fitting as a Problem of Coordinating Spatial Frames of Reference

All these instances of prospective control involve the individual acting directly on the object or some feature of the object with an empty hand. Once an object has been grasped, however, the properties of the hand change. Individuals need to gear their actions not just to the relation between the hand and object but also to the relation between the object and aperture. These dual demands can be conceptualized as a frame of reference problem or, more precisely, a problem of coordinating multiple frames of reference such as relating the body to an object and an object to another object. These have been referred to as problems involving body–object and object–object (aperture) relations, respectively (Lockman, 2000; Lockman & Ashmead, 1983). More broadly, the problem of coordinating multiple reference frames arises in numerous localization tasks, including tactile localization, where individuals must integrate information about the location of a tactile stimulus with respect to body anatomy along with information about the location of that part of the anatomy in external space (Heed, Buchholz, Engel, & Röder, 2015). For example, reconciling these competing frames of reference occurs in the body domain when we scratch an itch or swat a fly that we feel has landed on the skin.

To illustrate the coordination problem with respect to object fitting, consider the changing position of an object as an individual rotates it.

When an individual holds an object (e.g., a rod) in the hand, one end of that object extends toward the radial side of the palm and the other end extends toward the ulnar side. Despite rotation of the hand, these egocentric or anatomically based relations defining the position of the object relative to the hand remain stable, a constancy of sorts (see Section 5). By contrast, with respect to external space, the orientation of the object changes as the hand rotates, and it is this position that the individual must use to align the object with that of still another object/aperture external to the body (Lockman, 2000; Lockman & Ashmead, 1983). Coordinating these multiple and potentially competing frames of reference can lead to challenges for the young child during fitting tasks. This account predicts that the likelihood of success on these tasks can be manipulated by reducing or increasing the complexity of the frames of reference problem that the child needs to coordinate during fitting.

6.2 Hand Fitting

One way to simplify the frames of reference problem would be to eliminate the object altogether and require the child to fit their hand through an aperture. This is exactly what Street et al. (2011) did in a series of experiments with 18- to 24-month-old children using the posting task (see Section 3). Street et al. (2011) report a developmental dissociation between inserting the hand versus a handheld disc into a slot. Despite these tasks being formally the same, 18-month-old children preoriented the hand before inserting it into a horizontal or vertical slot, but they failed to do so when holding a disc. In contrast, 24-month-old children successfully preoriented the disc before insertion. Other investigators report that 10-month-old infants will insert their hands into a horizontal or vertical slot to contact an object located behind it (McKenzie, Slater, Tremellen, & McAlpin, 1993).

Collectively, these findings are consistent with a multiple frames of reference account. When the spatial demands associated with insertion are simplified and only body-object frames of reference need to be coded, children will succeed on certain kinds of insertion tasks. By 18 months of age, children can successfully orient their empty hand and insert it into an aperture. But when the same age children are required to insert objects into apertures and the spatial coding demands increase, performance will be challenged. Object fitting may thus require children to differentially use different types of spatial codes and switch between them as children grasp an object (a body or anatomy-based code) and then subsequently align the object (an external or environmentally based code) with respect to an aperture.

6.3 Object Fitting and Geometric Structure

Just as simplifying spatial coding demands can facilitate performance on fitting tasks, increasing those demands may impede performance on these tasks. One way to increase these demands is by manipulating the geometric structure of the object to be fitted. Objects can vary with respect to geometric structure along a number of dimensions—shape, symmetry, extent, number of major axes etc. Several studies suggest that as the geometric structure of the object increases in complexity, children will experience greater difficulty as they attempt to prealign and insert a block into a hole (see also Fragaszy & Cummins-Sebree, 2005; Fragaszy, Kuroshima, & Stone, 2015).

Consistent with this idea, Örnkloo and von Hofsten (2007) report that on a majority of trials, 14-month-old children succeed at inserting a cylindrical solid with circular ends into a corresponding hole, but even 26-month-old children often fail at inserting a right-triangular solid into a corresponding hole, especially when the solid and hole are not initially aligned. This pattern of results appears to be related to the geometric structure of the objects. Whereas the cylindrical object with a circular base afforded fitting in any orientation as long as the axis of elongation was held vertically, the right-triangular solid afforded fitting only in one orientation. Furthermore, when the task was to insert shapes of intermediate complexity (i.e., a square, rectangular solid, or equilateral triangle, see Fig. 2), which allowed several possible orientations for insertion, success occurred somewhat earlier, increasing dramatically between 18 and 24 months of age.

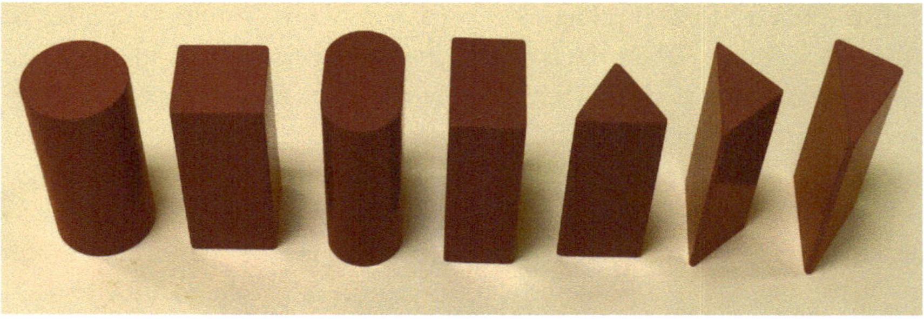

Figure 2 The different objects used in Örnkloo & von Hoftsen (2007, 2009). *Objects provided courtesy of Claes von Hofsten.*

Likewise, when objects are not symmetrical but irregularly shaped, 2-year-old children often encounter difficulty inserting objects into corresponding holes at ages when they succeed with more regularly shaped objects. Fragaszy et al. (2015) report that 3- and 4-year-old children succeed more often than 2-year-old children in fitting a "tomahawk-shaped object" into a matching groove. The problem is not that 2-year-old children are incapable of inserting objects comprising multiple axes into holes. The 2-year-old children are able to insert a bar (one major axis) or a cross-shaped object (i.e., a symmetrical object with two major axes) into a matching groove on a majority of trials.

Fragaszy et al. (2015) report related findings when alignments during fitting attempts are considered. Children are more likely to align the object's axis of elongation with a corresponding groove if that axis is part of a less geometrically complex structure. Specifically, they are more likely to align a simple bar alone than a bar that served as the shaft of the tomahawk-shaped object. In sum, children's alignment attempts and eventual success at fitting will be influenced by the object's geometric structure and hence the complexity of the frames of reference that they must coordinate.

6.4 Selecting Objects and Apertures for Fitting

Additional frame of reference problems involve comparing multiple objects to a single opening or a single object to multiple openings. These problems require children either to compare the geometric structure of objects to a single opening or the geometric structure of an object to several openings. In these tasks, children must compare some geometric properties (e.g., shape and/or size) along which objects and openings may vary.

When comparing two shapes (i.e., cylinder vs. square, rectangle vs. ellipsoid, isosceles vs. right-angled triangle; see Fig. 2), 20- to 40-month-old children are better at choosing between openings than objects: they are more successful in choosing which of two openings an object fits than when choosing which of two objects fit into a single opening (Örnkloo & von Hofsten, 2009). One possible explanation for this difference is that when children choose between multiple openings for a single object, they do not need to commit to a decision until after they grasp the object, unlike the case when children must choose between multiple objects for a single opening. Furthermore, geometric complexity influences children's performance. For instance, children are more successful selecting objects or openings when choosing between cylinder versus square shapes and rectangle versus ellipsoid shapes compared to isosceles versus right-angled triangle shapes. In addition, children improve dramatically between 20 and 40 months of age when choosing between cylinder/squares and rectangle/ellipsoids but show no significant improvement when choosing between isosceles and right-angled triangles.

In other work, investigators have examined how children use information about size when making object fitting judgments. Shutts et al. (2009) report that by 20 months but not 15 months of age, young children will observe size constraints when judging whether an object can fit into one of two openings or vice versa. When considered in relation to previously reviewed work on physical knowledge (see Section 4.3), these results suggest a dissociation between perception and action. Despite young infants showing sensitivity to the relation between object and opening size in studies on the perception of containment (Wang et al., 2004), difficulty with size judgments in action tasks involving fitting may not be that surprising given that children are still making scale errors when fitting their bodies into openings (DeLoache et al., 2004).

7. TOWARD A PROCESS APPROACH OF OBJECT FITTING

7.1 Prealignment

In parallel to questions in the reaching literature on infants' anticipatory hand adjustments (see Section 5.2), researchers have also asked, "When do children make anticipatory adjustments when the task is to fit an object into a hole?" As noted, there is a striking developmental dissociation between infants' ability to make appropriate anticipatory adjustments of the hand when reaching for objects and children's later developing ability to make corresponding types of anticipatory adjustments when attempting to align an object with a hole (see Section 5.2). Furthermore, although children may eventually succeed in fitting the object into a hole, the complexity of the object's geometric structure will often dictate the extent to which children make appropriate adjustments *before* the hand-held object contacts the hole.

Evidence in support of this idea comes from a number of studies. Örnkloo and von Hofsten (2007) highlight the complexity of this coordination problem, which often occurs in multiple spatial planes and thus involves the coordination of multiple frames of reference. Besides comparing eventual success at fitting, Örnkloo and von Hofsten (2007) examined the degree to which children between 14 and 26 months of age prealigned the elongated objects (see Fig. 2) when the objects initially contacted the hole. Prealignment was considered with respect to multiple spatial planes, that is, with reference to the object's axis of elongation, and with respect to its cross-section. These planes correspond to the object's vertical (upright) and horizontal (e.g., relative to a tabletop surface) orientations, respectively.

Developmentally, children solved the prealignment problem in the vertical plane before the horizontal one. Vertical prealignment of the object relative to the hole increased markedly between 18 and 22 months of age, but horizontal prealignment of the object (i.e., orienting the object's cross-section in relation to the hole) increased primarily between 22 and 26 months of age. Strikingly, despite the apparent salience of the axis of elongation and the results of prior studies suggesting that infants by this age possess physical knowledge about the conditions under which containment is permissible (Hespos & Baillargeon, 2006), 14-month-old children failed on about 25% of trials to orient the object vertically before attempting object insertion. At the other end of the age distribution, 26-month-old children experienced difficulty in prealigning some of the triangular (i.e., isosceles, right-angled) objects horizontally relative to the hole. Critically, these objects afforded insertion in only a small number of possible orientations. Likewise, Smith et al. (2014) report that when the task is to insert an object into a horizontal or vertical slot, 18-month-old and to some extent 24-month-old children are more successful at prealigning the axis of elongation of simple rectangular blocks than simple but nonrectangular and more complex shapes. In sum, these findings highlight the spatial challenges that children must master when integrating perceptual-cognitive abilities with manual action. The difficulty that young children often encounter when aligning objects in multiple spatial planes offers a window into how they attempt to analyze the three-dimensional structure of objects and how they incorporate this analysis, for better or for worse, into a plan for action.

7.2 Prealignment and Process

The issue of prealignment or anticipatory adjustments of the object before insertion has been of particular interest to investigators of fitting. As noted, prealignment can illuminate how children use visual information about object structure to guide manual action. When prealignment has been studied with children, researchers have tended to focus on the degree to which objects are aligned with apertures at the point when the object either first enters the aperture or contacts the surface surrounding it.

Such a focus, however, neglects consideration of the process of prealignment. The prealignment period extends from the time children grasp the object until that handheld object first contacts the aperture area. Children's manual adjustments during this period can reveal how they link their analysis of spatial structure (i.e., the object and its relation to the aperture) with the biomechanical properties of the arm-hand system. Crucially, the biomechanical properties of the arm-hand system permit objects to undergo different kinds of spatial transformations. Handheld objects can be translated in space as the arm extends, withdraws, or moves laterally and as the wrist extends and flexes. Handheld objects can also be rotated as the forearm rotates, as the wrist adducts and abducts, and as the fingers and thumb pivot and palpate against one another. To bring objects into alignment with apertures, the child must recruit some or all of these types of movements and coordinate their execution to achieve a spatial match. The process by which they do so can illuminate how the perception of object structure is rendered into spatial action.

Jung et al. (2015) employed this type of perception–action analysis to investigate object fitting in 16- to 33-month-old children. Jung et al. (2015) adapted high-speed motion capture technology (240 Hz) to track the spatial adjustments that children made as they transported a rod that was to be fit into a tabletop slot (Fig. 3). Movements were analyzed

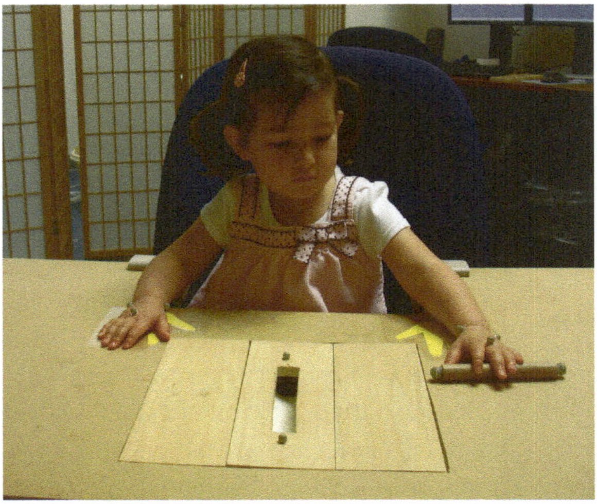

Figure 3 The experimental setup from Jung et al. (2015).

according to the types of spatial displacements that the rod underwent—namely, translations (lateral or forward/backward movement of the object independent of object orientation) and rotations (movement that results in a change of object orientation).

The results revealed striking developmental differences in how children orchestrated translations and rotations during object transport, although all children were able to fit the rod into the tabletop slot. Consistent with the results of prior work (Meyer, 1940; Örnkloo & von Hofsten, 2007; Street et al., 2011), children under 20 months of age did not coordinate translations and rotations. They transported the rod to the aperture, successfully performing the translational component of the task, but failed to orient the object appropriately in advance of contacting the area immediately surrounding the slot. They even failed when the object's initial orientation at the outset of a trial matched that of the slot only a short distance away, suggesting that a lack of spatial planning—characterized performance. Furthermore, although these younger children transported the rod to the slot, they did so inefficiently. They used much longer routes to translate the rod to the slot than did the older children. All told, the younger children's lengthy routes and their failure to preorient the rod had substantial costs. On average, children under 20 months of age took almost three times as long as the oldest child in the study to fit the object into the slot.

Between 20 and 24 months of age, children began to coordinate translations and rotations during object transport. During transport, they prospectively aligned the rod with the slot. They also made more efficient translations to the slot, traversing shorter routes than children under 20 months of age. Yet closer inspection of how the 20- to 24-month-old children coordinated translations and rotations while transporting the rod indicated that children still had not achieved optimal levels of efficiency. By comparison, 24- to 33-month-old children performed low to the surface translations, which resulted in even shorter transport routes. Moreover, the older children began to align the rod with the slot almost immediately after they grasped the rod. The results suggest that early in the third year, children quickly perceive the spatial disparity between an object and aperture and can immediately implement a plan of action in which they integrate translations and rotations to bring the object and aperture into alignment. Collectively, these findings indicate that when fitting objects with a simple geometric structure, children by the end of the second year progress from a two-step approach in which they perform translations and rotations sequentially to an integrated one in which they perform translations and rotations simultaneously.

When objects have a more complex spatial structure, however, children still evidence difficulty in coordinating translations and rotations as they transport the object for fitting, even at ages when they manifest the ability to do so with less geometrically complex objects. Jung, Kahrs, and Lockman (2018) presented 17- to 36-month-old children a rod, similar in dimension to the one used in the Jung et al. (2015) study, but the rod was now attached to a handle (see Fig. 4). Again, the task for children was to fit the rod into the slot. To do so, however, children had to use the handle to control the movement of the rod, a problem that arises in many common tool-use situations (Kahrs, Jung, & Lockman, 2013; Kahrs & Lockman, 2014; Lockman & Kahrs, 2017). Thus in this task, the complexity of the frames of reference problem increased. To accomplish fitting, children had to control the upright or vertical orientation of the handle and the horizontal orientation of the rod relative to the tabletop slot (see Fig. 4).

The key question focused on process — that is, how children oriented the major segments of the object (i.e., handle and rod) in orthogonal spatial planes as they transported the object to the slot. Use of motion-tracking technology in real time afforded insight into the dynamics of spatial coordination. The results indicated that this three-dimensional frames of reference problem created new challenges for children. Although all of the 17- to 36-month-old children successfully fit the distal segment of the object (i.e., the rod) into the slot, examination of the way in which children oriented the entire object during transport indicated that they prepared for

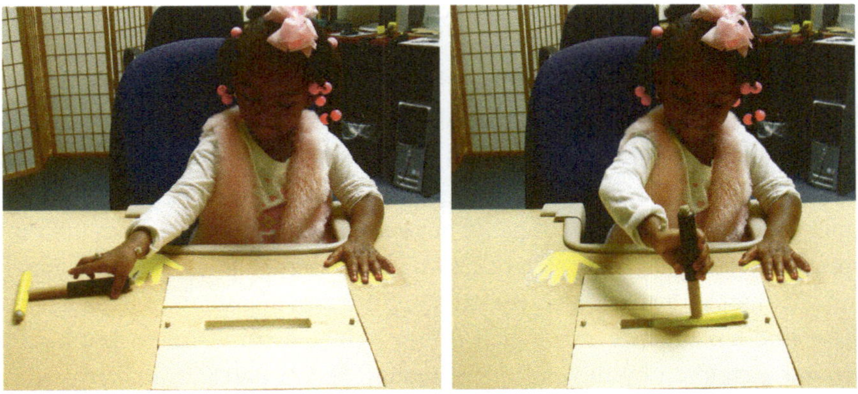

Figure 4 The experimental setup from Jung et al. (2018).

fitting by using different spatial strategies. Now, children between 17 and 30 months of age failed to prospectively align the rod with the slot, adopting a two-step approach similar to the children under 24 months of age in Jung et al. (2015) study. With the handled object, the 17- to 30-month-old children first oriented the handle in the upright or vertical plane before the object contacting the slot but only began to systematically orient the rod in the horizontal plane after the object had contacted the slot (Jung et al., 2018). In contrast, after 30 months of age, children began to prealign the orthogonal segments of the objects simultaneously. They oriented the handle vertically (i.e., perpendicular to the table) as they oriented the rod horizontally (i.e., relative to the slot), all in advance of the object contacting the slot. Furthermore, by 36 months of age, children had already initiated these simultaneous adjustments by the middle of the transport phase. Collectively, the results suggest there was a 6-month lag between the ability of children to prealign the rod when it was attached to a handle (Jung et al., 2018) and when children held the rod directly (Jung et al., 2015). Geometric complexity, particularly the dimensional structure of the object, influenced anticipatory adjustments.

Taken together, these findings underscore the value of using a process-based approach to understand how children relate perception and action in object fitting tasks. When preparing to fit objects into apertures, children need to gear their manual actions to an object's spatial structure. They need to exploit the action possibilities of the arm-hand system. They need to generate translation and rotational movements of the arms, wrist, and fingers to control the hand and, by extension, the object in it. And they need to integrate these different types of movements to achieve a match between the spatial structure of the object and that of the aperture.

By 3 years of age, children appear to have orchestrated all these elements to prepare for fitting. Over the course of just a few seconds, they can look at the object and aperture, register the spatial disparity between the two, and immediately implement an action plan to coordinate translations and rotations to bring the two into alignment along multiple dimensions. As this process-based account suggests, the dynamics of spatial coordination unfold even before the object contacts the area containing the aperture. Research on object fitting, thus, should focus not just on outcome measures such as whether or not children successfully fit a particular shape but also literally on the approach, or in other words, the transport or preparatory phase. Importantly, such a focus would highlight additional developmental changes that occur even after children become successful at prealigning and fitting objects into apertures. In the Jung et al. (2015, 2018) studies, the oldest children initiated the process of coordinating translations and rotations earlier in the transport phase than did the intermediate age children, although both groups prealigned the object with the slot. More generally, a process-based approach for object fitting can offer deeper insights into the dynamics of spatial planning and how these dynamics continue to change with development.

8. CONCLUSIONS AND FUTURE DIRECTIONS

In the foregoing review, we have argued for a process-based approach to understand the development of object fitting. Such an approach can advance understanding of how children prepare to fit an object into an aperture by considering it a problem of using action to coordinate multiple frames of reference. During object fitting, children need to integrate translational and rotational arm/hand movements to bring an object into alignment with an aperture. As development proceeds, this process becomes increasingly efficient, extending to objects with more complex geometric structures that extend into multiple spatial planes.

Impressively, children by the middle of the preschool period quickly plan and implement a spatial strategy to bring an object into alignment with an aperture (Jung et al., 2015, 2018). Nevertheless, a number of questions remain about the underlying processes by which they do so. Several investigators have suggested that to quickly prealign objects with apertures, especially those with a relatively complex spatial structure, children may perform mental rotation (Jung et al., 2015, 2018; Örnkloo & von Hofsten, 2009). Surprisingly, there is little work that directly relates the ability of young children to mentally rotate objects with their ability to fit objects into apertures. As noted, most work on object fitting has adopted an outcome approach based on whether children correctly select or insert an object into an aperture. In addition, in studies where prealignment of the object in relation to the aperture has been considered, investigators have just reported whether or not the object is aligned at the point of initial contact with the aperture area (see Section 1.2).

In contrast, the present review points to an alternate strategy for considering potential connections between fitting and mental rotation. By focusing on measures associated with the child's transport of the object to the aperture (e.g., at what point during transport the child begins to coordinate translational and rotational elements) and by using new measures of mental rotation developed for children in the later preschool years (Frick, Hansen, & Newcombe, 2013; Frick, Möhring, & Newcombe, 2014), investigators may be able to identify associations between particular parameters of object fitting and mental rotation. For instance, in fitting tasks, children who begin to coordinate object translations and rotations near the outset of the transport phase may be more likely to rely on mental rotation to formulate a plan of spatial action than children who do so later in the transport phase or not at all. More broadly, documenting a link between object fitting and mental rotation would be consistent with findings in the infancy period suggesting that motor processes may be involved in mental rotation (Frick et al., 2014; Frick & Wang, 2014; Möhring & Frick, 2013).

Given the possibility of linkages between object fitting and mental rotation, it is important to consider the issue of individual differences. Notably, investigators have not reported sex differences in object fitting performance during the preschool period. This conclusion holds when either outcome (success) or process variables are considered (Fragaszy et al., 2015; Jung et al., 2015, 2018; Örnkloo & von Hofsten, 2007, 2009; Shutts et al., 2009; Smith et al., 2014; Street et al., 2011). In contrast, some investigators report sex differences in mental rotation favoring males in the infancy period (Moore & Johnson, 2008, 2011; Quinn & Liben, 2008), whereas other investigators consistently find no sex differences in mental rotation ability in the infancy or preschool years (Frick et al., 2014). To the extent that object fitting performance and mental rotation skill are related, the absence of sex differences in object fitting during the preschool years challenges the idea that early sex differences in mental rotation ability are maintained throughout early childhood.

Beyond questions about mental rotation, it is also critical to examine other processes that are involved in object fitting. Although this review has highlighted how children attempt to incorporate their perception of an object's spatial structure into action, related questions about perception—action coupling can be raised. One such question centers on the real-time coupling of vision and action during object fitting. Little is known regarding where children direct visual attention as they formulate and implement a plan of spatial action or as they attempt to insert an object into an aperture. Examination of children's looking patterns might illuminate how they generate an action plan. Children, for instance, may glance back and forth between the object and aperture or take one look at the object and aperture before initiating a manual action. Subsequently, once children begin to transport the object to an aperture, their looking patterns to the object and aperture may illuminate how children use available perceptual information to guide action and/or to what extent children preplan a strategy to bring the object and aperture into alignment. Looking patterns may also shed light on how children analyze an object's spatial structure as they formulate a plan for action (Pereira et al., 2010; Smith et al., 2014). To address these types of process issues, the use of eye-tracking methods (e.g., Franchak, Kretch, Soska, & Adolph, 2011) in conjunction with other methods such as motion tracking and electromyography (EMG) would enable researchers to chart the real-time dynamics of perception and action.

Finally, a focus on process would also be of translational (as in application) relevance. Recent studies, some of which tested object fitting, have documented a compelling link between preschoolers' spatial construction skills and their kindergarten performance on spatial and mathematical tasks (Verdine et al., 2017). Other research indicates that when kindergarten and first-grade children are given daily experience with object assembly tasks over several months, they show improvements in spatial and mathematical test performance (Kim et al., 2018). These findings thus suggest developmental associations between tasks that require children to transform, rearrange, and fit objects in the preschool and kindergarten years and emerging STEM ability in the early elementary school years (see also Section 2.1). Greater attention to the process of object assembly, including object fitting, may lead to a deeper understanding of why these activities are associated with improved STEM performance in the early school years. Such a focus may provide targets for practice or intervention (Verdine et al., 2017).

To date, however, longitudinal predictions between preschool and kindergarten spatial and math performance have focused on the period between 3 and 5 years of age (Verdine et al., 2017). The work on the development of object fitting reviewed in this chapter opens up the possibility that meaningful parameters regarding spatial planning may be gathered from children even under 3 years of age. Such information might be useful for understanding not only how young children become spatial and mathematical thinkers but also how object fitting can serve as a model system for studying the real-time dynamics of perception and action.

ACKNOWLEDGMENTS

Preparation of this chapter was made possible in part with support from National Institutes of Health, 5R01HD086034, "Learning about hidden affordances."

REFERENCES

Adolph, K. E. (1997). Learning in the development of infant locomotion. *Monographs of the Society for Research in Child Development, 62*, 1–140.

Adolph, K. E. (2000). Specificity of learning: Why infants fall over a veritable cliff. *Psychological Science, 11*, 290–295.

Arterberry, M. E., & Kellman, P. J. (2016). *Development of perception in infancy : The cradle of knowledge revisited*. New York: Oxford University Press.

Ashton, T. S. (1951). *Iron and steel in the industrial revolution*. Manchester, UK: Manchester University Press.

Atkins, R. E. (1931). *The measurement of the intelligence of young children by an object-fitting test*. Minneapolis: The University of Minnesota Press.

Baillargeon, R., Spelke, E. S., & Wasserman, S. (1985). Object permanence in five-month-old infants. *Cognition, 20*, 191–208.

Barrett, T. M., & Needham, A. (2008). Developmental differences in infants' use of an object's shape to grasp it securely. *Developmental Psychobiology, 50*, 97–106.

Bayley, N. (1969). *Manual for the Bayley Scales of Infant Development*. New York: Psychological Corporation.

Bertamini, M., & Casati, R. (2015). Figures and holes. In J. Wagemans (Ed.), *The Oxford Handbook of perceptual organization* (pp. 281–293). Oxford: Oxford University Press.

Bertamini, M., & Croucher, C. J. (2003). The shape of holes. *Cognition, 87*, 33–54.

Bertamini, M., & Helmy, M. S. (2012). The shape of a hole and that of the surface-with-hole cannot be analyzed separately. *Psychonomic Bulletin & Review, 19*, 608–616.

Berthier, N. E., & Carrico, R. L. (2010). Visual information and object size in infant reaching. *Infant Behavior and Development, 33*, 555–566.

Bluff, L. A., Troscianko, J., Weir, A. A. S., Kacelnik, A., & Rutz, C. (2010). Tool use by wild New Caledonian crows *Corvus moneduloides* at natural foraging sites. *Proceedings of the Royal Society B: Biological Sciences, 277*, 1377–1385.

Brownell, C. A., Zerwas, S., & Ramani, G. B. (2007). "So big": The development of body self-awareness in toddlers. *Child Development, 78*, 1426–1440.

Bruner, J. S., & Koslowski, B. (1972). Visually preadapted constituents of manipulatory action. *Perception, 1*, 3–14.

Byrge, L., Sporns, O., & Smith, L. B. (2014). Developmental process emerges from extended brain-body-behavior networks. *Trends in Cognitive Sciences, 18*, 395–403.

Casasola, M. (2018). Above and beyond objects: The development of infants' spatial concepts. In J. B. Benson (Ed.), *Advances in child development and behavior* (Vol. 54, pp. 87–121). New York: Elsevier.

Casasola, M., Bhagwat, J., & Burke, A. S. (2009). Learning to form a spatial category of tight-fit relations: How experience with a label can give a boost. *Developmental Psychology, 45*, 711–723.

Casasola, M., Cohen, L. B., & Chiarello, E. (2003). Six-month-old infants' categorization of containment spatial relations. *Child Development, 74*, 679–693.

Chappell, J., & Kacelnik, A. (2002). Tool selectivity in a non-primate, the New Caledonian crow (*Corvus moneduloides*). *Animal Cognition, 5*, 71–78.

Corbetta, D., Thelen, E., & Johnson, K. (2000). Motor constraints on the development of perception-action matching in infant reaching. *Infant Behavior and Development, 23*, 351–374.

Corrow, S. L., Mathison, J., Granrud, C. E., & Yonas, A. (2014). Six-month-old infants' perception of the hollow face illusion: Evidence for a general convexity bias. *Perception, 43*, 1177–1190.

la Cour, L. T., Stone, B. W., Hopkins, W., Menzel, C., & Fragaszy, D. M. (2014). What limits tool use in nonhuman primates? Insights from tufted capuchin monkeys (*Sapajus spp.*) and chimpanzees (*Pan troglodytes*) aligning three-dimensional objects to a surface. *Animal Cognition, 17*, 113–125.

Dearborn, W. F., Anderson, J. E., & Christiansen, A. O. (1916). Form board and construction tests of mental ability. *Journal of Educational Psychology, 7*, 445–458.

DeLoache, J. S., Uttal, D. H., & Rosengren, K. S. (2004). Scale errors offer evidence for a perception-action dissociation early in life. *Science, 304*, 1027–1029.

Dilks, D. D., Hoffman, J. E., & Landau, B. (2008). Vision for perception and vision for action: Normal and unusual development. *Developmental Science, 11*, 474–486.

Fagard, J. (2000). Linked proximal and distal changes in the reaching behavior of 5- to 12-month old human infants grasping objects of different sizes. *Infant Behavior and Development, 23*, 317–329.

Fagard, J., & Jacquet, A. Y. (1996). Changes in reaching and grasping objects of different sizes between 7 and 13 months of age. *British Journal of Developmental Psychology, 14*, 65–78.

Fragaszy, D. M., & Cummins-Sebree, S. E. (2005). Relational spatial reasoning by a nonhuman: The example of capuchin monkeys. *Behavioral and Cognitive Neuroscience Reviews, 4*, 282–306.

Fragaszy, D. M., Kuroshima, H., & Stone, B. W. (2015). "Vision for action" in young children aligning multi-featured objects: Development and comparison with nonhuman primates. *PLoS One, 10*. Retrieved from http://journals.plos.org/plosone/article?id=10.1371/journal.pone.0140033.

Fragaszy, D. M., Stone, B. W., Scott, N. M., & Menzel, C. (2011). How tufted capuchin monkeys (*Cebus apella spp*) and common chimpanzees (*Pan troglodytes*) align objects to surfaces: Insights into spatial reasoning and implications for tool use. *American Journal of Primatology, 73*, 1012–1030.

Franchak, J. M., & Adolph, K. E. (2012). What infants know and what they do: Perceiving possibilities for walking through openings. *Developmental Psychology, 48*, 1254–1261.

Franchak, J. M., Kretch, K. S., Soska, K. C., & Adolph, K. E. (2011). Head-mounted eye-tracking: A new method to describe infant looking. *Child Development, 82*, 1738–1750.

Frick, A., Hansen, M. A., & Newcombe, N. S. (2013). Development of mental rotation in 3- to 5-year-old children. *Cognitive Development, 28*, 386–399.

Frick, A., Möhring, W., & Newcombe, N. S. (2014). Development of mental transformation abilities. *Trends in Cognitive Sciences, 18*, 536–542.

Frick, A., & Wang, S. (2014). Mental spatial transformations in 14- and 16- month-old infants: Effects of action and observational experience. *Child Development, 85*, 278–293.

Gesell, A., & Thompson, H. (1934). *Infant behavior: Its genesis and growth*. New York: McGraw-Hill.

Giralt, N., & Bloom, P. (2000). How special are objects? Children's reasoning about objects, parts, and holes. *Psychological Science, 11*, 497–501.

Goodale, M., & Milner, A. (1992). Separate visual pathways for perception and action. *Trends in Neurosciences, 15*, 20–25.

Goodale, M. A., Milner, A. D., Jakobson, L. S., & Carey, D. P. (1991). A neurological dissociation between perceiving objects and grasping them. *Nature, 349*, 154–156.

Granrud, C. E., Yonas, A., & Opland, E. A. (1985). Infants' sensitivity to the depth cue of shading. *Perception & Psychophysics, 37*, 415–419.

Habl, C., & Auersperg, A. M. I. (2017). The keybox: Shape-frame fitting during tool use in Goffin's cockatoos (*Cacatua goffiniana*). *PLoS One, 12*. Retrieved from http://journals.plos.org/plosone/article?id=10.1371/journal.pone.0186859.

Heed, T., Buchholz, V. N., Engel, A. K., & Röder, B. (2015). Tactile remapping: From coordinate transformation to integration in sensorimotor processing. *Trends in Cognitive Sciences, 19*, 251–258.

Hespos, S. J., & Baillargeon, R. (2001). Reasoning about containment events in very young infants. *Cognition, 78*, 207–245.

Hespos, S. J., & Baillargeon, R. (2006). Decalage in infants' knowledge about occlusion and containment events: Converging evidence from action tasks. *Cognition, 99*, 31–41.

von Hofsten, C., & Fazel-Zandy, S. (1984). Development of visually guided hand orientation in reaching. *Journal of Experimental Child Psychology, 38*, 208–219.

von Hofsten, C., & Rönnqvist, L. (1988). Preparation for grasping an object: A developmental study. *Journal of Experimental Psychology: Human Perception and Performance, 14*, 610–621.

Itard, J.-M.-G. (1801/1962). *The wild boy of Aveyron (Rapports et mémoires sur le sauvage de l'Aveyron)*. New York: M. P. Company.

James, K. H., Jones, S. S., Swain, S., Pereira, A., & Smith, L. B. (2014). Some views are better than others: Evidence for a visual bias in object views self-generated by toddlers. *Developmental Science, 17*, 338–351.

James, K. H., & Kersey, A. J. (2018). Dorsal stream function in the young child: An fMRI investigation of visually guided action. *Developmental Science, 21*. Retrieved from https://onlinelibrary.wiley.com/doi/epdf/10.1111/desc.12546.

James, T. W., Culham, J., Humphrey, G. K., Milner, A. D., & Goodale, M. A. (2003). Ventral occipital lesions impair object recognition but not object-directed grasping: An fMRI study. *Brain, 126*, 2463–2475.

Johnson, S. P. (2004). Development of perceptual completion in infancy. *Psychological Science, 15*, 769–775.

Johnson, S. P., & Aslin, R. N. (1995). Perception of object unity in 2-month-old infants. *Developmental Psychology, 31*, 739–745.

Johnson, S. P., & Hannon, E. E. (2015). Perceptual development. *Handbook of Child Psychology and Developmental Science, 2*, 63–112.

Jung, W. P., Kahrs, B. A., & Lockman, J. J. (2015). Manual action, fitting, and spatial planning: Relating objects by young children. *Cognition, 134*, 128–139.

Jung, W. P., Kahrs, B. A., & Lockman, J. J. (2018). Fitting handled objects into apertures by 17- to 36-month-old children: The dynamics of spatial coordination. *Developmental Psychology, 54*, 228–239.

Kahrs, B. A., Jung, W. P., & Lockman, J. J. (2013). Motor origins of tool use. *Child Development, 84*, 810–816.

Kahrs, B. A., & Lockman, J. J. (2014). Tool using. *Child Development Perspectives, 8*, 231–236.

Kaufman, J., & Needham, A. (2010). The role of surface discontinuity and shape in 4-month-old infants' object segregation. *Visual Cognition, 18*, 751–766.

Kellman, P. J. (1984). Perception of three-dimensional form by human infants. *Perception & Psychophysics, 36*, 353–358.

Kellman, P. J., & Spelke, E. S. (1983). Perception of partly occluded objects in infancy. *Cognitive Psychology, 15*, 483–524.

Kim, H., Duran, C. A. K., Cameron, C. E., & Grissmer, D. (2018). Developmental relations among motor and cognitive processes and mathematics skills. *Child Development, 89*, 476–494.
Knox, H. A. (1914). A scale, based on the work at Ellis Island, for estimating mental defect. *Journal of the American Medical Association, 62*, 741–747.
van Lawick-Goodall, J. (1968). The behaviour of free-living chimpanzees in the Gombe Stream Reserve. *Animal Behaviour Monographs, 1*, 161–311.
Libertus, K., Joh, A. S., & Needham, A. W. (2015). Motor training at 3 months affects object exploration 12 months later. *Developmental Science, 6*, 1058–1066.
Libertus, K., & Needham, A. (2010). Teach to reach: The effects of active vs. passive reaching experiences on action and perception. *Vision Research, 50*, 2750–2757.
Lockman, J. J. (1984). The development of detour ability during infancy. *Child Development, 55*, 482–491.
Lockman, J. J. (2000). A perception-action perspective on tool use development. *Child Development, 71*, 137–144.
Lockman, J. J., & Ashmead, D. H. (1983). Asynchronies in the development of manual behavior. *Advances in Infancy Research, 2*, 113–136.
Lockman, J. J., Ashmead, D. H., & Bushnell, E. W. (1984). The development of anticipatory hand orientation during infancy. *Journal of Experimental Child Psychology, 37*, 176–186.
Lockman, J. J., & Kahrs, B. A. (2017). New insights into the development of human tool use. *Current Directions in Psychological Science, 26*, 330–334.
MacGregor, N. (2011). *A history of the world in 100 objects*. London: Penguin Publishing Group.
McCarty, M. E., Clifton, R. K., Ashmead, D. H., Lee, P., & Goubet, N. (2001). How infants use vision for grasping objects. *Child Development, 72*, 973–987.
McKenzie, B., Slater, A., Tremellen, S., & McAlpin, S. (1993). Reaching for toys through apertures. *British Journal of Developmental Psychology, 11*, 47–60.
Meyer, E. (1940). Comprehension of spatial relations in preschool children. *The Journal of Genetic Psychology, 57*, 119–151.
Milner, A., & Goodale, M. (1995). *The visual brain in action*. Oxford: Oxford University Press.
Mix, K. S., & Cheng, Y. L. (2012). The relation between space and math. Developmental and educational implications. *Advances in Child Development and Behavior, 42*, 197–243.
Möhring, W., & Frick, A. (2013). Touching up mental rotation: Effects of manual experience on 6-month-old infants' mental object rotation. *Child Development, 84*, 1554–1565.
Montessori, M. (1912). *The montessori method*. New York: Frederick A. Stokes Company.
Montessori, M. (1914). *Dr. Montessori's own handbook*. New York: Frederick A. Stokes Company.
Moore, D. S., & Johnson, S. P. (2008). Mental rotation in human infants: A sex difference. *Psychological Science, 19*, 1063–1066.
Moore, D. S., & Johnson, S. P. (2011). Mental rotation of dynamic, three-dimensional stimuli by 3-month-old infants. *Infancy, 16*, 435–445.
Nardini, M., Atkinson, J., Braddick, O., & Burgess, N. (2008). Developmental trajectories for spatial frames of reference in Williams syndrome. *Developmental Science, 11*, 583–595.
Needham, A. (2016). *Learning about objects in infancy*. New York: Routledge.
Nelson, R., Thierman, J., & Palmer, S. E. (2009). Shape memory for intrinsic versus accidental holes. *Attention, Perception, & Psychophysics, 71*, 200–206.
Newell, C. D. (1931). The uses of the form board in the mental measurement of children. *Psychological Bulletin, 28*, 309–318.
Norman, D. A. (1988). *The psychology of everyday things*. New York: Basic Books.

Örnkloo, H., & von Hofsten, C. (2007). Fitting objects into holes: On the development of spatial cognition skills. *Developmental Psychology, 43*, 404–416.
Örnkloo, H., & von Hofsten, C. (2009). Young children's ability to solve spatial problems involving a choice. *European Journal of Developmental Psychology, 6*, 685–704.
Palmer, S. E. (1999). *Vision science: Photons to phenomenology*. Cambridge, MA: MIT Press.
Pereira, A., James, K., Jones, S., & Smith, L. (2010). Early biases and developmental changes in self-generated object views. *Journal of Vision, 10*, 1–13.
Piaget, J. (1936/1952). *The origins of intelligence in children (La naissance de l'intelligence chez l'enfant)*. New York: International Universities Press.
Piaget, J. (1937/1954). *The construction of reality in the child (La construction de réel chez l'enfant)*. New York: Basic Books.
Piaget, J., & Inhelder, B. (1948/1956). *The Child's conception of space*. London: Routledge & Kegan Paul Ltd.
Quinn, P. C., & Liben, L. S. (2008). A sex difference in mental rotation in young infants. *Psychological Science, 19*, 1067–1070.
Ransburg, N., Reiser, M., Munzert, J., Jovanovic, B., & Schwarzer, G. (2017). Concurrent anticipation of two object dimensions during grasping in 10-month-old infants: A quantitative analysis. *Infant Behavior and Development, 48*, 164–174.
Rigney, J., & Wang, S. H. (2015). Delineating the boundaries of infants' spatial categories: The case of containment. *Journal of Cognition and Development, 16*, 420–441.
Schmuckler, M. A., & Li, N. S. (1998). Looming responses to obstacles and apertures: The role of accretion and deletion of background texture. *Psychological Science, 9*, 49–52.
Schum, N., Jovanovic, B., & Schwarzer, G. (2011). Ten- and twelve-month-olds' visual anticipation of orientation and size during grasping. *Journal of Experimental Child Psychology, 109*, 218–231.
Seguin, E. (1866). *Idiocy: And its treatment by the physiological method*. New York: William Wood & Co.
Shutts, K., Örnkloo, H., von Hofsten, C., Keen, R., & Spelke, E. S. (2009). Young children's representations of spatial and functional relations between objects. *Child Development, 80*, 1612–1627.
Slater, A., Mattock, A., & Brown, E. (1990). Size constancy at birth: Newborn infants' responses to retinal and real size. *Journal of Experimental Child Psychology, 49*, 314–322.
Slater, A., & Morison, V. (1985). Shape constancy and slant perception at birth. *Perception, 14*, 337–344.
Smith, L. B., Street, S., Jones, S. S., & James, K. H. (2014). Using the axis of elongation to align shapes: Developmental changes between 18 and 24 months of age. *Journal of Experimental Child Psychology, 123*, 15–35.
Soska, K. C., Adolph, K. E., & Johnson, S. P. (2010). Systems in development: Motor skill acquisition facilitates three-dimensional object completion. *Developmental Psychology, 46*, 129–138.
Soska, K. C., & Johnson, S. P. (2008). Development of three-dimensional object completion in infancy. *Child Development, 79*, 1230–1236.
Soska, K. C., & Johnson, S. P. (2013). Development of three-dimensional completion of complex objects. *Infancy, 18*, 325–344.
Street, S. Y., James, K. H., Jones, S. S., & Smith, L. B. (2011). Vision for action in toddlers: The posting task. *Child Development, 82*, 2083–2094.
Sullivan, L. H. (1896). The tall office building artistically considered. *Lippincott's, 51*, 403–409.
Suzuki, A. (1966). On the insect-eating habits among wild chimpanzees living in the savanna woodland of Western Tanzania. *Journal of Primatology, 7*, 481–487.
Sylvester, R. H. (1913). The form board test. *The Psychological Monographs, 15*, 1–56.

Thelen, E. (1989). Self-organization in developmental processes: Can systems approaches work? In M. R. Gunnar, E. Thelen, M. R. Gunnar, & E. Thelen (Eds.), *Systems and development* (pp. 77—117). Hillsdale, NJ, US: Lawrence Erlbaum Associates, Inc.
Ungerleider, L. G., & Mishkin, M. (1982). Two cortical visual systems. In D. J. Ingle, M. A. Goodale, & R. J. W. Mansfield (Eds.), *Analysis of visual behavior* (pp. 549—586). Cambridge, MA: MIT Press.
Verdine, B., Golinkoff, R. M., Hirsh-Pasek, K., & Newcombe, N. S. (2017). Links between spatial and mathematical skills across the preschool years. *Monographs of the Society for Research in Child Development, 82*, 1—149.
Verdine, B. N., Golinkoff, R. M., Hirsh-Pasek, K., Newcombe, N. S., Filipowicz, A. T., & Chang, A. (2014). Deconstructing building blocks: Preschoolers' spatial assembly performance relates to early mathematical skills. *Child Development, 85*, 1062—1076.
Vrins, S., Hunnius, S., & van Lier, R. (2011). Volume completion in 4.5-month-old infants. *Acta Psychologica, 138*, 92—99.
Wang, S. H. (2011). Priming 4.5-month-old infants to use height information by enhancing retrieval. *Developmental Psychology, 47*, 26—38.
Wang, S. H., Baillargeon, R., & Brueckner, L. (2004). Young infants' reasoning about hidden objects: Evidence from violation-of-expectation tasks with test trials only. *Cognition, 93*, 167—198.
Weir, A. A. S., Chappell, J., & Kacelnik, A. (2002). Shaping of hooks in New Caledonian crows. *Science, 297*, 981.
Weir, A. A. S., & Kacelnik, A. (2006). A New Caledonian crow (*Corvus moneduloides*) creatively re-designs tools by bending or unbending aluminium strips. *Animal Cognition, 9*, 317—334.
Wentworth, N., Benson, J. B., & Haith, M. M. (2000). The development of infants' reaches for stationary and moving targets. *Child Development, 71*, 576—601.
Witherington, D. (2005). The development of prospective grasping control between 5 and 7 months: A longitudinal study. *Infancy, 7*, 143—161.
Young, H. H. (1916). The Witmer form board. *Psychological Clinic, 10*, 93—111.

CHAPTER THREE

The Development of Sensorimotor Intelligence in Infants

Claes von Hofsten[1] and Kerstin Rosander
Department of Psychology, Uppsala University, Uppsala, Sweden
[1]Corresponding author: E-mail: claes.von_hofsten@psyk.uu.se

Contents

Advances in Child Development and Behavior, Volume 55
ISSN 0065-2407
https://doi.org/10.1016/bs.acdb.2018.04.003

Abstract

Infancy is the most dynamic part of human development. During this period, all basic sensorimotor and cognitive abilities are established. In this chapter, we will trace some of the important achievements of this development with a focus on how infants achieve predictive control of actions, i.e., how they come to coordinate their behavior with the ongoing events in the world without lagging behind. With the maturation of the brain, new possibilities that have profound effects on cognition open up. Some of them are core abilities, i.e., they function at birth or very early in development. Important examples are the structured perception of objects and surfaces and the control of arm movements. Closely after birth, infants move their arms to the vicinity of objects in front of them demonstrating that they have some control of their arms and indicating that they perceive objects as such. Another example is the rapid onset of smooth-pursuit eye movements during the second month of life and the emerging ability to predict when and where an occluded moving object will reappear. At 4 months of age, out of sight is no longer of mind. The child's sensorimotor system is especially designed to facilitate the extraction of knowledge about the world including other people. In addition, the infant is endowed with motives that ensure that the innate predispositions are transformed into a system of knowledge for guiding actions predictively. By perceiving and acting on the world, infants develop their cognition and through developmental studies; we can learn more about these processes.

1. INTRODUCTION

Perception and action is at the base of our interaction with the world. No action could exist without perception, and perception relies ultimately on action (Bernstein, 1967). Together they form functional systems around which adaptive behavior develops. Perception is necessary both for planning actions and for guiding them toward their goals. For instance, active touch is required to perceive the form of an object through the haptic sense (Gibson, 1966). The hand must move over the object and feel its form, its bumps, and its indentations. The clearest example of the necessity of action for functional perception is vision itself. Our visual field consists of a very small foveal area, not larger than the thumb nail at arm's length, surrounded by a large peripheral visual field over which acuity rapidly deteriorates with increasing angular eccentricity. Already at 10°, acuity is only 20% of its foveal value. In spite of this, we have the illusion that we see everything equally well around us. A simple experiment shows that this is wrong. If one firmly fixates a word in a text, it is hardly possible to even read the neighboring words. The illusion of an equally clear visual field is created by the fact that we move the fovea to every single detail that we want to inspect and by doing this we can inspect everything with optimal resolution. This is also valid for young infants although the foveal receptor field is less distinct at this age (Banks & Bennett, 1988).

The same principles hold for all modes of perceiving. Perception is characterized by exploratory activities such as looking, listening, sniffing, tasting, and feeling (Gibson, 1966). It is equally valid that all actions have perceptual functions. Locomotion reveals the layout of the environment, manipulation reveals object properties, and social interaction is essential for person perception. Thus, by necessity, any executive action also involves exploratory actions. Cognition organizes perception and action into fluent and continuous behavior that anticipates what is going to happen next. In this view, cognition is based on both sensory and motor mechanisms. For example, the action of grasping and manipulation not only is a motor process but also connects sensory information about object properties with the integrated representation of motor and sensory properties of the action (Jeannerod, 2006).

In this chapter, we will first discuss the origins of perception, action, and cognition and explain why predictive control is crucial for all three domains. Organized behavior is only possible if movements are conceived ahead of time and their sensory effects anticipated. This is valid for all ages. The chapter discusses the behavior of neonates and concludes that their movements should be conceived as actions and not reflexes. We then review the early-appearing actions in development and point out how experience and maturation interact in the appearance of new modes of action. In particular, we discuss the predictive control of reaching, grasping, and manipulation. In a world like ours where objects go in and out of visibility, it is of paramount importance that we can represent them when they are out of sight. The chapter discusses when and how this appears in development. Finally, we discuss possible learning processes behind predictive control.

1.1 The Origins of Perception

It is an old insight that without any initial prestructuring of the sensory input, information about the environment would never be acquired. Thus, a pure "Tabula Rasa" is impossible. Not even Locke (1689), who invented the term in this context, believed in a completely unstructured sensory array but conceived of an innate 2-D structured image. Recent research, however, has demonstrated that vision is rather well structured from birth. This is remarkable since finely structured light does not project on the retina before birth. It can be argued that structured sensory input is present before birth for all the sensory organs except vision. In the case of vision, however, a simple but crucial change in the epigenetic process has enabled the fine structuring to start before birth. Shatz and colleagues (Shatz, 1992) showed in prenatal cats that waves of structured neural activity move back and forth over the retina and that this is quite sufficient for launching the fine mapping process of the visual field. There is evidence that neonates discriminate a correctly organized human face from a scrambled one (Johnson & Morton, 1991). Recent research also shows that the visual input at birth is structured in a way that makes it possible to discriminate emotional expressions in a seen face at a close distance (25 cm) (von Hofsten et al., 2014). Thus, if neonates can process visual input in such a detailed way, it is also possible that they can distinguish the subtle differences associated with emotional expressions.

In the context of action, perception of motion is of crucial importance. It is necessary for the monitoring of the dynamic world and the timing between actions and events. Neonates are sensitive to the direction of motion and turn their eyes and head to look at moving objects (von Hofsten, 1982). They are also sensitive to biological motion and discriminate it from nonbiological motion (Simion, Regolin, & Bulf, 2008).

To be able to act on the visual world, one must be able to segment the perceptual array into objects with inner unity and outer boundaries that exist over time (Spelke, 1998). Infants do this at a very early age by analyzing common and relative motion of surface parts. If, for instance, the center of a displayed object is occluded, 4-month-old infants perceive the unoccluded parts as belonging to the same object but only if the displayed object moves. If the parts move relative to each other, they are perceived as belonging to different objects (Kellman & Spelke, 1983). Similar results were obtained by von Hofsten and Spelke (1985) in a situation where 6-month-old infants reached for objects presented on a screen. They presented a smaller object in front of a larger one to which it was spatially connected. Infants reached for the edge of the closer object when the objects moved relative to each other and for the edge of larger and the more distant object when the two objects moved together.

Object perception becomes increasingly accurate and adapted to action over the first months of life. Young infants perceive objects in accord with the principles governing the motions of solid bodies. They divide perceptual arrays into units that move together, that move relative to one another, that maintain their size and shape over motion, and that act upon each other only on contact. To be perceived as an object, there must be well-defined and persistent outer boundaries. A heap of sand, for instance, is not perceived as an object (Huntley-Fenner, Carey, & Solimando, 2002). These findings suggest that a general representation of object unity and boundaries is interposed between representations of surfaces and representations of objects of familiar kinds. Perceived objects move on continuous and unobstructed paths.

1.2 The Origins of Action

Prestructuring is as important for the motor system as it is for the perceptual system. Without some initial structuring, self-produced movements would never emerge. In addition, the sensory input must make contact with the motor output and begin to form a loop so that information can be fed back into the system. Loops are necessary for modifying the system during ontogenesis toward more optimal functioning. Therefore, one of the most important aspects of action development is to form loops that enable the growing organism to regulate its own behaviors.

The most obvious way in which the child is prepared for action is the design of its body. It is clear that hands are made for grasping and manipulating objects, feet are made for walking, and eyes are made for looking. However, simply providing the hardware is not sufficient for establishing an action system. In addition, there needs to be some initial constraints on the movements produced to reduce the many degrees of freedom of the motor system (Bernstein, 1967). Thus, the arm and finger movements of neonates are organized into extension and flexion synergies that make the arm and the fingers extend and flex together (von Hofsten, 1989). This synergy simplifies the control problem and enables neonates to direct their arm movements in space. However, it prevents the neonate from grasping an object reached for because that would require them to flex the hand around the object while the arm is extended.

The motor system shows signs of being structured at around 2 months postconception. At this time the first fetal movements appear, such as arm movements, breathing movements, opening and closing of the mouth, yawning, sucking, and swallowing as observed through ultrasound registration (de Vries et al., 1982). Some of these synergies are rather complex, like those for breathing and swallowing. Synergies have both facilitating and constraining effects. Two studies, Zoia et al. (2007) and Myowa-Yamakoshi and Takeshita (2006), have provided some evidence of the very earliest co-ordination of the sensorimotor system. They found that the fetus moves its hands and legs to touch the walls of the amniotic sack, grasp the umbilical cord, and put the thumb in the mouth. At 22 but not 18 weeks of gestational age, the hand movements of a fetus are planned in the sense that those directed to the eye are smoother and more decelerated than those aimed toward the mouth (Zoia et al., 2007).

1.3 The Origins of Cognition

At birth, all cognition is expressed through action. It is here hypothesized to be the substrate from which all cognition originates. This was also Piaget's (1953). The starting point of development is not a set of reflexes triggered by external stimuli but a set of sensorimotor mechanisms activated by the child. To begin with, they may be primitive, but as long as there is a loop connecting the sensory side and the motor side, a window opens for refining the system through activity and experience and gearing it to the environment. Piaget (1953) called these loops circular reactions. Thus, the development of the nervous system and the development of action mutually influence each other in the process of forming increasingly complex and sophisticated action mechanisms. These mechanisms become increasingly future-oriented and integrated with each other.

There are a number of cognitive abilities needed to get the perception–action system to function. How are they established? One possibility is that infants learn to divide the light array at the retina into segments that correspond to different properties of the environment such as objects and surfaces and that infants have to learn all aspects of limb movements. Such a process would make the early part of development very extended indeed. Instead, several of these abilities are there to be used with no or very little learning because certain aspects of mature object representation may stem from intrinsic properties of humans' perceptual and cognitive systems. They are called core abilities or core knowledge of the environment (Spelke, 1998). The early perception of objects as bounded with inner unity and outer boundaries that exist over time is such a case.

1.4 The Necessity of Predictive Control

How to coordinate one's behavior with the ongoing events in the world without lagging behind is one of the most important problems that biological organisms must solve. The problem is that events always precede the feedback about them. The total delay for simple visual feedback in adults, for instance, is at least between 200 and 250 ms (Stevens, 2002). In infants, it is much longer. Gredebäck, Ornkloo, and von Hofsten (2006) found that the reaction time of 6-month-olds who tracked targets moving on abruptly changing trajectories was on the average close to 600 ms. The only way to overcome this problem is to anticipate what is going to happen next and use that information to compensate for the sensory lag. Infants do this from a very early age.

In cases where events in the world are too fast or unpredictable, the motor system elicits very fast reactions, i.e., reflexes. The prime example is the adjustment of balance after a perturbation of the motor system, i.e., postural reflexes. The reflex reaction time is around 50 ms, which is only a fraction of an ordinary reaction time (Nashner, Woollacott, & Tuma, 1979). However, even reflexes are too slow to solve the coordination problem. Most events in the outside world do not wait for us to act. Interacting with them requires us to move to specific places at specific times while being prepared to do specific things. This entails foreseeing the ongoing stream of events in the world as well as the unfolding of one's own actions. In preparation of a simple everyday action such as a handshake, one must aim that action in a precise way and time the encounter precisely. This demonstrates the importance of predictive control of actions.

Predictive control is possible because events are governed by rules and regularities. Core knowledge is about understanding these rules and to use them to regulate one's actions. There are three kinds of rules that in different ways underlie our ability to control our actions prospectively. One is about timing actions to the physical world, one about timing actions to the social world, and one about overcoming the programming delays of the motor system itself. Our mastery of the rules that make us perceive the world as being simultaneous with our actions is to be found both in the core knowledge that biology has equipped us with and in the acquisition of knowledge during development. The knowledge supplied by biology is most often not in the form of ready-made concepts but rather an awareness that facilitates the acquisition of concepts.

2. NEONATAL MOVEMENTS: REFLEXES OR ACTIONS?

The behavior of the neonates has traditionally been discussed in terms of reflexes rather than actions. According to Sherrington (1906), a reflex is a hardwired sensorimotor loop organized at a spinal or paraspinal level. A slight hit below the knee cap elicits a stretch reflex in both adults and newborns. Loss of support in neonates elicits the Moro response that makes the hands and arms stretch out rapidly in a reflex movement (Rönnqvist, 1995). If the neonate encounters something to hold on to during this response, the extension synergy is reversed into a flexion synergy and the encountered object is firmly grasped. It is a very fast and functional response and is also present in neonatal monkeys. The Moro response is a reflex according to the definition used by Sherrington (1906). Although such reflexes may serve important functions for the subject, they are stereotyped, elicited, and do not adjust to future states in a prospective way. This means, for instance, that reflexes do not adjust to meet other goals than those for which they were originally designed.

However, most neonatal behaviors cannot be adequately described as reflexes. On the contrary, they are goal-directed and flexible in the sense that they can be altered to gain advantages. This is valid for behaviors such as rooting, sucking, stepping, reaching, and grasping. It is also valid for some of the basic postural adjustments such as the asymmetrical tonic neck reflex (ATNR) (van der Meer, van der Weel, & Lee, 1995).

Rooting is traditionally described as a typical neonatal reflex. Rooting refers to the infant's search for the nipple of the breast. Mechanical stimulation in the area around the mouth makes the infant move his or her mouth toward the point of stimulation (Prechtl, 1958). However, rooting is not stereotyped. Odent (1979) showed that rooting does involve not just movements of the head and mouth but also explorative movements of the whole body with all the senses involved. Furthermore, rooting is not elicited when the infant touches itself (Rochat & Hespos, 1997) but only when an external object is the source of stimulation. These facts speak in favor of a far more sophisticated organization of this behavior than suggested by the reflex notion.

Sucking is probably the most precocious action of the newborn infant. Skilled sucking relies on a complex interaction of muscle contractions that are prospective in nature. Within a day or so after birth, the sucking system functions with amazing accuracy (Craig & Lee, 1999). There are two phases of sucking, one that creates a temporary vacuum in the mouth region and one the releases the milk from the nipple. A well-functioning sucking action relies on adjusting the change in sucking pressure to the flow of milk that is different from suck to suck. In other words, the newborn infant has to sense the upcoming flow of milk and adjust the sucking pressure to it ahead of time. Craig and Lee (op. cit.) found that neonates adjusted their sucking action in a precise and prospective way indicating that they anticipated the upcoming flow of milk.

Apart from using sucking to acquire food, neonates are also able to use it to gain other advantages, for instance, as a means to get access to the mother's voice (DeCasper & Fifer, 1980) or to regulate a visual event (Kalnins & Bruner, 1973). This shows that neonates can separate the perceived affordance of an event and the action used to fulfill what it invites. In other words, actions can be used as means rather than ends and they can be flexibly applied to a variety of problems.

If a neonate is supported upright under his or her arms and lowered toward a horizontal surface, he or she will step forward when the feet touch the surface. This is known as the stepping reflex. Recent studies of neonates indicate that this behavior is not a reflex (Barbu-Roth et al., 2009). Neonates were lowered toward a horizontal surface, on which a visual flow pattern was projected. When the pattern was translating backward providing visual information that the neonate was moving forward, the number steps elicited as the neonate was held above the surface were as many as when the feet touched the surface. When instead the flow pattern on the surface moved in a circular way or when it was stationary, the infants performed significantly fewer numbers of steps, indicating that the visual flow associated with forward motion made the neonate perform the stepping. This implies that the stepping is more than a reflex. It is elicited by the backward visual flow in addition to proprioceptive sensation (Barbu-Roth et al., op. cit).

Under certain conditions, neonates will reach for an object in front of them. The reaching is crudely aimed at the object, and there is no attempt to grasp it (von Hofsten, 1982). This action seems to have an explorative function. When the neonate looks at the object and reaches for it, the infant prepares him or herself for the encounter with the external event by pointing its feelers toward it. The reach does not end in a grasp (Fig. 1 and Video 1). This implies that the coordination of the exploratory system to a certain degree is preadapted. In an ingeniously designed study on neonates, van der Meer (1997) placed infants close to a beam of light passing in front of them. It should be stressed that the beam was totally invisible if nothing interrupted it. However, if the infant extended an arm forward, the hand interrupted the light beam and became brightly visible. When this happened, the infant stopped the hand for a moment in the beam. They would also increase the number of forward extensions of the arm into the beam and slow down the hand before entering it into the beam. These results demonstrate that neonates have certain ability to control the movements of the arms from information of the spatial layout of the nearby space. They move the arms in the direction of external visual targets and adjust the movements as to increase exposure to the targets.

Neonatal reaching has another very important function. When the hands move toward an object of interest, they enter into the visual field and the movements might then become controlled by visual information. Closing the visual–manual loop in this way is of crucial importance for the development of manual control. This is precisely what is needed for developing the system. It makes it possible for the infant to explore the relationship between commands and movements and between vision and proprioception and discover the possibilities and constraints of manual movements.

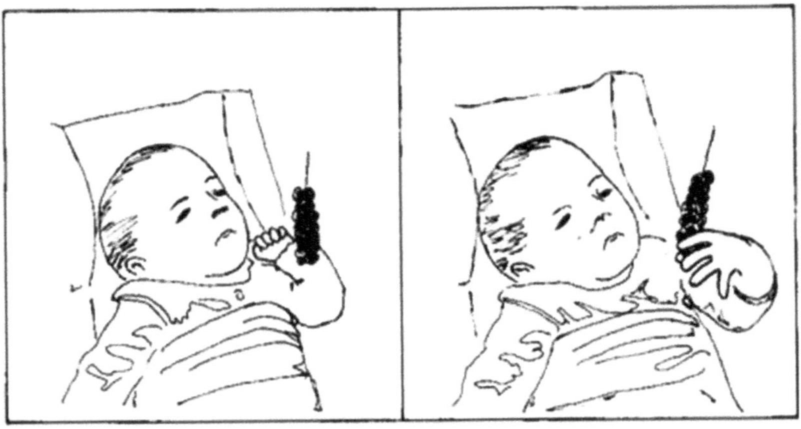

Figure 1 A newborn reach. Although the object is inside the hand, the infant does not flex around it. *From Cambridge University press, Encyclopedia of early childhood development, 2005.*

Summary: The sensorimotor system of the neonate is an action system. It is functional because the movements are initiated by the subject and they are goal-directed and flexible in the sense that they can be altered to gain advantages. This is the core knowledge on which the development of embodied cognition is based. The neonate is ready to interact with nearby objects by moving the hands closer to them. Thereby, they close the visual—manual loop. This makes it possible for the infant to explore the relationship between commands and movements and discover the possibilities and constraints of manual actions. In a similar way, one can argue that neonates' sensitivity to visual flow opens up a loop that makes it possible to control locomotion from visual input. Both locomotion and reaching are crucial for the interaction with the outside world. So is looking, and neonates are able to control gaze through saccades.

3. DEVELOPMENT OF ACTION IN EARLY INFANCY

The functioning action systems in the neonate give development a flying start. In the months ahead, new abilities are added with the maturation of the nervous system and altered by experience. We will point out the importance of basic orientation for the development of action and discuss how postural control is involved in all actions. The control of one's orientation relative to the environment is a prerequisite for all other functional activities (Gibson, 1966; Reed, 1996). We will apply this discussion to looking, reaching, grasping, and manipulation. They are excellent examples of how nature and nurture interact in the development of action systems and the emergence of embodied cognition.

3.1 Postural Control

This includes balancing the body relative to gravity and maintaining a stable orientation relative to the environment. As Reed (1996) stated, "maintenance of posture in the real world involves much more than simply holding part of the body steady; it is maintaining a set of invariant activities while allowing other activities to vary" (p. 88). Gravity is the frame of reference for all postural activities, but vision and proprioception provide important additional information about orientation.

Gravity is a stable and potent force, and when body equilibrium is disturbed, posture becomes rapidly uncontrollable. Therefore, any reaction to a balance threat has to be very fast and automatic. The vestibular system is especially designed for the control of balance, and several postural reflexes serve that purpose. However, balance is even better handled in a prospective way, because if the disturbances can be foreseen, there is no need for a fast reaction. Balance is also affected by the reactive forces of one's own movements. When a body part is moved, the point of gravity of the whole body is displaced. In addition, the movements themselves create momentums that tend to push the body out of equilibrium. These disturbances have to be compensated to maintain balance. Therefore, the effects of one's own movements must be foreseen and anticipated to maintain control of balance.

Posture is primarily controlled by the vestibular and the visual systems. Lee and Aronsson (1974) showed that 13- to 16-month-old infants who just had attained upright stance use visual information for maintaining balance. Special demands are associated with maintaining balance control during bodily activities such as reaching and walking. In particular, the individual must be able to take into account the contingencies between the limb movements and the reactive forces that arise during the movements. When grasping an object that resisted pulling, anticipatory postural activities are relatively rare before 13 months of age and only in 16- to 17-month-olds are they present in a majority of pulls (Witherington et al., 2002). As such anticipatory activities are dependent on vision, it is not surprising that walking independently is one of the clearest delays in the motor development of blind infants (Fraiberg, 1977). Fraiberg found that in a sample of blind children, 90% were delayed past the upper limits of sighted children as given by Bayley (1969) when walking independently across a room.

3.2 Looking

While neonates are able to control saccades, several studies on eye movements indicate that neonates have only limited ability to track a moving object smoothly. von Hofsten and Rosander (1996, 1997) recorded eye and head movements in unrestrained 1- to 5-month-old infants as they tracked a small live object oscillating in front of them along a horizontal path. They found that infants below 8 weeks of age tracked objects with saccadic eye movements, and from this age a substantial proportion of the tracking was smooth (von Hofsten & Rosander, 1997). In a later study, Rosander and von Hofsten (2002) placed 6- to 14-week-old infants in front of a moving object subtending visual angles of 2.5–35°. They found that the number of saccades was dependent on object size: At 6 and 9 weeks of age, there were more saccades for the smallest objects. There was no lag when infants tracked the object with smooth pursuit, implying that the upcoming motion was predicted. Smooth pursuit appeared simultaneously with the processing of motion information in the temporal–occipital border regions corresponding to MT/MST brain area in adults (Rosander, Nyström, Gredebäck, & von Hofsten, 2007). Longitudinal measurements show that whereas there is variability between the onset of smooth pursuit in different infants, the development within a single infant is completed within just a few weeks (see Fig. 2). This is one of the first signs of advanced predictive processing in development, and infants seem to be endowed with the ability to use motion information to control smooth eye movements in a prospective way.

3.2.1 Gradual and Abrupt Changes in Object Velocity

Two kinds of predictive processes have been observed in adult visual tracking (von Hofsten & Rosander, 1997). One uses the just seen motion to predict what will happen next through a process of extrapolation. Such predictions are in accordance with inertia that presumes that a motion with a certain speed and direction will continue with the same speed and

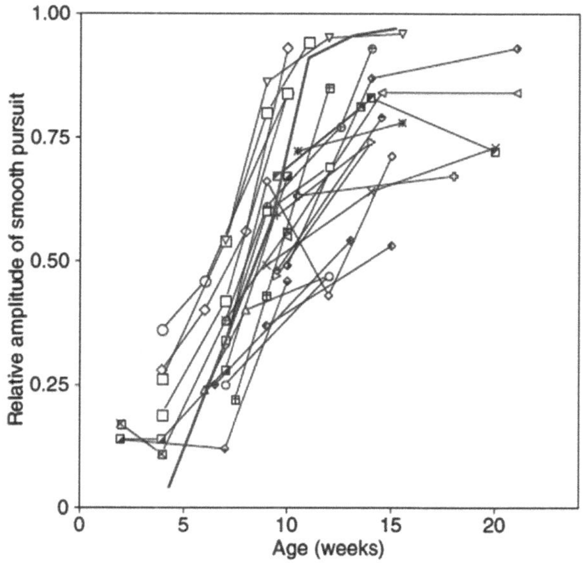

Figure 2 The relative amplitude of smooth-pursuit eye movements in 26 infants followed longitudinally over parts of the first 5 months of life. 0 means that no smooth pursuit is produced and 1.0 that all eye movements are smooth pursuit. As a comparison, the development of sensitivity to direction of motion (see Atkinson, 2000, pp. 28–42) is indicated by the *blue line. Elsevier, Encyclopedia of infant and early childhood development (2008).*

in the same direction unless it is affected by a force, in which case the motion will change gradually as in a sinusoidal motion. The extrapolation process is important for predicting object motion over short time windows, but it cannot handle prediction over longer periods. Such a predictive process relies on rules that certain events occur at certain times. An abruptly changing motion cannot be extrapolated because the changes do not reveal themselves in the just seen motion. Triangular motion is such a case. The object moves forward with constant velocity and at regular times the motion abruptly reverses. Prediction of these reversals cannot be accomplished through extrapolation but can be accomplished through a rule stating the periodicity of the reversals. To investigate the development of these two predictive processes, von Hofsten and Rosander (1997) studied visual tracking of sinusoidal and triangular motion functions. They found that tracking was well timed in the case of the sinusoidal motion from 2 months of age, but the tracking of the triangular motion lagged the target with about 200 ms at the reversals. At 5 months of age, the lagging decreased somewhat indicating that the infants started to have an idea of the periodicity but most of the lagging remained.

3.2.2 Vestibular–Visual Interaction During Looking

Both visual and vestibular mechanisms operate during head movements. The visual one aims at stabilizing gaze on the optic array by minimizing retinal slip (optokinetic response, OKR), while the vestibular one aims at stabilizing gaze in space (vestibuloocular response, VOR). Above 1 Hz the vestibular control dominates (Barnes, 1993). Below 1 Hz the visual and vestibular systems jointly contribute to gaze stabilization. In a study of the development of visual and vestibular gaze control in 3- to 18-week-old infants, Rosander and von Hofsten (2000) found that the vestibular control of smooth gaze adjustment functions earlier than the visual control. At 2 months, visual control improved dramatically, and at 3–4 months, head participation increased considerably. When the infant and the surrounding environment moved simultaneously, the eye gain could be well predicted by addition of the eye position signals in the OKR and VOR conditions.

Summary: Before 8 weeks of age, head movements are compensated by smooth counter rotations of the eyes, but external motion is handled with saccadic eye movements. At around 8 weeks of age, infants begin to track objects with smooth pursuit. Over just a few weeks, they develop this ability to an almost adultlike level. It shows that infants are endowed with ability to coordinate their eye movements with events in the world. They represent the upcoming motion through a neural predictive model that accords with inertia of objects.

4. REACHING, GRASPING, AND MANIPULATION

4.1 Reaching

4.1.1 Neural Aspects of Prereaching

The development of reaching during the first few months of life is dramatic. At around 7–8 weeks of age, the synergistic reaching characterized by simultaneous arm and finger extension is interrupted. Instead, the fingers flex when the arms extend (von Hofsten, 1984), and at the same time, the number of forward extended arm movements decreases. At 2 months of age, important changes take place in the organization of the nervous system. It has been well established that two separable systems are responsible for the control of the upper limb; one "proximal" motor system organized mainly on brainstem level and responsible for the gross movements of the arm and hand and one "distal" motor system organized cortically and responsible for the fine coordination of the hand. The change in the organization of arm and hand movements at this age indicates that the cortically "distal" motor system has started functioning but is not yet synchronized with the proximal motor system (Eyre, Miller, Clowry, Conway, & Watts, 2000; Kuypers, 1962, 1973). Consequently, coordination is adversely affected. After 2 months of age the hand starts to open again during the forward extension of the arm, but hand opening only occurs when the infant fixates the object (von Hofsten, 1984). The opening of the hand is not any longer just a part of an extension synergy but also a meaningful adaptive behavior in itself. The hand now starts to open as a preparation for grasping the object.

4.1.2 Can Prereaching Be Described as Motor Babbling?

The prereaching in the neonatal period is goal-directed. During the late part of the prereaching period, the infant tends to get the hand to the object during the forward extension. von Hofsten and Lindhagen (1979) studied this type of goal-directed behavior longitudinally in infants from 12 weeks of age. 3 successful movements were registered at 12 weeks of age, 10 were seen at 16 weeks, and as many as 60 at 18 weeks of age. The earliest reaches were typically jerky and circuitous, but at 18 weeks they were rather fluent and continuous. This transition from prereaching to reaching was also studied by Thelen et al. (1993) who found that each infant had his or her own individual way of moving his or her arms. The question is whether the prereaching period can be characterized as motor babbling, i.e., more or less random waving of the arms (e.g., Pulvermüller, Moseley, Egorova, Shebani, & Boulenger, 2014). The results of von Hofsten (1984), van der Meer (1997), von Hofsten and Lindhagen (1979), and Thelen et al. (1993) show that this is not the case. However, the variance decreases as the infants gain better control of the intrinsic dynamics of their arms.

4.1.3 Movement Units

Studies of reaching kinematics show that early reaches are rather segmented in contrast to adult reaches that often consist of a single bell-shaped velocity curve. von Hofsten (1979) defined movement units as segments of the reach, each consisting of an acceleration and a deceleration phase. The number of movement units decreased during the first months of successful reaching until most reaches were made up of only two or three movement units—the first to bring the hand near the target and the second and third to grasp it. The number of movement units reflects the predictability of a reaching action. Indeed, infants fixate the object and not the hand while reaching. When the movement accelerates, new energy is invested into the movement and a revised idea is implemented of how to continue. The information on which the revision of the plan is based is not only visual. Infants also reach successfully for objects in the dark within a week or two of reaching in the light (Clifton, Rochat, Litovsky, & Perris, 1991), suggesting that they can use proprioceptive information and memory of the object position to guide the reach. By 9 months, they preorient their hands to grasp objects in the dark (McCarty, Clifton, Ashmead, Lee, & Goubet, 2001) (Fig. 3).

4.2 Grasping

4.2.1 Hand Orientation

When reaching for an object, there are several problems that need to be solved in advance to have a smooth and efficient encounter with the object. The reaching hand needs to adjust to the orientation, form, and size of the object. The grasping action must be timed in such a way that the hand starts to close around the object in anticipation of and not as a reaction to encountering it. Such timing has to be planned and can only occur under visual control. By definition, tactually controlled grasping can only be initiated

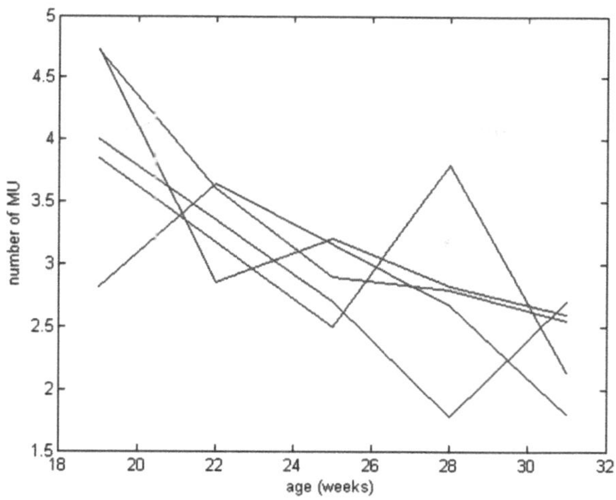

Figure 3 Number of movement units in a reach for five individual subjects at different ages. *From von Hofsten (1991).*

after contact and will induce an interruption in the reach-and-grasp action. This is not how early grasping is organized. On the contrary, it is planned during the approach to the object (von Hofsten & Rönnqvist, 1988). The emergence of prospective visual control of grasping is crucial for the development of manual skill.

When infants begin to reach successfully for objects they adjust the orientation of the hand to the orientation of a rod reached for (von Hofsten & Fazel-Zandy, 1984; Lockman, Ashmead, & Bushnell, 1984). Adjusting the opening of the hand to the size of an object is less crucial. Rather, it would also be possible to open the hand fully during the approach. von Hofsten and Rönnqvist (1988) found that 9-month-old infants, but not 5-month-old infants, adjusted the opening of the hand to the size of the object reached for ahead of grasping it. Recently, Mundinano et al. (2018) measured hand openings in infant marmoset grasping action. They found that visual information of the object is transferred via the pulvinar—MT pathway (Ffytche, Guy, & Zeki, 1995), which is also believed to function in human newborns. This action (the size of hand opening) was imprecise in those animals that were lesioned in the pulvinar tract. Thus, although predictive hand opening during reach was performed, visual information was essential for the final closing of the hand. In human infants, the ability to utilize this information develops between 5 and 9 months of age.

4.2.2 Timing of the Grasp

Another key to successful reaching is timing the grasp so that the fingers close around the object. von Hofsten and Rönnqvist (1988) monitored the timing of grasps in infants 13 months of age and younger. For each reaching movement, they determined when the distance between thumb and index finger started to diminish and when the object was encountered. They found that all the infants started to close the hand before that moment. For infants 9 months and younger, the hand first moved to the vicinity of the target and then started to close around it. For the 13-month-olds, however, the grasping action typically started during the approach, well before touch. In other words, at this age, grasping started to become integrated with the reach to become one continuous reach-and-grasp act.

4.2.3 Catching

The remarkable ability of infants to coordinate and time their manual actions relative to an external event is demonstrated in early catching behavior (von Hofsten, 1980, 1983; von Hofsten & Lindhagen, 1979; von Hofsten, Vishton, Spelke, Feng, & Rosander, 1998). von Hofsten and Lindhagen (1979) found that infants reached successfully for moving objects at the very age they began mastering reaching for stationary ones. Infants as young as 18 weeks of age were able to catch an object moving at 30 cm/sec. Further work showed that the reaches were aimed at the meeting point with the object and not toward the position where the object was seen at the beginning of the reach (von Hofsten, 1980). As a result, infants were very successful in catching the moving object. von Hofsten (1983) also found that 8-month-old infants successfully caught an object moving at 120 cm/sec. Given the speed of the moving object, the planning of such a reach must be initiated when the object is still well out of reach (Fig. 4). These studies show that infants predict the future position of a moving object, but they tell us little about the nature or limits of these predictions.

Systematic study of the principles guiding predictive reaching in infants requires variation of the spatial as well as the temporal properties of object motion. von Hofsten et al. (1998) presented 6-month-old infants with a live object that moved into reaching space on four different trajectories: Two linear trajectories that intersected out of reach at the center of the display and two trajectories containing a sudden perpendicular turn at the point of intersection. Shortly after the object had passed the intersection

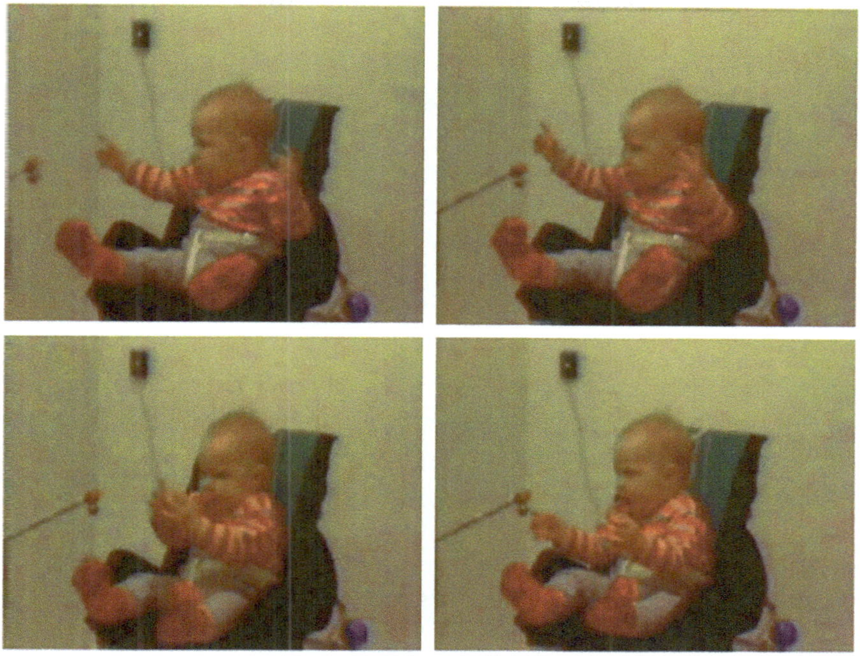

Figure 4 An 8-month-old infant attempting to grasp a fast-moving object that abruptly stops. Upper left: The object approaches from the right. The infant prepares to catch the object. Upper right: The object stops. Lower left: The infant closes the hands around the position where the object should have been if the motion had continued. Lower right: The infant discovers the true position of the object. *Elsevier, Encyclopedia of infant and early childhood development (2008).*

point, it arrived temporarily within reach. To catch the object while it was within reach, the action had to be planned before the object arrived at the intersection. Infants' tracking and reaching provided evidence for extrapolation of the object motion on linear paths, in accordance with inertia. This tendency was remarkably resistant to counterevidence, for it was persistent even after repeated observations of objects that suddenly turned at the point of intersection.

Summary: When infants begin to reach successfully for objects, the reaches are prepared in several different ways. The hand is turned in a way that facilitates grasping. The opening and closing of the hand is timed to the encounter with the object to be grasped. If the object to be grasped is moving, the reach is directed ahead of it toward the meeting point with it. This reflects advanced predictive control of action.

4.3 Manipulation

4.3.1 Fitting Objects Into Apertures

The development of skills in reaching and manipulation is closely related to such embodied cognitive skills as mental rotation and means—end relationships. When manipulating objects, the subjects must imagine the goal state of the manipulation and the procedures of how to get there. Örnkloo and von Hofsten (2007) studied how infants develop their ability to insert elongated blocks with various cross sections into horizontal apertures into which they fitted snugly. All objects had the same length, and the difficulty was manipulated by using different cross sections (circular, square, rectangular, elliptic, and triangular). The cylinder fitted into the horizontal aperture as long as its longitudinal axis was vertical. All the other objects had to be turned in specific ways to align the form of the cross section with the form of the aperture. The objects were presented both standing up and lying down.

Although infants younger than 18 months understood the task of inserting the blocks into the apertures and tried very hard, they had little idea of how to do it. They did not even place the blocks in a standup position when they were presented lying down but just placed them on the aperture and tried to press them in. The 22- and the 26-month-old children, however, systematically raised the horizontally placed objects when transporting them to the aperture and turned them appropriately before arriving there. They succeeded in getting them through the aperture. Fig. 5 shows that infants were rather unsuccessful before 22 months of age. The only block that they handled well at these ages

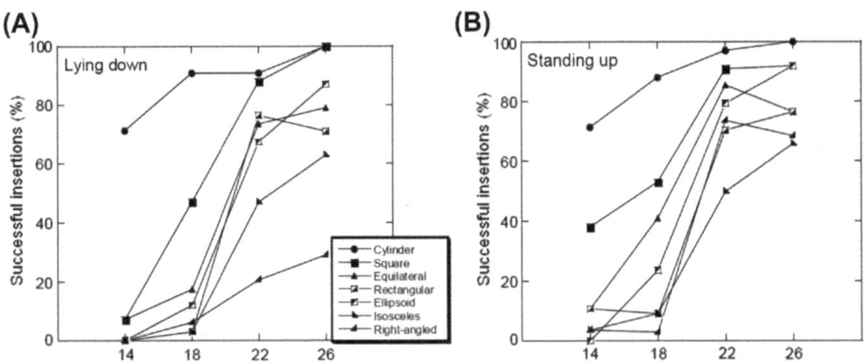

Figure 5 The percentage of successful insertions of objects of different shapes presented standing up (A) and lying down (B) at different ages. *Developmental Psychology (2007).*

was the cylinder. After 22 months, however, they succeeded very well with all the cross sections. The remarkable thing was that these adjustments were done ahead of the arrival of the block at the aperture. When the infants failed to orient the blocks appropriately ahead of time, they showed no tendency to succeed by trial and error. This result demonstrates a rather abrupt onset of perceptually guided adjustments relative to the aperture before carrying out the fitting action.

This achievement is the end point of several important developments that, in addition to mental rotation, include perception of the relation between the object and the aperture, anticipation of goal states, and an understanding of means—end relationships. These abilities are not independent of each other in a task like this and cannot be totally separated. Motor competence is expressed in actions, and actions rely on spatial perception and anticipations of goal states. The results indicate that a pure feedback strategy does not work for this task. The infants must have an idea ahead of time of how to orient the objects to make them fit. Such an idea can only arise if the infants can mentally rotate the manipulated object into the fitting position. The ability to imagine objects at different positions and in different orientations greatly improves the child's action capabilities. It enables them to plan actions on objects more efficiently, relate objects to each other, and plan actions involving more than one object. Thus, the perceptual representation is essential for the anticipatory action.

4.3.2 Planning Sequential Manual Actions

Claxton, Keen, and McCarty (2003) examined whether the planning of later parts of composite actions was reflected in the approach-to-grasp phase of infant reaching. Ten-month-old infants were encouraged to grasp a ball and then either to throw the ball into a tub or to fit it down a tube. Kinematic measures of the approach phase of the reach toward the ball showed that this part of the action was affected by what the infants intended to do with the ball after they picked it up. They reached for the ball faster if they were going to subsequently throw it as opposed to using it in a precision action. The perceptual aspects of the ball were the same and cannot account for these kinematic differences. This indicates that infants plan both phases of these actions in advance.

In a similar experiment, Chen, Keen, Rosander, and von Hofsten (2010) asked toddlers (18—21 months old) to build a tower of blocks (precise task) or to place the blocks into an open container (imprecise task). Two groups were distinguished with respect to whether they built high or low towers.

The high tower builders had a longer deceleration phase than the low tower builders. The former group thus had better visual control when placing blocks on the tower (Wu, Lin, Lin, Chang, & Chen, 2005). The kinematic differences between the groups remained a year later when all children could build high towers. By using two-stage tasks that involved sequential movements, the results demonstrated that toddlers engaged in movement planning beyond the available perceptual information and had the final goal of the entire sequence in mind. Finally, the sensitivity of this movement timing extended to separating among children of different skill levels, a difference that remained stable over 1 year between test sessions.

To test whether the demands of an action affect the planning of it as suggested by Claxton et al. (2003) and Chen et al. (2010), Gottwald et al. (2017) studied the planning of an action in a placement task. Fourteen-month-olds were asked to reach for an object and place it in a container with either a small or a large opening. The smaller the container opening and the longer the distance to it, the slower the infants were in the approach phase. Both factors influence the effort it takes to complete the action and therefore also the planning of it.

Summary: During the second year of life, infants come to master a number of important manipulatory skills. At 14 months of age, infants prepare composite actions globally by making adjustments of their later parts already at the onset. At 18–21 months of age, they combine blocks to construct a tower, and at 22 months of age, they succeed in inserting blocks with various cross sections into horizontal apertures. This reflects advanced cognitive abilities, such as mental rotation of objects, anticipation of goal states, and the understanding of means–end relationships.

5. REPRESENTING OBJECTS AND EVENTS

5.1 Occlusion of Objects

By 4 months of age, eye tracking data show that infants anticipate the reappearance of a moving object that is temporarily occluded. Gaze is shifted to the reappearance position ahead of time (Rosander & von Hofsten, 2004; von Hofsten, Kochukhova, & Rosander, 2007). von Hofsten et al. (2007) showed infants an object that oscillated with different velocities and amplitudes behind occluders of different widths (three factors), resulting in occlusion durations ranging from 0.2 to 1.7 s. In half of the passages, the infants predicted the reappearance of the object by shifting gaze to the opposite side of the occluder. The tendency to make such gaze shifts could not be explained by the passage of time since disappearance. Neither could it be fully explained in terms of occluder width. On the contrary, the latency of the predictive gaze shifts was determined by the time of object reappearance, and it was a function of all three factors manipulated. During occlusion, smooth pursuit stopped altogether. The results suggest that the infants maintain a representation of the moving object and shift gaze to the other side of the occluder when the conceived object was about to arrive there. Thus, we concluded that the infants tracked the occluded object in their "mind's eye." In support of this hypothesis are the findings that object velocity is represented in the frontal eye field of rhesus monkeys during the occlusion of a moving object (Barborica & Ferrera, 2003). Four-month-old infants represent object motion during occlusion in a similar way. Where the object is going to reappear after occlusion is a more open question. Kochukhova and Gredebäck (2007) showed 6-month-olds an object that disappeared behind a circular occluder. All infants predicted the object to reappear on the linear extension of its previous trajectory by moving gaze there, as expected from the law of inertia. However, after only one violation of this law by making the object reappear perpendicularly to the original path, the subjects began to move gaze to this position ahead of time.

From 4 months of age, infants shift gaze to the reappearing edge of an occluder. Thus, out of sight is not out of mind in infants of this age. This is an important accomplishment. In everyday life, objects move in and out of visibility and it is important to be able to keep track of them over periods of occlusion.

5.2 Reaching After Occlusion

Spelke and von Hofsten (2001) found that while infants reached predictively for a visible object, this was not the case when the object underwent a period of occlusion before it came within reach. They suggested that young infants represent both visible and hidden objects, and their object representations are similar to those used by adults to represent and attentively track objects. They suggested that the infants' object representations have the following properties. Representations are more precise, at all ages, when objects are visible than when they are hidden. Precise representations are required for reaching: To reach for an object, one must know where it is, how big it is, what shape it has, and how it is moving. When the object is invisible due to darkness, infants still maintain a representation vivid enough to support reaching (Clifton et al., 1991). In contrast, the less precise representations resulting from occlusion do not suffice to support reaching. As suggested by Munakata (2001), object representations are more precise in the dark than in the presence of a visible occluder because the occluder competes with the hidden object for attention. The precision of object representations under conditions of darkness and occlusion, therefore, can account for infants' different abilities to reach in the two situations.

6. LEARNING PROCESSES

6.1 Exploratory Actions

The special status of exploration is that it does not need to be attached to performing any immediate activity. Exploratory actions aim at gaining information about the world rather than affecting it. Most actions are, in fact, both exploratory and executive. We act to affect conditions in the outside world, and at the same time we learn about the objects and events involved in the actions and about the actions themselves. The learning process is associated with specific motives. They ensure that the appropriate kind of experience is encountered that provides the right kind of knowledge for adapting to the world. The motives are associated with one of the three specific sets of rules that infants must learn. Infants need to learn about the physical world, their own motor system so they can control their actions, and the social world and their relations to other people. These three basic needs are satisfied by motives to learn about objects and events in the surrounding environment and to learn about other people and to explore one's action capabilities.

6.1.1 Learning About the Physical World

When children master the basic actions on objects, they begin to learn more complex actions that may involve several objects. They also learn how one object could be used as a tool to act on another one. This development becomes very prominent in the second year of life. For instance, infants find it very attractive to build towers, put lids on pans, and insert objects into holes. They also begin to explore the relationship between different objects and between objects and support surfaces (Bourgeois, Khawar, Neal, & Lockman, 2005). When infants begin to use one object to act on another one, their action repertoire increases dramatically. This is of great significance for the development of object knowledge and spatial cognition and the start of tool use.

The only mode of action that is exclusively exploratory is looking. This is especially important for young infants who have limited action capabilities that they can use for interacting with the outside world. For them, looking is an extremely important way of finding out about the world. Infants focus all attention on something they perceive for the first time. One of the mechanisms by which objects and events become familiar to the infant can be described as statistical learning. Infants are very sensitive to regularities embedded in the spatial structures or the flow of events and learn about them very fast (Saffran, 2003). Recently, Monroy, Gerson, and Hunnius (2017) demonstrated that knowledge from statistical learning is used by 19-months-old infants to predict upcoming action. This is the kind of learning that Gibson called "learning of higher order variables" (Gibson, 1966).

We learn about objects by looking and acting on them. Other modalities, like the haptic one, always include actions on objects, which provide detailed information of object properties that are not accessible to vision. In the auditory domain, infants use sound-producing actions to explore the properties of objects by, for instance, banging on them (Kahrs, Jung, & Lockman, 2013). Another example of exploratory actions is sliding. Friction between an object and a surface can only be explored by sliding the object against the surface. Haptic exploration is also superior to vision for exploring textures. However, because haptic exploration relies on actions relative to an object or a surface, it is dependent on the development of relevant reaching and grasping capabilities.

When infants master reaching, they spend much time on exploring objects manually. For example, it is very fascinating to observe 5- to 6-month-old infants handling a piece of paper. They tear, pull, wrinkle, and mouth the paper with persistent energy. In a recent study where 11- and 13-month-olds were video-recorded in their homes for 1 h, Karasik, Adolph, Tamis-LeMonda, and Zuckerman (2012) found that the infants made contact with about 40 objects during that period, corresponding to a new object every 1.5 min. The motive to explore objects is closely related to the social motive of the child. Not only do children explore objects and events for their own benefit, but they also want to share their newly acquired knowledge with other people. Karasik et al. (2012) found that in a large majority of the cases, the infants in her study showed the objects to the parent who was present and they often carried the objects to them.

6.1.2 Learning About One's Own Actions

Infants have a strong motive to explore their own action capabilities. Before they master reaching, for instance, they spend hours and hours trying to reach for an object even at a stage when they fail most of the time. There is no external reward. The activity itself is rewarding. This fact was described by Harlow, Harlow, and Meyer, 1950, who found that rhesus monkeys would engage with mechanical puzzles for long periods of time without receiving any extrinsic rewards like food. On the contrary, the introduction of food in the puzzle situation tended to disrupt, not facilitate, the learned performances. Harlow (op cit.) postulated a strong and persistent manipulation drive to account for learning and maintenance of the puzzle performance. This is in accordance with early findings, showing that rats will cross an electrified grid simply for the privilege of exploring new territory (Nissen, 1930) and that monkeys learn complex discriminations specifically for the sake of inspecting the entrance room (Butler & Harlow, 1957). Thus, there is reason to believe that children have an intrinsic motivation toward mastering their actions. Singh, Barto, and Chentanez (2005) define intrinsic motivation as being driven to do something because it is just enjoyable. It leads organisms to engage in exploration, play, and other behavior driven by curiosity in the absence of explicit reward. These activities favor the development of broad competence rather than being directed to more externally directed and rewarded goals.

Infants will abandon established patterns of behavior in favor of new ones even when this implies a setback in movement efficiency. At the onset of walking, for instance, infants stubbornly try to walk at an age when they can locomote much more efficiently by crawling or sliding. There is no obvious external reward for walking. Moving is probably just very pleasurable. According to Adolph and Berger (2006), infants who have recently started to walk take more than 9000 steps during a day.

When new possibilities open up as a result of, for example, the establishment of new neuronal pathways, improved perception, or biomechanical changes, children are eager to explore them. At the same time, they are eager to explore what objects and events in their surrounding afford in terms of new modes of action (Gibson & Pick, 2000). The pleasure of moving makes children less focused on what is to be achieved and more on their movement possibilities. It makes children try many different procedures and introduces necessary variability into the learning process. When the infant discovers new procedures that improve the movement efficiency, for instance, by making the hand come closer to the goal in reaching or by placing the foot better in locomotion, this new procedure is reinforced.

6.1.3 Learning About Other People's Actions

From birth, infants are very attracted by faces, and from the first weeks of life, they engage in social interaction with their caregivers (Trevarthen, 1980). Such actions serve to establish strong bonds at an age when infants crucially depend on them. Then, infants understand basic communications mediated by facial gestures and use such gestures themselves (Johnson & Morton, 1991). These social abilities make infants able to learn and develop, not only from their own actions, but also from other people's actions. The role that other people play in this process is of extraordinary importance. Thus, infants' knowledge of the world develops primarily in two ways: through their own actions and through observation of other people's actions.

Recent research into the social aspects of motor control shows that there is a shortcut to the understanding of other people's actions. It is the *mirror neuron system* (MNS) mechanism and implies that the observation of a goal-directed action performed by another person activates the corresponding neural structure in the observer's own action system (Rizzolatti & Craighero, 2004). Consequently, the motor and cognitive structures associated with the action become available to the observer in the same way as in the performer. Most importantly, the subject who observes an action does not only see the movement of the performer but perceives also the goal and intention of his or her action. The adaptive value of such a mechanism for social interaction is obvious. The MNS provides a very efficient mechanism for the exchange of information between individuals when rapid response is necessary (von Hofsten & Rosander, 2015). It is as important in a cooperative as in a competitive situation. A necessary condition for a functioning MNS is mastery of the observed actions. This knowledge is integrated into the very structure of the neural system in such a way that the observation of an action gives rise to neural activation in the corresponding neurons as when the subject performs the action himself or herself. This is called "the direct matching principle."

There are two kinds of evidence for *mirror neurons* in infants. First, when an adult watches another person performing a goal-directed action, a specific desychronization of the EEG is observed within a certain frequency called the mu rhythm. Such desynchronization is observed in

8- and 9-month-old infants (Nyström, Ljunghammar, Rosander, & von Hofsten, 2011; Southgate, Johnson, Osborne, & Csibra, 2009). Secondly, when a subject performs an action, his or her gaze will shift to the goal of the action ahead of time. This also happens when someone else observes the action, indicating that the motor program that includes gaze shifting is also available to the observer. This is indirect evidence for *mirror neurons*. Rosander and von Hofsten (2011) showed that infants exhibit the same proactive gaze shifts as adults. Ten-month-olds watching a displacement action shift gaze proactively to the goal of that action. Fig. 6 shows how infants monitor their own and other people's displacement movements, with gaze arriving at the goal ahead of time in both these conditions.

The close connection between vision and manipulation also makes it possible to learn about object affordances by viewing other people manipulating objects. This is especially relevant when learning about the functions of tools. Kahrs and Lockman (2012) suggested that tool use may be a more continuous development than previously believed. It is rooted in the perception—action routines that infants employ to gain knowledge about their environment. They suggested that to learn more about tool use development, research should focus on the processes by which children detect and relate affordances between objects, coordinate spatial frames of reference, and incorporate early-appearing action patterns into instrumental behaviors. It is not only seeing the action itself that improves learning about it. Corbetta and Fagard (2017) found that infants who observe other people acting on objects learn more if they can see the model's face. Thus, social

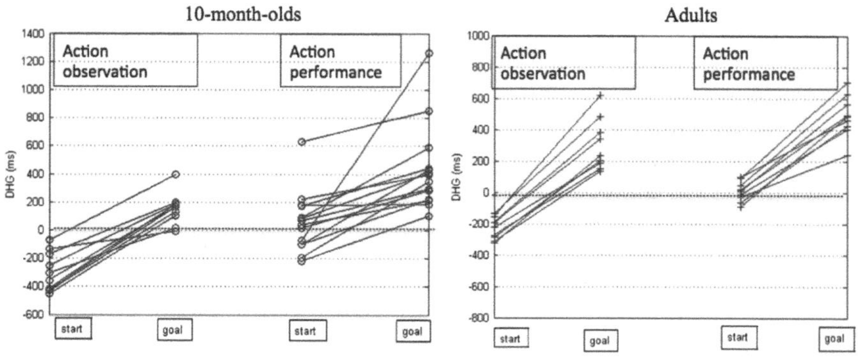

Figure 6 Observing (left) and performing (right) in 10-month-old infants and adults: means of the time difference between hand and gaze (DHG) in individual subjects at the start and at the goal. *Neuropsychologia (2011).*

signals conveyed by the face of a performer make infants more motivated in learning about the action in question.

7. CONCLUSIONS

Solving action problems includes both a spatial and a timing aspect. Planning movements requires an idea of how to act to accomplish a certain goal, how to adjust the action to a spatial context, and how to fit the action into the unfolding of other events. Efficient movements need to be conceived ahead of time such that the component movements are parts of a general plan. This requires anticipation of goal states.

A basic problem is that guiding actions requires information about what is going to happen next. There is no alternative to predictive control. Time is irreversible, and the only part of the action that is controllable is the one that has not yet been accomplished. Even a simple reach requires an ability to anticipate future events. If the object is out of reach, the action of attaining it will also involve whole body movements that will further extend action time. If the object is moving, the whole action has to be directed toward a point further ahead where the hand and the object will meet (von Hofsten, 1980, 1983).

Infants acquire many actions during the first 2 years of life. Some of the basic abilities are present at birth, such as sucking reaching, and looking. These are core abilities. The timing of actions seems to develop ahead of spatial abilities. For instance, young infants synchronize smooth eye movements to an external oscillating object but with insufficient gain. They catch moving objects at an age when they still build reaching movements with several corrections. The question is how sensorimotor intelligence becomes to be generally accessible to explicit thinking. The answer is strongly related to the child's ability to simulate an action in his or her mind. This develops gradually over infancy. At 2 years of age the child is able to mentally rotate a block before trying to fit it into an aperture and imagine a sequence of manipulations (at least two) ahead of time. According to Jeannerod (2001), the motor system is part of a simulation network that is activated under a variety of conditions in relation to action. One of the important functions of this simulation process is to shape the motor system in anticipation of execution. Through this process, cognition and action are tied closer to each other. The present review of action development shows that cognition is rooted in the sensorimotor intelligence expressed in infancy.

SUPPLEMENTARY DATA

Supplementary data related to this article can be found online at https://doi.org/10.1016/bs.acdb.2018.04.003.

REFERENCES

Adolph, K. E., & Berger, S. A. (2006). Motor development. In W. Damon & R. Lerner (Series Eds.) & D. Kuhn, R. S. Siegler (Vol. Eds.), *Handbook of child psychology: Vol. 2: Cognition, perception, and language* (6th ed., pp. 161–213). New York: Wiley.

Atkinson, J. (2000). *The developing visual brain*. New York, NY: Oxford University Press Inc.

Banks, M. S., & Bennett, P. J. (1988). Optical and photoreceptor immaturities limit the spatial and chromatic vision of human neonates. *Journal of the Optical Society of America, 5*, 2059–2079.

Barborica, A., & Ferrera, V. P. (2003). Estimating invisible target speed from neuronal activity in monkey frontal eye field. *Nature Neuroscience, 6*, 66–74.

Barbu-Roth, M., Anderson, D. I., Desprès, A., Provasi, J., Cabrol, D., & Campos, J. J. (2009). Neonatal stepping in relation to terrestrial optic flow. *Child Development, 80*(1), 8–14.

Barnes, G. R. (1993). Visual-vestibular interaction in the control of head and eye movement: The role of visual feedback and predictive mechanisms. *Progress in Neurobiology, 41*, 435–472.

Bayley, N. (1969). *Bayley scales of infant development*. New York: Psychological Corporation.

Bernstein, N. (1967). *The coordination and regulation of movements*. Oxford: Pergamon.

Bourgeois, K. S., Khawar, A. W., Neal, S. A., & Lockman, J. J. (2005). Infant manual exploration of objects, surfaces, and their interactions. *Infancy, 8*, 233–252.

Butler, R. A., & Harlow, H. F. (1957). Discrimination learning and learning sets to visual exploration incentives. *The Journal of General Psychology, 57*, 257–264.

Chen, Y., Keen, R., Rosander, K., & von Hofsten, C. (2010). Task demands affect infants' reaching kinematics. *Child Development, 81*, 1846–1858.

Claxton, L. J., Keen, R., & McCarty, M. E. (2003). Evidence of motor planning in infant reaching behavior. *Psychological Science, 14*, 354–356.

Clifton, R., Rochat, P., Litovsky, R., & Perris, E. (1991). Object representation guides infants' reaching in the dark. *Journal of Experimental Psychology: Human Perception and Performance, 17*, 323–329.

Corbetta, D., & Fagard, J. (2017). Editorial: Infants' understanding and production of goal-directed actions in the context of social and object-related interactions. *Frontiers in Psychology*. https://doi.org/10.3389/fpsyg.2017.00787.

Craig, C. M., & Lee, D. N. (1999). Neonatal control of sucking pressure: Evidence for an intrinsic tau-guide. *Experimental Brain Research, 124*, 371–382.

DeCasper, A. J., & Fifer, W. P. (1980). On human bonding: Newborns prefer their mothers' voices. *Science, 208*, 1174–1176.

Eyre, J. A., Miller, S., Clowry, G. J., Conway, E. A., & Watts, C. (2000). Functional corticospinal projections are established prenatally in the human foetus permitting involvement in the development of spinal motor centres. *Brain, 123*, 51–64.

Ffytche, D. H., Guy, C. N., & Zeki, S. (1995). The parallel visual motion inputs into areas V1 and V5 of human cerebral cortex. *Brain, 118*(Pt. 6), 1375–1394.

Fraiberg, S. (1977). *Insights from the blind*. New York: Basic Book.

Gibson, J. J. (1966). *The senses considered as perceptual systems*. New York: Houghton Mifflin.

Gibson, E. J., & Pick, A. (2000). *An ecological approach to perceptual learning and development*. Oxford: Oxford University Press.

Gottwald, J. M., de Bortoli, A., Lindskog, M., Nyström, P., Ekberg, T. L., von Hofsten, C., et al. (2017). Infants prospective control of reaching based on the difficulty of future actions: To what extent can infants' multistep actions be explained by Fitt's law? *Developmental Psychology, 53*, 4–12.

Gredebäck, G., Ornkloo, H., & von Hofsten, C. (2006). The development of reactive saccade latencies. *Experimental Brain Research, 173*, 159–164.

Harlow, H., Harlow, M., & Meyer, D. (1950). Learning motivated by a manipulation drive. *Journal of Experimental Psychology, 40*, 228. https://doi.org/10.1037/h0056906.

von Hofsten, C. (1979). Development of visually guided reaching: The approach phase. *Journal of Human Movement Studies, 5*, 160–178.

von Hofsten, C. (1980). Predictive reaching for moving objects by human infants. *Journal of Experimental Child Psychology, 30*, 369–382.

von Hofsten, C. (1982). Eye-hand coordination in newborns. *Developmental Psychology, 18*, 450–461.

von Hofsten, C. (1983). Catching skills in infancy. *Journal of Experimental Psychology: Human Perception and Performance, 9*, 75–85.

von Hofsten, C. (1984). Developmental changes in the organization of pre-reaching movements. *Developmental Psychology, 20*, 378–388.

von Hofsten, C. (1989). The organization of arm and hand movements in the neonate. In C. von Euler (Ed.), *The neurobiology of early infant behavior* (pp. 129–142). London: MacMillam.

von Hofsten, C. (1991). Structuring of early reaching movements: A longitudinal study. *Journal of Motor Behavior, 23*, 280–292.

von Hofsten, C., & Fazel-Zandy, S. (1984). Development of visually guided hand orientation in reaching. *Journal of Experimental Child Psychology, 38*, 208–2194.

von Hofsten, C., Kochukhova, O., & Rosander, K. (2007). Predictive occluder tracking in 4-month-old infants. *Developmental Science, 10*, 625–640.

von Hofsten, C., & Lindhagen, K. (1979). Observations on the development of reaching for moving objects. *Journal of Experimental Child Psychology, 28*, 158–173.

von Hofsten, C., & Rönnqvist, L. (1988). Preparation for grasping an object: A developmental study. *Journal of Experimental Psychology: Human Perception and Performance, 14*, 610–621.

von Hofsten, C., & Rosander, K. (1996). The development of gaze control and predictive tracking in young infants. *Vision Research, 36*, 81–96.

von Hofsten, C., & Rosander, K. (1997). Development of smooth pursuit tracking in young infants. *Vision Research, 37*, 1799–1810.

von Hofsten, C., & Rosander, K. (2015). On the development of the mirror neuron system. In G. Rizolatti, & P. Ferrari (Eds.), *New frontiers in mirror neuron research. Chapter 15* (pp. 270–320). Oxford University Press.

von Hofsten, C., & Spelke, E. S. (1985). Object perception and object directed reaching in infancy. *Journal of Experimental Psychology: General, 114*, 198–212.

von Hofsten, C., Vishton, P., Spelke, E. S., Feng, Q., & Rosander, K. (1998). Predictive action in infancy: Tracking and reaching for moving objects. *Cognition, 67*, 255–285.

von Hofsten, O., von Hofsten, C., Sulutvedt, U., Laeng, B., Brennen, T., & Magnussen, S. (2014). Simulating newborn face perception. *Journal of Vision, 14*(13), 16, 1–9.

Huntley-Fenner, G., Carey, S., & Solimando, A. (2002). Objects are individuals but stuff doesn't count: Perceived rigidity and cohesiveness influence infants' representations of small groups of discrete entities. *Cognition, 85*, 203–221.

Jeannerod, M. (Jul, 2001). Neuroimage. *Neural simulation of action: a unifying mechanism for motor cognition, 14*(1 Pt 2), S103–S109.

Jeannerod, M. (2006). *Motor cognition: What actions tell the self.* Oxford University Press, ISBN 978-0-19-856965-7.

Johnson, M. H., & Morton, J. (1991). *Biology and cognitive development: The case of face recognition*. Oxford: Blackwell. Kalins & Bruner.

Kahrs, B. A., Jung, W. P., & Lockman, J. J. (2013). Motor origin of tool use. *Child Development, 84*, 810–816.

Kahrs, B. A., & Lockman, J. J. (2012). Tool use of objects emerge continuously [French]. *Enfance, 64*(1), 61–72.

Kalnins, I. V., & Bruner, J. S. (1973). The coordination of visual observation and instrumental behavior in early infancy. *Perception, 2*, 307–314.

Karasik, L. B., Adolph, K. E., Tamis-LeMonda, C. S., & Zuckerman, A. L. (2012). Carry on: Spontaneous object carrying in 13-month-old crawling and walking infants. *Developmental Psychology, 48*, 389–397.

Kellman, P. J., & Spelke, E. S. (1983). Perception of partly occluded objects in infancy. *Cognitive Psychology, 15*, 438–524.

Kochukhova, O., & Gredebäck, G. (2007). Learning about occlusion: Initial assumptions and rapid adjustments. *Cognition, 105*, 26–46.

Kuypers, H. G. J. M. (1962). Corticospinal connections: Postnatal development in the rhesus monkey. *Science, 138*, 678–680.

Kuypers, H. G. J. M. (1973). The anatomical organization of the descending pathways and their contribution to motor control especially in primates. In J. E. Desmedt (Ed.), *New developments in electromyography and clinical neurophysiology* (Vol. 3, pp. 38–68). New York: S. Karger.

Lee, D. N., & Aronsson, E. (1974). Visual proprioceptive control of standing in human infants. *Perception & Psychophysics, 15*, 529–532.

Locke, J. (1689). *A essay concerning human understanding*. London: The Buffet.

Lockman, J. J., Ashmead, D. H., & Bushnell, E. W. (1984). The development of anticipatory hand orientation during infancy. *Journal of Experimental Child Psychology, 37*, 176–186.

McCarty, M. E., Clifton, R. K., Ashmead, D. H., Lee, P., & Goubet, N. (2001). How infants use vision for grasping objects. *Child Development, 72*(4), 973–987.

van der Meer, A. L. H. (1997). Keeping the arm in the limelight: Advanced visual control of arm movements in neonates. *European Journal of Paediatric Neurology, 4*, 103–108.

van der Meer, A. L. H., van der Weel, F. R., & Lee, D. N. (1995). The functional significance of arm movements in neonates. *Science, 267*, 693–695.

Monroy, C., Gerson, S., & Hunnius, S. (2017). Infants motor proficiency and statistical leaning for actions. *Frontiers in Psychology, 8*. article 2142.

Munakata, Y. (2001). Graded representations in behavioural dissociation. *Trends in Cognitive Science, 5*(7), 309–315.

Mundinano, I. C., Fox, D. M., Kwan, W. C., Vidaurre, D., Teo, L., Hommen-Ludiye, J., et al. (January 3, 2018). Transient visual pathway critical for normal development of primate grasping behaviour. *Proceedings of the National Academy of Sciences of the United States of America*.

Myowa-Yamakoshi, M., & Takeshita, H. (2006). Do human fetuses anticipate self-oriented actions? A study by four-dimensional (4D). *Ultrasonography Infancy, 10*(3), 289–301.

Nashner, L. M., Woollacott, M. H., & Tuma, G. (1979). Organization of rapid responses to postural and locomotor-like perturbations of standing man. *Experimental Brain Research, 36*, 463–476.

Nissen, H. W. A. (1930). A study of exploratory behavior in the white rat by means of the obstruction method. *The Pedagogical Seminary and Journal of Genetic Psychology, 37*, 361–376.

Nyström, P., Ljunghammar, T., Rosander, K., & von Hofsten, C. (2011). Using mu rhythm perturbations to measure mirror neuron activity in infants. *Developmental Science, 14*, 327–335.

Odent, M. (1979). The early expression of the rooting reflex. In L. Carneza, & L. Zichella (Eds.), *Emotion and reproduction* (Vol. 20B). London: Academic Press.
Örnkloo, H., & von Hofsten, C. (2007). Fitting objects into holes: On the development of spatial cognition skills. *Developmental Psychology, 43*, 403–416.
Piaget, J. (1953). *The origins of intelligence in the child*. New York: Routledge.
Prechtl, H. F. R. (1958). The directed head turning response and allied movements of the human infant. *Behaviour, 13*, 212–242.
Pulvermüller, F., Moseley, R. L., Egorova, E., Shebani, Z., & Boulenger, V. (2014). Motor cognition-motor semantics: Action perception theory of cognition and communication. *Neuropsychologia, 55*, 71–84.
Reed, E. S. (1996). *Encountering the world: Towards an ecological psychology*. New York: Oxford University Press.
Rizzolatti, G., & Craighero, L. (2004). The mirror-neuron system. *Annual Review of Neuroscience, 27*, 169–192.
Rochat, P., & Hespos, S. J. (1997). Differential rooting reponses by neonates: Evidence for an early sense of self. *Early Development and Parenting, 6*, 105–112.
Rönnqvist, L. (1995). A critical examination of the Moro response in newborn infants – symmetry, state relation underlying mechanisms. *Neurospsychologia, 33*(6), 713–726.
Rosander, K., & von Hofsten, C. (2000). Visual-vestibular interaction in early infancy. *Experimental Brain Research, 133*, 321–333.
Rosander, K., & von Hofsten, C. (2002). Development of gaze tracking of small and large objects. *Experimental Brain Research, 146*, 257–264.
Rosander, R., & von Hofsten, C. (2004). Infants' emerging ability to represent object motion. *Cognition, 91*, 1–22.
Rosander, K., & von Hofsten, C. (2011). 10-month-olds have a developed action plan to be applied when observing others. *Neuropsychologia, 49*, 2911–2917.
Rosander, K., Nyström, P., Gredebäck, G., & von Hofsten, C. (2007). Cortical processing of visual motion in infants. *Vision Research, 47*, 1614–1623.
Saffran, J. R. (2003). Statistical language learning: Mechanisms and constraints. *Current Directions in Psychological Science, 12*, 110–114.
Shatz, C. J. (September 1992). The developing Brain. *Scientific American*, 35–41.
Sherrington, C. S. (1906). *The integrative action of the nervous system*. New Haven: Yale University Press.
Simion, F., Regolin, L., & Bulf, H. (2008). A predisposition for biological motion in the newborn baby. *Proceedings of the National Academy of Sciences of the United States of America, 105*, 809–813.
Singh, S., Barto, A., & Chentanez, N. (2005). Intrinsically motivated reinforcement learning. In L. K. Saul, Y. Weiss, & L. Bottou (Eds.), *Advances in neural information processing systems 17: Proceedings of the 2004 conference*. Cambridge, MA: The MIT Press.
Southgate, V., Johnson, M. H., Osborne, T., & Csibra, G. (2009). Predictive motor activation during action observation in human infants. *Biological Letters, 5*(6), 769–772.
Spelke, E. S. (1998). Nativism, empiricism, and the origins of knowledge. *Infant Behaviour and Development, 21*(2), 181–200.
Spelke, E. S., & von Hofsten, C. (2001). Predictive reaching for occluded objects by six-month-old infants. *Journal of Cognition and Development, 2*, 261–282.
Stevens, S. S. (2002). *Handbook of experimental psychology*. Wiley.
Thelen, E., Corbetta, D., Kamm, K., Spencer, I. P., Schneider, K., & Zernicker, R. F. (1993). The transition to reaching: Mapping intention and intrinsic dynamics. *Child Development, 64*, 1058–1099.
Trevarthen, C. (1980). The foundations of intersubjectivity: Development of interpersonal and cooperative understanding in infants. In D. Olsen (Ed.), *The social foundations of language and thought: Essays in honor of J.S. Bruner* (pp. 316–342). New York: W.W. Norton.

de Vries, J. I. P., Visser, G. H. A., & Prechtl, H. F. R. (1982). The emergence of fetal behavior. I. Qualitative aspects. *Early Human Development, 23*, 159–191.
Witherington, D. C., von Hofsten, C., Rosander, K., Robinette, A., Woollacott, M. H., & Bertenthal, B. I. (2002). The development of anticipatory postural adjustments in infancy. *Infancy, 3*(4), 495–517.
Wu, C. Y., Lin, K. C., Lin, K. H., Chang, C. W., & Chen, C. L. (2005). Effects of task constraints on reaching kinematics by healthy adults. *Perceptual and Motor Skills, 10*, 983–994.
Zoia, S., Blason, L., D'Ottavio, G., Bulgheroni, M., Pezzetta, E., Scabar, A., et al. (2007). Evidence of early development of action planning in the human foetus: A kinematic study. *Experimental Brain Research, 176*, 217–226.

CHAPTER FOUR

Are Different Actions Mediated by Distinct Systems of Knowledge in Infancy?

Peter M. Vishton
Department of Psychological Sciences, College of William & Mary, Williamsburg, VA, United States
E-mail: vishton@wm.edu.

Contents

Abstract

This chapter considers why studies of infant looking and reaching often suggest different patterns of cognitive and perceptual development. In some cases, convergent results have emerged from studies of infant looking and reaching, but differences are

Advances in Child Development and Behavior, Volume 55
ISSN 0065-2407
https://doi.org/10.1016/bs.acdb.2018.05.003

common. The most typical results suggest less adult-like perception and cognition in studies of reaching than in studies of looking. Several reaching studies, however, do not fit this pattern, suggesting that reaching actions may be mediated by distinct systems of knowledge and information processing. Comparisons of research on other behaviors, such as crawling and walking, also suggest that infant knowledge systems vary across actions. Research on how adult size perception differs between verbal and reaching response behaviors is considered and used as a template to interpret the developmental results. Like adults, when infants prepare to engage in particular actions, they seem to shift their sensitivity to particular sources of information and to process that information in action-relevant ways. These tendencies suggest that distinct knowledge systems mediate different actions in infancy.

1. INTRODUCTION

What do infants know, and when do they know it? This fundamental question has motivated decades of research on infant cognitive and perceptual development. One clear conclusion from this body of work is that our understanding of the development of infant perception and cognition is directly tied to how we address these questions. This chapter considers evidence that when infants engage in different types of actions, our answers to these questions must change. If infants reach for and interact with a display, they seem to know—and not know—different things than when they merely view it.

One of the cornerstones of Piaget's theory of infant development was the apparent lack of object permanence in children younger than 8 months of age (Piaget, 1954). Around 4 months of age, infants begin to make successful reach-to-grasp actions directed at nearby visible objects. But if an object of interest is covered with an uninteresting cloth, children younger than 8 months often stop reaching for it. Piaget inferred that infants in this age group lack the ability to maintain a mental representation of an object unless it is directly visible. Later work, based on looking time measures, contradicted Piaget's conclusions about the development of object permanence. For instance, Baillargeon's (1987) "drawbridge" study presented 3.5-month-olds with an event in which a solid, rotating panel appeared to pass through a solid box. Infants looked longer at this "impossible" event, relative to baseline control levels. This pattern of looking emerged even though the rotating panel completely blocked the infants' view of the solid box. Baillargeon concluded that 3.5-month-olds do possess the ability to mentally represent an object, even when it is not directly visible.

If you ask a 4-month-old whether an occluded object continues to exist using a reaching measure, the answer is no. If you ask the same question using a looking measure, however, the answer is yes. The standard interpretation of these sets of disparate findings is that young infants do possess mental representations of hidden objects; what they lack is the ability to use those mental representations to coordinate actions toward hidden objects (but see Clifton, Rochat, Litovsky, & Perris, 1991). According to this interpretation, the difference in the results of the reaching and looking measures is due to a difference in the relative difficulty of the two tasks. Munakata (2001) has proposed a graded representation strength model of these different looking and reaching results. She assumes that the neural representation of a visible object is quantitatively stronger than that associated with a hidden object. If a smaller amount of representation strength is needed to coordinate looking than reaching actions, then perhaps hidden object representations for young infants fall between the two thresholds. The representations are strong enough to support relatively simple looking actions, but not strong enough to support the more demanding task of reaching.

In this chapter, I will argue for an alternative interpretation of such task-related differences. When study participants prepare to act on a target display, as opposed to simply viewing that display, a variety of evidence suggests that they alter how they process incoming sensory information. This seems to be true for both adult and infant populations. The shift in the perceptual "mode of processing" associated with action preparation increases sensitivity to some sources of information while suppressing other sources. What do infants know and when do they know it? By adding an action dimension to these "what" and "when" questions of development, a more complete understanding may emerge.

When infants' behaviors are guided by characteristics of the environment on a principled basis, many have described it as indicating infants "knowledge" about the world, and I will adopt this terminology here. There are good arguments for characterizing infant perception and action without invoking the concept of knowledge, which implies conscious, domain-general thought. While I do not intend to evoke these concepts when I use this term, I will nonetheless use it to connect with the literature considered here.

1.1 Chapter Outline

In the first section, I discuss measures of looking and reaching that have been used to characterize infant and adult knowledge about objects. This includes the reasoning used to infer early infant knowledge based on infant looking times and the concept of "violation of expectation" (VOE). I then discuss studies of adult visually guided reaching behaviors and resulting inferences about the information processing (and knowledge) inherent in these actions. The results of these studies provide a template for considering results from the developmental literature. I end this section with a description of the information processing inherent in the development of visually guided reaching in infants and young children.

In the second section, I consider groups of studies that suggest strong similarities in the course of development for looking and reaching, such as research on infant understanding of containment and occlusion events (Feigenson & Carey, 2003; Hespos & Baillargeon, 2006; 2008; Van de Walle, Carey, & Prevor, 2000). In the third section, I review studies that suggest different courses of development for looking and reaching behaviors, including the A-not-B error and depth perception (Arterberry, Bensen, & Yonas, 1991; Baillargeon & Graber, 1988; Bertin & Bhatt, 2006; Bhatt & Bertin, 2001; Cuevas & Bell, 2010). Many of these studies have suggested that infants perform in a more advanced, "adult-like" fashion when looking measures are used as compared to object reaching and search tasks.

In the fourth section, I review evidence that infants rely on different sources of information when performing looking and reaching behaviors. I discuss studies from my own group on infants' perceptions of object boundaries (Vishton, Ware, & Badger, 2005), and studies that have compared different components of the same overall infant action such as future-oriented reaching for moving objects (Berthier et al., 2001).

In the fifth section, I consider additional evidence that infants and young children process information differently when engaged in different actions, based on comparisons of behaviors other than reaching and looking. For instance, experienced 11-month-old crawlers will reliably avoid steep slopes, but when these same children stand up to walk, they ignore this slope information (Adolph, Bertenthal, Boker, Goldfield, & Gibson, 1997).

I will conclude by considering several predictions that emerge from a theory of action-specific knowledge. As action capabilities emerge and humans gain expertise with them, specific perception—cognition—action systems develop. Understanding the information-processing architecture of these subsystems is important for understanding development, and for any theory of the overall function of the human perception—cognition—action system. It is during development that we will be best able to explore the underlying architecture of these systems (e.g., Karmiloff-Smith, 1995).

2. MEASURES OF LOOKING AND REACHING

2.1 Measures of Infant Looking Time and Violation of Expectation

Three characterizations of the development of perception and cognition have been extensively replicated over the past several decades. First, very young infants perceive and make some sense of the world around them. Second, infants and young children perceive and reason about the world differently than adults do. Third, as infants mature and acquire experience they become increasingly adult-like in their perception and cognition. Many findings from developmental science have sought to characterize the ordered list of emerging perceptual and cognitive capacities associated with this development of increasingly adult-like behaviors.

From the day that they are born, indeed for at least several weeks before they are born, infants exhibit a tendency to habituate in their response to repeated stimuli (Fantz, 1964; Leader, Baillie, Martin, & Vermeulen, 1982). For instance, if a typical infant is shown a salient, colorful object, he/she will look at it for some period of time before looking away. If the same object is repeatedly shown on successive trials, then he/she will look at it for progressively shorter amounts of time before looking away. This consistent habituation of the looking-time response demonstrates that infants can see and encode at least some aspects of visual stimuli in a form that influences future behavior. Some rudimentary memory mechanisms must already be functional, enabling the infant to compare what is currently being seen with what has been seen in the past.

Also very reliable is the tendency of infants to exhibit "dishabituation"—a recovery of looking time duration or other response to a stimulus—if the habituation display is replaced with a new stimulus that is different in some way that the child can detect. The well-supported inference in this area is that infants tend to look longer at objects and events that are novel and/or events that are unexpected. This theoretical tool has been applied very fruitfully to explore how young infants perceive and reason about their surrounding environment.

By 3.5 months of age, infants' looking behaviors suggest that they expect solid objects not to pass through one another (Baillargeon, 1987). If an event is presented that seems to have violated this "solidity and cohesion" principle, infants will look longer at the event relative to baseline control conditions in which a violation does not take place (Spelke & Kinzler, 2007). Prior to 3.5 months, this tendency is not apparent in infant behaviors, suggesting that some cognitive or perceptual capacity that supports the behavior emerges around this age.

By 4.5 months of age, infants seem to expect that objects will fall downward in the absence of support (Needham & Baillargeon, 1993). Events in which a hand pushes an object beyond the edge of some supporting surface and the object remains in the same vertical location (i.e., it does not fall down) inspire longer looking times. Such looking times are always considered relative to carefully designed control events that are nearly identical but do not contain this violation of a "support" principle. Prior to 4.5 months, this tendency is not apparent, suggesting that this is the age at which this perceptual/cognitive capacity develops.

Hundreds of experiments of this type have explored infant development in this fashion, resulting in a detailed, largely self-consistent literature on the developmental progression of infant perception and cognition (for review see Spelke & Kinzler, 2007). A pervasive but largely implicit inference that has often been made is that looking-time measures provide the most accurate assessment of infants' perceptual and cognitive abilities at a given age because they are the most sensitive. A looking-time study places a minimum of demands on infant participants in terms of action planning and execution. According to this reasoning, infants possess object permanence by 3.5 months of age, but their ability to demonstrate this ability can be masked in a reaching study by the distraction and difficulty associated with performing the more complex task of planning and executing visually guided reaching actions. If an adult were given a demanding set of distractor tasks, his/her performance on any particular task would be diminished and errors would occur. It stands to reason that the same would be true of infants and young children as well.

Ramachandran and Blakeslee (1998) somewhat fancifully pointed out that if you want to prove pigs can talk, then you only need one talking pig. While many philosophers of science would take issue with this, there is a parallelism to infant research worth noting. As long as some measure, in some experimental context indicates that infants of a particular age possess some perceptual or cognitive ability, that has been taken as sufficient evidence that the ability is present by that age.

The vast majority of this work has relied on looking tendencies of infants, but other indicators of arousal have been used as well. In some studies, heart rate or sucking frequency has been used (e.g., Eimas, Siqueland, Jusczyk, & Vigorito, 1971). Levels of brain activation have also been measured (e.g., Wilcox & Biondi, 2015). In almost all cases, however, these studies rely on the same VOE reasoning used to determine what an infant can and cannot perceive and/or what an infant does and does not know.

Looking and reacting to experimenter-controlled events is certainly not the only set of behaviors available to an infant, however. When other behaviors are considered, many results that are not predicted by these VOE studies have emerged. Infant object-directed reaching studies have provided several examples of this. Before considering them, however, it is worth placing them in context with a consideration of some characteristics of adult object-directed reaching behaviors. A wide range of research has suggested that adult visual perception processes make use of different information processing during object-directed reaching behaviors, as compared with verbal response or other consciously mediated perceptual judgment behaviors. These studies of adults provide a template that we can use to consider developmental research. Do infants similarly alter their information processing when they engage in different actions?

2.2 Measures of Adult Object-Directed Reaching

When adults reach for objects, they engage in a variety of precise information processing, typically in an unconscious, automatic fashion. Perception of the distance and direction to an object relative to the current position of the hand are critical to coordinating an effective grasping action. Adult reaches typically involve the movement of the hand along a relatively straight path from its starting location to the target (for review see Jeannerod, 1988). In a typical reach, the hand accelerates smoothly through the first half of the movement and decelerates during the second half. This implies that the distance and direction of the hand movement to the target is determined before the movement onset. If an adult view of the target is removed at the onset of a reach—for example, by abruptly turning off the lights at the onset of movement—the hand still exhibits a trajectory with these kinematic characteristics (Paulignan, MacKenzie, Marteniuk, & Jeannerod, 1997).

The size of the object is also visually registered and mediates the shape of the grip used during the reach. Marteniuk, Leavitt, MacKenzie, and Athenes (1990) attached precise position sensors to participants' fingers and wrists and recorded their movements as they made precision grasps using the thumb and index finger. They presented participants with disk-shaped targets of varying sizes and found a canonical grip formation that was precisely mediated by the size of the target. During the first part of the action, the fingers moved apart from one another, until they reached a maximum grip aperture

(MGA) about half way through the reach. The grip then closed during the second half of the movement until it made contact with the target. The Pearson correlation between the diameter of the disk target and the MGA was quite linear and very high, around 0.99.

The shape of the object is also taken into account during a reaching action. For instance, if the reaching target is an irregular shape, the thumb and index finger are not placed randomly, but instead positioned at opposing positions on the shape, so as to afford a stable grip (Goodale, Meenan, Bülthoff, Nicole, Murphy, & Racicot, 1994). Studies of the force applied to an object when it is grasped and lifted indicate that the approximate weight of an object is also included in the action plan associated with the grasp (Brenner & Smeets, 1996). When lifting an egg shell, far less force is applied than when lifting a heavy metal object, for instance. These many detailed aspects of a "simple" reach-to-grasp movement are computed outside of our awareness in most cases, but they are both complex and essential to the performance of efficient, successful actions.

Vishton et al. (2007) performed several studies on how our conscious perceptions of target size are altered when we prepare to perform a reaching action. The interpretation applied in those experiments provides a template for better understanding how infants' perception and cognition might be altered when they prepare to perform a reaching action as well.

In these studies, participants were asked to repeatedly choose which of two disks seemed larger. A standard, 28-mm diameter disk was always presented, along with a second disk that varied between 27 and 33 mm in diameter. In some cases, participants were asked to verbally state which disk appeared larger. In others, participants were asked to reach out and grasp the disk that they perceived to be larger. When the pairs of disks were presented on a plain background, participants were very accurate in both the verbal and grasp selection tasks.

The experimenters also presented the disks on a background that induced the Ebbinghaus illusion (Fig. 1). The illusion background made the standard 28-mm disk seem larger and the comparison disks seem smaller. When participants engaged in a verbal response task to indicate which disk was larger, the illusion exerted a 9% effect on perceived size of the disks. That is, the comparison disk needed to be approximately 3 mm larger than the 28-mm standard disk to reliably cause participants to verbally choose it as larger. When participants engaged in a grasp response task, however, the magnitude of the illusion effect was reduced by about 40%. Note here that it is not merely the grip formation that is resistant to the illusion, a

Figure 1 The Ebbinghaus illusion as presented to participants by Vishton et al. (2007). The two central disks are identical in size and constructed from thin plastic such that they can be grasped and lifted. When assessed by a verbal response choice task, the surrounding arrays of circles printed on paper cause participants to perceive the central disk on the left as approximately 9% larger than the central disk on the right. The magnitude of the illusion is reduced by approximately 40% when participants indicate their choices by grasping or touching the selected disk.

finding that has been obtained in several studies (e.g., Aglioti, DeSouza, & Goodale, 1995). Preparing to reach for a target changed participants' conscious perception of relative size. When a 30-mm comparison disk was presented to participants in the illusion background condition, they would verbally state that the 28-mm disk appeared larger. When the same display appeared in the grasp response task condition, participants' hands would typically make the opposite response, indicating that the 30-mm disk seemed larger. Even when making the same perceptual choice, with the same display, when participants were engaged in a reaching behavior, their perceptions of the display were qualitatively altered.

These studies also replicated results obtained by Aglioti et al. (1995), showing that the effect of the illusion on the MGA produced during the grasp was significantly smaller than that obtained for the verbal response task. Agilioti et al. described that result as evidence for the presence of a second, largely independent, somewhat illusion-resistant visual processing stream associated with the parietal cortex. The magnitude of illusion reduction for the Vishton et al. disk choice measure was approximately the same as that seen for the MGA measure, but the changes they identified did not merely affect the grasp formation.

Others have identified related changes in distance perception associated with changes in action intention (e.g., Witt, Proffitt, & Epstein, 2005). Based on these results, Vishton et al. (2007) argued that the preparation to reach engages an alternative "mode" of visual processing. In any particular context, human vision exhibits certain information-processing characteristics. Of the many sources of information available for perceptual processing, some are picked up, whereas others are ignored. By carefully controlling a range of stimuli and observing human performance, experimenters can precisely characterize what information is used and how it relates to perceptual outcomes. The mode of processing approach suggests that these characteristics are malleable, perhaps on a moment-to-moment basis, when participants prepare to engage in different action tasks. For instance, stereopsis cues to size and distance are extremely effective across the relatively small range of distances that are encountered for reaching actions (Cutting & Vishton, 1995). For large distances, however, stereopsis information is not useful, due to physical limitations imposed by the distance between the two eyes and the limits of human retinal acuity. Human vision seems to incorporate this fact by relying more heavily on stereopsis when engaged in reaching actions than when engaged in nonreaching behaviors. An increased weighting of stereopsis information and a corresponding reduction in weighting of nonstereopsis depth information would result in a reduction in the magnitude of illusions caused by that nonstereopsis information.

In the Vishton et al. grasping and touching experiments, the information that causes the Ebbinghaus illusion—presumably the relative size of circles in the display—is somewhat suppressed. In general, preparing to reach for a stimulus can change how the reacher perceives it. An analogous process may take place for infants and children as well. Action planning stimulates a wide range of changes in patterns of neural activity. Reaching-relevant information presumably becomes more salient. Information that is not relevant to action control may be reduced in salience. Infant perception and cognition may change just as has been established in adult participants.

2.3 Measures of Infant Object-Directed Reaching

What information do infants and young children use to guide their reaching for objects? Human infants typically begin to successfully grasp nearby, visible targets by around 4 months of age (von Hofsten, 1991). Even before this age the foundations of visually guided reaching seem to be present. For instance, von Hofsten (1982) has shown that even newborn infants make systematic prereaching movements that bring their hands toward a visible target.

While 4-month-olds typically make successful reach-to-grasp actions, the actions are initially not mediated by target properties as they are in adults. These reaching characteristics emerge in the first 2 years of development (Konczak & Dichgans, 1997). Lockman, Ashmead, and Bushnell (1984) demonstrated that 9-month-olds rotate the hand to account for the orientation of a long, thin target object during a grasping action. By 9 months of age, infants scale their grips to the size of targets (von Hofsten & Rönnqvist, 1988; Siddiqui, 1995), but the scaling is less precise than that of adults and typically incorporates a larger-than-needed grip.

The development of visually guided action clearly develops over an extended period of childhood, but even very young infants' reaching is controlled on the basis of many sources of information gathered from the environment—many of the same sources that have been shown to influence looking behaviors in VOE studies. As with studies that measure looking time, experimenters have been able to create situations in which the reaching behaviors of infants can be used to infer how the infant perceived and reasoned about displays. The information processing that is implicated by such studies suggests what infants know (and do not know) at particular ages.

2.4 Looking Time Versus Looking Location and Reaching Location Versus Reaching Duration

In this chapter, except where specifically noted, measures of "looking" refer to the amount of time an infant spends looking at a display before looking away. This measure is taken as an assessment of how much a particular display attracts the attention of an infant. Recent work, however, has made increasing use of eye trackers to record not just *whether* an infant looks at a display, but *where* the infant directs his/her fixations. In studies in which display objects move, the visual tracking behaviors of infants can be monitored as well.

For most studies, researchers have focused on looking duration and reach location, but this could, in principle, be reversed. The amount of time an infant spends reaching for and interacting with a display can provide a measure of how much it attracts the infant's attention (e.g., Mandler, Fivush, & Reznick, 1987). Where an infant looks can be taken as a measure of where an infant believes a hidden object to be located (e.g., Cuevas & Bell, 2010; Hofstadter & Reznick, 1996). While there are exceptions that I will note, in general, this chapter adheres to the historical tendency to focus on looking durations and reach locations. Whether it is the looking versus reaching distinction or the duration versus location distinction that is most important is an issue that remains to be resolved.

3. EVIDENCE FOR SIMILAR DEVELOPMENT OF REACHING AND LOOKING BEHAVIORS

Several lines of research have compared infant reaching and looking measures and obtained very similar results. These parallel patterns of development suggest that reaching and looking may be governed by a single information processing system.

3.1 Occlusion and Containment

In the key conditions of their experiment, Hespos and Baillargeon (2001) showed infants events in which a tall target object was lowered behind an occluder that was shorter than the target object. As such, when the bottom of the target object made contact with the support surface behind the occluder, its motion should have stopped, and much of the object should have remained visible. A hidden hole in that support surface, however, enabled the target object to move downward until only the very top of it remained visible. The 4.5-month-old participants in this experiment looked reliably longer at this event than at relevant control events (e.g., taller occluder or shorter target object). The results suggest that infants at this age are able to reason about the relative heights of objects to develop expectations about what this occlusion event should look like. When those expectations were violated, it attracted the infants' attention, and thus longer looking times.

Interestingly, if the event involves a target object being placed into a container rather than behind an occluder, 4.5-month-olds do not exhibit this consistent-looking preference. Around 7.5 months of age, however, infants seem to develop the ability to reason about containment events in the same way that they reason about occlusion events at 4.5 months of age.

Hespos and Baillargeon (2006) developed a clever reaching-based study that asked all of these same questions about infant object reasoning. In these studies, infants were shown a tall frog target object. The frog was placed behind an occluding screen. When the screen was removed, infants saw a tall and short occluder; frog legs protruded from each. The short occluder was too short to have hidden the tall frog. If infants were able to reason about the relative heights of the frog target and the occluders, then infants should have inferred that there was only one frog target and that it was located behind the tall occluder. When the display was moved within reach, 6-month-olds consistently reached more frequently for the tall occluder, relative to baseline preferences (e.g., without prior view of the tall frog target). However, if the target frog appeared to have been placed into a container rather than behind an occluder, 6-month-olds did not exhibit this preferential reaching tendency. The 7.5-month-olds in their study did exhibit the preference, however. This developmental decalagé—reasoning about relative size first with occlusion events and only later with containment events—thus seems to occur across both looking and reaching measures.

Note that these looking and reaching studies were not completely parallel. The 4.5-month-olds exhibited adult-like size reasoning for looking measures with the occlusion events. There was no corresponding reaching task for 4.5-month-olds. However, for 6-month-olds, we would expect continued adult-like looking preferences with occlusion. The 6-month-old reaching performance matches this prediction. At 7.5 months of age, the looking data suggest an onset of adult-like size reasoning with containment events. The 7.5-month-old reaching performance matches this prediction as well.

The same research team found strong similarities in the development of infant reasoning about object support (Hespos & Baillargeon, 2008). A series of studies had already explored infant understanding of support relations using looking-time tasks (for review see Baillargeon, Gertner, & Wu, 2010). When 3.5- to 4.5-month-olds watched a hand release a target object, they seemed to expect the object to fall, looking longer than baseline comparison levels if the object remained floating, seemingly unsupported in space. If the target object was placed adjacent to a support platform, this preference was not present. Only 5.5-month-old infants exhibited an increase in looking in this adjacency condition. At this age, however, infants do not seem to differentiate between full support of an object (100% of object base supported) and partial support (only 15% of the object supported). Only at 6.5 months of age do infants seem to reason about support in a way that takes into account both the *kind* and *amount* of support provided in events of this type.

Hespos and Baillargeon (2008) explored infants' understanding of object support using a reaching measure as well. Anyone who has spent time around infants will have seen how they enjoy reaching for objects that can be picked up, handled, and placed in the mouth. If an object is firmly attached to a wall, it can be touched, but not manipulated. It stands to reason that if infants are given the choice of reaching for an attached versus unattached object, they will tend to choose the unattached target. If an object is suspended in space—not supported from below—then it is likely attached to the background wall. This reasoning enabled the researchers to explore when infants perceive an object as supported (and thus unattached) versus unsupported (and thus attached). They presented infants with displays containing pairs of objects, e.g., one supported by a shelf and another attached to the background. Infants at 5.5 months of age preferred to reach for the supported target. This was true regardless of whether the support was full, or only partial. Only at 6.5 months of age did infants take into account the amount of support provided, reaching more for targets with full support.

These results with the reaching studies are especially compelling given the opposite preference present in the looking studies. In the looking studies, infants were especially attracted to displays that seemed to violate the physical principles of support. In these reaching studies, the infants reached away from these targets, grasping displays that did not exhibit a violation.

3.2 Object Individuation

Another parallel pattern of looking and reaching studies has been found in the domain of object individuation. If an object moves behind an occluder panel and then another object emerges from the other side, is it the same object? If it looks exactly the same, then adults and infants seem to believe that it is. If the second object looks different from the first, however, adults reason that there must be two objects behind the occluder that are emerging one at a time.

To test infants' perceptions of this type of event, Xu and Carey (1996) habituated infants to two different objects, alternately emerging from behind a central occluder panel. For instance, a toy truck would emerge from the left of the occluder and then move back out of view. Next, a toy duck would emerge from the right and then move back out of view. Experimenters habituated infants to this repeating sequence of events and then lowered the occluder to reveal either one or two objects. Adults have a clear inference in this situation that there should be two objects—a duck and a truck. If there is only one object, this would constitute a clear VOE event. For infants as old as 10 months of age, however, it does not. If the duck and truck are shown simultaneously during the habituation, then 10-month-olds seem to expect two objects behind the occluder panel (i.e., they look longer if there is only one). When the objects are shown one at a time, however, infants do not express this looking behavior. For a 10-month-old, apparently it's reasonable for a toy duck to spontaneously turn into a toy truck (and vice versa) during the period of time when the object is occluded. By 12 months of age, the looking pattern changes, aligning with adults' intuitions about this occlusion event.

Van de Walle et al. (2000) developed an object search task to address this same question using a more active measure of infant behavior (also see Feigenson & Carey, 2003). Infants watched as an experimenter placed one or two objects into an opaque box. The box was presented such that infants could not look inside, but could only explore it by placing their hand in through a small opening on one end. When infants were allowed to search the box, 10- and 12-month-olds reached into the box an appropriate number of times. That is, if one object had been hidden, then infants retrieved one object and tended not to search the box a second time. If two objects had been placed in the box, then the infants were significantly more likely to continue searching the box, even when the second object had been surreptitiously removed by the experimenters.

To compare their results directly with those of Xu and Carey (1996), these experimenters ran a second experiment in which two objects were removed from the box, one at a time, and then placed back into the box. For instance, the experimenter might reach into the box and remove a cookie monster toy, show it to the infant, and then place it back inside. Next, the experimenter would reach in again and show the infant a toy helicopter before placing it back in the box. After this series of events, the 10-month-olds searched the box as if there were only one toy contained within it. The 12-month-old participants, however, searched the box as if there were two objects (Van de Walle et al., 2000).

If an adult saw a cookie monster toy removed from a box and then placed back inside, and then saw a toy helicopter removed and placed back inside, a clear inference would result. The adult would presume that two objects were in the box. Alternatively, if the same cookie monster toy were shown and then returned twice, no such inference would result. This pattern was produced by the 12-month-olds, but not the 10-month-olds, just as in the earlier looking-time studies. For object individuation, reaching and looking seem to be mediated by the same knowledge system.

4. EVIDENCE FOR LATER DEVELOPMENT OF REACHING THAN LOOKING BEHAVIOR

Several lines of research have found similar results when infant looking and reaching measures have been compared. Many others, however, have found differences. The most common results have suggested more adult-like perception and cognition when based on looking relative to reaching behaviors.

4.1 Object Permanence

Several lines of research have suggested that the perceptual and cognitive processes that support infant looking behaviors are more adult-like than those that support visually guided reaching behaviors. I have already mentioned the earliest example of this with object permanence. Piaget (1954) noted that infants younger than 8 months of age consistently fail to reach for target objects if they are placed out of view. Yet Baillargeon (1987) and many others have found evidence that infants engage in strikingly complex and adult-like reasoning about those hidden objects if looking measures are used.

Several other lines of research have produced a similar pattern of outcomes, all of which suggest that looking measures produce more adult-like perception and cognition than reaching. This might be because looking and reaching inspire the activation of different systems of knowledge, but it could also be that looking simply provides a more sensitive measure of infant knowledge. Perhaps the planning and execution of a reaching action consumes some of a finite pool of mental resources, reducing the ability of the infant to engage in his/her best possible analysis of the presented displays and events. Looking involves looking. Reaching involves looking as well as reaching.

Clifton et al. (1991) found that although 6.5-month-olds infants fail to reach for objects when they are behind some occluding surface, they reach for audible objects in the dark. And those reaching actions were not uncoordinated swipes into the darkness. During reaches under normal illumination conditions, a small object was associated with a particular sound and a large object with a different sound (e.g., a bell and a buzzer). When that sound was played in the dark, the infant reaching was guided by the target size implied by the sound. For the large object sound, the hands were spread laterally during the reach. For the small object sound, the reaches were more likely to involve one hand extending, while the other remained back near the infant's trunk. The result suggests that infants' limitation in the classic Piagetian task was not their inability to see the object, but rather a distraction caused by the sight of the occluder.

A related result was obtained by Jonsson and von Hofsten (2003) in their study of 6-month-olds' performance in catching a moving target. If the moving object passed behind an occluder, the frequency and accuracy of future-oriented reaching declined precipitously. If the room lights were turned off, however, during the time that the object would have been behind the occluder, the decline in reaching performance was significantly smaller. The loss of the ability to see the object seems to matter for object catching, but the presence of a visible occluder seems to matter more. All of this work suggests that the relative delay in the cognition-supporting reaching relative to looking may result from extra challenges present in reaching studies rather than the presence of a different system of knowledge.

Piaget described the early development of so-called object permanence as relatively fragile, as evidenced by infants' failures on the classic A-not-B task. In this paradigm, researchers typically study infants between 8 and 12 months of age, who are able to retrieve objects hidden behind an occluder. Two hiding locations are used, referred to as A and B respectively. Children watch an adult hide an object in location A and successfully retrieve it several times. On the key test trials, the experimenter switches to hiding the target object in the B location. All of this is performed in full view of the infants, who watch each step. Even after a delay of only several seconds, however, many infants incorrectly search in the A location.

VOE studies relying on looking time suggest that infants are able to track the location of hidden objects, however. Baillargeon and Graber (1988) showed 8-month-olds a series of events on a stage with two separate occluding panels and a nearby object. The occluding panels were moved laterally such that one of the panels hid the object. In some cases, the object was placed so as to be hidden behind the panel on the left, and in others hidden by the panel on the right. A hand reached in from the side of the display. After lingering there for 15 s, it reached behind the nearest occluder and retrieved an object. The experimenters recorded how long the infant looked at the display before looking away for 2 continuous sec. In the "possible" case, the object was retrieved from the same panel behind which it had been hidden. In the "impossible" case, the experimenters surreptitiously switched the location of the object, without revealing this to the infant. For instance, in some trials, the object would have been hidden behind the occluder on the left, but then retrieved from the occluder on the right. Eight-month-olds looked significantly longer at these impossible trials, providing strong evidence that they are adept at tracking the location of a hidden object as long as this ability is measured using a looking-time VOE method.

Other versions of the A-not-B task have explored infants' understanding using a visual tracking methodology (e.g., Cuevas & Bell, 2010). In the looking version of the A-not-B task, the object was hidden in the A location repeatedly but an adult caregiver restrained the arms of the infant so that she could not search for it manually. After the experimenter prompted the infant (e.g., "Where is it?") the subsequent visual fixation was likely to be in the direction of hiding location A. When the experimenter switched to hiding the target in the B location, infants were still likely to make an initial fixation in the direction of location A. Thus, with looking location (see note above about looking duration vs. location) infants seem to make the A-not-B error. Cuevas and Bell tracked the development of object search behaviors between 5 and 10 months of age and found lower error rates for looking than for reaching. Again, it seems that infants' performance is more adult-like when the task involves looking rather than reaching.

Keen (2003) presented 2-year-olds with an object search task in which a ball rolled down a ramp, behind an occluder containing four doors. The task of the child was to open the correct door to find the ball. Adults have no difficulty in this task, reasoning that the ball should roll down the ramp until it runs into an obstacle. When Keen placed a barrier on the ramp, however, 2-year-olds did not use it to infer that the ball would stop at the door adjacent to it. This was true even though the top of the barrier remained visible throughout the task. The result is striking given the looking time VOE evidence indicating that infants can reason about solidity and cohesion as early as 3.5 months of age. Fully 20 months later, they seem unable to apply that knowledge in a search task. When a behavioral measure such as this involves several steps—tracking the occluded movement of the ball, considering how the occluder will affect it, and then after several seconds grasping and opening one of several doors—the knowledge inherent in looking behaviors can be strikingly different from that apparent in more complex action tasks.

4.2 Depth Perception

Another example of this tendency of looking behaviors to be more adult-like than reaching behaviors is present in research on infant depth perception. Yonas et al. have extensively studied depth perception using a preferential reaching task (for review see Kellman & Arterberry, 2006). Infants between 5 and 7 months of age exhibit a consistent tendency to reach for the nearer of two surfaces (see also von Hofsten & Spelke, 1985). If an infant is sensitive to a depth cue suggesting that one surface is closer, then a reaching preference will be observed. This method has been used to suggest that 7-month-old infants are sensitive to static, monocular sources of depth information such as occlusion, height-in-field, familiar size, etc., whereas 5-month-olds are not. Infants at both ages, however, are sensitive to binocular and motion-based sources of depth information. All of these results apply when infants are engaged in reaching actions. Do the same results apply when the infants are merely looking at a display? One study has suggested a similar course of development for looking behaviors, with sensitivity to monocular sources of depth information emerging between 5 and 7 months of age (Arterberry et al., 1991). Several other looking studies, however, have presented evidence for much earlier sensitivity to monocular information when looking behaviors are assessed.

Shuwairi (2009), for example, presented 4-month-olds with 2D images of cubes that were constructed to be "possible" or "impossible" figures. In the impossible case, a normal 2D image of a 3D cube was altered such that more distant surfaces seemed to partially occlude closer surfaces. Four-month-olds' spontaneous preferences for these impossible images, relative to similar possible images, suggests that they perceived that something was unusual and novel in them. It further suggests that they were able to infer a global 3D structure by integrating static, monocular 2D information across the image.

In another line of work, Bhatt and Bertin (2001; Bertin & Bhatt, 2006) presented 3-month-old infants with pairs of images containing collections of small, geometric figures that adults perceive as 3D rectilinear objects. On one side, all of the depicted objects in the image were identical, whereas on the other side, one target object was different. When alterations were made to the figures that created the illusion of a change in the 3D shape of the object (i.e., shifting the location of line intersections and the shading of the figures), infants exhibited a looking preference. When carefully matched alterations were made to the figures that did not change implied 3D shape, infants did not exhibit a consistent looking preference. These preferential looking studies suggest that infants are sensitive to shading and line-intersection depth cues as early as 3 months of age, well before it influences their preferential reaching at 7 months.

4.3 Interpreting the Meaning of Reaching-Specific Delays in Development

Research on both object permanence and depth perception suggest a delayed pattern of development for infant reaching relative to infant looking. While this pattern of results is consistent with the notion that infants engage different knowledge systems for reaching and looking tasks, there is an alternative explanation based on task difficulty. Reaching may simply be a more difficult task than looking.

A similar challenge has been present in reasoning about loss of cognitive function associated with brain injury (Shallice, 1988). Consider a patient who suffers damage to a region of the inferior temporal cortex (area IT) and thereafter is unable to recognize faces. The patient retains the ability to recognize everyday objects, but not faces. Are face and object recognitions mediated by different information processing systems? Perhaps, but there is an alternative interpretation possible that is analogous to the present comparison of looking and reaching behaviors. Perhaps distinguishing different categories of objects is easier than distinguishing individual faces. Faces are typically very similar to one another, with the same features in approximately the same configuration. Perhaps face and object recognitions are computed by a common network of brain regions rather than two separate systems, and area IT is a part of this common network. If the system still functions, but at a reduced level of ability, then it may retain the ability to perform simple tasks, while losing the ability to perform those that are more difficult. Indeed, the reasoning about the role that the "fusiform face area" plays in recognition of configural, nonface stimuli has been a subject of much research (e.g., Gauthier, Skudlarski, Gore, & Anderson, 2000).

In developing theories of cognitive structure, neurologists typically reason on the basis of more than one patient with more than one pattern of injury and associated deficits (but see Vishton, 2005). In the current example, if a second patient could be identified, who retained the ability to recognize faces while losing the ability to recognize objects after suffering an injury to a different part of the brain, then a "double dissociation" would be found. Such double dissociations cannot be easily explained on the basis of task difficulty: recognizing faces cannot be both harder and easier than recognizing objects.

To argue for the existence of different knowledge systems for reaching and looking behaviors in infants, an analogous dissociation is needed. This section has identified several cases in which infant looking outperforms infant reaching in terms of adult-like reasoning. In the next section, I will argue that infants are sometimes more adult-like in their reaching than in their looking.

5. EVIDENCE FOR DISTINCT DEVELOPMENT OF REACHING AND LOOKING BEHAVIORS

Some research has suggested that reaching and looking behaviors are governed by distinct information processing systems. The patterns of results suggest that when infants are engaged in a reaching task, they are less influenced by some sources of visual information and more influenced by others. Reaching infants do not seem to know less than infants in a VOE task; they seem to know different things.

5.1 Object Boundary/Gestalt Perception

An extensive series of studies has explored how infants parse their visual input—how they determine where object boundaries are located, and how they decide when two different parts of a display are connected. Often this has been referred to as Gestalt perception, in that it explores how infants group separate stimuli into perceptual units. Kellman and Spelke (1983) presented 4-month-old infants with a display that consisted of a central occluder and two protruding rod parts. If the edges of the two rod pieces are aligned, with the same color and surface features, most adults perceive them as a single object placed behind an occluder. Four-month-olds only seem to perceive the display in this way if the two parts are shown moving together in unison (i.e., exhibiting common motion). Additional work has shown that after habituation to a similar display, 2-month-olds exhibited the opposite preference (Johnson & Aslin, 1995), suggesting that this "perceptual completion" ability emerges between 2 and 4 months of age.

When Kellman and Spelke (1983) presented these same displays without the common motion of the visible rod pieces, the preference for the split rod did not emerge. Common motion seems essential to perceptual completion for 4-month-olds. In a subsequent experiment, in which common motion was present but the two visible parts of the display differed in color and shape, infants still looked longer at a split display than at a connected object. Later studies have found that edge alignment and relative proximity also influence perceptual completion. If the top and bottom figures are substantially misaligned or if the central occluder separates the visible rod pieces by too much distance, then the preference for the split display does not emerge (Johnson & Aslin, 1995, 1996; Smith, Johnson, & Spelke, 2003). In all cases, however, motion information seems to play a primary role in perceptual completion with these displays.

Needham and Baillargeon (Needham, 1999; Needham & Baillargeon, 1997) explored infant perception of object boundaries based on how participants looked at "move-apart" and "move-together" events. In general, they presented displays that could have consisted of a single, connected object or two separate, adjacent objects. After presenting a display to infants and allowing them to look at it for several seconds, a hand emerged from the side, grasped one part of the display and pulled it to the side. In some cases, the entire display would move—the move-together event. In others, only part of the display would move, whereas the other part would remain stationary—the move-apart event. If an infant perceived the initial display as a single, connected object, then they should have expected the move-together event. The move-apart event should therefore generate a VOE and longer looking time as compared with the move-together event. Conversely, if the infant perceived the initial display as two separate, adjacent parts, then the move-together event should result in longer looking times relative to the move-apart event. By exploring when infants of different ages exhibited these preferences, these researchers have explored how infants perceive, or fail to perceive, the presence of object boundaries.

Based on this method, 8-month-olds seem to rely on differences in shape and color to decide when two display parts are connected. When two adjacent display parts differed in shape and color, infants looked longer at the move-together event than at the move-apart event. If the two object parts were identical in shape and color, however, then it was the move-apart event that produced longer looking (Needham & Baillargeon, 1997). Eight-month-olds also make use of spatiotemporal information in this paradigm. Needham and Baillargeon (1997) presented infants with displays consisting of two adjacent pieces with identical color and shape. After a thin board was lowered between the two display parts and then removed, infants subsequently looked longer at the move-together event, suggesting that this board event caused infants to perceive the display as two separate objects. Infants also seem to make use of information about object support to parse visual inputs. If one display part is suspended above the presentation stage, and if that part is touching the other display part, adults infer that the two parts must be connected. (Otherwise the floating display part would have fallen down onto the stage.) Eight-month-olds seemed to make this same inference after familiarization with a display constructed in this manner, looking longer at a subsequent move-apart event (Needham & Baillargeon, 1997).

Younger infants only make use of some of this information. With 4-month-olds, when two display parts differed in shape, infants looked longer at the move-together event, suggesting they perceived the initial display as consisting of two separate parts. A difference in color, however, has not seemed sufficient to produce a perception of two separate objects at this age (Needham, 1999a). In another study, when 4.5-month-old infants were briefly familiarized with one object before it was placed adjacent to another, the memory of having seen the individual object was sufficient to cause longer looking at the move-together event (Needham & Baillargeon, 1998).

The looking time studies conducted with the center-occluded rod and with the move-apart and move-together events suggest a largely consistent pattern of development. Infants develop the ability to use nonmotion information (e.g., shape and color) in isolation sometime between 4 and 6 months of age. Nonmotion information can influence the interpretation of the motion information during this age range, but when spatiotemporal or motion information suggests one parsing of the display while color and shape information suggest another, it is the spatiotemporal or motion information that determines infants' perception.

Infant object-directed reaching across this age span suggests a different use of these information sources. Vishton et al. (2005) presented 8- and 9-month-olds with long narrow displays consisting of two wooden blocks. In the *connected* condition, the blocks were attached together to form one object (16 cm wide, 2 cm in height and depth). In the *split* condition, the two blocks sat next to one another, but were not connected. (Two 8-cm blocks, placed adjacent to one another resulted in display that was identical in appearance.) In the *gap* condition, a space of approximately 1 cm was left between two slightly smaller display parts (approximately 7.5 cm wide), resulting in a display of the same 16-cm width, but with a visible separation between the two parts.

In these object-directed reaching studies, the experimenter held the display block(s) with two hands, tapped the display part(s) against the table surface, and allowed the infant to view it for several seconds. If the display consisted of a single object, this presentation provided common motion information. When the display consisted of two separate pieces (either the *adjacent* or *gap* conditions), the two pieces were moved separately from one another, providing separate motion information as well as a clear spatial separation between the two parts. Once the infant had viewed the display for several seconds, the experimenter would place the display (either one piece or the two parts) onto a marked position on a display board, which was immediately slid across the table to where the infant could reach out and grasp the display.

When the two display parts were of the same color, shape, and texture, and when experimenters showed the two display parts undergoing common motion, 8- and 9-month-olds tended to aim their one-handed reaches for the middle of the display. When experimenters showed a two-part display undergoing separate motion and/or when there was a visible gap left between the two display parts, these infants aimed their reaches away from the center of the display, closer to the display ends. These one-handed reaches directed away from the display center were perhaps aimed for the centers of one of the two display parts. Regardless, the infants' pattern of reaching provides a clear indication of how they perceived the display. For a one-object display, one-handed reaches are directed near the middle of the object. For a two-object display, those reaches are significantly shifted away from the middle. Based on this, we can explore what information is necessary to generate a perception of object connectedness and separation.[1]

Whereas the 8- and 9-month-olds in the Vishton et al. (2005) study seemed to make use of visible separation or separate motion information to perceive an object boundary, when the same study was conducted with 6- and 7-month-olds, a different pattern emerged. With the *connected* display, reaches were again directed near the middle. If a visible *gap* was left between the two parts of the display, reaches away from the center were frequent. These two results were similar to what was found with 8- and 9-month-olds. In the *split* condition, however, when the two display parts were moved separately and then placed adjacent to one another, the 6- and 7-month-olds reached for the center of the display in approximately the same way they did with the *connected* display. It was as if, in the 5 s

[1] It is worth noting that this result applies with these particular display dimensions and participant ages. In a separate study, which made use of larger displays and older children, a different pattern of reaching emerged (Needham, 1999b). In that study, after handling a 24 × 3 × 3 cm single-object display, 9.5- and 12.5-month-old participants tended to use one hand as in the Vishton et al. (2005) study. However, if the participants instead handled two separate 12 × 3 × 3 cm display parts, then when the experimenters later placed them adjacent to one another, 12.5-month-olds commonly made two-handed reaches, making contact near the ends of the display, away from the center. No such shift between one- and two-handed reaching was found in the Vishton et al. study.

between the separate motion presentation and the onset of the reach, the 6- and 7-month-olds forgot that there were two separate parts and treated the display as a single, connected object.

Vishton et al. (2005) also conducted a looking time, VOE study with these displays using the move-apart versus move-together method. When infants were shown separate motion, they looked longer at the move-together event than at the move-apart event. How many objects did infants perceive to be present in the *split* motion condition? When the experimenters asked the infants using reaching, the answer was one object; when they asked the infants using looking-time behaviors, the answer was two.

Thus far, the Vishton et al. (2005) results are similar to other findings suggesting more advanced performance in looking than in reaching studies. For looking purposes, it seems that 6- and 7-month-olds remember the composition of a display longer than they can for reaching purposes. An additional experiment with 6- and 7-month-olds suggests something different, however. Vishton et al. conducted a version of their reaching experiment using a display constructed from two blocks that differed in color and shape—a blue rectilinear block and a red cylinder. The 6- and 7-month-olds consistently reached away from the center of the displays, regardless of what spatiotemporal information was presented. Even if common motion information presented by the experimenter indicated that the display consisted of a single, connected object, the infants still reached away from the center.

No looking time study was conducted with these stimuli with the shape and color differences, but the predictions from the looking time, VOE literature seem clear. When common motion, spatiotemporal information indicates that two display parts are connected, even if there is a difference in color and shape, we would expect that infants would perceive a single, connected object. Infants would be expected to look longer at a split display, as in the center-occluded object studies. Infants would also be expected to look longer at the move-apart event. Nonetheless, their reaching indicates a perception of two separate display parts.

In VOE studies, many factors influence infants' perception of object boundaries. Across several studies, motion and spatiotemporal information seemed to be the most powerful influences. If two display parts move together, infants tend to perceive them as connected. Infants seem to perceive the two display parts as not connected if the following conditions hold: (1) the two display parts move separately, (2) one part is presented in isolation, (3) a visible gap is present between two parts, or (4) a thin board is inserted between them.

In the Vishton et al. (2005) reaching study, infants were sensitive to motion information, but shape and color exerted a stronger influence. This pattern of results is difficult to interpret without suggesting a different process of object boundary perception for infants engaged in looking versus reaching tasks. The result is consistent with the adult studies of Vishton et al. (2007) that suggest engaging in a reaching behavior changes the nature of human perception, rendering certain sources of information (i.e., shape and/or color) more salient, whereas rendering other sources (i.e., motion) less salient.

Kaufman, Mareschal, and Johnson (2003) presented a similar argument, based on a review of looking time, VOE studies. The center-occluded object studies suggested that motion information was the primary and perhaps only source of information that influenced infant object boundary perception. No effects of shape or color similarity have been identified in that line of research. For instance, when the top and bottom portions of the center-occluded object greatly differed in shape and color, common motion information still inspired longer looking in the split object test trials.

In the studies of the move-apart versus move-together events, however, several results have suggested that shape and color differences do influence infant object boundary perception. Kaufman et al. (2003) argued that this may be due to different sizes of stimuli typically used in these two lines of research. The objects used in the move-apart versus move-together studies reviewed here were quite large (approximately 30 × 10 × 10 cm), whereas the rod parts of the center-occluded rod displays were only about 1.3 cm in diameter. The large objects were ungraspable by young infants, whereas the small rod would have been graspable. Perhaps for stimuli that afford a grasping action, a different set of brain systems became more active. This difference could then have resulted in selective encoding or weighting of different sources of display information as different segments of the visual cortex were used (e.g., Milner & Goodale, 2006).

The Vishton et al. (2005) stimuli were all graspable. In some procedures, grasping was encouraged. In the looking time studies, the objects were presented slightly beyond the infants' reach. Perhaps these differences resulted in a shift in the pattern of neural activation such as that proposed by Kaufman et al. (2003). Vishton et al. did not vary color and shape separately, but it would be reasonable to expect that information sources that are more important for grasping (i.e., shape) would exert a greater effect than those that do not (i.e., color).

5.2 Comparing Different Aspects of the Same Action

Studies of infant reaching have produced results that are not easy to predict based on existing studies of infant looking. Up to this point, I have contrasted experiments that involve only looking or reaching. Some of the most compelling evidence that different actions inspire different information processing comes, however, from examining different aspects of the same action. When an infant engages in a particular action, one aspect of the action suggests one pattern of perception and cognition, whereas another aspect of the same action suggests a different pattern of perception and cognition. This is true in some cases with the same display and the same infant at nearly the same moment in time.

Berthier et al. (2001) presented a set of experiments exploring how 9-month-olds visually track and catch a ball as it rolls past them. To succeed at this task, infants cannot reach for the current location of the target object, but must be "prospective" or "future-oriented" in their action control. They must reach ahead of the object, along its path of future motion, so that the hand and the object arrive at some place at the same moment in time. If the path of a rolling ball is unobstructed and fully visible, even 4-month-olds are capable of succeeding at this task (von Hofsten, 1983).

Berthier et al. (2001) placed an occluder panel between the infants and the path of the ball. This occluder blocked the infant's view of approximately 13 cm of the ball's horizontal motion as it approached. Infants were still effective at catching the ball in this situation. For some conditions of the experiment, the infant watched as an experimenter placed a barrier along the path that the ball would travel. The barrier was placed behind the occluder and was tall enough that it could still be seen protruding above it. When the barrier was in place, it would always stop the ball; the ball would disappear behind the occluder and not reemerge on the other side. Although the frequency of infant reaches during these barrier trials declined substantially, infants still made frequent reaches in the barrier condition (44% of trials). Moreover, the timing and general kinematics of these reaches were virtually identical to those observed when the barrier was not present.

Taken together, these two distinct measures suggest the presence of different systems of knowledge guiding two different aspects of the same object-directed reaching behavior. The infants' choice of whether to reach was influenced by the presence of the barrier, but when the infant did choose to reach, another system was engaged. This action implementation system considered the location and velocity of the ball, but not the presence of obstacles along the path of the motion. This implementation system does not seem to know about principles of solidity and cohesion.

A similar distinction in action choice and action implementation has been identified in 2-year-old children by DeLoache, Rosengren, and Uttal (2004), who were the first to characterize "scale errors." After encouraging children to play with full-size versions of several toys for 15 min (e.g., a sliding board, chair, and child-sized car), these experimenters took participants for a short walk outside of the play area. While they were out of the room, other experimenters removed the full-sized toys and replaced them with miniature replicas. In the subsequent play session with the miniature toys, about half of the children produced at least one behavior in which they attempted to use the miniatures in the same way that they had used the full-sized toys. For instance, a child might try to climb into the tiny car or slide down the tiny sliding board. These actions were always unsuccessful, as the objects were far too small to support the chosen behaviors.

When watching the children perform these scale error behaviors, however, it is clear that they mentally register the actual size of the targets. When they pick up the tiny car, they do not reach for it with two hands, spread far apart as they would have with the full-size car. Instead, they make a well-coordinated, one-handed reach with the fingers scaled to the approximate size of the toy. In terms of the choice of what actions to perform, children seem to sometimes ignore the sizes of objects. The implementation of these chosen actions, however, seems to engage a different system of knowledge that clearly does consider object size.

An analogous pattern has occasionally been suggested in the A-not-B domain as well. Some infants have been reported to reach to an incorrect location while simultaneously looking at the correct location. This has not been carefully documented, but such a result would parallel the pattern observed in the Berthier et al. (2001) and DeLoache, Uttal, and Rosengren (2004) studies. Different systems of knowledge may operate at different times (e.g., Vishton et al., 2007), but in at least some instances, they seem to be activated simultaneously and operate in parallel within the same infant brain.

6. DIFFERENCES BETWEEN ACTIONS OTHER THAN LOOKING AND REACHING

Comparisons of infant looking and reaching behaviors suggest the presence of different systems of knowledge, but these are not the only pairs of behaviors that have shown this pattern. Between 4 and 7 months of age, infants typically learn to sit independently and thereafter learn about their environment from this posture. Between 6 and 10 months of age, infants typically learn to shift onto their bellies and crawl. When they do so, it seems that they forget some of the things they had clearly learned while in that sitting position. When they return to a sitting posture, however, the knowledge returns. When they stand up and walk several months later, they again seem to need to relearn for this new behavior (Adolph & Joh, 2009). There is a surprising lack of generalization of knowledge across these different postures and actions.

This line of thought is closely associated with Karen Adolph and her collaborators, who have studied how infant motor development affects their action choices. In one study, 9-month-olds were seated on the edge of a support surface, with an attractive target suspended some distance in front of them. If the target was close, the infants would lean forward, reach out, and grasp it. When the target was located too far away, engaging in a sufficient forward lean and reach would cause the infant to fall forward, off of the support surface (Adolph, 2000). (Experimenters would gently catch the infant to prevent injury in this case.)

After presenting a series of trials to identify the maximum distance at which the infant could successfully retrieve an object, the experimenter would present a randomized series of test trials with the object located at a safe distance, near the maximum distance limit, and beyond the limit. These 9-month-olds had an average of 104 days of sitting experience prior to the study. They responded to these test trials very appropriately. When the object was close enough, a reaching action was very likely. When the object was too far, infants only rarely attempted a reach (Adolph, 2000).

These same infants also participated in the same set of tasks while in a crawling posture at the edge of the same table. The experimenters again determined the distance limit for the child to reach away from the support surface and obtain the object without falling. Test trials were then administered around this limit. These same infants who had been so accurate in the seated version of the task were surprisingly bad at the task when performing it from the crawling posture. They often fell off of the table and showed very little improvement over the course of the study. The infants were all relatively inexperienced with crawling (average of 45 days). Even though the apparatus and task were essentially the same, when a different task posture was adopted, the infants seemed to have lost the ability to recognize a situation that would produce a fall (Adolph, 2000).

This pattern has emerged from studies of other pairs of motor behaviors. Kretch and Adolph (2013) constructed an apparatus with an adjustable height "cliff." When the cliff was low, it was easy for crawling or walking infants to move from the upper to lower platforms. When the cliff was adjusted to be higher, the infants could not descend without falling. (Again, the infants were gently caught to prevent injury whenever they tried to descend.) Novice crawlers were very error prone, producing many falls. Experienced crawlers learned to perceive when the step could be safely descended and when it should be avoided. When the infants started to walk, however, this learning process had to be repeated, seemingly from scratch. As with the reaching study, simply changing the posture of the infant seems to change their knowledge about affordances in their surroundings.

Adolph (1995) found the same pattern of results with an adjustable sloped walkway. If you ask an infant whether a slope is too steep to safely traverse, his/her answer depends on his/her current postural state. An experienced crawler who is a novice at walking will safely avoid falling down a steep slope when crawling. When that same infant stands up, however, he/she will fall down a slope that is too steep to even have been traversed while crawling. All of this work builds on extensive studies of infants crawling on a fixed-height visual cliff that was covered with a sturdy piece of transparent glass to prevent falls (e.g., Bertenthal, Campos, & Kermoian, 1994; Gibson & Walk, 1960).

Adolph and Joh (2009) describe these findings in terms of "learning sets" (after Harlow, 1949). According to this theory, infants fail to generalize from crawling to walking tasks because the physical constraints that govern the two tasks are very different. Both crawling and walking are means of locomotion achieved by exertion of the body, but there are few other similarities. The balance demands are different when on four versus two limbs. The resting and starting positions of the limbs are different. The muscle groups and the ways in which those muscle groups are activated to create movement are very different. And, of course, the structure of affordances is different. How big does a gap need to be to afford passing through it? What is the maximum height of a vertical step before it cannot be traversed? How many toys can be carried without hindering successful forward movement? Given all of these differences, it seems quite sensible that different, largely independent learning processes would take place for the two different types of actions. Those independent learning processes may result in two distinct sets of knowledge that are accessed whenever the child prepares to perform a particular action.

7. PREDICTIONS AND CONCLUSIONS

A great deal of research has been directed at characterizing what infants know and do not know at different points in their development. If our exploration of this topic focuses on only one behavior, such as looking, then the results of that research might be summarized as an ordered list, specifying the ages at which infants first develop an understanding of various principles that govern the world around them. When studies of other behaviors, such as reaching, are considered, however, the results become more complex. In many cases, such as those summarized here, the study of particular action behaviors seems to suggest that different systems of knowledge mediate various behaviors. Looking is only one of many behaviors.

To be sure, some studies have found close agreement between reaching and looking measures. Many other studies have simply found that reaching behaviors lag behind looking in their apparent development, perhaps because reaching is more difficult to perform, and thus more likely to distract study participants. A growing number of studies, however, do not fit well into either of these categories. Reaching performance is not worse than looking performance, but it instead seems to function according to different knowledge and inherent information processing.

When considered in the context of studies of adult perception, cognition, and action, the presence of action-specific perceptual and cognitive processes is not surprising. Different human behaviors are mediated by an enormously complex set of neural subsystems. Many of these subsystems are specifically associated with the performance of particular action behaviors. If knowledge is a property that emerges from brain activity, and if different parts of the brain are associated with different tasks, it would be surprising if there were *no* different knowledge systems associated with different behaviors.

If different action systems are mediated by distinct systems of knowledge in infancy, how should developmental science account for it? First, it seems clear that our theories should consider not just what infants seem to know or what principles form the foundations of infant cognition and perception. Rather the theories should account for infant knowledge and foundations on an action-by-action basis. Some principles might be found to govern all behaviors, but that is an inherently empirical question.

It is typically not difficult to develop a reaching-based study to assess any question that might be addressed using looking, VOE measures. The only clear exception is for the study of development prior to 4 months of age, when infants are typically not able to control successful object-directed reaching behaviors. If the results of the reaching experiment match those of a looking-time study, then a powerful piece of convergent evidence is obtained. If the results of the reaching experiment differ from those of the looking study, there is no cause for alarm. Indeed, it is the comparisons of reaching and looking performance in cases where the results diverge that are potentially the most interesting.

Some of the most exciting action-based research has suggested ways in which action development may influence the knowledge that guides looking performance. For instance, Sommerville, Woodward, and Needham (2005) habituated 3-month-olds to a display consisting of two objects, placed on two different platforms (e.g., a toy bear and a ball). Infants watched a hand reach in from the side of the display and grasp one of the objects (e.g., the ball). Once infants were familiar with this repeated event, test trials were conducted in which the positions of the objects were switched from one platform to the other. On alternate test trials, infants saw the hand either reach for the same location (i.e., a different object) or the same object (i.e., in a different location).

Woodward (1998) had previously found that 6-month-olds, but not 5-month-olds, look longer at the test trials in which the hand grasps a different object. She interpreted this result as suggesting that infants in this age range are developing intuitions about other humans having preferences and intentions. Even if the hand changes its path of motion, moving to a different end location in the display, this does not generate as much of a VOE as a human changing his/her intention. At no point in that earlier research was there a hint that 3-month-olds should produce this pattern of results.

Sommerville et al. (2005) tested whether accelerating infants' reaching experience would lead to enhanced performance in the hand intention task. This work was based on earlier work in which prereaching 3-month-olds were given experience with Velcro "sticky mittens" (Needham, Barrett, & Peterman, 2002). One part of the Velcro was sewn onto the mittens, whereas the corresponding side was attached to toys. When infants played with these, they were able to make contact with the toys and cause them to adhere to the mittens. As such, they were able to lift and manipulate the object several weeks before they would typically have been able to. Half of the 3-month-olds in the Sommerville et al. (2005) study were given experience with the sticky mittens, whereas the others were not. Even after only 200 s of sticky mitten experience, 3-month-olds performed like 6-month-olds on the hand intention task. The 3-month-olds who did not have the sticky mitten experience exhibited a significantly less adult-like interpretation of the displays.

Action may not only be driven by different systems of knowledge but also may create them. Indeed, the development of knowledge itself may be driven by the development of action abilities (e.g., Gibson, 1969). Most researchers think of the brains of young infants as being less capable than those of older infants. Studies of infant perception and cognition certainly support this assertion. While this may be true to some extent, it may alternatively be the smaller action repertoire of young infants that drives these findings. I have argued that an understanding of infant knowledge development can only be achieved by considering how the knowledge changes in the context of different actions. Based on results such as these, it seems increasingly likely that an understanding of infant action development may provide the most direct path to understanding infant knowledge itself.

This chapter has argued for the presence of distinct, action-specific systems of knowledge in infancy. As research in this area progresses, however, it may be that the term infant "knowledge" should be abandoned, or at least defined more carefully. The term knowledge implies a set of facts, skills, and/or principles that are possessed by someone. Knowledge, as we usually conceive of it, is inherently task- and context-general. The idea that someone could "know" something at one moment in time, then not know it a few seconds later, and then know it again a few seconds after that violates the typical definition of the term.

For early research in this area, based largely on a single behavioral measure, the term was sensible. Indeed, as long as a single, coherent set of principles could be used to predict infant behaviors at different ages, those principles could be appropriately described as infant knowledge. As an increasing body of findings suggests the presence of context- and action-specific principles of perception and cognition, however, the use of the term has become increasingly problematic.

Rather than asking what infants know and when they know it, a more precise theoretical language seems appropriate. Developmental experiments can characterize the information processing of infants in a particular context, detailing what information is picked up and how that information influences infants' behaviors. The computations and inferences that take place between the perception and action control can be characterized. Additional studies can test and refine those characterizations. As infants develop, the changes in these perception and action processes can be described. Certainly infants know things, but that knowledge seems to be an outcome rather than a starting point for infant behavior. Knowledge seems not to be a static representation in the head, but rather the outcome of an emergent process that brings together many aspects of perceptual, cognitive, and motor functioning.

ACKNOWLEDGMENTS

The author thanks Jennifer Stevens, Natalie Brito, Kaitlyn Brunick, and Evan Jones for their valuable contributions to this work. The author also thanks Jodie Plumert for tremendous help in refining the presentation of this material. Address correspondence to Peter M. Vishton, Department of Psychological Sciences, College of William & Mary, Box 8795, Williamsburg, VA 23187-8795, USA. Vishton may be contacted electronically at vishton@wm.edu or http://wmpeople.wm.edu/site/page/pmvish/petermvishton.

REFERENCES

Adolph, K. E. (1995). Psychophysical assessment of toddlers' ability to cope with slopes. *Journal of Experimental Psychology: Human Perception and Performance, 21*, 734.

Adolph, K. E. (2000). Specificity of learning: Why infants fall over a veritable cliff. *Psychological Science, 11*, 290–295.

Adolph, K. E., Bertenthal, B. I., Boker, S. M., Goldfield, E. C., & Gibson, E. J. (1997). Learning in the development of infant locomotion. *Monographs of the Society for Research in Child Development, 62*.

Adolph, K. E., & Joh, A. S. (2009). Multiple learning mechanisms in the development of action. In A. Woodward, & A. Needham (Eds.), *Learning and the infant mind* (pp. 172–207). New York: Oxford University Press.

Aglioti, S., DeSouza, J. F. X., & Goodale, M. A. (1995). Size-contrast illusions deceive the eye but not the hand. *Current Biology, 5*, 679–685.

Arterberry, M. E., Bensen, A. S., & Yonas, A. (1991). Infants' responsiveness to static-monocular depth information: A recovery from habituation approach. *Infant Behavior and Development, 14*, 241–251.

Baillargeon, R. (1987). Object permanence in 3½-and 4½-month-old infants. *Developmental Psychology, 23*, 655.

Baillargeon, R., & Graber, M. (1988). Evidence of location memory in 8-month-old infants in a nonsearch AB task. *Developmental Psychology, 24*, 502.

Baillargeon, R., Li, J., Gertner, Y., & Wu, D. (2010). How do infants reason about physical events?. In *The Wiley-Blackwell handbook of childhood cognitive development* (2nd ed., pp. 11–48).

Bertenthal, B. I., Campos, J. J., & Kermoian, R. (1994). An epigenetic perspective on the development of self-produced locomotion and its consequences. *Current Directions in Psychological Science, 3*, 140–145.

Berthier, N. E., Bertenthal, B. I., Seaks, J. D., Sylvia, M. R., Johnson, R. L., & Clifton, R. K. (2001). Using object knowledge in visual tracking and reaching. *Infancy, 2*, 257–284.

Bertin, E., & Bhatt, R. S. (2006). Three-month-olds' sensitivity to orientation cues in the three-dimensional depth plane. *Journal of Experimental Child Psychology, 93*, 45–62.

Bhatt, R. S., & Bertin, E. (2001). Pictorial cues and three-dimensional information processing in early infancy. *Journal of Experimental Child Psychology, 80*, 315–332.
Brenner, E., & Smeets, J. B. J. (1996). Size illusion influences how we lift but not how we grasp an object. *Experimental Brain Research, 111*, 473–476.
Clifton, R. K., Rochat, P., Litovsky, R. Y., & Perris, E. E. (1991). Object representation guides infants' reaching in the dark. *Journal of Experimental Psychology: Human Perception and Performance, 17*, 323.
Cuevas, K., & Bell, M. A. (2010). Developmental progression of looking and reaching performance on the A-not-B task. *Developmental Psychology, 46*, 1363.
Cutting, J. E., & Vishton, P. M. (1995). Perceiving layout and knowing distances: The integration, relative potency, and contextual use of different information about depth. In *Perception of space and motion* (pp. 69–117).
DeLoache, J. S., Uttal, D. H., & Rosengren, K. S. (2004). Scale errors offer evidence for a perception-action dissociation early in life. *Science, 304*(5673), 1027–1029.
Eimas, P. D., Siqueland, E. R., Jusczyk, P., & Vigorito, J. (1971). Speech perception in infants. *Science, 171*, 303–306.
Fantz, R. L. (1964). Visual experience in infants: Decreased attention to familiar patterns relative to novel ones. *Science, 146*, 668–670.
Feigenson, L., & Carey, S. (2003). Tracking individuals via object-files: evidence from infants' manual search. *Developmental Science, 6*, 568–584.
Gauthier, I., Skudlarski, P., Gore, J. C., & Anderson, A. W. (2000). Expertise for cars and birds recruits brain areas involved in face recognition. *Nature Neuroscience, 3*, 191.
Gibson, E. J. (1969). *Principles of perceptual learning and development.* New York: Appleton-Century Crofts.
Gibson, E. J., & Walk, R. D. (1960). The"visual cliff". *Scientific American, 202*, 64–71.
Goodale, M. A., Meenan, J. P., Bülthoff, H. H., Nicolle, D. A., Murphy, K. J., & Racicot, C. I. (1994). Separate neural pathways for the visual analysis of object shape in perception and prehension. *Current Biology, 4*, 604–610.
Harlow, H. F. (1949). The formation of learning sets. *Psychological Review, 56*, 51.
Hespos, S. J., & Baillargeon, R. (2001). Infants' knowledge about occlusion and containment events: A surprising discrepancy. *Psychological Science, 12*, 141–147.
Hespos, S. J., & Baillargeon, R. (2006). Decalage in infants' knowledge about occlusion and containment events: Converging evidence from action tasks. *Cognition, 99*, B31–B41.
Hespos, S. J., & Baillargeon, R. (2008). Young infants' actions reveal their developing knowledge of support variables: Converging evidence for violation-of-expectation findings. *Cognition, 107*, 304–316.
Hofstadter, M., & Reznick, J. S. (1996). Response modality affects Human infant delayed-response performance. *Child Development, 67*, 646–658.
Jeannerod, M. (1988). *The neural and behavioural organization of goal-directed movements.* Clarendon Press/Oxford University Press.
Johnson, S. P., & Aslin, R. N. (1995). Perception of object unity in 2-month-old infants. *Developmental Psychology, 31*, 739.
Johnson, S. P., & Aslin, R. N. (1996). Perception of object unity in young infants: The roles of motion, depth, and orientation. *Cognitive Development, 11*, 161–180.
Jonsson, B., & Von Hofsten, C. (2003). Infants' ability to track and reach for temporarily occluded objects. *Developmental Science, 6*, 86–99.
Karmiloff-Smith, A. (1995). *Beyond modularity: A developmental perspective on cognitive science.* MIT press.
Kaufman, J., Mareschal, D., & Johnson, M. H. (2003). Graspability and object processing in infants. *Infant Behavior and Development, 26*, 516–528.
Keen, R. (2003). Representation of objects and events: Why do infants look so smart and toddlers look so dumb? *Current Directions in Psychological Science, 12*, 79–83.

Kellman, P. J., & Arterberry, M. E. (2006). Infant visual perception. In D. Kuhn, R. S. Siegler, W. Damon, & R. M. Lerner (Eds.) (6th ed.,*Cognition, perception, and language: Vol. 2. Handbook of child psychology* (pp. 109–160). Hoboken, NJ: Wiley.
Kellman, P. J., & Spelke, E. S. (1983). Perception of partly occluded objects in infancy. *Cognitive psychology, 15*, 483–524.
Konczak, J., & Dichgans, J. (1997). The development toward stereotypic arm kinematics during reaching in the first 3 years of life. *Experimental Brain Research, 117*, 346–354.
Kretch, K. S., & Adolph, K. E. (2013). Cliff or step? Posture-specific learning at the edge of a drop-off. *Child Development, 84*, 226–240.
Leader, L. R., Baillie, P., Martin, B., & Vermeulen, E. (1982). The assessment and significance of habituation to a repeated stimulus by the human fetus. *Early Human Development, 7*, 211–219.
Lockman, J. J., Ashmead, D. H., & Bushnell, E. W. (1984). The development of anticipatory hand orientation during infancy. *Journal of Experimental Child Psychology, 37*, 176–186.
Mandler, J. M., Fivush, R., & Reznick, J. S. (1987). The development of contextual categories. *Cognitive Development, 2*, 339–354.
Marteniuk, R. G., Leavitt, J. L., MacKenzie, C. L., & Athenes, S. (1990). Functional relationships between grasp and transport components in a prehension task. *Human Movement Science, 9*, 149–176.
Milner, D., & Goodale, M. (2006). *The visual brain in action*. Oxford University Press.
Munakata, Y. (2001). Graded representations in behavioral dissociations. *Trends in Cognitive Sciences, 5*, 309–315.
Needham, A. (1999a). The role of shape in 4-month-old infants' object segregation. *Infant Behavior and Development, 22*, 161–178.
Needham, A. (1999b). How infants grasp two adjacent objects: Effects of perceived display composition on infants' actions. *Developmental Science, 2*, 219–233.
Needham, A., & Baillargeon, R. (1993). Intuitions about support in 4.5-month-old infants. *Cognition, 47*, 121–148.
Needham, A., & Baillargeon, R. (1997). Object segregation in 8-month-old infants. *Cognition, 62*, 121–149.
Needham, A., & Baillargeon, R. (1998). Effects of prior experience on 4.5-month old infants' object segregation. *Infant Behavior and Development, 21*, 1–24.
Needham, A., Barrett, T., & Peterman, K. (2002). A pick-me-up for infants' exploratory skills: Early simulated experiences reaching for objects using 'sticky mittens' enhances young infants' object exploration skills. *Infant Behavior and Development, 25*, 279–295.
Paulignan, Y., MacKenzie, C., Marteniuk, R., & Jeannerod, M. (1997). Influence of object position and size on human prehension movements. *Experimental Brain Research, 114*, 226–234.
Piaget, J. (1954). *The construction of reality in the child*. New York: Basic.
Ramachandran, V. S., & Blakeslee, S. (1998). *Phantoms in the brain. Probing the mystery of the human mind*. New York: W. Morrow & Co.
Shallice, T. (1988). *From neuropsychology to mental structure*. Cambridge University Press.
Shuwairi, S. M. (2009). Preference for impossible figures in 4-month-olds. *Journal of Experimental Child Psychology, 104*, 115–123.
Siddiqui, A. (1995). Object size as a determinant of grasping in infancy. *The Journal of Genetic Psychology, 156*, 345–358.
Smith, W. C., Johnson, S. P., & Spelke, E. S. (2003). Motion and edge sensitivity in perception of object unity. *Cognitive Psychology, 46*, 31–64.
Sommerville, J. A., Woodward, A. L., & Needham, A. (2005). Action experience alters 3-month-old infants' perception of others' actions. *Cognition, 96*, B1–B11.
Spelke, E. S., & Kinzler, K. D. (2007). Core knowledge. *Developmental Science, 10*, 89–96.

Van de Walle, G. A., Carey, S., & Prevor, M. (2000). Bases for object individuation in infancy: Evidence from manual search. *Journal of Cognition and Development, 1*, 249–280.

Vishton, P. M. (2005). Using kitchen appliance analogies to improve students' reasoning about neurological results. *Teaching of Psychology, 32*, 106–109.

Vishton, P. M., Stephens, N. J., Nelson, L. A., Morra, S. E., Brunick, K. L., & Stevens, J. A. (2007). Planning to reach for an object changes how the reacher perceives it. *Psychological Science, 18*, 713–719.

Vishton, P. M., Ware, E. A., & Badger, A. N. (2005). Different Gestalt processing for different actions? Comparing object-directed reaching and looking time measures. *Journal of Experimental Child Psychology, 90*, 89–113.

von Hofsten, C. (1982). Eye-hand coordination in newborns. *Developmental Psychology, 15*, 450–461.

von Hofsten, C. (1983). Catching skills in infancy. *Journal of Experimental Psychology: Human Perception and Performance, 9*, 75.

von Hofsten, C. (1991). Structuring of early reaching movements: A longitudinal study. *Journal of Motor Behavior, 23*, 280–292.

von Hofsten, C., & Rönnqvist, L. (1988). Preparation for grasping an object: A developmental study. *Journal of Experimental Psychology: Human Perception and Performance, 14*, 610.

von Hofsten, C., & Spelke, E. S. (1985). Object perception and object-directed reaching in infancy. *Journal of Experimental Psychology: General, 114*, 198.

Wilcox, T., & Biondi, M. (2015). Object processing in the infant: Lessons from neuroscience. *Trends in Cognitive Sciences, 19*, 406–413.

Witt, J. K., Proffitt, D. R., & Epstein, W. (2005). Tool use affects perceived distance but only when you intend to use it. *Journal of Experimental Psychology: Human Perception and Performance, 31*, 880–888.

Woodward, A. L. (1998). Infants selectively encode the goal object of an actor's reach. *Cognition, 69*, 1–34.

Xu, F., & Carey, S. (1996). Infants' metaphysics: The case of numerical identity. *Cognitive Psychology, 30*, 111–153.

FURTHER READING

Brownell, C. A., Zerwas, S., & Ramani, G. B. (2007). "So Big": The development of body self-awareness in toddlers. *Child Development, 78*, 1426–1440.

Clearfield, M. W., Diedrich, F. J., Smith, L. B., & Thelen, E. (2006). Young infants reach correctly in A-not-B tasks: On the development of stability and perseveration. *Infant Behavior and Development, 29*, 435–444.

Craton, L. G. (1996). The development of perceptual completion abilities: Infants' perception of stationary, partially occluded objects. *Child Development, 67*, 890–904.

DeLoache, J. S., LoBue, V., Vanderborght, M., & Chiong, C. (2013). On the validity and robustness of the scale error phenomenon in early childhood. *Infant Behavior and Development, 36*, 63–70.

Hespos, S., Gredebäck, G., Von Hofsten, C., & Spelke, E. S. (2009). Occlusion is hard: Comparing predictive reaching for visible and hidden objects in infants and adults. *Cognitive Science, 33*, 1483–1502.

Kavšek, M., Yonas, A., & Granrud, C. E. (2012). Infants' sensitivity to pictorial depth cues: A review and meta-analysis of looking studies. *Infant Behavior and Development, 35*, 109–128.

Lee, J. H., & van Donkelaar, P. (2002). Dorsal and ventral visual stream contributions to perception-action interactions during pointing. *Experimental Brain Research, 143*, 440–446.

Spelke, E. S., Kestenbaum, R., Simons, D. J., & Wein, D. (1995). Spatiotemporal continuity, smoothness of motion and object identity in infancy. *British Journal of Developmental Psychology, 13*, 113–142.

Vishton, P. M., Rea, J. G., Cutting, J. E., & Nuñez, L. (1999). Comparing effects of the horizontal-vertical illusion on grip scaling and judgment: Relative vs. absolute, not perception vs. action. *Journal of Experimental Psychology: Human Perception and Performance, 25*, 1659–1672.

von Hofsten, C., & Fazel-Zandy, S. (1984). Development of visually guided hand orientation in reaching. *Journal of Experimental Child Psychology, 38*, 208–219.

Wraga, M., Creem, S. H., & Proffitt, D. R. (2000). Perception-action dissociations of a walkable Müller-Lyer configuration. *Psychological Science, 11*, 239–243.

CHAPTER FIVE

Action Errors: A Window Into the Early Development of Perception–Action System

Matthew J. Jiang and Karl S. Rosengren[1]
Department of Psychology, University of Wisconsin, Madison, WI, United States
[1]Corresponding author: E-mail: krosengren@wisc.edu

Contents

Abstract

In this chapter, we explore an interesting class of behaviors, referred to as action errors, which, we argue, provide a window in to the early development of the perception–action system. As we examine these behaviors, we discuss how acquisition of motor and cognitive skills interact at particular periods of development to make children more likely to perform action errors. However, we also provide evidence that even adults perform action errors under certain task demands. We argue that it is fruitful to examine the developing perception–action system in terms

Advances in Child Development and Behavior, Volume 55
ISSN 0065-2407
https://doi.org/10.1016/bs.acdb.2018.04.002

of the dynamic interplay of constraints within the environment, the individual child, and the task that they are attempting to complete. This interaction of constraints is dynamic and multiply determined, which is why action errors do not occur whenever a child sees a photograph of an object, views a tiny chair, or interacts with grandparents over interactive media. We argue, however, that not all constraints are weighted equally in the emergence of a specific behavior. Rather, the child's goal or intention plays a key role in organizing factors that lead to a specific behavior.

1. INTRODUCTION

Young children exhibit incredible variability in behavior over the first few years of life, as they explore the complex dynamics between their growing and changing bodies and the environment. As children acquire greater control of their developing bodies, they gain sufficient control over their muscles to coordinate limbs and joints in purposeful actions, enabling them to successfully initiate and complete a desired course of action. However, successful completion of any action also involves accurately perceiving what the environment affords for action. While some of these affordances may be derived from adaptation to environmental pressures over the course of human evolution, others may need to be learned in an increasingly designed and technologically complex environment. In this manner the developing perception—action system is also influenced by gains in cognitive skills related to executive function, conceptualization, and learning more generally. While much of the gains in the perception—action system may lead to an overall decrease in variability in behavior as children develop and acquire preferences for particular forms of action (e.g., crawling, walking, running), variability in behavior is common as children acquire new skills. Children often exhibit a wider range of behaviors than adults as they come to learn what the environment affords for their actions, and some of these behaviors are quite interesting to explore from a researcher's perspective.

In this chapter, we explore an interesting class of behaviors, referred to as action errors, which, we argue, provide a window into the early development of the perception—action system. As we examine these behaviors, we discuss how acquisition of motor and cognitive skills interacts to lead children at particular periods of development to be more likely to perform action errors than children at other periods of development and adults. However, we will also provide evidence that even adults perform action errors under certain task demands.

We begin this chapter by defining what we mean by the term action error and distinguish these types of errors from other motor errors. We then provide evidence for different types of action errors—grasp, scale, and media errors—and then describe, based on current evidence, the likely developmental time course of these behaviors. We then turn to explain how a study of action errors may illuminate interesting aspects of the development of the perception–action system. In this explanation, we outline how action errors emerge from a dynamic interaction of constraints within the environment, the developing child, and the tasks that they are attempting to accomplish. We also highlight that to understand the development of the perception–action system, it is important to consider cognitive development and symbolic understanding.

2. WHAT ARE ACTION ERRORS?

We define action errors as a class of behaviors that involve attempts to perform a desired action, but the behaviors cannot be successfully carried out because aspects of the environment do not afford the desired action. A prototypical example of an action error is when a young child attempts to sit unsuccessfully in a tiny doll-sized chair that is way too small to accommodate his or her body. DeLoache, Uttal, and Rosengren (2004) labeled these behaviors, "scale errors," as it appears that when children perform these actions they do not take in to account the scale of the object with respect to the size of their bodies. Two other forms of action errors have been proposed by Rosengren and French (2011), Rosengren et al. (2018): grasp errors and media errors. Grasp errors are defined as actions where an individual attempts to pick up or grasp at an object that is depicted on a two-dimensional surface, such as a photograph, or an electronic screen. An example of this behavior is when a young child attempts to pick up a toy that is shown in a photograph (DeLoache, Pierroutsakos, Uttal, Rosengren, & Gottleib, 1998). Media errors occur when an individual attempts an action with some form of technology that cannot be completed because the action is attempted through the media. An example of this behavior occurs when a child tries to pass or receive something from an individual interacting with the child using interactive technology. In the sections that follow, we first justify the use of the label "error" with respect to these behaviors, contrast these behaviors with other types of errors, and then provide an outline of what we know about these behaviors with respect to their developmental time course.

2.1 Why Call These Behaviors "Errors"?

Is it appropriate to label children's unsuccessful actions as "errors?" The term "error" often conjures up the idea of a mistake or a blunder. Our use of "error" is deliberate and is based on the work of James Reason, a human factors researcher, who defined an error as "an occasion in which a planned sequence of mental or physical activities fails to achieve its intended outcome and when these failures can't be attributed to intervention of chance agency" (Reason, 1990, p. 9). We label the behaviors as "action errors," as our focus is on physical activities that fail to achieve an intended outcome. A central part of the use of the term "error" to describe these behaviors is that behavior is goal-directed. That is, in attempting these actions, a young child is intending to perform a specific action to accomplish a desired outcome. For example, in performing a scale error with a tiny chair, the child acts as to actually sit in the chair but is unsuccessful owing to the small size of the chair with respect to their own body. The issue is that the child is *intentionally* making an attempt to fit his or her onto an object that is too small to accommodate him or her. Children who perform grasp errors are also *intentionally* attempting to pick up a photographed or pictured object. Reason's definition of "error" can be appropriately applied to both these scenarios, as children are executing a planned sequence of motor actions that fail to achieve an intended outcome.

2.2 Action Errors Versus Motor Errors

Action errors differ from a number of other types of motor errors. For example, a child might attempt to throw a bean bag into a bucket. However, their attempt misses the target. Errors such as this may stem from lack of skill on the part of the child. As they become more proficient at tossing the bean bag in to the bucket, but miss only every once in a while, the miss may be due to random variability within their motor system. Schmidt (1982, pp. 201–202) has referred to these types of motor behaviors as "errors in execution." A key difference from our view of action errors is that these errors do not involve an attempt to accomplish a goal that is not afforded by aspects of the environment. Errors of execution may be reduced by practice, heightened attention to the goal, or specific training with respect to sports.

Schmidt (1982, pp. 201–202) also discussed "errors in selection." He defines these errors as a situation where an individual chooses a course of action, initiates the action, but the action is wrong for the particular environmental situation. In this case, they are wrong in terms of the action leading to an undesirable outcome and not wrong because the environment does not afford the action. For example, a tennis player may expect that his or her opponent is going to attempt to hit a drive past his or her on the left side of the court and so the player starts to move in that direction. However, the opponent hits a drop shot to the right side of the court and the tennis player is unable to return the shot because they have chosen the wrong action for this particular situation. Errors in selection can be reduced by choosing to change the action that was initiated (e.g., the tennis player could start moving left and then correct their movement to move to the right) or potentially delaying the initial action until more information is available (e.g., waiting until it is clear where the opponent plans to hit the tennis ball).

Both errors in execution and selection were framed by Schmidt (1982) in terms of motor programs. For errors in execution he suggested that the error stems from variability in the motor system. For errors in selection, he suggested that the error stems from choice of the wrong motor program. Neither of these errors was viewed by Schmidt as stemming from aspects of the perception–action system, rather they focus only on the function of the motor system. In contrast, we view action errors as stemming from the interaction of cognition and the perception–action system.

2.3 Action Errors Versus Slips of Action

Action errors are conceptually different from another form of errors involving actions. For example, Norman (1981) labeled another class of behaviors that involve action but are not intended as "slips of actions." We want to emphasize that the key part of this definition is that these action slips are unintended. These behaviors have generally been studied in adults performing routine, everyday tasks, such as taking a shower or making coffee (Heckhausen & Beckmann, 1990; Norman, 1981; Reason & Mycielska, 1982).

Slips of action are common when a desired action deviates from some sort of routine behavior that has been carried out on numerous occasions. For example, an individual might use the same walking route almost every day to go from home to his or her office and back home at the end of the day. However, one day he or she may want to stop on the way home to buy a gallon of milk. A slip of action occurs when the individual completes his or her daily routine and fails to stop to buy milk. The distinction between action errors and slips of action hinges on whether the "error"—attempting to sit in tiny chair or failing to buy milk—is intended. In the case of attempts to sit in the tiny chair, the action, sitting, is intended. In the case of failing to buy milk, the action, continuing to walk home without the milk, is not intended.

Norman (1981) suggested that slips of actions appear to result from: (1) conflicts between different possible actions or thoughts, (2) mixing up the sequence of a particular action sequence, and/or (3) selection of an appropriate action but in a situation or context where the action is inappropriate for the context or situation in some manner. The third group of slips of action seem similar to what we have defined as action errors, but the two actions differ in terms of whether the action itself is intended or not. Norman (1981) has suggested that these action slips are most likely caused by multiple factors, with potentially different factors playing roles in the different types of action slips.

Human factors researchers have been particularly interested in action slips, as even a minor action slip may have serious consequences if it occurs while driving a car or flying a plane (Botvinick & Blysma, 2005). Researchers have also been interested in action slips under the assumption that by understanding the characteristics of them and the situations where they occur, researchers can gain insight in to the processes and mechanisms involved in the control of routine behaviors that involve a series of steps or sequences (Heckhausen & Beckmann, 1990; Schwartz, 1995). Similarly, we suggest that by studying action errors, we may gain insight in the development of the perception–action system more generally. Slips of actions and action errors may also have some characteristics in common—an issue we will pursue further in a later section.

3. SPECIFIC TYPES OF ACTION ERRORS

As described in the introduction, three different types of action errors have been identified: grasp errors, scale errors, and media errors. In this section, we provide a review of research describing each of these different types of action errors and then provide a tentative time course for their developmental progression.

3.1 Grasp Errors

Of the action errors that we have described, grasp errors were the first to be documented formally (DeLoache et al., 1998), although anecdotal reports of their occurrence were reported quite a bit earlier (Murphy, 1978; Ninio & Bruner, 1978). They have also been documented to occur earlier in development than the other types of action errors. As described above, we define these behaviors as attempts to pick up or grasp an object that is depicted on a two-dimensional surface. We refer to these behaviors as "errors" because the two-dimensionality of the pictures does not enable the successful performance of the action, and from all appearances, they are intentional actions. Although the original work by DeLoache et al. (1998) described young children's grasp errors while young infants were interacting with realistic photographs of common objects and toys, these behaviors can occur with touch pads, video monitors, and other forms of technology.

DeLoache et al. (1998) reported four studies investigating the manual exploration of color photographs in infants between the ages of 9 and 19 months. In the first three studies, they found that all 10 9-month-olds explored the photographs as if they were real objects. Eight of the 10 children were reported to attempt to grasp at the pictured object, with a number of infants making repeated attempts to grasp the depicted objects in the photograph. This finding that some infants are highly persistent in making action errors is consistent with results found by other investigators (Rosengren, Schein, & Gutiérrez, 2010) and will be discussed in further detail in a later section. A second study presented 9-month-olds simultaneously with actual toys and photographs of the same toy. The infants overwhelmingly made their initial reach toward the real object rather that the photograph and spent much more time interacting with the real object than the photograph, suggesting that children can perceptually differentiate real objects from their photographic referent and that they prefer the real objects over the photographs. An additional study by these researchers established that manual exploration of photographs decreased from 9 to 19 months of age and was replaced by pointing at the depicted objects.

A final study in this initial report examined whether manual exploration of photographs could be found in a culture where photographs were not at all common. For this study, DeLoache et al. (1998) examined whether Beng infants, from a culture living in the Ivory Coast, would also manually explore photographs. They provided picture books containing photographs of both Western infant toys and common objects found in the Beng culture to 8- to 18-month-old infants. DeLoache et al. (1998) reported that the Beng infants behaved similarly to the 9-month-olds in the United States, manually exploring and attempting to grasp some of the depicted objects.

DeLoache et al. (1998) interpret young infants' manual exploration, and attempts to grasp at objects in the photographs, as indicative of young infants' uncertainty of what a photograph affords for action. They further suggest that it is through experience with investigating the nature of photographs that children acquire a concept of "picture." Part of this concept involves understanding that a picture or photograph can both be an object in itself but can also represent something else (i.e., the depicted object). This is a central part of DeLoache's model of dual representation (DeLoache, 2000; DeLoache, Miller, & Rosengren, 1997). We suggest that learning about the dual nature of symbols is a key aspect to the decline of action errors, a point we return to in a later section.

The existence of grasp errors, and whether they occur in many if not all children, is not without controversy. Yonas, Granrud, Chov, and Alexander (2005) argue that children actually do not grasp at pictures and treat objects and photographs differently. Note though, DeLoache et al. clearly do state that infants prefer the real object to its photographic referent. Others have questioned what it means when infants sometimes grasp at objects in photographs and whether this indicates that infants must learn what pictures and photographs afford for action (Ziemer, Plumert, & Pick, 2012).

Part of the discrepancy in whether children can be interpreted as making grasp errors can be explained by differences in methodology and part can be explained by different theoretical orientations. From an empirical perspective, we would argue that given highly realistic photographs, young infants do make grasp errors, at a relatively high rate under some conditions (Rosengren & French, 2011). Indeed, if one examines the behavior of young infants to objects and their photographic referents, one finds that the same actions are in fact attempted with the real object and the depicted one. Figs. 1 and 2 provide examples of three infants performing actions that lead them to successfully grasp an object and unsuccessfully attempt to grasp a depicted object. As can be seen in Fig. 1, the infants are using the same hand configurations for both the real object (Fig. 1A) and object depicted in the photograph (Fig. 1B). Fig. 2 shows, with the same infant captured in successive frames, that the sequence of actions directed toward the real object (Fig. 2A) and depicted one (Fig. 2B) are highly similar.

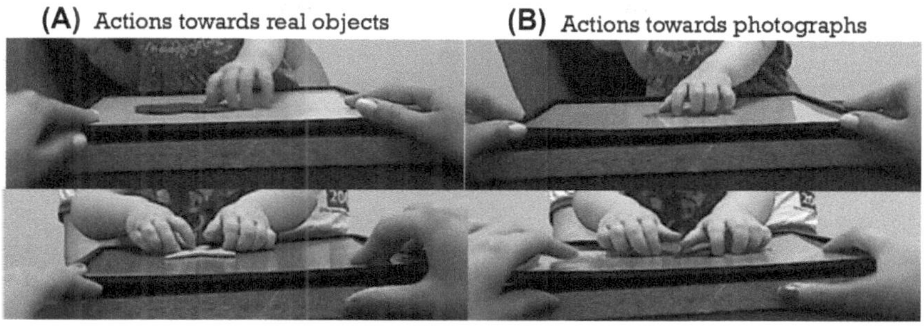

Figure 1 Examples of two young infants' behavior directed toward real objects (A) and photographs of objects (B).

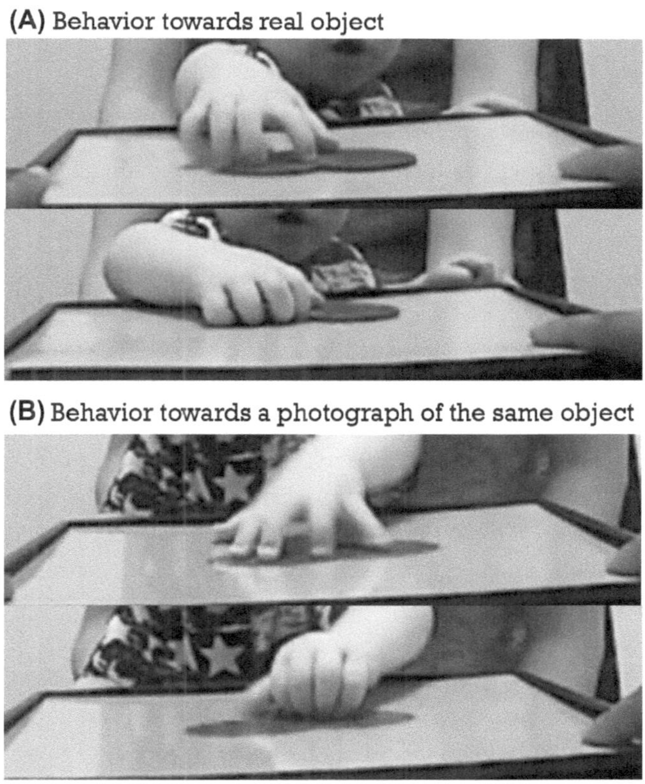

Figure 2 An example of the same infant picking up a real object (A) and making similar hand movements to the same object depicted in a photograph (B). The figure demonstrates similar sequential actions directed toward the object and photograph.

Furthermore, there is anecdotal evidence that adults perform grasp errors under certain conditions. One example was reported to the second author. In this report, another researcher explained that she was late to run an experiment and went to grab a pencil to have a participant complete a survey. She grasped at what she thought was a pencil, only to find that it was in fact a photograph of a pencil. Another anecdotal example of a grasp error was provided by the editor of this volume. One day she was in a hurry cleaning up her desk, and she went to grasp an object that she wanted to throw away. However, the object turned out to be a picture on a flyer rather than a real object. We have also confirmed that under time constraints, adults in a laboratory study can be induced to make grasp errors (Rhoad, Bruton, French, Gutiérrez, & Rosengren, 2012).

Grasp errors have not only been found in humans. Certain species of primates (e.g., baboons) have been shown to grasp at food items depicted in photographs (Bovet & Vauclair, 1998; Parron, Call, & Fagot, 2008). Parron et al. (2008) suggest that the baboons failed to process the photographs as representations and treated the photograph as if it were a real banana, in some cases, actually eating a photograph of a real banana. Taken together, these and related studies suggest that manual exploration of photographs (e.g., grasp errors) are sometimes produced by infants between the ages of 8 and 15 months (DeLoache et al., 1998) and that they are more likely to occur when infants are presented with highly realistic two-dimentional representations (Pierroutsakos & DeLoache, 2003).

An important thing to note with respect to grasp errors is that infants' behavior appears to be elicited by a representation depicted on a two-dimensional surface. Children's reach to the representation is visually guided—in that the action is accurately directed to the space on the surface where the object is depicted. Finally, the perceptual information present in the depiction leads children to act in a similar way as with certain real objects (see Figs. 1 and 2).

While we would argue that the evidence does support that young infants (and certain species of primates) commit grasp errors, the meaning of these behaviors is still controversial. As mentioned above, there are theoretical reasons for this controversy. On the one hand, supporters of James Gibson's ecological perspective argue that infants have no difficulty distinguishing photographs from real objects (Yonas et al., 2005) and that infants rarely if ever make grasp errors and when they do make grasp errors it stems from the complex self-organization "from elements of the environment, infant, and task coming together in the moment" (Ziemer et al., 2012, p. 496).

We agree that the grasp errors, and indeed all of the action errors that we describe here, are relatively rare but argue that even rare events can shed insights into development of the perception–action system. Where we differ from these other researchers is with respect to the elements of the infant that come to play when these behaviors are observed. Gibson et al. (Gibson, 1971; 1979; Kennedy, 1974) argued there was sufficient information in the environment for infants to accurately perceive what pictures afford for action, suggesting that learning was not necessary. In contrast, we argue that one element of the infant that needs to be considered in the production of action errors is the cognitive development of the young infants, an aspect of the child that is generally not considered from an ecological perspective. We address this issue in more detail in a later section.

3.2 Scale Errors

As in grasp errors, anecdotal reports of children doing odd things with objects led to the formal study of scale errors. In one case, the second author observed one of his children attempting to get in to a tiny car (see Fig. 3) and another one of his children attempting to sit on a tiny chair. Likewise, Judy DeLoache reported that she sometimes observed children in her studies of symbolic reasoning attempting to climb in and sit on furniture in the small scale models used in her research. These observations led us to formally investigate whether these behaviors could be elicited in a controlled environment.

In the original study of scale errors, children between 15 and 30 months of age were first presented with appropriately child-sized toys (i.e., ones

Figure 3 Child-sized car with occupant (right) and child-sized car and miniature toy replica (left). For much of the 1990s, the Cozy Coupe, made by Little Tikes, was the best-selling car in the world with over 450,000 sold in 1998 (http://www.nytimes.com/1998/10/21/automobiles/very-big-seller-in-a-very-small-market.html).

designed for 2- to 3-year-olds) including a version of the car (see right side in Fig. 3), a slide, and a chair. The children were encouraged to play with the toys and then left the room with an experimenter. While the children were gone, another experimenter switched each of the child-sized toys with miniature replica toys and then the children returned to the room (see the toy shown on the far left of Fig. 3). The child's behavior was video-recorded as they spontaneously, or with an experimenter prompting, interacted with the replica toys. Later studies have shown that scale errors occur without any form of prompting. Of the 54 children included in the study, 25 (46%) attempted to climb into the tiny car, sit in the tiny chair, or slide down the tiny slide with children performing between zero and four scale errors. A follow-up study presented the replica objects along with the child-sized toys to a group of eight children. When prompted to "sit in the chair," "go down the slide," or "drive the car" all of these children chose the larger object. This suggests that when presented simultaneously, children have no difficulty perceiving which of the objects affords the requested action. But why then do children sometimes attempt to act on the miniature toys? We return to this issue shortly.

Since the original laboratory study, scale errors have been reported using slightly different laboratory conditions (Brownell, Zerwas, & Ramani, 2007; DeLoache, LoBue, Vanderborght, & Chiong, 2013), observational studies in preschool classrooms seeded with miniature replica toys (Rosengren, Carmichael, Schein, & Anderson, 2009; Rosengren et al., 2010), retrospective online surveys of parents (Ware, Uttal, & DeLoache, 2010), and a prospective parental diary study (Rosengren, Gutiérrez, Schein, & Anderson, 2009). Rates of scale errors vary greatly across these methods with retrospective reports providing the lowest estimate (18% of 220 parents reported at least one scale error; Ware et al., 2010) and prospective reports providing the highest estimate (97% of 30 parents reported at least one scale error; Rosengren, Gutiérrez,etal., 2009). Observational studies in preschool classrooms provide estimates ranging from 53% (Rosengren, Carmichael, et al., 2009) to 88% (Rosengren et al., 2010) depending on the age of the children observed in the classroom. Additional laboratory studies report similar rates as the original laboratory study (Brownell, Zerwas, & Ramani, 2007; DeLoache et al., 2013). These studies provide strong evidence using very different methods and independent research teams that young children do attempt actions on objects that are too small to accommodate their bodies. In addition, many of these studies have reported that some children persist in their attempts to perform these actions. We return to the issue of individual differences when we explore why children might commit action errors in a later section.

Similar to what we have argued for grasp errors, scale errors are also visually guided. In video records, it can be clearly seen that children visually guide and align their bodies, so as to complete the desired action. In this manner, there exists a tight coupling between the perception of the object and action being attempted.

Researchers (Casler, Eshleman, Greene, & Terziyan, 2011; Ware, Uttal, Wetter, & DeLoache, 2006) have also shown that young children make scale errors involving two objects. For example, Ware et al. (2006) found that children make scale errors with dolls, attempting to fit relatively large dolls into chairs or cars that were way too small to accommodate the dolls. Casler et al. (2011) also found that children make scale errors with tools. In a series of studies, children sometimes chose a tool that was too large or too small to accomplish the task. For example, children would sometimes attempt to get a large toy fish out a fish tank using a net that was way too small to complete the task. They also sometimes attempted to use a net that was way too big to get a small toy fish out of a small fish tank as well. To our knowledge, Casler et al. are the first to show that scale errors can occur when the target object is substantially smaller or bigger than the child's body or tool. She and her colleagues (Casler, Hoffman, & Eshleman, 2014) have also shown that under speeded conditions adults can be induced to make scale errors with tools. Casler et al. argue that scale errors with tools are elicited by teleofunctional (purpose-based) reasoning, suggesting that cognitive reasoning plays an important role in their occurrence.

3.3 Media Errors

Interactive media errors are the least studied of the three action errors described in this chapter, but they also have been reported anecdotally. For example, a collaborator of both authors reported (Kirkorian, personal communication) that during an interactive video chat with her young niece, her niece retrieved a book and attempted to sit on her aunt's lap. The problem was that the two were separated by many miles and a computer screen! Instead of actually sitting on her aunt's lap, she sat on the computer keyboard. This is one example, similar to a number of different types of interactive media errors that we have been collecting in a prospective diary study with parents of children over a 6-month interval (Rosengren et al., 2018).

Use of digital media by young children has increased dramatically in recent years. At present, nearly all families in the United States with children younger than 8 years have some sort of digital media that is used by children (Rideout, 2017). Almost 80% of families in this category own a tablet computer, with roughly 40% reporting that their child under the age of 8 years has his or her own tablet. As the use of digital media by children continues to increase, we expect that the occurrence of different types of media errors will also increase.

As in grasp and scale errors, interactive media errors involve attempts by young children to perform a desired action that the media does not enable the child to complete successfully. In one of the few published reports of media errors, Pierroustakos and Troseth (2012) reported evidence of children manually exploring information presented on digital screens. Similar to both grasp and scale errors, the researchers showed that infants appeared to differentiate between three-dimensional objects from objects in two-dimensional screens and preferred interacting with real objects when presented statically in the real world or on a digital screen. However, the evidence does suggest that young children do display grasping behaviors toward objects appearing on a digital screen but to a much lesser extent than they do toward three-dimensional objects (Ziemer & Snyder, 2016). In this case, we have chosen to include these behaviors in the media category, even though they involve attempts to grasp objects that are not graspable. We would argue that these behaviors could be categorized as either grasp or media errors. Indeed, grasp errors can occur across different kinds of media (print, digital) whereas some media errors only can involve digital media (e.g., attempts to hand something to someone viewed on a digital screen).

In our prospective diary study that is investigating media errors (as well as grasp and scale errors), we have found that about 30% of our sample has reported that their child performed at least one media error over a 6-month interval, with the most common form of media error occurring while children were engaged with interactive media. For example, parents reported that their children attempted to share their dinners over video-chat sessions and attempted to grab items out of television broadcasts. With the proliferation of different types of digital media, parents have also reported that children confuse the affordances of different digital mediums, with some children treating traditional laptop screens as touch screens. In these cases, some children would persist, attempting to "play" videos by touching the corresponding button on the screen. We do not include these latter behaviors as action errors as they stem more from lack of information about what the technology itself is capable of and not really from a lack of understanding of what the technology itself is capable of in terms of action.

As in grasp and scale errors, there appear to be large individual differences in children's production of media errors. We suggest that media errors clearly show that some children do not understand what electronic media afford for action. In this sense, we suggest, as we have for grasp errors, that children must learn what the media afford for actions, and that this is not spontaneously perceived by young children. We suggest that, just as with grasp and scale errors, children must explore what different electronic media and technology afford for action. A recent anecdote about a young child, whose family bought a digital smart assistant (e.g., Alexa) for the home, reinforces this idea of exploration. The parent reported that their 2-year-old child had begun to talk to coasters and other cylindrical devices in the home that looked similar to the digital assistant, exploring whether they would respond to his inquiries (Rosenwald, 2017).

3.4 Tentative Developmental Time Course of Different Action Errors

The time course of different action errors is driven by a number of different factors. First, children must have acquired certain motor skills to attempt the actions. To perform a grasp error, children must be able to reach and successfully grasp objects. This behavior requires a certain level of fine motor skill that is not present in many young infants before about 8 months of age. For this reason, we can place the initial onset of these behaviors around this time period. We have demonstrated that there are large individual differences in the production of action errors. Some of these individual differences stem from differential experiences available for young children. For example, there is large variation in the extent that parents provide books or read to their children. There is also wide variation in families with respect to whether photographs and other two-dimensional images are available for children to look at and manually interact with in homes. Clearly, without providing stimuli that might elicit grasp errors (e.g., picture books with realistic images of small toys or food) these behaviors will not be observed. We would suggest that depending on children's experiences, those children with more rather than less experience interacting with and exploring photographs and other two-dimensional displays will learn more quickly what pictures and photographs afford for action. At the same time, gains in cognition, most notably, the acquisition of symbolic understanding and improvements in executive function, likely also lead to a decrease in the propensity to make grasp errors. These factors likely lead to the early emergence of grasp errors around 8 months of age, an increase in their likelihood over the next 6–8 months, and then a decrease in their frequency as children gain sufficient experience exploring photographs and make gains in cognitive development.

Like grasp errors, scale errors are also limited at first by fine and gross motor skills and experience with the environment. To make many of the scale errors that have been reported, such as attempting to climb in to a tiny car or sit on a tiny seat, requires children to be able to successfully stand, sit, and walk. These are skills that generally emerge around the first year of life and improve substantially over the next 6–8 months of life. For this reason we would expect the earliest scale errors to occur around this period of time, which is around the time period that researchers have documented their first appearance (Rosengren, Carmichael, et al., 2009; Rosengren, Gutiérrez, et al., 2009). As in grasp errors, scale errors require an environment that contains miniature toys that are similar to some degree to more child- and adult-sized functional objects in the environment. That is, children need to experience both appropriately scaled chairs, slides, and cars and miniature versions of similar objects to make scale errors. As in grasp errors, the frequency in the production of scale errors will likely increase and then decrease as children explore the affordances of objects of different sizes and as they achieve gains in symbolic understanding and cognition.

The developmental time course for various types of scale errors involving the child's own body (e.g., body scale errors: DeLoache et al., 2004; Brownell et al., 2007), children interacting with dolls and other objects (e.g., object scale errors: Ware et al., 2006), and functional tools (e.g., tool scale errors: Casler et al., 2011) appears to be somewhat different. At present, evidence suggests that body scale errors emerge first, followed by object scale errors, and then tool scale errors. This progression is parallel to advances in fine motor skills and cognition. Specifically, controlling two objects to attempt to fit a large doll into a tiny high chair involves greater fine motor skill than attempting to sit on a tiny rocking chair. Likewise, using a tool in a functional manner requires both relatively sophisticated fine motor skill and some specific conceptual knowledge about what the tool is designed to accomplish.

At present, media errors have not been explored to the same extent as the other action errors discussed in this chapter. However, we would argue that similar factors are at play in the developmental time course of these behaviors. That is, a certain level of fine motor skill is required to use a tablet or other electronic device. This level of fine motor skill comes in after children acquired the ability to reach and grasp objects but requires a level of fine motor control that goes beyond the ability to reach and grasp. At present, some children are beginning to interact with tablets and smart phones around 8 months of age, but most children are not likely being exposed on a regular basis to these devices until a year and a half or older. Thus, we would expect media errors to emerge sometime around the first year of life, increase in likelihood over the second year of life, and then decrease in frequency in children over the age of 3 years. Like the other action errors described, the developmental time course will be determined in part by exposure to particular stimuli in the environment (e.g., smart phones, tablets) and the child's level of cognitive development. One factor that also seems to come in to play with respect to media errors is their social experience. That is, a number of the reports that we have received from parents involve media errors where children are interacting with other people remotely using technology. Thus, this form of action error also requires the development of interactive social skills, such as sharing toys, food, or other interesting objects with another person; these are skills that are emerging over the second year of life into the toddler period.

4. HOW MIGHT ACTION ERRORS INFORM US ABOUT THE DEVELOPMENT OF THE PERCEPTION–ACTION SYSTEM?

To address this question, it is important to examine why children might produce action errors. As described earlier, Ziemer et al. (2012) have suggested that grasp errors occur owing to a complex interaction of factors in the environment, infant, and task. We have argued a similar point about motor behavior more generally (Rosengren & Braswell, 2003; Rosengren, Savelsbergh, & van der Kamp, 2003; Savelsbergh, van der Kamp, & Rosengren, 2006), suggesting that the interaction of environmental, organismic (i.e., individual), and task constraints lead to both the production of a specific behavior in a particular situation and provide important sources of variability in the behavior. From this perspective, constraints are viewed as factors that both limit and facilitate certain behaviors (Newell, 1986). One can think of these constraints as similar to a canal that both limits water to moving in a certain direction and also facilitates the movement in water in that direction.

4.1 Constraints on Action Errors

In terms of environmental constraints, we have already mentioned that for action errors to occur the environment must contain certain objects. For grasp errors, realistic two-dimensional depictions of three-dimensional objects must be present in the environment to elicit an attempted grasp. It is also true that infants likely need to have experience with grasping actual objects in the real world. For scale errors, the environment must contain appropriate-sized objects and miniature versions of similar objects. Given DeLoache et al.'s (2013) finding that when presented with the appropriately scaled and tiny replica version of a car, chair, or slide children choose the appropriately scaled item, we would suggest that scale errors are unlikely to occur when the environment contains both an appropriately scaled object and a highly similar replica miniature in close proximity. Although some researchers have suggested that the familiarity with the actual appropriately sized object and tiny replica version of the same object may increase the likelihood of scale errors, our own experience based on parental diaries and observations in preschool classrooms suggests that children need to merely recognize the tiny object as a member of a class of objects (e.g., chairs) that is familiar. For media errors, certain forms of technology need to be present in the environment and available for children to interact with. Taken together, the idea is that the developing perception—action system cannot be separated from the environment in which the child is developing.

Organismic constraints include such things as the individual child's body size, his or her rate of growth and physical maturation, his or her past experiences, and his or her cognitive development. We have already discussed at length the role of experience, and in particular children's exploration of what the environment affords for action, as a key aspect in the production of action errors and the decline in frequency of them over time. In the next section, we examine in more depth aspects of cognitive development that may play an important role in action errors. In particular, we focus on conceptual development, symbolic understanding, and aspects of executive functioning.

Task constraints are another factor that might influence the production of action errors. For young children, the task is the behavior that is intended. For grasp errors, the task involves picking up something. For scale errors, the task involves sitting on or climbing in to an object. For media errors the task involves interacting with someone or something. A key issue is that in all cases the task involves an intended action. In our view, this goal or intended action serves to organize the behavior in the moment.

4.2 Conceptual Development and Symbolic Understanding

We suggest that conceptual development plays a relatively large role in the emergence of children's action errors. In many ways, aspects of conceptual development can be described as learning what the environment affords for action, but we argue that it is also important to recognize that certain items in the environment are objects that can be picked up to be explored or eaten. Other objects in the environment can be sat in or on or slid down. One reason why we argue that acquiring these concepts is important for eliciting action errors is based on an explanation provided by DeLoache et al. (2004). Their explanation is derived in part from Milner and Goodale's (1995; see also Glover, 2004) theory of two different neural pathways, labeled as the dorsal and ventral streams. DeLoache et al. (2004) suggested that scale errors might occur because in young children the ventral stream, which processes information relevant for object recognition, and the dorsal stream, which processes information relevant for the control of action, are not fully integrated. They suggest that when a child perceives a tiny scale replica (e.g., a small chair), this visual information activates parts of the brain associated with visual recognition of the representation of the larger object or class of objects that the small object represents (more general concept of chair). They suggest that this representation also activates an action plan associated with the larger object or category (e.g., sitting). The action, even though it cannot be completed successfully, is visually guided in a manner that is appropriate for the scale of the object.

Converging evidence for this overall explanation is provided by research that has shown that motor and cognitive systems are coupled (Barsalou, Kyle Simmons, Barbey, & Wilson, 2003; Tucker & Ellis, 1998; 2001). For example, viewing an object such as a key has been found to activate, in some situations, the motor behavior commonly associated with that object (Klatzky, Pelligrino, McCloskey, & Doherty, 1989). Additional brain imaging studies have shown that motor areas in the brain are activated in concert with related conceptual areas when individuals view objects (e.g., a hammer) with a strongly associated motor action (e.g., hammering; Martin, 2001; Martin & Chao, 2001; Simmons, Martin, & Barsalou, 2005).

We argue that action errors in general may occur when a conceptual representation of an object or an event activates an action plan commonly associated with that object or event. In adults, however, the action plan is generally inhibited in situations where it is not appropriate owing to characteristics of the object or context. In the case of a photograph, the symbolic aspect of the photograph, that the photograph is a representation of an object and not a real object to be grasped, serves to inhibit the associated action plan. In young children whose inhibitory skills are not as well developed, inhibition of the activated action plan does not occur, and a grasp error results. Similarly, for scale errors, when children view a small replica object (e.g., a tiny chair) from a category of objects the child is familiar with (e.g., chairs in general), the visual stimuli activates a representation (e.g., concept of chair) that also activates an action plan (e.g., sitting) associated with that conceptual representation. In adults, this behavior is inhibited, but it is not so in young children. Although less well investigated, we suggest a similar argument can be made for media errors. In this case, interacting with a person over interactive video may activate a script associated with social interaction (e.g., giving another person a toy) that activates the specific action plan associated with that script (e.g., attempting to pass the toy to the person depicted on the screen). In adults, the activated action plan is inhibited but not in young children who are just learning what the interactive media affords for action. The fact that adults under task demands that require a rapid response commit grasp (Rhoad et al., 2012) and scale errors (Casler et al., 2014) suggests that lack of inhibitory control is one factor associated with the production of action errors. This aspect of executive function undergoes substantial development over the first few years of life, the same time period where action errors occur.

Symbolic understanding may also be important for the developmental progression of action errors. Acquiring knowledge that a photograph is a representation (e.g., symbol) of something else may help children inhibit the motor action associated with object depicted. DeLoache (2000) has referred to this issue as the problem of dual representation. Dual representation refers to the idea that a symbol can both represent something and be an object in and of itself. Although most of DeLoache's research has focused on young children's difficulty with understanding that scale models can represent a larger space, the dual representation model can be applied to children's difficulty in understanding that a photograph can both be an object and a representation of an object. Likewise, tiny replica objects can both be representations of larger objects, as is the case for doll furniture, and can also be objects themselves. Recognizing that small replica objects can have these dual roles—as a symbol and as an object—may lead slightly older children to inhibit the action plans associated with the larger object. Likewise, learning that video can represent an individual in a different time and or place may lead children to inhibit the behaviors associated with media errors.

As we have mentioned, researchers from an ecological perspective generally do not advocate that cognitive representations are needed to explain aspects of motor behavior, arguing that even infants and young children accurately perceive what the environment affords for action (e.g., Yonas et al., 2005). The argument is that perception and action are tightly coupled in the moment and there is no need to invoke cognitive representations in the guidance of action (Thelen & Smith, 1994). Rather, behavior is self-organized in the moment from the interaction of environmental, individual, and task constraints.

We argue, however, that the child's goal acts as an overall cognitive constraint that serves to organize the behavior at a higher level of functioning (see Rosengren et al., 2003 for a more detailed argument). In addition, we argue that symbolic understanding serves as an additional constraint on children's behavior that cannot be reduced to self-organization in the moment. Evidence in support of this argument comes from the "shrinking room study" (DeLoache et al., 1997). This study was designed to test DeLoache's dual representation model. In this task, children were presented with a symbolic task where they were shown a small toy hidden in a scale model, instructed that the model represented a larger space, and then asked to find a corresponding larger toy in the same location in the larger space. Before understanding that the small space represents the larger space, young children (under about age of 3 years) generally have little difficulty remembering where the object was hidden originally (~80% accurate in retrieval), but generally fail to find the object in the larger space (~20% successful). However, in the shrinking room study, the symbolic relation between the scale model and the larger space is broken by convincing children that the large room was shrunk to the scale model (or vice versa). By shrinking the room, the task becomes a memory task involving the "identical" but shrunken room. When this occurs, children respond similarly to the memory task, finding the hidden toy in the shrunken room at about the same rate as is found in older children in the symbolic task. Thus, by removing the symbolic aspect of the task, young children are able to perform successfully.

It is not clear how the results of this study can be interpreted without invoking the importance of symbolic understanding in older children. Likewise, we argue that it is more parsimonious to argue that conceptual representations and symbolic understanding are involved in the decline of action errors with age and experience than to suggest that they can be entirely explained in terms of self-organization. Instead we argue that children learn that objects can be both objects and representations and that this realization leads children to inhibit actions that have been activated along with conceptual representations.

To some extent, this argument is similar to one that Norman (1981) proposed for slips of action. Norman described one form of action slips, those that result from a thought that was not meant to be performed but that gets carried out anyway. He suggested that the thought causes the action in these cases. In this way, aspects of the action errors we have described in young children may be similar to some action slips in adults. Norman also points out that many action slips are caught at the time they are made, while others are caught just before their occurrence. He suggests that catching a slip that has been started requires some monitoring mechanism. As most of the action errors we have observed unfold unimpeded, it is likely that this monitoring mechanism is either not present or poorly developed in most young children who perform action errors. Norman (1981) proposed that action slips could be described as part of an activation-trigger-schema (ATS) system where once a high level schema (representation) is triggered, lower level action sequences get triggered, and the action is performed.

4.3 Individual Differences and Executive Function

The large individual differences in the performance of action errors also implicate issues of executive function and inhibitory control. Some children appear to perform different types of action errors rarely, while other children perform action errors persistently in a single session and over an extended period of time (Rosengren et al., 2009). Children who perform particular action errors rarely or only on one occasion may have relatively advanced executive functioning and may quickly learn that a photograph, tiny object, or video image does not afford actions normally associated with the object depicted, the larger object, or live individual. In contrast, children who persistently perform action errors, either in a single session, or over time, may not attend to affordances of the situation, effectively learn from their failed attempts to perform intended actions, or fail to inhibit motor actions activated by representations. We have collected some preliminary evidence suggesting that the frequency of children's grasp errors is related to measures of inhibitory control (Rhoad et al., 2012).

4.4 The Developing Perception—Action System

We argue that it is fruitful to examine the developing perception—action system in terms of the dynamic interplay of constraints within the environment, the individual child, and the task that they are attempting to complete. This interaction of constraints is dynamic and multiply determined, which is why action errors do not occur whenever a child sees a photograph of an object, views a tiny chair, or interacts with grandparents over interactive media. We argue, however, that not all constraints provide equal weight in the emergence of a specific behavior. Rather, the child's goal or intention to act plays a greater role in organizing factors to lead to a specific behavior.

Eleanor Gibson (1970, 1992) argued that visual input drives learning through the perception of affordances in the environment. These perceived affordances also provide the context in which children and adults act on the environment. Adolph and Kretch (2015) suggest that an important aspect of development involves perceptual learning. In the process of perceptual learning, children come to identify what the environment affords for action. By exploring the environment, the child can more effectively perceive what in the environment affords action. With development, and physical growth and maturational changes of their bodies, children must continue to explore the nature of affordances. In our view, this exploration is also guided by important changes in children's cognitive and symbolic understanding. To the extent that affordances can be viewed as possibilities for action that are dependent on the characteristics of the individual and properties of the environment, it is important to consider children's cognitive and symbolic understanding of the world to be an important aspect of perceiving the possibilities for action. Technology and manufactured artifacts have made this exploration both more interesting and more challenging for young children, as they are confronted with stimuli that provide different types of affordances than their perceptual systems have evolved to pick up. In this way, the interaction between the child and environment in some cases may lead to a misperception of affordances.

5. CONCLUSION

Based on the evidence that we and others have collected, we argue that all or almost all children likely perform action errors over the course of early development. From prospective diary studies, observations in preschools, and laboratory studies we have found that if certain stimuli are made available to young children over a course of time the likelihood that they will perform an action error is relatively high. This is not to say that action errors are common or frequent. However, we do argue that their existence—even fleeting existence—indicates that children must actively explore the environment to determine what it affords for their own actions on a particular object, their actions involving more than one object, and their actions involving technology and media. We would strongly suggest that our perceptual apparatus has not evolved to spontaneously pick up the affordances of tiny manufactured objects, photographs, or technology and that children must explore with their bodies and hands what these artifacts afford for action. However, we argue that the developing perceptual—action system cannot be completely understood without considering how young children's cognitive development and symbolic understanding influence the learning of what the environment affords for action.

ACKNOWLEDGMENTS

The writing of this chapter was supported in part by a core grant to the Waisman Center from the National Institute of Child Health and Human Development (U54 HD090256). The opinions expressed are those of the authors and do not represent views of the National Institute of Child Health and Human Development.

REFERENCES

Adolph, K. E., & Kretch, K. S. (2015). Gibson's theory of perceptual learning. In H. Keller (Developmental Section Ed) (Ed.), *International encyclopedia of social and behavioral sciences* (2nd ed., Vol. 10, pp. 127—134). New York: Elsevier.

Barsalou, L. W., Kyle Simmons, W., Barbey, A. K., & Wilson, C. D. (2003). Grounding conceptual knowledge in modality-specific systems. *Trends in Cognitive Sciences,* 7(2), 84—91.

Botvinick, M. B., & Bylmsa, L. M. (2005). Distraction and action slips in an everyday task: evidence for a dynamic representation of the task context. *Psychonomic Bulletin & Review, 12*, 1011—1017.

Bovet, D., & Vauclair, J. (1998). Functional categorization of objects and of their pictures in baboons (*Papio anubis*). *Learning and Motivation, 29*, 309—322.

Brownell, C. A., Zerwas, S., & Ramani, G. B. (2007). "So Big": The development of body self-awareness in toddlers. *Child Development, 78*, 1426—1440.

Casler, K., Eshleman, A., Greene, K., & Terziyan, T. (2011). Children's scale errors with tools. *Developmental Psychology, 47*, 857–866. http://dx.doi.org/10.1037/a0021174.
Casler, K., Hoffman, K., & Eshleman, A. (2014). Do adults make scale errors too? How function sometimes trumps size. *Journal of Experimental Psychology General, 143*, 1690–1700.
DeLoache, J. S. (2000). Dual representation and young children's use of scale models. *Child Development, 71*(2), 329–338.
DeLoache, J. S., LoBue, V., Vanderborght, M., & Chiong, C. (2013). On the validity and robustness of the scale error phenomenon in early childhood. *Infant Behavior & Development, 36*, 63–70.
DeLoache, J. S., Miller, K. F., & Rosengren, K. S. (1997). The credible shrinking room: very young children's performance with symbolic and nonsymbolic relations. *Psychological Science, 8*(4), 308–313.
DeLoache, J. S., Pierroutsakos, S. L., Uttal, D. H., Rosengren, K. S., & Gottlieb, A. (1998). Grasping the nature of pictures. *Psychological Science, 9*(3), 205–210.
DeLoache, J. S., Uttal, D. H., & Rosengren, K. S. (2004). Scale errors offer evidence for a perception-action dissociation early in life. *Science, 304*(5673), 1027–1029.
Gibson, E. J. (1970). The development of perception as an adaptive process. *American Scientist, 58*, 98–107.
Gibson, E. J. (1992). How to think about perceptual learning: twenty-five years later. In H. L. Pick, P. van den Broek, & D. C. Knill (Eds.), *Cognition: Conceptual and methodological issues* (pp. 215–237). Washington, DC: American Psychological Association.
Gibson, J. J. (1971). The information available in pictures. *Leonardo, 4*(1), 27–35.
Gibson, J. J. (1979). *The ecological approach to visual perception*. Boston: Houghton Mifflin.
Glover, S. (2004). What causes scale errors in children. *Trends in Cognitive Science, 8*(10), 440–442.
Heckhausen, H., & Beckmann, J. (1990). Intentional action and action slips. *Psychological Review, 97*, 36–48.
Kennedy, J. M. (1974). *A psychology of picture perception*. San Francisco, CA: Jossey-Bass.
Klatzky, R. L., Pelligrino, J. W., McCloskey, B. P., & Doherty, S. (1989). The role of motor representations in semantic sensibility judgments. *Journal of Memory and Language, 28*, 56–77.
Martin, A. (2001). Functional neuroimaging of semantic memory. *Handbook of Functional Neuroimaging of Cognition, 1*(3), 153–186.
Martin, A., & Chao, L. L. (2001). Semantic memory and the brain: structure and processes. *Current Opinion in Neurobiology, 11*(2), 194–201.
Milner, A. D., & Goodale, M. A. (1995). *The visual brain in action*. Oxford: Oxford University Press.
Murphy, C. M. (1978). Pointing in the context of shared activity. *Child Development, 49*, 371–389.
Newell, K. M. (1986). Constraints on the development of coordination. In M. Wade, & H. T. A. Whiting (Eds.), *Motor skill acquisition in children: Aspects of coordination and control* (pp. 341–360). Dordrecht: Martinus Nijhof.
Ninio, A., & Bruner, J. (1978). The achievement and antecedents of labeling. *Journal of Child Language, 5*, 1–15.
Norman, D. A. (1981). Categorization of action slips. *Psychological Review, 88*, 1–15.
Parron, C., Call, J., & Fagot, J. (2008). Behavioural responses to photographs by pictorially naïve baboons (*Papio anubis*), gorillas (*Gorilla gorilla*) and chimpanzees (*Pan troglodytes*). *Behavioural Processes, 78*, 351–357.
Pierroutsakos, S. L., & DeLoache, J. S. (2003). Infants' manual exploration of pictorial objects varying in realism. *Infancy, 4*, 141–156.

Pierroutsakos, S. L., & Troseth, G. L. (2012). Video verite: infants' manual investigation of objects on video. *Infant Behavior & Development, 26*, 183–199.

Reason, J. (1990). *Human error*. Cambridge: Cambridge University Press.

Reason, J. T., & Mycielska, K. (1982). *Absent minded? The psychology of mental lapses and everyday errors*. Englewood Cliffs, NJ: Prentice Hall.

Rhoad, A., Bruton, C. M., French, J. A., Gutiérrez, I. T., & Rosengren, K. S. (May 2012). Evidence for grasping errors in adults. In *Poster presented at the association for psychological science, Chicago, IL.*

Rideout, V. J. (2017). *The common sense census: Media use by kids age zero to eight*. San Francisco, CA: Common Sense Media.

Rosengren, K. S., & Braswell, G. (2003). Learning to draw and to write: issues of variability and constraints. In G. Savelsbergh, K. Davids, J. van der Kamp, & S. Bennett (Eds.), *Development of movement coordination in children: Applications in the field of ergonomics, health sciences and sport* (pp. 56–74). London: Routledge.

Rosengren, K. S., Carmichael, C., Schein, S. S., Anderson, K. N., & Gutiérrez, I. T. (2009). A method for eliciting scale errors in preschool classrooms. *Infant Behavior and Development, 32*(3), 286–290.

Rosengren, K., & French, J. A. (March 2011). Action errors in childhood: the role of representations and inhibitory control. In *Invited symposium presentation at the Biennial Conference for the Society on Research on Child Development, Montreal, Canada.*

Rosengren, K. S., Gutiérrez, I. T., Anderson, K. N., & Schein, S. S. (2009). Parental reports of children's scale errors in everyday life. *Child Development, 80*(6), 1586–1591.

Rosengren, K. S., Kirkorian, H., Choi, K., Jiang, M. J., Raimer, C., Tolin, E., et al. (2018). *Scale errors and beyond: A diary study of children's action errors with toys, photographs, and screens* (in preparation).

Rosengren, K. S., Savelsbergh, G. J., & van der Kamp, J. (2003). Development and learning: a TASC-based perspective of the acquisition of perceptual-motor behaviors. *Infant Behavior and Development, 26*(4), 473–494.

Rosengren, K. S., Schein, S. S., & Gutiérrez, I. T. (2010). Individual differences in children's production of scale errors. *Infant Behavior and Development, 33*(3), 309–313.

Rosenwald, M. S. (March 2, 2017). How millions of kids are being shaped by know-it-all voice assistants. *The Washington Post*. Retrieved from https://www.washingtonpost.com/local/how-millions-of-kids-are-being-shaped-by-know-it-all-voice-assistants/2017/03/01/c0a644c4-ef1c-11e6-b4ff-ac2cf509efe5_story.html?utm_term=.466f0f3acbc7.

Savelsbergh, G. J. P., van der Kamp, J., & Rosengren, K. S. (2006). Functional variability in perceptual-motor development. In K. Davids, S. J. Bennett, & K. Newell (Eds.), *Variability in the movement system: A multi-disciplinary approach* (pp. 185–198). Urbana-Champaign: Human Kinetics.

Schmidt, R. A. (1982). More on motor programs. In J. S. Kelso (Ed.), *Human motor behaviour: An introduction* (pp. 189–217). Hillsdale, NJ: Lawrence Erlbaum Associates.

Schwartz, M. F. (1995). Re-examining the role of executive functions in routine action production. In J. Grafman, K. J. Holyoak, & F. Boller (Eds.), *Annals of the New York Academy of sciences: Vol. 769. Structure and functions of the human prefrontal cortex* (pp. 321–335). New York: New York Academy of Sciences.

Simmons, W. K., Martin, A., & Barsalou, L. W. (2005). Pictures of appetizing foods activate gustatory cortices for taste and reward. *Cerebral Cortex, 15*(10), 1602–1608.

Thelen, E., & Smith, L. B. (1994). *A dynamic systems approach to the development of cognition and action*. Cambridge: MIT Press.

Tucker, M., & Ellis, R. (1998). On the relations between seen objects and components of potential actions. *Journal of Experimental Psychology: Human Perception and Performance, 24*(3), 830.

Tucker, M., & Ellis, R. (2001). The potentiation of grasp types during visual object categorization. *Visual Cognition, 8*(6), 769–800.

Ware, E. A., Uttal, D. H., & DeLoache, J. S. (2010). *Developmental Science, 13*, 28–36.

Ware, E. A., Uttal, D. H., Wetter, E. K., & DeLoache, J. S. (2006). Young children make scale errors when playing with dolls. *Developmental Science, 9*, 40–45.

Yonas, A., Granrud, C. E., Chov, M. H., & Alexander, A. J. (2005). Picture perception in infants: do 9-month-olds attempt to grasp objects depicted in photographs? *Infancy, 8*(2), 147–166.

Ziemer, C. J., Plumert, J. M., & Pick, A. D. (2012). To grasp or not to grasp: infants' actions towards objects and pictures. *Infancy, 17*, 479–497.

Ziemer, C. J., & Snyder, M. (2016). A picture you can handle: infants treat touch-screen images more like photographs than objects. *Frontiers in Psychology, 7*.

CHAPTER SIX

Timing Is Almost Everything: How Children Perceive and Act on Dynamic Affordances

Jodie M. Plumert*,[1] and Joseph K. Kearney[§]
*Department of Psychological and Brain Sciences, The University of Iowa, Iowa City, IA, United States
[§]Department of Computer Science, The University of Iowa, Iowa City, IA, United States
[1]Corresponding author: E-mail: jodie-plumert@uiowa.edu

Contents

Advances in Child Development and Behavior, Volume 55
ISSN 0065-2407
https://doi.org/10.1016/bs.acdb.2018.05.002

Abstract

A key challenge for the developing perception–action system is learning how to move the self in relation to other moving objects. This often involves perceiving and acting on affordances or possibilities for action that depend on the relation between the characteristics of the individual and the properties of the environment (Gibson, 1979). This chapter overviews our program of research on perceiving and acting on dynamic affordances (i.e., possibilities for action that vary over time). Our goal is to bridge the divide between basic and applied research by using road crossing as a model system for studying how children's ability to perceive and act on dynamic affordances undergoes change with age and experience. The basic task is for participants to cross virtual roads with continuous traffic either on foot or on a bicycle. This work reveals that children's gap choices and crossing motions are less tightly linked than those of adults. Children often choose the same size gaps as adults but time their entry into those gaps less tightly than adults. As a result, children typically end up with less time to spare than adults when they clear the path of the vehicles. Improvement in gap selection and movement timing occurs gradually over development, indicating the perception–action system undergoes continuous change well into adolescence. As in other areas of development (e.g., face perception, word recognition), this kind of gradual developmental change appears critical for the fine-tuning of the system. The late development of these skills may explain also why adolescent pedestrians, cyclists, and drivers continue to be at risk for collisions when crossing roads. Further work aimed at better understanding the developmental mechanisms underlying these changes will inform the fields of both developmental science and injury prevention.

1. INTRODUCTION

1.1 We Perceive to Act and Act to Perceive

A fundamental tenet of the ecological approach to perception is that perception and action are tightly intertwined. We use available perceptual information to guide action, and we use action to make perceptual information available. A key challenge for the developing perception–action system is to learn how to finely tune or coordinate perception and action (including dynamic adjustment of actions on the basis of perceptual information). Becoming a skilled pedestrian, for example, involves improved use of visual information to guide gap decisions and to time crossing movements. Unlike the development of perceptual skills (vision, audition) and motor abilities (walking, running), this perception–action tuning process involves a long period of development (Plumert, Kearney, & Cremer, 2007). As we note at the end of the chapter, this kind of gradual, continuous change depends both on experience with performing perception–action tasks and maturation of relevant brain structures. Furthermore, experience and maturation have bidirectional influences on each other—experiences shape brain development and brain maturation enables new experiences.

An important part of this tuning process is perceiving and acting on affordances, or possibilities for action that depend on the relationship between the characteristics or skills of the perceiver and the properties of the environment (Gibson, 1979). This is an inherently relational concept, meaning that possibilities for action depend on *both* the characteristics of the organism and the structure of the environment (e.g., water offers a surface of support for a water bug but not for a human). Thus, changes in the environment and changes in the organism (or both) lead to changes in possibilities for action. For developing organisms, affordances change as body dimensions and motor skills develop (Adolph, 2008). Affordances also change with experience because opportunities for action expand as organisms become more skilled at perception—action tasks.

Our work focuses on how children and adults perceive and act on dynamic affordances, or affordances that vary with time (see also Fajen, 2013). Time-varying affordances often involve moving the self relative to other moving objects, such as crossing a gap in traffic or stepping onto a moving escalator. Perceiving affordances is more complex when objects are moving than stationary because affordances change over time when objects are moving. Actions that are possible at one moment in time may not be possible a short time later. We use road crossing as a model system for studying how the ability to perceive and act on dynamic affordances undergoes change with development and experience. This is a good model system because the perceiver must choose a possibility for action (a gap to cross) from a stream of possibilities (a series of gaps) and then act on this decision at the right time.

A gap affords crossing if the individual's (projected) crossing time is less than the temporal size of the gap (Lee, Young, & McLaughlin, 1984). To successfully coordinate movement through the gap, individuals must cut in closely behind the lead vehicle in the gap, while crossing before the tail vehicle reaches their line of travel. Importantly, given the dynamic nature of traffic, gap decisions and crossing movements must be tightly linked in time. That is, selecting a gap that affords crossing can lead to poor outcomes if the individual delays too long before moving, and precisely, coordinating movement can also lead to poor outcomes if the individual selects a gap that is too small to afford safe crossing. This means that children must accurately judge both the size of the temporal gap and the time required to cross to choose a safe gap. Thus, both overestimation of gap size and underestimation of crossing time can contribute to errors in judging whether a gap is sufficiently large to afford safe crossing. The potential for such errors makes road crossing a very-high-stakes skill that virtually all children need to learn to function adaptively in everyday life.

Studying how children cross roads can also inform our understanding of an important public health issue—traffic safety. In 2015 alone, there were 8000 pedestrian injuries and 5000 cyclist injuries involving collisions with motor vehicles in children between the ages 5 and 14 years (National Highway Traffic Safety Administration, 2017). Pedestrian and cyclist injuries during childhood peak during the 10- to 14-year-old range, suggesting that there may be an increase in vulnerability for pedestrian and cyclist injuries involving motor vehicle crashes at the ages when children commonly cross roads without parental supervision (Wills et al., 1997). Motor vehicles are involved in approximately one-third of all bicycle-related brain injuries and in 90% of all fatalities resulting from bicycle crashes (Acton et al., 1995; Rivara & Aitken, 1998). Many of these collisions occur at intersections (Ashbaugh, Macknin, & VanderBrug Medendorp, 1995; Wachtel & Lewiston, 1994; Wang & Nihan, 2004). Our work aims to advance understanding of the factors that contribute to these pedestrian and cyclist fatalities and injuries.

1.2 Chapter Organization

We start with a description of the bicycling and pedestrian simulators, along with a description of the basic road-crossing task. We then cover our older work on how child and adult cyclists cross roads and then our newer work on how child and adult pedestrians cross roads. We then discuss work in progress comparing how children cross roads on foot versus bike. We end by discussing how this program of research on perception–action informs the fields of developmental science and traffic safety.

2. THE BICYCLING AND PEDESTRIAN SIMULATORS

The primary instrument for our work is a large-screen virtual environment that can be configured as either a bicycling simulator or a pedestrian simulator (Figs. 1 and 2). The virtual environment consists of three large screens placed at right angles relative to one another, forming a three-walled room (10-feet wide × 14.2-feet long × 8-feet tall). Currently, our setup includes three stereo projectors that rear-project images onto the front and side

Figure 1 Photograph of a rider crossing the road in the bicycling simulator.

Figure 2 Photograph of a pedestrian crossing the road in the pedestrian simulator.

screens and a fourth that front-projects stereo images onto the floor (note that all of our previously published work on cyclist road crossing used nonstereo displays). When configured as a bicycling simulator, a bicycle mounted on a stationary frame sits 5 feet from the front and side screens. The bike is instrumented to sense both steering angle and rear wheel rotation. This information is combined with virtual terrain information to render the graphics corresponding to the bicyclist's real-time trajectory through the virtual environment. We also generate appropriate dynamic forces on the rider's pedaling, taking into account rider and bicycle mass and inertia, virtual terrain slope, ground friction, and wind resistance. This enables a riding experience that realistically incorporates many of the real-world dynamics of bicycling.

When configured as a pedestrian simulator, the virtual environment consists of an open floor bounded by the front and side screens. The length of the side screens allows participants to physically walk across a virtual one-lane road, thereby engaging similar perceptual-motor processes as in real road crossing. Optical motion-tracking cameras detect the position and orientation of a helmet worn by participants, which ensures that images are rendered correctly for the participant's eye point. Participants wear shutter glasses, allowing them to experience the virtual environment in stereo. Hence, when participants stand at the edge of the roadway, the cars appear as 3D images as they pass through the volume of the simulator.

These state-of-the-art bicycling and pedestrian simulators have allowed us to safely and systematically study how children and adults cross roads with traffic. The realism of the virtual environment provides a high level of ecological validity, making it possible to draw conclusions about the development of perception–action skills in the context of a real-world problem—crossing roads with traffic. At the same time, we are able to present road-crossing challenges to our participants without concern for their safety. This combination of realism and safety makes virtual environment technology a unique tool for understanding the development of perception and action (see Loomis, Blascovich, & Beall, 1999 for a discussion of immersive virtual environments as a basic research tool in psychology).

3. THE ROAD-CROSSING TASK

The basic task for participants is to cross a virtual road with continuous cross traffic without being "hit" by a vehicle. Typically, a single lane of continuous traffic travels at residential area speeds (25 or 35 mph) and approaches from the left-hand side. The temporal gaps between vehicles are usually randomly ordered and range in size from uncrossable to easily crossable (e.g., 2–5 s, on the half second). Bicyclists ride up to each intersection and attempt to cross without being "hit" by a car. Once they reach the other side, they continue riding to the next intersection. Similarly, pedestrians stand at the edge of the roadway and attempt to cross without being "hit" by a car. Once they reach the other side, the traffic ceases to be generated and they walk back across the empty road to the starting position. Bicyclists typically cross 6–12 intersections and pedestrians typically make 12–20 crossings.

One thing to note about our road-crossing task is that we present children with more challenging road-crossing conditions than they are likely to encounter in the real world. Even our "normal traffic density" intersections involve a relatively tight range of gap sizes, and children have to choose a gap to cross because the cross traffic is continuous. Why not just present participants with road traffic conditions that mimic exactly those encountered in real life? In a nutshell, we have found that presenting children and adults with more challenging road-crossing situations is critical for revealing developmental and individual differences. Through observations of literally thousands of trials, we consistently see that both children and adults will always take the large gaps, especially if they come early in a sequence of gaps. More interesting is how children and adults respond to gaps that are more ambiguous in size. Across many studies, we have found that the most interesting behavior occurs in response to these more ambiguous gaps. For example, after a riding experience with a risky virtual peer, child cyclists are more willing to take ambiguous size gaps (Babu et al., 2011). While we readily acknowledge that children (and even adults) take tighter gaps in the simulator than they would in real life, we believe that the patterns of findings reveal important developmental and individual differences in perceiving and acting on dynamic affordances.

4. KEY MEASURES OF GAP DECISIONS AND MOVEMENT TIMING

Our focus is on the two broad components of perceiving and acting on gap affordances: gap decisions and movement timing. In terms of gap decisions, we are interested in the size of the gap accepted on each trial and the likelihood of accepting or rejecting each gap seen. We use mixed-effects logistic regression to model the likelihood of accepting gaps of different sizes, and whether gap choices are moderated by fixed factors such as age and condition. In terms of movement timing, we are especially interested in how participants time their entry into the gap relative to the lead car and how much time to spare they have when they clear the roadway. These measures are important because precise timing of entry (i.e., cutting in close behind the lead vehicle in the gap) allows for a greater margin of safety (i.e., time to spare relative to the tail vehicle in the gap) when participants clear the path of the cars, provided that they cross the road in a timely manner. The positions (i.e., x and y coordinates) of the participant and cars are recorded at every timestep of the simulation and used to calculate the following gap selection and movement timing variables for each participant for each trial:

Gap accepted. The size (in seconds) of the gap crossed.

Timing of entry. The time (in seconds) between the pedestrian or rider and the tail of the lead car in the gap at the moment the pedestrian or rider enters the path of the traffic.

Crossing time. The time (in seconds) from entering to clearing the path of the traffic.

Time to spare. The time (in seconds) between the pedestrian or rider and the front of the tail car in the gap at the moment the pedestrian or rider clears the path of the traffic.

Collisions. Crossings in which the time to spare is less than zero.

Each measure is averaged over the total number of trials, giving us robust measures of performance in the road-crossing task. We also compute measures such as variability of timing of entry by calculating the standard deviation of timing of entry over all trials. Together, these measures of gap acceptance and movement timing yield a fine-grained picture of how children and adults perform the road-crossing task.

5. BICYCLING ACROSS ROADS

5.1 Crossing Single Versus Multiple Lanes of Traffic

We started this program of research with the simplest case in which children and adults crossed a single lane of traffic coming from the left-hand side, with randomly ordered gaps of varying sizes (Plumert, Kearney, & Cremer, 2004). Our primary goal was to examine age differences in decisions about gap affordances. We focused on 10- and 12-year-olds both for basic and applied reasons. In terms of basic research issues, the ability to coordinate self-movement and object movement appears to undergo developmental change up until at least 12 years of age (Hoffmann, Payne, & Prescott, 1980; Savelsbergh, Rosengren, van der Kamp, & Verheul, 2003). For example, ball-catching skills continue to improve across middle to late childhood, even under simple circumstances (Savelsbergh et al., 2003). In terms of applied issues, bicycling injuries increase from age 5 to 9 years and peak between 10 and 14 years (National Center for Statistics and Analysis, 2017 (NHTSA), 2017). Even when injury rates are adjusted for current amount of bike riding (both time and distance), children in late childhood and early adolescence remain most at risk (Hamann, Peak-Asa, & Lynch, Ramierz, Torner, 2013; Thompson, Thompson, & Rivara, 1990). In this study and virtually all of our other work on road crossing, college-age adults are included as a comparison group.

Children and adults performed our basic road-crossing task in the bicycling simulator. To our surprise, we found that 10- and 12-year-old children and adults chose almost exactly the same size gaps to cross (approximately 4 s on average). However, children consistently had less time to spare than adults when they cleared the path of the tail car in the gap. When we looked back at what children and adults were doing before crossing, we saw that children delayed initiation of crossing relative to adults. This resulted in less time to spare when children cleared the path of the approaching car. These findings are consistent with earlier work by other researchers on child pedestrians' road crossing (Barton & Schwebel, 2007; Lee et al., 1984; Pitcairn & Edelmann, 2000; te Velde, van der Kamp, Barela, & Savelsbergh, 2005). This pattern of results indicates that 10- and 12-year-old children's gap decisions and crossing motions are less well matched than those of adults, even in simple road-crossing situations.

We have also examined how children and adults choose gaps and time movement in more complex road-crossing tasks; namely, crossing two lanes of opposing traffic (Grechkin, Chihak, Cremer, Kearney, & Plumert, 2013). Judging gap affordances when crossing multiple lanes of opposing cross traffic is a challenging task because the gaps approach from opposite directions and cannot be observed simultaneously, unlike the case when gaps approach from the same direction. When judging whether a pair of near- and far-lane gaps affords safe crossing, individuals must accurately perceive the size of each individual gap and the overlap between the two gaps. Each individual gap must be sufficiently large for safe crossing and the overlap between the two gaps must be sufficiently large for safe crossing. The relationship between the opening of the near and the far gaps provides riders with two qualitatively different opportunities for crossing. When the far gap opens before or with the near gap, the temporal crossing interval when both lanes are clear of vehicles appears as an "aligned" gap pair spanning both lanes of traffic (Fig. 3). Conversely, in a "rolling" gap pair, the near-lane gap opens before the far-lane gap (Fig. 4). If the temporal offset is sufficiently large, the cyclist can enter the near-lane gap before the far-lane gap opens, allowing the rider to cut in closely behind the lead car in the far-lane gap.

Twelve- and 14-year-olds and adults crossed a series of 12 intersections in the bicycling simulator. Given that the earlier work had shown that

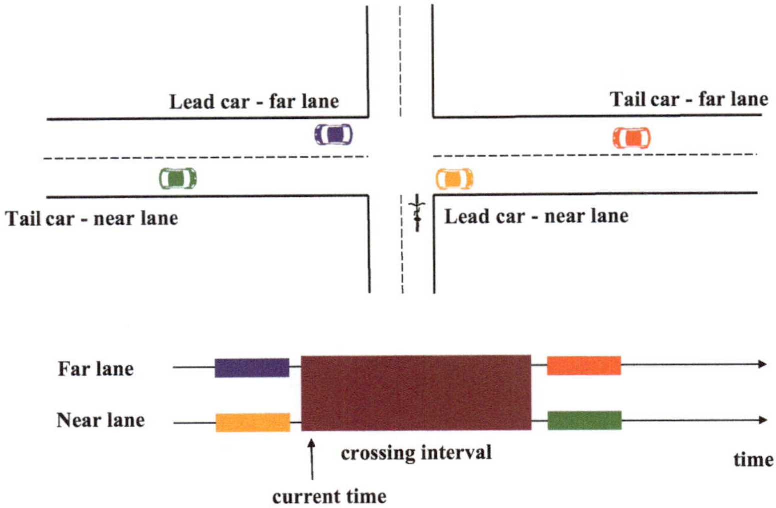

Figure 3 Diagram illustrating a cyclist crossing a pair of aligned gaps. The cyclist enters the near-lane gap when both lanes of traffic are simultaneously open. Although this configuration of gaps may appear safer, the time interval for crossing is shorter than in the rolling gaps case.

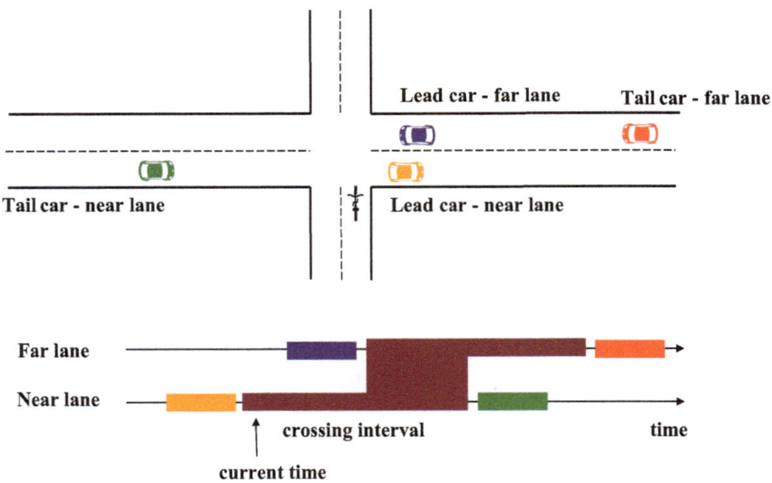

Figure 4 Diagram illustrating a cyclist crossing a pair of rolling gaps. The cyclist enters the near-lane gap before the far-lane gap opens, thereby allowing the cyclist to cut in closely behind the lead car in the far lane when the far-lane gap opens. This results in a longer overall time interval for crossing than in the aligned gaps case.

10- and 12-year-olds are less adept than adults in timing their movement when crossing a single lane of traffic restricted to the near lane (Plumert et al., 2004), we shifted the child age range to 12- and 14-year-olds because we expected that 10-year-olds would have substantial difficulty crossing two lanes of relatively dense, opposing traffic. Each intersection had a continuous stream of cross traffic approaching from opposite directions in both the near and far lanes, corresponding to crossing a busy road. The gaps in both lanes ranged between 1.5 and 6.5 s and were randomly ordered. Because two overlapping large gaps were rarely available, the participants had to make difficult choices in selecting reasonably safe pairs of gaps for crossing.

In contrast to our earlier work on crossing a single lane of traffic, we observed significant age differences in gap selection. Although all age groups preferred rolling over aligned gap pairs, this preference was stronger for adults. This is consistent with research by Barton and Schwebel (2007) who found that adult pedestrians were more likely than child pedestrians to enter the near lane before the far lane was completely open. All age groups showed similar preferences for the near-lane gap sizes, but 14-year-olds chose larger far-lane gap sizes than 12-year-olds. Children were also less skillful than adults in timing their entry into the gaps. Twelve- and 14-year-olds significantly delayed their entry into both the near lane and the far lane compared with adults. Twelve-year-olds' less skillful timing combined with their riskier far-lane gap choices resulted in significantly less time to spare than adults when they cleared the path of the cars. Unlike the 12-year-olds, 14-year-old cyclists compensated for their poorer movement timing skills by choosing larger far-lane gaps, resulting in similar time to spare as adults when they cleared the path of the cars.

5.2 Changes in Crossing Behavior With Experience

How do gap choices and crossing behavior become more finely tuned with experience? In particular, how does experience with operating near the limits of the perceptual-motor system affect gap choices and crossing behavior? Experiences that push the perceptual-motor system near the limit may be especially informative for learning about the boundary between success and failure and for bringing actions more tightly in line with decisions. Over time, such experiences should lead to more finely tuned decisions and actions. Although pushing road-crossing actions too close to the limit in the real world can have dire consequences, experience with varying safety margins may be informative. Such experience may be particularly useful for cases in which individuals have to precisely coordinate their decisions and actions (e.g., crossing dense traffic during rush hour).

We examined these questions by asking 10- and 12-year-old children and adults to cross high-density traffic (Plumert, Kearney, Cremer, Recker, & Strutt, 2011). We chose this task because crossing high-density traffic is likely to push the perceptual-motor system close to the limit. We were particularly interested in how high-density traffic affects gap choices and movement timing, and how experience with crossing high-density traffic leads to change in gap choices and movement timing. Children and adults crossed 12 intersections with a single lane of continuous cross-traffic coming from their left-hand side. In the control condition, participants encountered normal-density traffic at all intersections. In the high-density condition, participants encountered a set of four intersections with high-density traffic sandwiched between two sets of four intersections with normal-density traffic. At the high-density intersections, riders initially encountered a series of 6–8 uncrossable gaps (1.5 and 2 s), followed by pairs of successively larger gaps (starting with 3-s gaps and increasing by the half second) interspersed with four uncrossable gaps. The gaps all appeared in a continuous stream of traffic, making the traffic pattern difficult to detect. The end result was that participants had to wait for considerably more gaps to pass before crossing at the high-density than at the normal-density intersections.

As in our previous work with single-lane crossing, we found no age differences in gap choices, but significant age differences in time to spare. Consistent with pedestrian research (Guth, Ashmead, Long, Wall, & Ponchillia, 2005), both children and adults took much smaller gaps when faced with high-density than normal-density traffic. They also cut in more closely behind the lead car in the gap when crossing the high-density intersections, suggesting that both children and adults adjusted their actions to more closely match their (risky) decisions. Nonetheless, children were also "hit" on 20% of high-density intersections, indicating that although they attempted to bring their actions closer in line with their decisions, they were often unsuccessful at doing so.

We also found that after experience with high-density traffic, both children and adults continued to take tighter gaps at later intersections with lower-density traffic. At the group level, participants in the high-density traffic condition were more likely to accept very tight 3-s gaps during the last than the first set of intersections than were participants in the normal-density traffic condition. At the individual level, participants who took smaller gaps and waited for less time when confronted with high-density traffic were also significantly more likely to take very tight 3-s gaps during the last set of intersections. One explanation for these findings is that participants became more skilled as a result of their experience with taking tight gaps during the high-density intersections. Hence, a more tightly tuned perception–action system may have contributed to a greater willingness to take very tight gaps at the last set of intersections, even when larger ones were readily available. Another possible explanation is that the experience of crossing high-density traffic may have increased participants' willingness to take greater risks, perhaps due to heightened arousal or impatience. Note, however, that the two explanations offered above are not necessarily mutually exclusive—a highly tuned perception–action system coupled with a willingness to engage in risky behavior may have created the right conditions for some children and adults to accept very tight gaps.

Experience with the road-crossing task also resulted in improvements in 10-year-olds' movement timing across the session in both the high-density and control conditions. Across the session, 10-year-olds cut in closer behind the lead car and crossed the intersection more quickly. As a result, they improved their safety margins by 25% by the last set of intersections. One general factor that seems to play an important role in perceptual-motor change is gaining better control over motor actions (Adolph & Berger, 2006). In our case, this involves learning to better control the bicycle. Generally speaking, better control over the bicycle makes it possible to ride at a higher speed with better steering. As noted previously, 10-year-olds showed significant changes in their crossing speed across the session. In addition, 10-year-olds exhibited a large (45%) and significant decline in veering while crossing from the first to the last set of intersections. Quite likely, better control over the bike made it easier for the 10-year-olds to bring their crossing movements tightly in line with the visual information. Hence, they cut in more closely behind the lead car in the gap, leaving them with a greater safety margin relative to the trailing car in the gap at the end of the session than at the beginning.

Another general factor that seems to play an important role in producing change in perceptual-motor functioning is learning to better anticipate consequences of actions. von Hofsten (2007, see also this volume) argues that a major hallmark of perceptual-motor development is the ability to anticipate what is going to happen next and to use this information to guide behavior. In our case, timing of movement relative to the lead car in the gap requires prospective control over movement. That is, to tightly cut in behind the lead car, individuals need to anticipate exactly when to begin moving. In situations such as our virtual road-crossing task, experience crossing small gaps gives children valuable practice in learning how to precisely time their motions with respect the approach of the lead vehicle in the gap. Improvements in the ability to synchronize self-motion with the motion of the traffic may have led to better prospective control over the timing of their movement later in the session. In sum, these types of gains in movement timing over short-term timescales may help produce the developmental changes seen over longer-term timescales.

5.3 Intercepting Moving Gaps on the Run

We have also studied how children synchronize self-movement and object movement when intercepting a moving gap on the run (Chihak, Grechkin, Kearney, Cremer, &, Plumert, 2014; Chihak et al., 2010). This task allows us to study synchronization of self-movement and object movement independent of movement initiation and gap selection (see also Louveton, Bootsma, Guerin, Berthelon, & Montagne, 2012; Louveton, Montagne, Berthelon, & Bootsma, 2012). Our initial study examined how well 10- and 12-year-old children and adults adjust their motions to intercept a moving gap (Chihak et al., 2010). At each intersection, riders attempted to pass without stopping between two red blocks moving from left to right (Fig. 5). Using an adaptive scenario technique, block arrival times were timed such that participants needed to speed up or slow down to intercept the gap. This meant that the timing of the block arrival times for the speed up and slow down trials were keyed to the individual's riding speed during

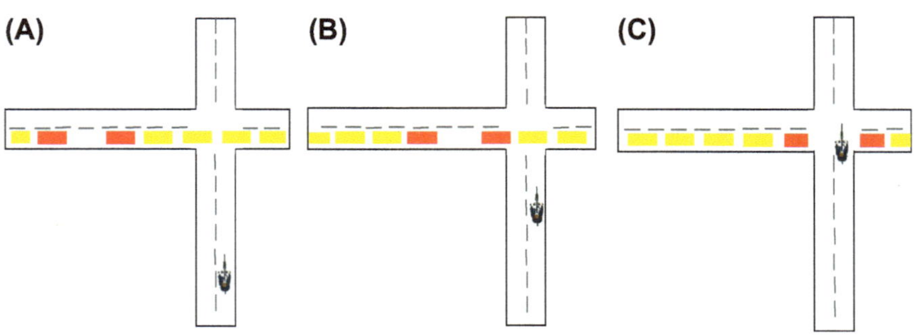

Figure 5 Diagram illustrating the gap interception task. The task for the rider is to intercept the moving red blocks without stopping. Panels A, B, and C depict the rider and blocks as the rider moves toward the interception point.

the approach to each intersection. As in our road-crossing studies, we found that children timed their entry relative to the lead block in the gap less tightly than adults. Children also exhibited significantly more variability in their approach to the intersection and in the amount of time they had to spare. Thus, although children did not have to select the gap to cross or initiate movement from a stop, they still synchronized self-movement and object movement less skillfully than did adults.

We have also used the gap interception task to address the question of how interceptive actions become more finely tuned with experience (Chihak et al., 2014). Numerous studies have shown that adults exhibit more finely tuned interception skills with practice, even over relatively short time periods (Camachon, Jacobs, Huet, Buekers, & Montagne, 2007; Montagne, Buekers, Camachon, de Rugy, & Laurent, 2003), and that varied practice experiences are more beneficial than identical practice experiences (Huet et al., 2011). We examined how giving 10-year-olds and adults consistent versus variable practice with speeding up or slowing down to intercept the gap affected their performance on the interception task. The block timings during the first eight intersections were adjusted such that participants either had to speed up on all trials (speed up condition), slow down on all trials (slow down condition), or to speed up on half of the trials and slow down on half of the trials (variable condition).

On slow-down trials, 10-year-olds in the variable condition slowed down far less on the approach to the intersection than did 10-year-olds in the slow-down condition, whereas on the speed-up trials, 10-year-olds in the variable condition sped up less on the approach to the intersection than did 10-year-olds in the speed-up condition. As a consequence, children in the variable condition required less speed correction immediately before intercepting the gap on slow-down trials and more speed correction on speed-up trials. Adults' interceptive actions were precisely timed regardless of condition. This suggests that children who experienced both slow-down and speed-up trials used a "split-the-difference" approach whereby they averaged their previous experiences with the two trial types as they attempted to intercept the gap at each successive intersection. This was beneficial in the slow-down trials but detrimental in the speed-up trials. These findings suggest that children may have more difficulty than adults with integrating their past experience with on-line information to coordinate self-movement and object movement.

5.4 Individual Differences in Gap Decisions and Movement Timing

We have also used an individual differences approach to better understand the mechanisms underlying gap decisions and movement timing in road crossing. We have been particularly interested in the role of inhibitory control, a facet of executive functioning critical for adaptive functioning across many tasks (Steinberg, 2005). The ability to tightly synchronize self-movement and object movement may be related to inhibitory control because it requires a high level of self-regulation—the rider must not begin to move too soon or too late. Moreover, the rider must begin to move based on the anticipated position of the vehicle relative to the path of travel. This ability to move the self in relation to an anticipated object position is likely to require a high degree of concentration and control. We have examined the role of individual differences in inhibitory control in a series of two studies, one that examined how inhibitory control was related to road-crossing performance in typically developing children and one that examined how children with Attention-Deficit Hyperactivity Disorder (ADHD) crossed roads compared with their counterparts without ADHD.

In the first study (Stevens, Plumert, Cremer, & Kearney, 2013), we asked 10- and 12-year-old typically developing children to cross roads using our high-density traffic scenario (Plumert et al., 2011). We chose this scenario to elicit individual differences in inhibitory control, as waiting for an acceptable gap at the high-density intersections requires patience and self-control. While children were riding, parents completed the Early Adolescent Temperament Questionnaire–Revised (EATQ-R; Ellis & Rothbart, 2001), a measure of temperament for children between 9 and 16 years of age. As in other work, we found that older children timed their entry into the roadway more precisely (i.e., cut in more closely behind the lead car in the gap) than did younger children. Likewise, male participants timed their entry into the intersection more precisely than did female participants and also had more time to spare when they cleared the intersection. This is consistent with other work on child pedestrian road crossing, showing that boys miss fewer opportunities to cross and time their entry into the roadway more skillfully than girls (Barton & Schwebel, 2007). We also found significant links between temperamental characteristics and bicycling behavior. Interestingly, 10-year-olds with higher parent-reported inhibitory control timed their movement more precisely when they entered the intersection and had more time to spare when they cleared the intersection than did their counterparts with lower inhibitory control. Thus, it appears that 10-year-olds characterized by higher levels of internal self-regulation exhibited more mature road-crossing skill in our task. In fact, 10-year-olds with higher inhibitory control looked exactly like the 12-year-olds with respect to timing of entry and time to spare.

In our second study (Nikolas et al., 2016), we asked 10- to 14-year-olds with and without ADHD to bicycle across virtual roads using our high-density traffic scenario. Parents completed several questionnaires to assess ADHD symptomatology (inattention and impulsivity) and temperamental characteristics (inhibitory control). First, as in previous work (Stevens et al., 2013), we found that both ADHD and non-ADHD children were more likely to take tight gaps at the high-density intersections than the normal-density intersections. However, ADHD youth were more likely to select smaller gap sizes following exposure to high-density traffic than non-ADHD youth, suggesting that ADHD youth may have more difficulty modulating their behavior in response to changing traffic conditions. Second, ADHD youth timed their entry into the roadway less tightly than non-ADHD youth and exhibited greater variability in their timing of entry compared with non-ADHD youth. Consequently, they also had significantly less time to spare than non-ADHD youth. Third, some specificity emerged when examining associations between ADHD symptom dimensions and bicycling outcomes. Hyperactive-impulsive symptoms specifically predicted selection of smaller gap sizes, whereas both inattention symptoms and poorer inhibitory control among all youth predicted less tight timing of entry and less time to spare when crossing. Together, these studies indicate that individual differences in attention and inhibitory control are predictive of individual differences in timing of entry into the gap. This suggests that executive functioning skills play a critical role in deciding when to act.

5.5 Summary

Two key findings from this program of research on child cyclists' road crossing are that (1) there are few age differences in gap choices and (2) there are systematic developmental and individual differences in how children time their movement relative to the lead car in the gap. Given that the lead vehicle in the gap acts as a gate to crossing, keying movement relative to the lead vehicle is critical for tightly synchronizing self-movement and object movement. We consistently find that 10- to 14-year-old cyclists time their movement relative to the lead vehicle less tightly and more variably than do adult cyclists, both in the road-crossing task and in the interception task. These difficulties in timing movement relative to the lead car when entering the roadway almost always result in less time to spare relative to the tail car when exiting the roadway. Given that children do not adjust their gap choices to match their timing skills, child cyclists almost always engage in riskier road-crossing behavior than do adult cyclists. Furthermore, children with deficits in inhibitory control appear to engage in even more risky road-crossing behavior and may be particularly at risk for collisions with motor vehicles.

6. CROSSING ROADS ON FOOT

Our most recent work has focused on how child pedestrians cross roads with continuous traffic. Previous work shows that both gap selection and movement timing are problems for younger child pedestrians (Barton & Schwebel, 2007; Connelly, Conaglen, Parsonson, & Isler, 1998; Demetre et al., 1992; Lee et al., 1984; Schwebel, Gaines, & Severson, 2008; te Velde et al., 2005; Young & Lee, 1987). In a classic early study, Lee et al. (1984) devised a road-crossing task in which 5- to 9-year-old children crossed a "pretend road" setup parallel to an actual road. Children watched the cars on the actual road and crossed the pretend road when they felt that they could safely reach the other side of the pretend road (i.e., before the oncoming vehicle on the real road crossed their line of travel). Although children were generally cautious, they sometimes accepted gaps that were too tight for safe crossing. Researchers have also used virtual environment technology to study how child pedestrians cross roads (e.g., Chaddock, Neider, Lutz, Hillman, & Kramer, 2012; Morrongiello, Corbett, Milanovic, Pyne, & Vierich, 2015; Schwebel et al., 2008). For example, in Schwebel et al. (2008), 7- to 9-year-old children and adults stood on a pretend curb and watched two-way moving traffic displayed on three large monitors. When they thought it was safe to cross, participants stepped down off the curb onto a pressure plate that initiated the movement of an avatar in the virtual environment. The avatar crossed the road at a constant speed (based on each participant's own walking speed) while the participant stood and watched. Children experienced significantly more hits and close calls than adults and also exhibited significantly longer movement initiation delays than did adults.

6.1 Limitations of Past Research

Although this research has yielded valuable information about components of children's road-crossing skills, there are several limitations to this work. The "pretend road" task developed by Lee et al. (1984) involves having children watch traffic on a real road but cross a pretend road setup parallel to the real road. Because children are standing at the edge of the pretend road, they view the traffic on the real road from a distance, making it difficult to precisely time initiation of movement relative to the traffic on the real road. In Connelly et al. (1998), 5- to 12-year-old children stood at a roadside and indicated the last possible moment that they would cross (i.e., made go/no-go decisions). However, for obvious ethical reasons, children were not asked to act on their decisions. In the virtual road-crossing task developed by Schwebel et al. (2008), children trigger the movement of an avatar by stepping off a curb. Although the speed of the avatar is matched to their own baseline walking speed, children view the consequences of their action in the third person and cannot adjust the speed of the avatar while it is crossing the road. Other work using virtual environment technology relies on treadmill interfaces (Chaddock et al., 2012) or head-mounted displays (Morrongiello et al., 2015), which limit natural movement and vision.

Our immersive pedestrian simulator overcomes these problems because participants physically walk across a virtual roadway with a full field of view, thereby engaging similar perceptual-motor processes as in real road crossing. To our knowledge, the only other large-screen pedestrian simulator in the world in which pedestrians physically walk across a virtual roadway has been developed by Dommes et al. in France (Dommes, Cavallo, Dubuisson, Tournier, & Vienne, 2014), which they have used to study how older pedestrians cross roads (Dommes et al., 2014, 2015). The goal of our initial study on pedestrian road crossing was to systematically examine developmental changes in how children coordinate their decisions and actions when crossing roads on foot. To study this developmental trajectory in fine-grained detail, we examined road crossing in children between the ages of 6 and 14 years, along with an adult comparison group. We were particularly interested in the ability to align decisions and actions as movement timing abilities progressively improve.

6.2 Extended Development of Child Pedestrian Road-Crossing Skills

Children and adults performed our basic road-crossing task in which they physically crossed a virtual roadway in our large-screen, stereo pedestrian simulator. To our surprise, although the task was relatively simple (crossing a single lane of 25 mph traffic), adult-like gap choices and movement timing were not observed until age 14 years. On the movement timing side, we observed steady developmental change in children's timing of entry relative to the lead car in the gap up to age 14 years. With increasing age, children timed their entry more tightly and exhibited less variability across trials. As noted earlier, keying movement relative to the lead car in the gap is critical for tightly coordinating self-movement and object movement because the lead car acts as a gate to crossing. On the gap selection side, we observed clear developmental change both in terms of gap thresholds and sensitivity. Before age 12, children's gap choices were more risky and less discriminating than those of older children and adults. Coupled with their poorer timing of entry, 6-, 8-, and 10-year-olds' gap choices resulted in significantly less time to spare and more collisions than 14-year-olds and adults. Interestingly, 12-year-olds' gap acceptance thresholds were significantly more conservative than those of both the younger and older age groups. As a result, although they timed their entry into the roadway less tightly than 14-year-olds and adults, 12-year-olds did not differ from the 14-year-olds and adults in time to spare. The prolonged developmental course in movement timing skills may be particularly important for explaining continued risk for pedestrian injuries in early adolescence, especially in challenging situations such as high-density traffic.

6.3 Summary

The finding that movement timing skills continue to develop well into adolescence in a pedestrian road-crossing task is consistent with our earlier findings with the bicycling road-crossing task. Even with a well-practiced motor skill such as walking, children aged 12 years and under timed their entry into the gap less tightly and more variably than 14-year-olds and adults. Interestingly, 12-year-olds compensated for their poorer movement timing skills by choosing larger gaps. Our previous work with 12- and 14-year-old cyclists crossing two lanes of opposing traffic parallels this developmental pattern (Grechkin et al., 2013). Unlike 12-year-olds, 14-year-olds compensated for poorer movement timing skills by choosing larger far-lane gap sizes when performing the complex task of bicycling across two lanes of opposing traffic. These findings fit with our expectation that this pattern of results would appear earlier in development in a pedestrian task, given that walking is a more direct and experienced form of movement than bicycling.

7. WORK IN PROGRESS: COMPARING PEDESTRIAN AND BICYCLIST ROAD CROSSING

One important question our work raises is the developmental trajectory of pedestrian and cyclist road-crossing skills. In other words, how does the ability to tightly link decisions and actions compare when children of different ages walk versus bicycle across roads? On the one hand, it is possible that children at a given age show similar levels of skill across pedestrian and cyclist road crossing because the perceptual information specifying the gaps remains the same across walking and bicycling. In other words, the road-crossing problem is essentially the same across the two tasks. This would suggest that any difficulties children have with choosing gaps that are well matched to their crossing abilities should appear at the same age in both pedestrian and cyclist road crossing. On the other hand, it is possible that children at a given age show greater skill in matching their gap decisions with their crossing abilities when walking than bicycling across traffic because the modes of locomotion are different. In particular, interaction with the environment is indirect when bicycling (i.e., mediated through a mechanical device) but is direct when walking. In addition, children typically have several more years of experience with walking than with bicycling. This would suggest that children of a given age may exhibit tighter links between decisions and actions while walking than while bicycling across roads.

7.1 A Comparison of Bicycling and Walking Across Roads

We have begun to address these questions in our current work comparing how children choose gaps and time movement in pedestrian and cyclist road-crossing tasks. We have chosen to study 8-, 10-, and 12-year-olds because our previous work indicates that pedestrian and cyclist road-crossing skills are undergoing substantial changes across these ages. Adults will be included as a comparison group. Children perform both a pedestrian and bicyclist road-crossing task, counterbalanced across participants. (This is possible because we have a pair of identical simulators—one configured as a bicycling simulator and the other as a pedestrian simulator.) The road-crossing scenario is identical for both the pedestrian and bicycling task, including the roadway and the traffic. This means that the visual information remains the same across both tasks, whereas the mode of locomotion varies. While children are performing the road-crossing tasks, parents fill out questionnaires about their child's temperament and bicycling and pedestrian experience.

Our preliminary observations indicate that 8- and 10-year-olds have far more difficulty with the bicycling than the pedestrian task. The 8-year-olds in particular seem to have more difficulty controlling the bike, which impairs their timing of entry into the gap and consequently leaves little time to spare on exiting the roadway. This contrasts with the 12-year-olds who exhibit far greater control over the bicycle and hence more precise timing of entry. Although data collection is still ongoing and statistical analyses need to be conducted, our observations indicate that road-crossing skill develops earlier for walking than for bicycling. This is consistent with the idea that gap affordances depend on the relationship between the characteristics of the individual and the properties of the environment. In this case, the properties of the environment remain constant, but the characteristics of the individual vary (skill in walking vs. bicycling). Given younger children's less skillful bicycling than walking, the possibilities for action are different for bicycling than walking. Two interesting questions are whether younger children's gap decisions reflect these differences in movement skill and whether experience transfers from one mode of locomotion to the other.

7.2 Implications for Novice Drivers

This work also has potentially important implications for explaining the spike in novice drivers' crash rates on earning a provisional driver's license (Mayhew, Simpson, & Pak, 2003). We propose that this problem exists because driving is a new mode of action that requires learning a modified coupling of perception and action. Namely, although the perceptual information specifying the movement of the cars remains the same across walking, bicycling, and driving, the action required to move the individual in relation to those cars is different. For individuals to tightly synchronize their own movements in relation to those of the cars, they need experience with learning how to control the forces governing movement. The simplest case is learning to control self-movement in relation to other moving objects while walking. The most difficult case is learning to control the movement of the self in relation to other moving objects while driving. In this case, the vehicle extends in all directions around the individual, and the ratios between control actions (e.g., pushing the brake or accelerator) and resulting forces (e.g., vehicle slowing or acceleration) are large (i.e., small depression of the brake or accelerator results in large change in speed). This framework explains why a period of experience with driving is needed before young drivers accurately perceive and act on driving affordances.

8. TIMING IS (ALMOST) EVERYTHING

A consistent finding from this program of research is that children time their entry into the gap less tightly and less consistently than college-age adults, both when walking and bicycling across roads. We have also seen that children with lower inhibitory control time their entry into the roadway less tightly than children with higher inhibitory control and that children with ADHD also show poorer timing of entry than their typically developing counterparts. What accounts for this pattern of findings? One possibility is that children intentionally leave a larger berth because they are taught not to enter the roadway until the lead car has completely passed their line of travel. However, one might also expect that this kind of caution would be accompanied by choosing larger gaps to cross than adults. We do not see children taking larger gaps than adults, although these larger gaps are readily available.

Another possibility is that children are less adept at anticipating when the oncoming vehicle will arrive at their line of travel. In earlier unpublished work, we asked 10- and 12-year-olds and adults to judge the time-to-arrival of a single vehicle traveling at either 25 or 35 mph. Children and adults sat on the bike in the bicycling simulator and watched as a vehicle traveling from right to left in the far lane disappeared behind two gridlocked buses in front of them (Fig. 6). Their task was to push a button on the handlebar when they thought the front of the car was immediately in front of them (the car never reappeared from behind the buses). Both children and adults made highly accurate time-to-arrival judgments, indicating that they are able to anticipate when an oncoming vehicle will arrive at their line of travel. These findings suggest that age differences in timing of entry into the gap are the result of children's difficulty with using information about the time-to-arrival of the oncoming vehicle to prospectively create a motor program for initiating movement (see also von Hofsten in this volume). This explanation is consistent with findings reported earlier that 10-year-olds with higher inhibitory control exhibit better timing of entry (and more time to spare) than their counterparts with lower inhibitory control (Stevens et al., 2013), and that typically developing children exhibit better timing of entry than do children with ADHD.

Yet another possibility is that children leave a larger berth between themselves and the lead vehicle (or block) because their timing is simply more variable. We have consistently found that children's timing of entry

Figure 6 Screenshot of the time-to-arrival task. Children and adults watch a car coming down the roadway that disappears behind the buses. Their task is to press a button when they judge that the front of the car will reach their line of travel.

relative to the lead vehicle is more variable than that of adults, which means that the distribution of timing of entry across a set of road-crossing trials is broader for children than for adults. As a consequence, even if a child and an adult are aiming for the same temporal point in a gap, the child will have a much greater risk of colliding with the lead vehicle in the gap than the adult due to higher variability in timing (Fig. 7). Given high variability in timing, a conservative approach is to aim for a later time of entry to avoid a potential collision with the lead vehicle in the gap. Of course, if children leave a wider berth between themselves and the lead vehicle in the gap to account for their greater variability in timing, then they should also choose larger gaps to give themselves more time relative to the tail vehicle in the gap. Their failure to do so suggests that children are not fully taking into account their poorer timing skills when choosing gaps.

Importantly, these three explanations are not mutually exclusive and may operate at different points in development or play different roles for particular developmental disorders. For example, all three of these factors may be at work for young children crossing roads (e.g., 6-year-old pedestrians), but difficulties with prospective control over movement or high variability in the motor timing system may be at play for older children (e.g., 10-year-old pedestrians) and children with executive function deficits (e.g., children with ADHD). In fact, some have hypothesized that timing deficits constitute a distinct causal pathway of ADHD (Sonugua-Barke, Bitsakou, & Thompson, 2010; Zelaznik et al., 2012). Furthermore, timing deficits appear across neurodevelopmental disorders such as ADHD and

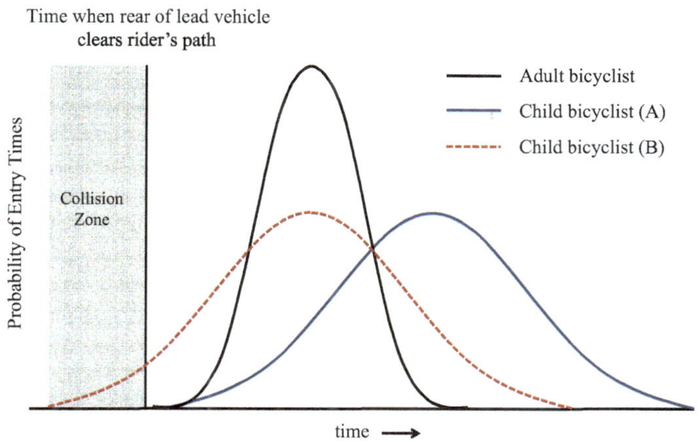

Figure 7 Potential consequences of movement timing variability profiles for collisions with the lead vehicle. Child bicyclists A and B illustrate how a wider probability distribution of entry times impacts potential collisions with the lead vehicle when aiming to enter the roadway at an earlier (A) or later (B) time. The adult bicyclist illustrates how a tighter probability distribution of entry times impacts potential collisions with the lead vehicle when aiming to enter the road at the same time as child bicyclist A.

autism, and in other conditions such as schizophrenia and Parkinson's disease (Allman & Meck, 2012). This suggests that impairments in the corticostriatal and corticocerebellar brain networks underlying sensorimotor synchronization may be common across these disorders (Valera et al., 2010).

9. IMPLICATIONS FOR UNDERSTANDING THE DEVELOPMENT OF THE PERCEPTION–ACTION SYSTEM

One of the most noteworthy findings from our work is the long developmental time course of children's road-crossing skills, both for walking and bicycling across roads. Even when walking across a single lane of traffic, we do not see adult-like gap decisions and movement timing until age 14 years. Another important characteristic of the developmental changes we observe is that they are quantitative rather than qualitative in nature. Although children are "hit" more often than adults in both the pedestrian and bicycling tasks, such failures are rare (except for the high-density traffic scenario). Children and adults perform the tasks similarly, but children do so less skillfully than adults. The primary change with increasing age is gradual improvement in choosing gaps and timing movement, and in tightly and consistently linking gap decisions and movement timing. In terms of the developing perception—action system, we see these specific improvements with age in the road-crossing task as part of more general improvements in moving the self in relation to other moving objects. As noted earlier, a key aspect of this improvement is precisely synchronizing self-movement and object movement. These gradual, continuous age changes in decision-making and movement timing skills highlight the prolonged developmental processes in tasks that require precise tuning of perception and action.

What underlies these developmental changes in children's ability to precisely time their movements in relation to other moving objects? We suggest that these developmental changes involve both brain development and movement experience. One late-maturing brain structure critical for the precise timing of movement is the cerebellum (Ivry & Keele, 1989; Keele & Ivry, 1990). Neuroimaging studies also show that the cerebellum is recruited most heavily for motor tasks such as the ones used in our work that require individuals to pay close attention and concentrate (for a review, see Diamond, 2000). Given that the cerebellum continues to mature up until at least puberty (Tiemeier et al., 2010), it seems likely that the differences between children and adults are at least partly due to differences in cerebellar functioning. Furthermore, there are significant connections between the cerebellar cortex and the prefrontal cortex, a brain structure involved in decision-making and executive functioning (Diamond, 2000). Given our findings showing that inhibitory control (a component of executive functioning) is related to timing of entry in both typically developing and ADHD children, it seems likely that developmental changes in the cerebellar—prefrontal cortex network play an important role in the developmental time course of children's movement timing skills.

Experience with moving the self in relation to other objects also plays an important role in the development of children's movement timing skills. As noted earlier, we see changes in children's movement timing over the course of even a single session (Plumert et al., 2011). Contemporary views of perceptual-motor development suggest that short-term learning experiences accumulate to produce long-term developmental changes in the perception—action system (Berthier, Rosenstein, & Barto, 2005; Newell, Liu, Mayer-Kress, 2001; Thelen & Smith, 1994). These short-term experiences with performing tasks that require precise timing of movement (e.g., road crossing, ball catching, and obstacle avoidance) likely accumulate over time to create long-term changes in the perception—action system. At this point, however, it is not known how much experience is required to create these lasting changes. Our previous work examining how constant and variable practice impacts gap interception skills suggests that children are much less adept than adults at precisely zeroing in on which perceptual invariants are relevant to optimal task performance (Chihak et al., 2010). Children may require significant amounts of practice with dynamic perception—action tasks to develop sensitivity to these higher-order perceptual invariants (e.g., constant bearing angle).

Note that brain development and movement experience must work hand in hand to produce change in the perception—action system. Much like the reciprocal relationship between perception and action, developmental change in brain structures makes new experiences with performing actions possible and experience with performing actions provides input necessary to make further brain development possible. An important question for future work is to understand how such interactions between brain development and movement experience produce the kinds of changes we see in the perception—action system.

10. IMPLICATIONS FOR ROAD-CROSSING SAFETY

As we noted at the beginning of this chapter, a major goal of this program of research is to better understand the risk factors for injuries and fatalities involving child pedestrians and bicyclists. Although a multitude of factors likely contribute to such injuries and fatalities, our work shows that immature perceptual-motor skills and impaired inhibitory control are risk factors for collisions while crossing roads. Of particular importance are the findings that children's gap choices and movement timing are less well matched than those of adults, and that children with poorer inhibitory control also exhibit less precise movement timing skills. What implications do these findings have for prevention? One approach to intervention is to improve children's movement timing skills by teaching them to more tightly time their entry into the gap. As noted earlier, however, movement timing skill may require considerable practice to improve and have limited malleability due to brain maturation constraints. As such, this approach may not be a useful target for intervention.

Another approach to intervention is to improve children's gap decisions by teaching them to choose larger gaps. We believe that this may be a more useful approach for improving children's road-crossing safety, both for typically developing children and for children with impairments in inhibitory control (e.g., children with ADHD). We have already seen in our work that older children seem to spontaneously adopt this strategy, which allows them to compensate for their poorer movement timing skills (Grechkin et al., 2013; O'Neal et al., 2018). We have recently been exploring ways to use computer-generated agents as road-crossing partners, which can be programmed to only choose large gaps for crossing (Jiang et al., 2018). Providing children with experience crossing roads with "safe" virtual peers may be a useful technique for training children to choose larger gaps. Other work by Schwebel et al. (2008) has shown that virtual reality can be an effective tool for training road-crossing skills in children.

11. CONCLUSIONS

This program of research provides a fine-grained picture of the development of movement timing skills in road crossing, and how the ability to tightly link decisions and actions changes throughout development. The prolonged developmental course of movement timing skills may be particularly important for explaining continued risk for pedestrian and cyclist injuries in early adolescence, especially in challenging situations such as high-density traffic. More generally, this work informs our understanding of development by showing how gradual, continuous change in even basic perception—action skills occurs well into adolescence (Plumert et al., 2007). This is consistent with other work showing the same kinds of slow, gradual change into early adolescence in areas such as spoken word recognition (Rigler et al., 2015), face perception (Baudouin, Gallay, Durand, & Robichon, 2010; de Heering, Rossion, & Maurer, 2012), and object recognition (Jüttner, Wakui, Petters, Kaur, & Davidoff, 2013), as well as memory for location (Plumert, 2008). Unlike the dramatic developmental changes seen in infancy and early childhood when skills first come on line, this kind of gradual developmental change appears critical for the fine-tuning of the system. Without such fine-tuning, cognitive and perceptual systems would not be able to function at adult levels. Further work is needed across all domains of cognitive and perceptual development to understand the mechanisms underlying this kind of developmental change.

ACKNOWLEDGMENTS

The authors are Jodie M. Plumert, Professor of Psychological and Brain Sciences, and Joseph K. Kearney, Professor of Computer Science. For correspondence concerning this article, contact Jodie M. Plumert at jodie-plumert@uiowa.edu. This research was supported by grants from the National Institute of Child Health and Human Development (R01-HD052875), the National Science Foundation (BCS-1251694, CNS-0750677, CNS-1305131, EIA-0130864, IIS 00−02535), the U.S. Department of Transportation, Research and Innovative Technology Administration (Prime DFDA No. 20.701, Award No. DTRT13-G-UTC53), and the National Center for Injury Prevention and Control/Centers for Disease Control and Prevention (R49/CCR721682, R49/CE001167).

REFERENCES

Acton, C., Tomas, S., Nixon, J., Clark, R., Pitt, W., & Battistutta, D. (1995). Children and bicycles: What is really happening? Studies of fatal and non-fatal bicycle injury. *Injury Prevention, 1*, 86−91.

Adolph, K. E. (2008). Learning to move. *Current Directions in Psychological Science, 17*, 213−218.

Adolph, K.E., Berger, S.A. (2006). Motor development. In W. Damon & R. Lerner (Series Eds) & D. Kuhn & R. S. Siegler (Vol Eds), *Handbook of child psychology: Vol 2: Cognition, perception, and language* (6th ed.). New York: Wiley, pp. 161−213.

Allman, M. J., & Meck, W. H. (2012). Pathophysiological distortions in time perception and timed performance. *Brain, 135*, 656−677.

Ashbaugh, S. J., Macknin, M. L., & VanderBrug Medendorp, S. (1995). The Ohio bicycle injury study. *Clinical Pediatrics, 34*(5), 256−260.

Babu, S., Grechkin, T., Chihak, B., Ziemer, C., Kearney, J., Cremer, J., et al. (2011). An immersive virtual peer for studying social influences on child cyclists' road-crossing behavior. *IEEE Transactions on Visualization and Computer Graphics, 17*, 14−25.

Barton, B. K., & Schwebel, D. C. (2007). The roles of age, gender, inhibitory control, and parental supervision in children's pedestrian safety. *Journal of Pediatric Psychology, 32*(5), 517−526.

Baudouin, J. Y., Gallay, M., Durand, K., & Robichon, F. (2010). The development of perceptual sensitivity to second-order facial relations in children. *Journal of Experimental Child Psychology, 107*, 195−206.

Berthier, N. E., Rosenstein, M. T., & Barto, A. G. (2005). Approximate optimal control as a model for motor learning. *Psychological Review, 112*, 329−346.

Camachon, C., Jacobs, D. M., Huet, M., Buekers, M., & Montagne, G. (2007). The role of concurrent feedback in learning to walk through sliding doors. *Ecological Psychology, 19*(4), 367−382.

Chaddock, L., Neider, M. B., Lutz, A., Hillman, C. H., & Kramer, A. F. (2012). Role of childhood aerobic fitness in successful street crossing. *Medicine and Science in Sports and Exercise, 44*(4), 749−753.

Chihak, B. J., Grechkin, T. Y., Kearney, J. K., Cremer, J. F., & Plumert, J. M. (2014). How children and adults learn to intercept moving gaps. *Journal of Experimental Child Psychology, 122*, 134−152. https://doi.org/10.1016/j.jecp.2013.12.006.

Chihak, B. J., Plumert, J. M., Ziemer, C. J., Babu, S., Grechkin, T., Cremer, J. F., et al. (2010). Synchronizing self and object movement: How child and adult cyclists intercept moving gaps in a virtual environment. *Journal of Experimental Psychology: Human Perception & Performance, 36*, 1535−1552.

Connelly, M. L., Conaglen, H. M., Parsonson, B. S., & Isler, R. B. (1998). Child pedestrians' crossing gap thresholds. *Accident Analysis & Prevention, 30*, 443−453.

Demetre, J. D., Lee, D. N., Pitcairn, T. K., Grieve, R., Thompson, J. A., & Ampofo-Boatneg, K. (1992). Errors in young children's decisions about traffic gaps: Experiments with roadside simulations. *Br J Psychol, 83*, 189–202.

Diamond, A. (2000). Close interrelation of motor development and cognitive development and of the cerebellum and prefrontal cortex. *Child Development, 71*, 44–56.

Dommes, A., Cavallo, V., Dubuisson, J. B., Tournier, I., & Vienne, F. (2014). Crossing a two-way street: Comparison of young and old pedestrians. *Journal of Safety Research, 50*, 27–34.

Dommes, A., Le Lay, T., Vienne, F., Dang, N. T., Beaudoin, A. P., & Do, M. C. (2015). Towards and explanation of age-related difficulties in crossing a two-way street. *Accident Analysis & Prevention, 85*, 229–238.

Ellis, L. K., & Rothbart, M. K. (2001). Revision of the Early Adolescent Temperament Questionnaire. In *Poster presented at the 2001 Biennial Meeting of the Society for Research in Child Development, Minneapolis, Minnesota.*

Fajen, B. R. (2013). Guiding locomotion in complex, dynamic environments. *Frontiers in Behavioral Neuroscience,* 7(85), 1–15.

Gibson, J. J. (1979). *The ecological approach to visual perception*. Boston, MA: Houghton Mifflin.

Grechkin, T. Y., Chihak, B. J., Cremer, J. F., Kearney, J. K., & Plumert, J. M. (2013). Perceiving and acting on complex affordances: How children and adults bicycle across two lanes of opposing traffic. *Journal of Experimental Psychology: Human Perception & Performance, 39*, 23–36.

Guth, D., Ashmead, D., Long, R., Wall, R., & Ponchillia, P. (2005). Blind and sighted pedestrians' judgments of gaps in traffic at roundabouts. *Human Factors, 47*, 314–331.

Hamann, C., Peek-Asa, C., Lynch, C. F., Ramierz, M., & Torner, J. (2013). Burden of hospitalizations for bicycling injuries by motor vehicle involvement: United States, 2002 to 2009. *Journal of Trauma and Acute Care Surgery, 75*(5), 870–876.

de Heering, Rossion, B., & Maurer, D. (2012). Developmental changes in face recognition during childhood: Evidence from upright and inverted faces. *Cognitive Development, 27*, 17–27.

Hoffman, E. R., Payne, A., & Prescott, S. (1980). Children's estimates of vehicle approach times. *Human Factors, 22*, 235–240.

von Hofsten, C. (2007). Action in development. *Developmental Science, 10*, 54–60.

Huet, M., Jacobs, D. M., Camachon, C., Missenard, O., Gray, R., & Montagne, G. (2011). The education of attention as explanation of variability of practice effects: Learning the final approach phase in a flight simulator. *Journal of Experimental Psychology: Human Perception and Performance, 37*(6), 1841–1854.

Injury Prevention & Control, Injury Prevention & Control: Data & Statistics (WISQARS). Centers for Disease Control and Prevention. Retrived from http://www.cdc.gov/injury/wisqars/index.html.

Ivry, R. B., & Keele, S. W. (1989). Timing functions of the cerebellum. *Journal of Cognitive Neuroscience, 1*, 136–152.

Jiang, Y., O'Neal, E. E., Rahimian, P., Yon, J. P., Plumert, J. M., & Kearney, J. K. (2018). *Joint action in a virtual environment: Crossing roads with risky vs. safe human and agent partners* (Manuscript submitted for publication).

Jüttner, M., Wakui, E., Petters, D., Kaur, S., & Davidoff, J. (2013). Developmental trajectories of part-based and configural object recognition in adolescence. *Developmental Psychology, 49*, 161–176.

Keele, S. W., & Ivry, R. B. (1990). Does the cerebellum provide a common computation for diverse tasks? A timing hypothesis. *Annals of the New York Academy of Sciences, 608*, 179–211.

Lee, D. N., Young, D. S., & McLaughlin, C. M. (1984). A roadside simulation of road crossing for children. *Ergonomics, 12*, 1271–1281.

Loomis, J. M., Blascovich, J. J., & Beall, A. C. (1999). Immersive virtual environment technology as a basic research tool in psychology. *Behavior Research Methods, Instruments, & Computers, 31*, 557–564.

Louveton, N., Bootsma, R. J., Guerin, P., Berthelon, C., & Montagne, G. (2012). Interception crossing considered as intercepting a moving traffic gap: Effects of task and environmental constraints. *Acta Psychologica, 141*, 287–294.

Louveton, N., Montagne, G., Berthelon, C., & Bootsma, R. J. (2012). Intercepting a moving traffic gap while avoiding collision with lead and trail vehicles: Gap-related and boundary-related influences on drivers' speed regulations during approach to an intersection. *Human Movement Science, 31*, 1500–1516.

Mayhew, D. R., Simpson, H. M., & Pak, A. (2003). Changes in collision rates among novice drivers during the first months of driving. *Accident Analysis & Prevention, 35*(5), 683–691.

Montagne, G., Buekers, M., Camachon, C., de Rugy, A., & Laurent, M. (2003). The learning of goal-directed locomotion: A perception–action perspective. *Quarterly Journal of Experimental Psychology, 56A*(3), 551–567.

Morrongiello, B. A., Corbett, M., Milanovic, M., Pyne, S., & Vierich, R. (2015). Innovations in using virtual reality to study how children cross streets in traffic: Evidence for evasive action skills. *Injury Prevention, 21*, 266–270.

National Center for Statistics and Analysis. (2017). *Children: 2015 data. (Traffic Safety Facts. Report No. DOT HS 812 383)*. Washington, DC: National Highway Traffic Safety Administration.

Newell, K. M., Liu, Y. T., & Mayers-Kress, G. (2001). Time scales in motor learning and development. *Psychological Review, 108*, 57–82.

Nikolas, M., Elmore, A., Franzen, L., O'Neal, E., Kearney, J. K., & Plumert, J. M. (2016). Risky bicycling behavior among youth with and without attention-deficit hyperactivity disorder. *Journal of Child Psychology and Psychiatry, 57*, 141–148. https://doi.org/10.1111/jcpp.12491.

O'Neal, E. E., Jiang, Y., Franzen, L. J., Rahimian, P., Yon, J. P., Kearney, J. K., et al. (2018). Changes in perception–action tuning over long time scales: How children and adults perceive and act on dynamic affordances when crossing roads. *Journal of Experimental Psychology: Human Perception and Performance, 44*, 18–26.

Pitcairn, T. K., & Edelmann, T. (2000). Individual differences in road crossing ability in young children and adults. *British Journal of Psychology, 91*, 391–410.

Plumert, J. M. (2008). Children's thinking is not just about what's in the head: Understanding the organism and environment as a unified system. In R. V. Kail (Ed.), *Advances in child development and behavior* (pp. 373–417). San Diego, CA: Academic Press.

Plumert, J. M., Kearney, J. K., & Cremer, J. F. (2004). Children's perception of gap affordances: Bicycling across traffic-filled intersections in an immersive virtual environment. *Child Development, 75*, 1243–1253.

Plumert, J. M., Kearney, J. K., & Cremer, J. F. (2007). Children's road crossing: A window into perceptual-motor development. *Current Directions in Psychological Science, 16*, 255–258.

Plumert, J. M., Kearney, J. K., Cremer, J. F., Recker, K. M., & Strutt, J. (2011). Changes in children's perception-action tuning over short time scales: Bicycling across traffic-filled intersections in a virtual environment. *Journal of Experimental Child Psychology, 108*, 322–337.

Rigler, H., Farris-Trimble, A., Greiner, L., Walker, J., Tomblin, J. B., & McMurray, B. (2015). The slow developmental time course of real-time spoken word recognition. *Developmental Psychology, 51*, 1690–1703.

Rivara, F. P., & Aitken, M. (1998). Prevention of injuries to children and adolescents. *Advances in Pediatrics, 45*, 37–72.

Savelsbergh, G., Rosengren, K., van der Kamp, J., & Verheul, M. (2003). Catching action development. In G. Savelsbergh, K. Davids, J. van der Kamp, & S. J. Bennett (Eds.), *Development of movement co-ordination in children: Applications in the fields of ergonomics, health sciences, and sport* (pp. 191–212). New York: Routledge.

Schwebel, D. C., Gaines, J., & Severson, J. (2008). Validation of virtual reality as a tool to understand and prevent child pedestrian injury. *Accident Analysis & Prevention, 40*, 1394–1400.

Sonuga-Barke, E., Bitsakou, P., & Thompson, M. (2010). Beyond the dual pathway model: Evidence for the dissociation of timing, inhibitory, and delay-related impairments in attention-deficit/hyperactivity disorder. *Journal of the American Academy of Child & Adolescent Psychiatry, 49*, 345–355.

Steinberg, L. (2005). Cognitive and affective development in adolescence. *Trends in Cognitive Sciences, 9*, 69–74.

Stevens, E., Plumert, J. M., Cremer, J. F., & Kearney, J. K. (2013). Preadolescent temperament and risky behavior: Bicycling across traffic-filled intersections in a virtual environment. *Journal of Pediatric Psychology, 38*, 285–295.

te Velde, A. F., van der Kamp, J., Barela, J. A., & Savelsbergh, G. J. P. (2005). Visual timing and adaptive behavior in a road-crossing simulation study. *Accident Analysis & Prevention, 37*, 399–406.

Thelen, E., & Smith, L. B. (1994). *A dynamic systems approach to the development of cognition and action*. Cambridge, MA: MIT Press.

Thompson, D. C., Thompson, R. S., & Rivara, F. P. (1990). Incidence of bicycle-related injuries in a defined population. *American Journal of Public Health, 80*, 1388–1390.

Tiemeier, H., Lenroot, R. K., Greenstein, D. K., Tran, L., Pierson, R., & Giedd, J. N. (2010). Cerebellum development during childhood and adolescence: A longitudinal morphometric MRI study. *Neuroimage, 49*, 63–70.

Valera, E. M., Spencer, R. M. C., Zeffiro, T. A., Makris, N., Spencer, T. J., Faraone, S. V., et al. (2010). Neural substrates of impaired sensorimotor timing in adult attention-deficit/hyperactivity disorder. *Biological Psychiatry, 68*, 359–367.

Wachtel, A., & Lewiston, D. (1994). Risk factors for bicycle-motor vehicle collisions at intersections. *ITE (Institute of Transportation Engineers) Journal, 64*(9), 30–35.

Wang, Y., & Nihan, N. L. (2004). Estimating the risk of collisions between bicycles and motor vehicles at signalized intersections. *Accident Analysis & Prevention, 36*, 313–321.

Wills, K. E., Christoffel, K. K., Lavigne, J. V., Tanz, R. R., Schofer, J. L., Donovan, M., et al. (1997). Patterns and correlates of supervision in child pedestrian injury. *Journal of Pediatric Psychology, 22*, 89–104.

Young, D. S., & Lee, D. N. (1987). Training children in road crossing skills using a roadside simulation. *Accident Analysis & Prevention, 19*, 327–341.

Zelaznik, H. N., Vaughn, A. J., Green, J. T., Smith, A. L., Hoza, B., & Linnea, K. (2012). Motor timing deficits in children with attention-deficit/hyperactivity disorder. *Human Movement Science, 31*, 255–265. https://doi.org/10.1016/j.humov.2011.05.003.

FURTHER READING

Plumert, J. M., & Kearney, J. K. (2014b). How do children perceive and act on dynamic affordances in crossing traffic-filled roads? *Child Development Perspectives, 8*, 207–212. https://doi.org/10.1111/cdep.12089.

Schwebel, D. C., Plumert, J. M., & Pick, H. L. (2000). Integrating basic and applied developmental research: A new model for the twenty-first century. *Child Development, 71*, 222–230.

te Velde, A. F., van der Kamp, J., & Savelsbergh, G. J. P. (2008). Five- to twelve-year-olds' control of movement velocity in a dynamic collision avoidance task. *British Journal of Developmental Psychology, 26*(1), 33–50.

CHAPTER SEVEN

Physical Growth, Body Scale, and Perceptual-Motor Development

Karl M. Newell*[,1] and Michael G. Wade[§]
*Department of Kinesiology, University of Georgia, Athens, GA, United States
[§]School of Kinesiology, University of Minnesota, Minneapolis, MN, United States
[1]Corresponding author: E-mail: Kmn1@uga.edu

Contents

Abstract

In this chapter we consider from the theoretical framework of the ecological approach to perception and action, the relations between physical growth and body scale in the context of children's perceptual-motor development. Body scale and the timescale of its change through growth are shown to relate to the emergence and dissolution of the fundamental skills in infancy, the perception of what an environment affords functionally for action, together with the emergent pattern of movement coordination. A central issue in typical and atypical motor development is the mapping of the timescale of adaptive change in the acquisition of perceptual-motor skill to the accompanying timescale of change in physical growth.

Advances in Child Development and Behavior, Volume 55
ISSN 0065-2407
https://doi.org/10.1016/bs.acdb.2018.04.005

1. PHYSICAL GROWTH, BODY SCALE, AND PERCEPTUAL-MOTOR DEVELOPMENT

Child development encompasses change in many different facets of behavior and biology. None are perhaps so obvious to the eye of an observer than the progressions of physical growth and perceptual-motor skill that occur in the formative years of life. It is the case, however, the physical growth (Malina, Bouchard, & Bar-Or, 2004) and perceptual-motor skill acquisition (Haywood & Getchell, 2009; Sugden & Wade, 2013) have been studied in a relatively independent way in the field of child development. This is in spite of the fact that physical growth leads to scale changes in the body form at each moment in time in the life span that a child engages in action. Growth is considered here at the whole-body level though it is related to change in both principle and practice at the level of the organ, cell, and molecule (Malina et al., 2004; Shuttleworth, 1939; Tanner, 1962).

In our view, the theme of this chapter is timely because there is now a theoretical framework and considerable accompanying experimental study of the relations between physical growth, body scale, and perceptual-motor skill. The central theoretical contribution toward this approach has been and still is the emerging framework of the ecological approach to perception and action (Michaels & Carello, 1981; Turvey, 1992). This framework draws on Gibson's (1979) theory of direct perception and the biophysical perspective of Bernstein (1967, 1996) to address the issue of movement coordinative structures and control of the system degrees of freedom. These theoretical influences on perception and action have articulated the beginnings of a principled role for body scale in movement skills, including that of children's perceptual-motor development. Cognitive theory has also recognized the problem with a contrasting consideration through what is called embodied cognition (Clark, 1997), but it has had little to say directly about physical growth, body scale, and perceptual-motor skill development.

Here, we consider the core theoretical developments in the relations between physical growth, body scale, and perceptual-motor skills in the context of children's motor development. The first section examines the pattern of physical growth in children and its influence on the mechanical constraints and the development of the fundamental movement forms. We discuss the central issue of the relation of the timescale of growth to the timescale of change in the acquisition of a perceptual-motor skill

(Newell & Liu, 2014; Newell, Liu, & Mayer-Kress, 2009), the importance of which is enhanced and more apparent in periods of rapid growth (e.g., adolescence). The second section examines the complementary notion of the information for action in the fundamental perceptual-motor skills that emerge from the evolving fit (niche) of the growing child with the environment. Throughout, we discuss some practical and clinical issues arising from the consideration of body scale more broadly in child development. These include childhood obesity, clumsiness in adolescence, scaling of equipment for perceptual-motor skills, and the broader layout of the environmental context for safe play, physical activity, and sport.

2. PHYSICAL GROWTH AND BODY SCALE PATTERNS IN CHILD DEVELOPMENT

There is a longstanding tradition in child development to describe the fundamental properties of postnatal body scale and physical growth patterns in terms of population indices of children's height and weight from birth through to maturity. The most recognized and authoritative charts of children's physical growth are those of the US Centers for Disease Control (CDC—Centers for Disease Control and Prevention, 2000) and the World Health Organization (WHO, 1995). There are important similarities and differences between these widely used approaches to children's growth charts in terms of the representative subject population, together with how the data were collected and depicted. Indeed, there is still considerable discussion, if not debate, as to what on the surface seems a straightforward problem of a valid description of body scale in child development and its change over time.

Fig. 1 shows a single representative example of these growth charts from the WHO (1995) in the form of the height for age (5–19 years) in boys and girls, independently. The figure shows what is generally interpreted as continuous nonlinear growth in child development and provides the percentile cutoffs, in addition to the mean for each age group. This graphical representation of children's physical growth depicted as variable by age represents the standard approach in growth charts. A comprehensive summary of the many details of description and inference arising from the charting of children's physical growth is presented in Malina et al. (2004).

It is axiomatic that the height and weight of an individual tend to be correlated to some greater or lesser degree. It follows, therefore, that there

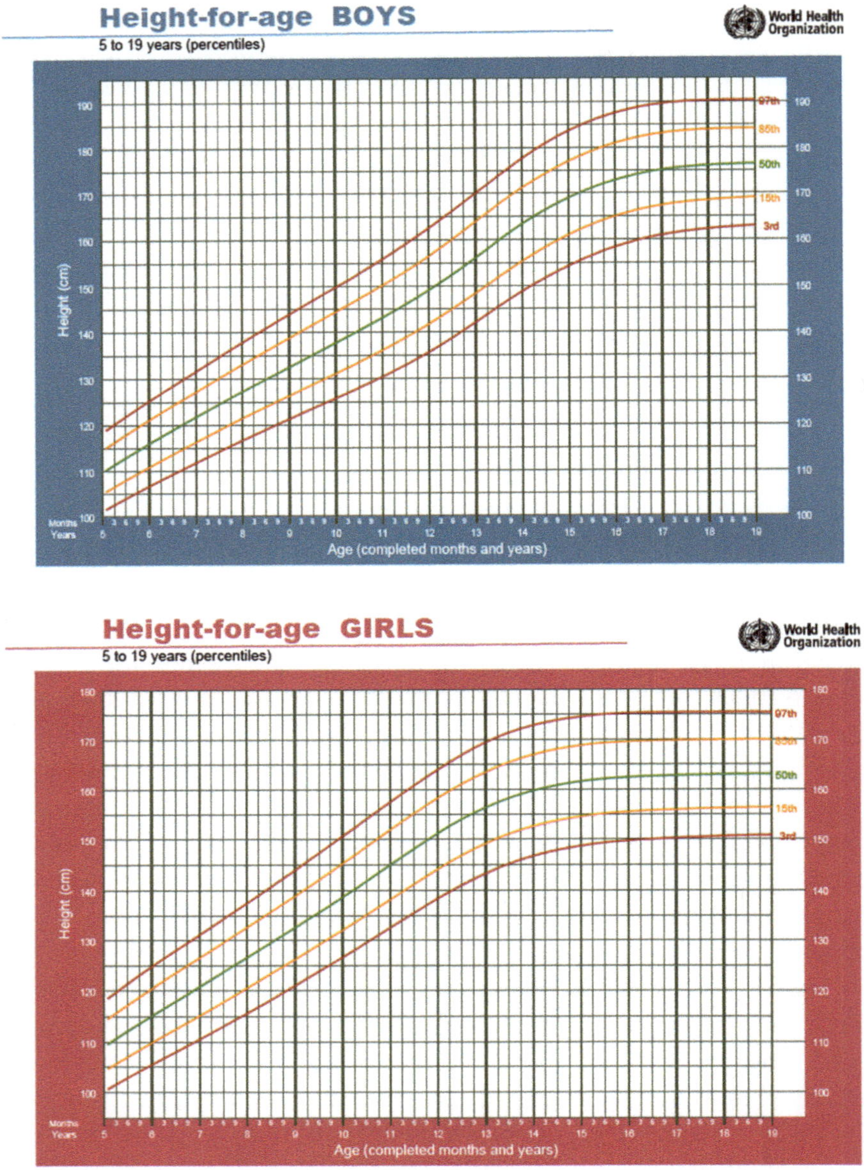

Figure 1 Height-for-age boys/girls (5–19 years). *Adapted with permission from World Health Organization. (1995). Physical status: The use and interpretation of anthropometry. Geneva: World Health Organization, Technical Report series, No. 854.*

have been several efforts to produce formal scaling links of their relation to provide a more complete characterization of the growing three-dimensional body form in child development. The height and weight indices have been combined in a ratio following the discussion of Adolphe Quetelet (1842) that, in effect, provides an index of weight per unit height.

Indeed the charting of the ratio of children's height and weight in terms of what is now known as the body mass index (BMI) has increasingly become the worldwide gold standard for describing body size and children's growth patterns in development. BMI is defined as body mass/body height^2 and expressed in units of Kg/m^2. A BMI of 19 and 25, respectively, is typically used as cutoffs to characterize under- and overweight but there are many considerations and caveats to the validity and reliability of these criteria (Malina et al., 2004). The BMI is relatively straightforward to calculate even in clinical health settings but the method has its limitations for understanding the change of body size and form over time. Moreover, it is clear that the worldwide obesity crisis is having an as yet not fully understood influence on the population norms for children's height and weight and their health implications.

Another human biology approach to body form and scale is the tripartite somatotype scheme of Sheldon, Stevens, and Tucker (1940). This scheme has been used, particularly in the physical activity community, to represent body size and shape of children and adults in a way that has reference to the constructs of fatness, thinness, and muscularity. Sheldon proposed to characterize the body form through what was known as the different germ layers of embryonic development, namely: endomorph (digestive system—softness, roundness, fat), mesomorph (muscle and heart—bony, rugged, muscularity), and ectomorph (skin and nervous system—linear fragility), and following Galton (1904) he linked this level of description to the behavior and personality of the individual. The somatotype classification thus involves the measurement of more dimensions of body form than the more popularly used BMI. It is based on a three-category assessment of the body dimensions with each on a scale of 1—7. Petersen (1967) has developed an atlas of growth charts for somatotyping children in the Sheldon framework.

It is relevant to the focus of this chapter that the somatotype characterization of the body form accounts for a modest amount of variance in predicting in which Olympic event an individual athlete may perform (Malina et al., 2004). This finding implies a relation between somatotype profile and high-level achievement in the performance of a particular set of perceptual-motor tasks. Furthermore, the level of the correlation within a sport tends to be activity or sport specific. Thus, the somatotype analysis indicates that the effect of body scale on performance and skill is task specific.

Our purpose here, however, is not to reiterate the many established operational details and nuances of interpretation of the physical growth charts for child development (Malina et al., 2004). Rather, we draw on them to the degree necessary to remind us of the central relevant features of children's growth as backdrop to the interpretation of their influence on body scale and perceptual-motor skill development. We now emphasize a few key inferences from the growth charts that inform about the role of body scale in children's perceptual-motor development and that we use and build on throughout the remainder of the chapter.

First, growth curves such as those shown in Fig. 1 are based on averaged data of a population age group and are often reflective of only cross-sectional data. It is well established that averaging data over time, such as in learning curves (Newell, Liu, & Mayer-Kress, 2001), can produce a mean trajectory that does not represent the pathway of change of any of the participants. This same principle on the limitations of averaging data also holds for understanding the timescales of change in children's physical growth trajectories.

Second, as we noted previously with respect to Fig. 1, the growth curve trajectories imply that the change in height and weight in development is continuous. There has been an emerging body of evidence led by Michelle Lampl's research program that challenges this fundamental assumption about the continuity of the trajectory of change in a way that has significant relevance for the development of the mapping of perception and action (Lampl, 2009, 2012; Lampl, Veldhuis, & Johnson, 1992). A central point of contrast to the traditions of the CDC and WHO growth charts is that the Lampl analysis of the change in body stature is over a much shorter timescale of observation (as short as every 24 h). The outcome from this finer grained analysis of infant growth is that discontinuities and saltations (abrupt variations) in standard body size indices were observed. Importantly, this shorter timescale for measuring growth gets closer to the timescale of relevance for linking to movement coordination and control in the development of perceptual-motor skills. It also follows as a consequence that the continuity/discontinuity debate of growth in child development needs to be investigated at the level of shorter timescale observations of individual data (Newell et al., 2009).

Third, the rate of change in growth and motor development is nonlinear (nonproportional) from birth to maturity (Malina et al., 2004; Savelsbergh, van der Maas, & van Geert, 1999). As a consequence, children do not remain at the same percentile of the population growth chart through the range of years of childhood. Furthermore, there are in essence two spurts within the overall growth trajectory from birth to maturity where there is an increment in the rate of change of body scale. These growth spurts are in the first 2 months of life and again during adolescence and are more readily seen by plotting the velocity of the respective growth curve over age.

Fourth, the growth trajectories through development are different for boys and girls. In general, these show that girls tend to mature earlier than boys as revealed in a range of developmental growth measures. The expected BMI trajectory for girls during the growth spurt (age 9—12 years) varies substantially depending on whether they are growing at the 10th or 85th percentile (CDC growth chart, 2000). For girls, the maximum annual change in weight and BMI is more than 100% greater at age 10 when comparing low versus high growth patterns.

The general height/weight growth data provide fundamental indices of the change in body scale with development but their interpretation tends to rest on an assumption of uniform relative growth across body segments and subsystems. The assumption of proportional change in the length and weight of the individual body segments (e.g., torso, legs, arms, head) does not, however, hold as we now discuss. The dynamic properties of nonlinear change in the evolving scale of body segments have relevance for understanding the movement coordination and control of children's body segments in perceptual-motor skill development.

2.1 Relative Size in Growth and Motor Development

Movement and performance outcome in physical activity, including the activities of daily living, are significantly determined by body scale (McMahon & Bonner, 1983). Moreover, change in the size and form of the body during childhood is a foundational factor in the change of movement organization and its outcome in physical activities (Malina et al., 2004; Newell, 1984; Riddiford-Harlan, Steele, & Baur, 2006). Nevertheless, there has been little study of the effects of the informational and mechanical constraints that arise from physical growth in children's development (Lebiedowska & Polisiakiewicz, 1997; Newell & Cesari, 1998).

One limiting factor to the development of understanding in this research area is that many studies on the effect of body scale on performance are driven by the allometric assumption of a standardized ratio of change in the physical properties of the sensorimotor system (McMahon & Bonner, 1983), an assumption that is now also being additionally challenged by the changes in body form due to the obesity epidemic. These obesity-induced adaptations include, in addition to general body weight gain, changes in body composition, relative growth size, and challenges to the scaling of muscle strength to body length and mass.

One major influence of the change in the absolute and relative sizes of body segments is on the moment of inertia of each body segment (Jensen, 1981, 1986; Newell, 1984), and the resulting more global whole-body moment(s) of inertia from the movement system considered as a collective. Given the formula for the moment of inertia of each body part, it can be viewed as an index of its resistance to acceleration in movement. The index is of the form $y = ml^2$ where m is mass and l is the respective body segment length. It follows that the changing moment of inertia of body segments and the whole body during growth is an important problem for theories of movement and action to accommodate (Bernstein, 1967).

Significant changes in height, weight, and BMI occur in children's body scale and form during the growth spurt of adolescence (2000 http://www.cdc.gov/growthcharts). For example, average annual change in stature in boys and girls is more than 50% greater during the adolescent "growth spurt" than just prior to it. Thus, it is during adolescence that the more rapid rates of change in body scale and growth properties occur. This growth spurt is especially relevant in the context of the early work by Jensen (1981) who reported that even small changes in size (e.g., limb length) of the body can lead to significantly greater order of magnitude influences on the mechanical constraints (e.g., moment of inertia) of movement in physical activity due to the inherent relations of Newton's laws of motion. The effect of the change in the length of body segments has a great effect on the moment of inertia due to the squaring of the length term in the equation.

Jensen (1981) investigated the growth in the height and weight properties of adolescents over a 1-year time interval of growth and development. He showed that as a consequence of growth the moment of inertia of the centroidal transverse axis reflected individual increases from 12% to 57%

(mean 30.8%), while the increments for the longitudinal centroidal axis ranged from 8% to 92% (mean 33.5%). For most of the children the percent changes in moment of inertia far exceeded the percent change in age, height (mean 4.7%) and mass (mean 15.6%). Jensen proposed an alternative whole-body index that was the product of mass multiplied by the square of the standing height—a transformation of the BMI ratio. Jensen (1981) found no relation between body somatotype and the amount of change in the moment of inertia but this relational property deserves further experimental study.

The changing inertial constraints of the system due to physical growth in development are an evolving dynamic constraint to which the perceptual-motor system must continually adapt and compensate for in action. This challenge is present particularly during the major growth spurts due to the more rapid rate of growth change. The consequence of this change in system organization does not reside only at the mechanical level but also in terms of the perception of body-relevant information in action (as we take up in a subsequent section). The general consideration is that the functional and structural biology of the human system is evolving in a nonlinear way at all levels of analysis—whole body, organism, molecular, and cellular (Newell, 1984).

The growth charts for height and weight provide a basic understanding of growth at the macroscopic whole-body level of analysis, but it follows also that the strength of the respective muscle groups is also developing in ways to accommodate the evolving moments of inertia that follow growth. The cross section of muscle is usually taken as an index of strength and thus strength scales as a squared term to the linear increments of limb length. However, the mapping of strength to both height and weight in a developmentally relevant timescale is a poorly understood problem.

In general, it appears that the timescale of the increments of strength in development is often too slow for the increments of height and weight in the sense that it lags behind them. This is consistent with the nonproportional scaling of strength to body length and the greater level of change required to maintain the scaling relation of earlier performance before the growth spurt. A good example of this influence is in the decline in skill level that young elite gymnasts often show as they pass through puberty. It is hypothesized that the decline in performance is due in part to the failure to keep strength increments sufficient and on the appropriate timescale with changes in body length, mass, and the resulting moments of inertia.

2.2 Allometry—The Problem of Relative Size

Fig. 2 shows the often-reproduced schematic of Robbins et al. (1928) that strikingly drives home the magnitude of the problem of relative physical growth on mechanical constraints in child development. The figure reflects the changes in human form and proportions through the fetal and infant stages up to adulthood. Through growth and development the head and upper parts of the body become proportionately smaller, whereas the lower parts become correspondingly larger. The length of a newborn's head is about one-quarter of body height, whereas it is about one-eighth the height in the adult. Thus, not only does the absolute height and weight of the individual change during development but also the proportional size of given limbs or body features to the total body changes. Furthermore, the *rate or timescale* at which these changes occur also varies. For example, height and weight undergo transitory periods of fast and slow increases (Shuttleworth, 1939). These properties of relative growth in infancy are consistent with the finding that supporting the torso and head in young infants while sitting leads to earlier than typical age onset of reaching behavior (Carvalho, Tudella, Caljouw, & Savelsbergh, 2008; Out, van Soest, Savelsbergh, & Hopkins, 1998).

The paleontologist Edward Drinker Cope (1885) argued that from an evolutionary perspective the body size increases during phylogeny is a result of changes in body form. This became a recognized principle in

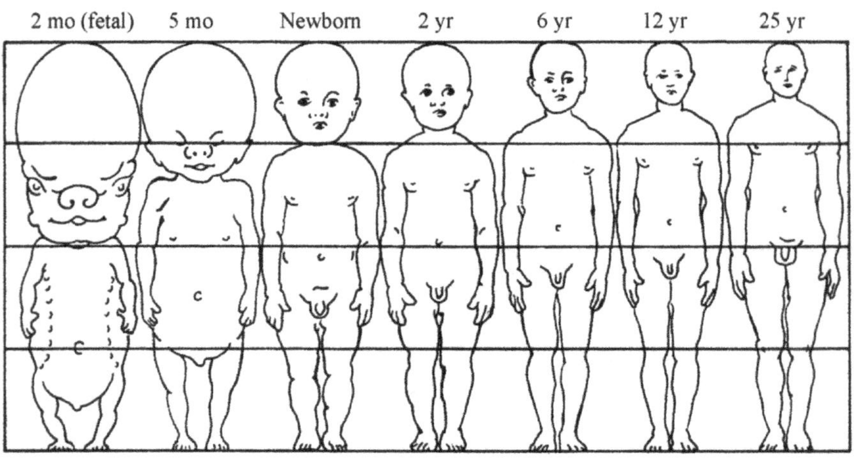

Figure 2 Changes in form and proportion of human body during fetal and postnatal life. *From Robins, W. J., Brody, S., Hogan, A. G., Jackson, C. M., & Greene, C. W. (1928). Growth. New Haven, Conn: Yale University Press.*

evolutionary biology and was later expressed with the development of power-law equations of the type, $y = mx^b$, with y representing say brain weight or heart volume, and x representing body size within a particular class of species. This scaling formulation in turn led to empirical studies on the effects of growth and body size differences in humans (Brody, 1945), organ weights, and somatic measurements in primates (Stahl, 1962).

The study of the dimensions of organisms and the effects of size on their proportions is called allometry (Gould, 1966). A working definition of allometry is still due to Huxley (1932) who proposed it to mean "relative growth." As an example, McMahon (1975) has likened the relative growth concept as two separate investment accounts growing ($$s) in a bank, at two different rates of interest. This begs the question as to what impact differential physical growth rates have on the development of movement coordination and control across the life span of humans, and especially in children and youth.

Allometric equations (*allometry* "by a different measure," compared with *isometry*, "geometric similarity by the same measure") are now an important methodology to make sense of the relative growth across a range of anatomical and physiological properties. Isometry or geographical similarity represents a directly proportional increase in two measures. For example arm spread is directly proportional to height as illustrated by da Vinci's drawing of "Vitruvian Man." While isometry may hold for humans both within and between ethnic populations the same does not hold for the wide range of quadrupeds. Here the principle of "elastic similarity" applies simply because both bone length and bone width must be factored into allometric equations to account for the wide range of sizes of a particular species. In the case of humans worldwide, this is less of a problem either within or between ethnic populations. In the development of newborns to adulthood, there is only a slight change in isometry the degree to which varies with the body segments being contrasted. The log–log framework is the classic formal method to show the scaling and critical points of the many properties of body and movement forms (see McMahon & Bonner, 1983 for many examples).

The major period of physical growth in boys and girls is from birth to puberty where the gender-based differences are relatively limited though persistent. Typically females are in advance of males when compared with the onset timing of the postpubertal changes across a range of physical properties such as height, weight, muscular development, and strength. It is during adolescence that the physical development of males rapidly outpaces females both in height, weight, and strength. Accordingly, motor skills requiring strength and speed produce an ever-widening gender gap in perceptual-motor performance in this age range (Malina et al., 2004).

2.3 Body Size, Form, and the Emergence of Perceptual-Motor Skills

When considering relative growth from an allometric perspective, it is perhaps obvious that young children showing different rates of anatomical and physiological development will experience differential success or failure in learning and performing a variety of perceptual-motor tasks. This is because changes in body size, including limb length and mass, are related to changes in strength and physiological capacity the influence of which depend on the demand characteristics of the specific task. In early classic infant motor development studies, Shirley (1931) and Bayley (1936) found that infants with proportionally longer legs who were not overweight tended to walk earlier than did children with proportionally shorter legs. Norval (1947) observed a similar relationship with newborns of the same weight in that an increase of body length of 1 inch led (on average) to an earlier onset (by 22 days) of voluntary walking. These early demonstrations of the role of body scale in channeling the mechanical constraints in the emergence of the fundamental infant movement patterns have not been emphasized and built on sufficiently in motor development.

In another striking and more contemporary example of body size effects on the appearance and dissolution of a fundamental movement pattern in infancy, Thelen and colleagues investigated the so-called "disappearing" step reflex in infancy. In a series of three experiments, and with a large sample of infants measured at 2–4 and 6 weeks of age, changes in body weight and frequency of stepping were recorded, and limb mass was manipulated by adding small weights to the babies' limbs (Thelen & Fisher, 1982; Thelen, Fisher, & Ridley-Johnson, 2002). The experiment counteracted the effects of mass by having the babies "step" while their lower body was submerged in water. The results led to the interpretation that the normal "disappearance" of the stepping reflex was a consequence of asynchronous development of muscle mass and bone length. The disappearance and subsequent reappearance of stepping was a direct consequence of changes in both muscle strength and changes in limb length. This experimental outcome provides a case study example of the strong role of body scale on the emergence and disappearance on the fundamental motor skills. Indeed, when provided with sufficient postural support or tactics to counter the mechanical or biomechanical constraints, infants demonstrated that the stepping reflex had not disappeared but was a consequence of relative changes (increments) in bone length and mass.

Similar results on the influence of body scale on the development of perceptual-motor skills have been forthcoming with respect to an infant's ability to reach and grasp objects and intercept moving objects. Babies at 4 months, with appropriate postural support, were reasonably accurate in reaching and contacting both stationary and slow-moving objects (cf. von Hofsten, 1979; von Hofsten & Lindhagen, 1979). Furthermore, newborns have been shown to purposely control their arm movements in the face of external forces and that development of visual control of arm movements is underway soon after birth (Van der Meer, van der Weel, & Lee, 1995).

A general expectation is that young babies afforded such support "know" the absolute distance of objects within reasonable limits but that their motor control often lacks the necessary precision. Skills requiring this level of coordination and control were not thought possible by the early scholars of children's motor development (Bayley, Gesell, Halverson, Shirley), particularly those driven by the tenets of maturation theory. In a very real sense the capacity for such skilled activity was dormant in the system until the physical growth (the strength and stability of postural support) of the individual "unlocked" the ability to execute such skilled activity.

These findings can be interpreted within Newell's (1986) framework of the confluence of task, performer, and environmental constraints as a dynamic interrelationship that influences skilled activity. Indeed, the differential rates of physical growth are a first-order consideration for control and coordination in the developing movement repertoire in infancy. Changes in physical growth are in essence the extrinsic aspects of body scale, which is the scaled relationship between rates of change of height, weight, and associated changes in strength, flexibility, and energy cost. These extrinsic aspects of body scale are influenced by both the mechanical and physiological changes in human growth and development.

3. THE EFFECTS OF OBESITY ON BODY SCALE

With an abundance of food available, especially in the western world, and the relative availability of inexpensive sources of protein, fats and carbohydrates, the incidence of obesity and type 2 diabetes is a major health problem both in North America and perhaps to a lesser extent in Europe (Ogden, 2016). Too much food intake that is not balanced by a sufficient level of physical activity has produced a situation where the typical allometric power-law equations can lack reliable predictive power because of increased weight and reduced relative strength that impacts an individual's BMI. In considering the role of obesity in skilled performance, careful consideration must be directed at the nature of the actual skill activity.

The epidemic of children's obesity has led to a significant, added set of physical constraints on children's performance and level of physical activity. The low levels of physical activity are strongly implicated as a causal factor in the epidemic of childhood obesity (Kaplan, Liverman, & Kraak, 2005; Troiano, Flegal, Kuczmarski, & Campbell, 1995). Indeed, the increased body weight and the associated changes in body shape provide additional constraints (e.g., mechanical inertial) to performance beyond those arising from the standard developmental growth properties of height and weight. These additional constraints and their influences on children's physical functioning and capacity have seen limited direct study (see D'Hondt, Deforche, De Bourdeaudhuij, & Lenoir, 2008; Riddiford-Harlan et al., 2006 for exceptions). This is a significant gap in our knowledge of children's physical capacity that has both theoretical and practical ramifications for engagement in physical activity and the general physical and health education of children and youth.

Castetbon and Andreyeva (2012) investigated the role of obesity and motor skills in a large sample of 4- to 6-year-old children in the United States. They reported no significant reduction in overall coordination and fine motor skills in obese young children. Motor performance was, however, adversely affected for those skills that were directly related to the need to transport or translate body position (so-called whole-body movement tasks). This finding perhaps comes as no surprise as it highlights the importance of designating what exactly defines the level of coordination required to perform the skill (Sugden & Wade, 2013).

Castetbon and Andreyeva (2012) used the Bruininks-Oseretsky test (BOTMI—Bruininks & Bruininks, 2007) and the Movement Assessment Battery for Children (MABC—Henderson, Sugden, & Barnett, 2007) to record overall skill level, along with building blocks and tracing for fine motor skills and skipping and jumping for gross motor skills. They concluded that skilled activities such as hopping in both boys and girls, and jump distance for girls were directly influenced by body weight. There was no significant relationship for the fine motor skills and body weight. This is a likely a reflection of a higher level of coordination and force output required of the selected gross motor skills, compared with the fine motor skill activities. The designation fine or gross motor skill in this study seems less to do with the level of coordination and more to do with the activity itself (e.g., small limb vs. large limb). For example, juggling might be a fine motor skill requiring a high level of coordination compared with tracing or building a tower out of 10 wooden blocks. Again, the nature of the task and coordination level involved is a key element in this kind of analysis.

There is growing evidence that an increment in BMI is positively correlated with changes in the movement pattern exhibited in the fundamental skills of locomotion, posture, and prehension (Hills & Parker, 1991; Pathare, Haskvitz, & Selleck, 2013). However, these negative effects of obesity on movement coordination, control, and skill may be mediated by the change in other body scale variables (e.g., mechanical and fitness) that also occur with changes in BMI. Thus, for example, efforts to determine the formal scaling impact of increments of growth in height and weight can be confounded by the parallel losses of relative strength (Challis, 2018).

King, Challis, Bartok, Costigan, and Newell (2012) investigated the influence of selected body scale (height, body mass, BMI), body composition (Body Fat %), mechanical (moment of inertia—MI), and strength (S) variables as predictors of the control of postural motion in adolescents. 125 healthy adolescents (65 boys, 60 girls) with a wide range of BMI (13.8–31.0 kg/m^2) performed a battery of tests that assessed body composition, anthropometry, muscular strength, and postural control. Multiple measures of postural motion variability were derived for analysis with body scale, mechanical, and strength variables separately for boys and girls. BMI, height, and body mass, considered both separately and collectively, were poor and/or inconsistent predictors of movement variability in all three postural tasks. However, the ratio of strength to whole-body moment of inertia showed the highest positive correlation to most postural variability measures in both boys and girls. These findings support the hypothesis that lower strength to mechanical constraint ratio compromises the robustness of the strength to body scale relation in movement and postural control of the developing child.

Finally, it should be remembered that adolescence is the critical period of development in which the prevalence of clumsiness increases with respect to the execution of skills requiring a range of coordination and control solutions (e.g., Keogh & Sugden, 1985; Sigmundsson, 2005). Clumsiness in adolescence is poorly documented or understood but it is logical to assume that it is related to the rapid growth spurt of this developmental period. A working hypothesis is that this accelerating change in body size during adolescence is more rapid than the capacity of the perceptual-motor system to adapt to these rapid growth changes. The net effect is an increased propensity for clumsiness in adolescence—a property further magnified by the additional constraints arising from the enhanced physical scaling properties of obesity (e.g., BMI changes).

It follows that the additional changes in body weight that arise from obesity are enhancing the torque and work demands on the evolving system of the adolescent to achieve the same physical performance and/or action goals (Challis, in press; Jensen, 1981). Thus, for example, increments in BMI beyond traditional standardized growth patterns provide an extra physical burden on the developing child, the effects of which are poorly understood. It should not go unnoticed that the dropout rate from participation in physical activity is greatest during the period of adolescence, though clearly other factors beyond the increased inertial constraints from body size, contribute to participation rates (Kaplan et al., 2005).

The current state of research on motor skills with respect to growth and development, especially pre- and postadolescence, is in need of at least two foci. First, a focus on an understanding of the contemporary limitations on children's motor skill abilities during the adolescent growth spurt, an area of research that has received only limited empirical attention. And second, a focus on isolating the relative contribution of standard physical growth and obesity factors on the changing inertial constraints on motor skills during the growth spurt in adolescence. In both of these lines of research, there will be a need to disentangle the relative effects of age and body size to move beyond the descriptive correlation of these variables that has driven most studies to date in this area.

4. GROWTH AND THE STRUCTURE—FUNCTION RELATION IN PERCEPTUAL-MOTOR SKILLS

The classic CDC and WHO growth charts for children from birth to maturity with their emphasis on the variables of height and weight lead to a consideration of the emerging physical structure of the developing body form. The word structure as used in this context is often taken, however, as a static property of body form perhaps because its timescale of change is relatively long or even viewed to be nonexistent over a given time interval. Thus, for example, the length of a child is typically assumed to be constant over short durations of observation (say 1 h or 1 day—though again consider Lampl, 2009, 2012).

Structural and functional constraints to human movement in action can be distinguished by their relative timescales of change (Kugler, 1986; Kugler, Kelso, & Turvey, 1980; Newell, 1984). Thus, structures at all levels of analysis of the system (whole body, organ, cellular, and molecular) should not be viewed as impervious to change but rather an element that undergoes a much slower rate of change than is typically associated with functional processes. Indeed, in traditional interpretations, biological structures at all levels of analysis are viewed to not change within the timescale of consideration. Height and weight are then in the short term interpreted as static structures although in the long term of the growth charts of development there is clearly change over time in the form of body size. Consider, for example, the significant increase in the height of astronauts after only 2—3 weeks in the gravity-free environment of space reflects the role of environmental constraints on biological structures. Relatedly, there is a smaller but robust difference in an individual's height on earth between the time of getting out of bed in the morning and going to bed at night.

Thus, the distinction between structure and function in the human body in action is relatively speaking, a qualitative distinction. The body scale growth indices are both structural and functional according to the timescale under consideration. This leads to the proposition that the body scale indices through growth not only reflect structural boundaries of the system but also provide related functional information for the individual in perceptual-motor skills (Kugler & Turvey, 1987; Kugler et al., 1980).

We conclude this section on children's growth and body scale with a quote from McMahon and Bonner (1983) as a lead in to the relation of form and function in the following section on body scale and information for action in the development of perceptual-motor skills.

> *Something tells the organism how much space it has. Goldfish remain small in a bowl but grow big to a relatively large dimension in a lake. Something quite parallel, we assume, tells the liver or muscle cell the size of the organism it lives in so it can adjust its metabolic rate and other biological activities accordingly, so that it can fit in with the other cells and do its job. It may be a physical truth that space is unbounded, but does not appear to be a biological*

> *truth. The fact that boundaries exist and may be perceived through unconscious mechanisms - the boundaries of the cell membrane, of the skin, of the fish tank- means that, as far as biology is concerned, space is bounded and finite. The body is subject to the dumb perceptions of bounded-ness and the limitations of size - the laws of scale - and this will never change. Among the special faculties of life, it appears that only imagination is unbounded (p. 243).*

5. BODY SCALE AND THE DEVELOPMENT OF PERCEPTION AND ACTION

There is a second perspective of body scaling that must be considered, namely what we refer to as "intrinsic" body scaling. That is, the individual child's ability to organize and scale her or his actions to the perceived demands of opportunities for action, referred to by Gibson (1979) as "affordances." This intrinsic body scaling is not tied directly to the biomechanical or physiological state of the individual at any specific point in the trajectory of growth and development, but reflects how the individual's movement ability relates to the opportunities for action present in the environment. Furthermore, it influences whether an action will be successful or not at any particular point in time. The development of this capacity is taken up in this section on body scale and information for perceptual-motor skills.

The central theoretical contribution toward the role of body scale in perceptual-motor skills has been the emerging framework of the ecological approach to perception and action (Michaels & Carello, 1981; Turvey, 1990, 1992; Turvey, Shaw, Reed, & Mace, 1981). As we noted in the introduction, the foundation for this framework draws on Gibson's (1979) theory of direct perception and the biophysical perspective of Bernstein (1967, 1996) in relation to movement coordinative structures and control of the system degrees of freedom. These theoretical influences on perception and action have provided the beginnings of a principled role for body scale in movement skills, including that of children's perceptual-motor development. This role encompasses the complementary influences of body scale on the perception of information for action and the form of the emergent movement coordination structure.

Our focus here is not to present the theory of the ecological approach to perception and action but to emphasize the core constructs that relate to the physical growth and body scale influence on the development of perceptual-motor skills. We have seen from the developmental literature that body scale and the timescale of its change (growth) relate to both the emergence and dissolution of the fundamental skills in infancy. Here the emphasis in the context of body scale is on the perception of what an environment affords an individual functionally for action, together with its influence on the emergent pattern of movement coordination. A synthesis of this approach in the context of perceptual-motor skills in typical and atypical child development may be found in Sugden and Wade (2013) and Wade and Kazeck (2018).

5.1 Ecological Approach to Perception and Action

The core radical idea of Gibson (1979) was that the perception of information for action is direct. That is, the information is available in the interactions with the environment—it needs to be detected and picked up by the perceptual systems rather than processed for meaning by a higher brain center. This leads to the position that the world is perceived without an elaboration of sensory input as held by the more traditional, and still-dominant information processing and cognitive theory approaches to perception. In Gibson's (1979) view, perception and action are intimately linked in a reciprocal fashion as reflected in the Gibson admonition that one perceives to move and one moves to perceive.

Gibson held that through action an individual perceives meaningful information from the environment sensitive to the invariant properties as revealed in ambient light, shadows, and the many other elements and contrasts that structure the world that we see. The theory holds that similar principles provide information from the other perceptual systems about the individual in the world (see Turvey & Carello, 1995, 2011 on dynamic touch). In particular, the perceptual system is sensitive to what the environment affords for action or what has been called the opportunities for action: namely, affordances. Thus, as Fig. 3 schematic from Michaels and Carello (1981) depicts, perception and action can only be considered with respect to each other and in terms of the environmental niche in which the individual resides. A key property in forming the niche in the perception—action interface is the body scale of the individual.

It is important to note that the affordance construct is functional in the sense of specifying the individual's opportunities for action. Thus, the structural properties of the layout of the world and those of the individual map to generate invariant informational properties that specify the potential actions available to the individual. In short, the information for action is present in the niche of the individual within the environment.

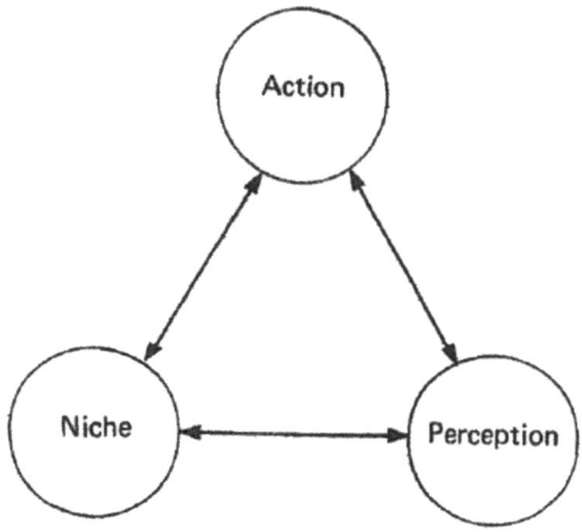

Figure 3 Schematic of the coimplicative relations among actions, perceptions, and the environmental niche. *Adapted with permission from Michaels, C. F., & Carello, C. (1981). Direct perception. Englewood Cliffs, NJ: Prentice-Hall, Fig 6-14.*

There are now variations in interpretation on the meaning of the affordance concept (cf. Chemero, 2009). At the heart of debate is the relation of an affordance to its dual construct "*effectivity*"—that is, the animal's disposition for action (Michaels & Carello, 1981; Turvey et al., 1981). Development plays a significant role in forming a child's "*effectivities*" but this has not been an empirical issue, although clearly, the child's dispositions for actions change as a function of growth and development.

A key principle of affordances is that the pickup of information about the individual relative to the environment is based on the invariant properties of the interactions that specify the affordances. This requires what Eleanor Gibson (1982, 1988) referred to as the education of attention to these invariant properties. Thus, engagement in activity can narrow the focus of attention to the invariant properties that can lead to a change in perceptual-motor behavior and what we know more generally as adaptation and learning. This provides the basis for Michaels and Isenhower (2008) to interpret learning also as direct within the ecological framework.

These principles lead to the role of information for perceptual-motor skill acquisition as body relative or body scaled in children's development. The pursuit of the informational invariants that specify an affordance has been the resulting perceptual-motor research agenda that we subsequently discuss. Experimentally this research on information for affordances, including a number of studies with young children, has addressed a broad range of physical activities or task constraints: walking, running, climbing, reaching, grasping, and aperture passing.

5.2 Task Constraints

The ecological approach to perception and action gives emphasis to the "fit" of the individual with the environment. In this view, the action system is defined over the organism, environment, and goal of the action. Expressed another way, it is the confluence of the constraints of organism, environment, and task that channel the information and movement dynamics in action (Newell & Jordan, 2007; Newell, 1986). These three categories of constraint coalesce to provide the boundary conditions at each level of analysis of the system in action.

Task constraints are reflected in an action goal and rules (where present, such as in some sports) that provide additional boundary conditions on how the goal of the action is to be realized. The task constraints can be self-determined by the individual as in play or by an external source of the environment in goal-directed activity. The task constraints of the movement outcome and the movement dynamics can also be time dependent or independent.

The affordance construct of Gibson (1979) provides information about the function for action and holds some parallels to the notion of the constraints of a task goal. This includes both the functional outcome (goal) of the action and the related movement coordinative structure. In some cases, such as in certain sports (e.g., gymnastics), the movement structure is the goal of the task.

5.3 Body-Scaled Information for Affordances

We now consider the experimental examination of the body-scaled information for affordances in representative perception–action examples. Emphasis is given where available to experiments with children in the context of the theory that was primarily investigated initially in studies with young adults. In general, the affordance studies support the powerful impact of information for action through development, including the motor abilities of infants. They also reflect the rapid gains in cognitive development as a function of achieving independent walking that in turn permits exploration of the environment—which has led to this transition being viewed as the single most critical milestone in motor development (Anderson et al., 2013).

Stair climbing and hurdle crossing. The classic experiment on information for affordances is that of Warren (1984) who studied in young adults the perceptual judgments of the climbability/nonclimbability of stairs that varied in their riser height. The critical riser height of climbable stairs was body scaled in that it mapped to an invariant ratio 0.88 R/L, where R is riser height and L is leg length. Furthermore, the visually preferred riser height was predicted by the minimal energy expenditure of climbing. This scaling relation holds parallels to the role of leg length in the equation from Alexander (1992) for the transition from walking to running.

Thus, the relative size of riser height to leg length was acting as a control parameter in moving the system through the dynamic landscape of stable/unstable states for the climbing task. The study was interpreted as providing evidence for the scale of the animal—environment fit as determining the information for affordances (climability/nonclimability) that also mapped to the minimum energy expenditure during climbing. Thus, riser height specifies the movement coordination mode that satisfies the same functional goal of climbing the stairs.

The results of the Warren (1984) experiments rest on leg length scaled to riser height as the control variable for the affordance. There are indications that limb length as a scalar breaks down in atypical populations where the mapping of the biological subsystems to body size is different than in the typical healthy undergraduate population. In this context, Konczak, Meeuwsen, and Cress (1992) found in older adults that the Warren (1984) equation (0.88 R/L) overestimated the critical point for transition (0.76 R/L) in determining the change of coordination mode in climbing stairs. Presumably the flexibility and strength of the older age group were less than that of the young adults even to the same leg length and this adaptation mediated the scaling ratio properties of the critical point of the transition of the movement coordinative structure. The Konczak et al. (1992) study shows that the body scaling of climbing mode with leg length rests on certain assumptions about the functional physiological capacity (e.g., strength, flexibility) of the system. Thus, it follows that leg length may be more realistically viewed as a beginning view to the scaling problem rather than a general account. We anticipate this limitation likely holds in the investigation of information for affordances with children, even at the level of the individual.

The intrinsic capacity concerning body-scaled behavior was the focus of an initial developmental investigation by Adolph, Eppler, and Gibson (1993) who examined infant crawlers (8.5-month-old infants) and early walkers (14-month-old infants) in deciding if they can walk downslopes of different angles or cross gaps of different widths. They found that infants learn to perceive affordances for locomotion over slopes and that learning may begin by the fine-tuning of exploratory activity. The crawlers were more hesitant in exploring the possibilities for action on the sloping walkway. Several studies have been conducted with children to investigate if there are developmental influences on the body-scaled information for affordances in stair climbing and similar locomotory (transport) activities (e.g., Kretch & Adolph, 2013; Ulrich, Thelen, & Niles, 1990).

Ulrich et al. (1990) investigated the body-scaled relation of riser height to body scale in infants who were beginning independent locomotion. The younger infants acted on the small and medium riser heights, whereas the older infants acted on all the sets of riser height studied. The findings were taken as early evidence that very young children perceive distinctions among the affordances offered by the environment and that their motor abilities and experiences are related to their perceptions. However, the anthropometric measures of the infant body segments did not scale robustly to the choice of riser step height, as in R/L ratio of the Warren (1984) study.

In a related but different activity to stair climbing, Kretch and Adolph (2013) investigated in infants the probability of falling and the severity of a potential fall in deciding whether to cross a bridge under different conditions (height, width). For crawlers and walkers the decision to cross (ascend/descend) the bridge was driven by the probability of falling—not the scale of the drop off. The findings support the conclusion that experienced crawlers and walkers perceive affordances for locomotion independent of the severity of a potential fall.

Aperture passing. Warren and Whang (1987) extended the stair climbing body scale protocol to the visual guidance of young adults walking through apertures of different widths (gaps) to determine the aperture/shoulder (A/S) ratio that marked the transition from frontal walking to walking with body rotation. An A/S ratio of 1.30 mapped to the critical point for body turning in young adults. They also determined that static monocular information was sufficient for judging passability of the aperture. It has since been shown that the passability of apertures is different when walking between two people versus two objects such that more space and greater caution are needed for a task constraint with human obstacles (Hakney, Cinelli, & Frank, 2015).

The role of children's body scale in aperture passing has been investigated by Franchak, Celano, and Adolph (2012) by determining young walker's sensitivity to the need to rotate the shoulders in passing through horizontal opening apertures of different widths and to the need to duck under (reduce functional height) in a vertical scaled opening. The verbal judgments of the children accurately predicted whether openings required gait modifications. The differences between horizontal and vertical openings were interpreted as the walkers accounting for the scaling decisions to body dimensions in walking. Franchak, van der Zalm, and Adolph (2010) found that the perceptual judgments of whether a doorway could be passed were enhanced when the children made judgments either before or after walking through doorways of varying widths. This led to the interpretation that action performance and experience facilitates affordance perception (see also Franchak & Adolph, 2012).

The aperture passing affordance paradigm has been extended to older children (6—14 years) and dynamic contexts including the affordance for crossing roads as a function of the size of the gap between moving cars (O'Neal, Plumert, McClure, & Schwebel, 2016; O'Neal et al., 2018). This protocol brings a temporal property to the affordance problem previously studied through *tau* gaps by David Lee and colleagues (Demetre et al., 1992; Young & Lee, 1987). The findings showed that children's ability to perceive and act on dynamic affordances undergoes a prolonged period of development and that attentional lapses contribute to risky decisions in the dynamic protocol. Witt and colleagues (Sugovic, Turk, & Witt, 2016) have reported obesity-related effects on children's perception of distance properties of the environment.

Finally, and in the context of a case study of a naturally evolving timescale property of body size, Franchak and Adolph (2013) investigated the adaptive responses of women through pregnancy to the perception of the passability of doorways of different apertures, including those that were no longer passable due to increments in belly girth and weight. The accuracy of passability estimates was very high and matched that of nonpregnant women. The accuracy of the passability estimates was also high in the artificial increment of girth by a "pregnant pack," though experience in the testing context facilitated recalibration of the action possibilities.

Reaching. The act of prehension provides natural contexts in which to investigate the information for affordances in the development of perception and action. The boundaries on the affordances of reaching and grasping can be examined simultaneously in the same prehensile act (e.g., picking up an object) or in separate reaching and grasping action protocols.

Johnson and Wade (2007, 2009) investigated the judgment of action capabilities in reaching in both typically developing children and those at risk for Developmental Coordination Disorder (DCD). In the 2007 study the typical and atypical groups were asked to make a decision on two judgment tasks. First, their maximum vertical reach to a suspended ball, raised or lowered until each individual judged their reaching extent was achieved; and second, their maximum sitting height as a stool was either raised or lowered until each individual judged their sitting height was reached. In the 2008 study two groups of children similar to the 2007 study were asked to judge their maximum horizontal reach (HR_{max}), both one-handed and two-handed, under conditions of variation in foot length (standard vs. short), and variation in support surface (rigid vs. compliant). Both studies concluded that DCD children were less adept at detecting changes in the limits of their action capabilities. Making adjustments to the experimentally imposed constraints was a characteristic of the typically developing children, but something that the DCD children experienced with difficulty.

In a more recent study, Wilmut, Du, and Barnett (2017) compared static and dynamic judgments of typical and atypical (DCD) participants (matched ages 7–29 years) making visual estimates of the passability through an aperture (Experiment 1) and then actually walking through the same apertures (Experiment 2). The results showed that making static perceptual judgments (Experiment 1) was not that different with the DCD group underestimating judgments relative to the typically developing participants. In other words scaling to body size while stationary appears essentially the same when merely looking from afar. When actively asked to walk through the aperture the DCD participants showed a reliably larger critical ratio than their typically developing peers. Wilmut et al. (2017) concluded that the relationship of body scaling is different between static and dynamic contexts with the fundamental differences between the typical and atypical participants residing in the dynamic perception–action relationship.

Ishak, Franchak, and Adolph (2014) found that infants, 7-year-olds, and adults all showed sensitivity to changes in the scaling of the environment when reaching through openings of various sizes. There were, however, age-related trends in the accuracy of the reaching action. The younger children were more likely to attempt to reach through impossible openings. This study provides additional evidence for the role of learning and experience in developmental trends for the affordance of reaching.

Grasping. In a series of studies on the development of grasping Newell, Scully, Tenenbaum, and Hardiman (1989a, Newell, Scully, McDonald, Baillargeon, 1989b, Newell, McDonald, and Baillageon, 1993) examined the role of object size in the development of grip configurations in infant and young children. In experimental grasping protocols, they showed that young children's grip configuration for picking up an object was dependent on the ratio of the body scale (hand length) to the object size. Fig. 4 from Newell et al. (1993) depicts the frequency of a grip configuration (top—one or two hands) and bottom (number of digits with one hand) dependent on the object/hand length ratio. The data reveal

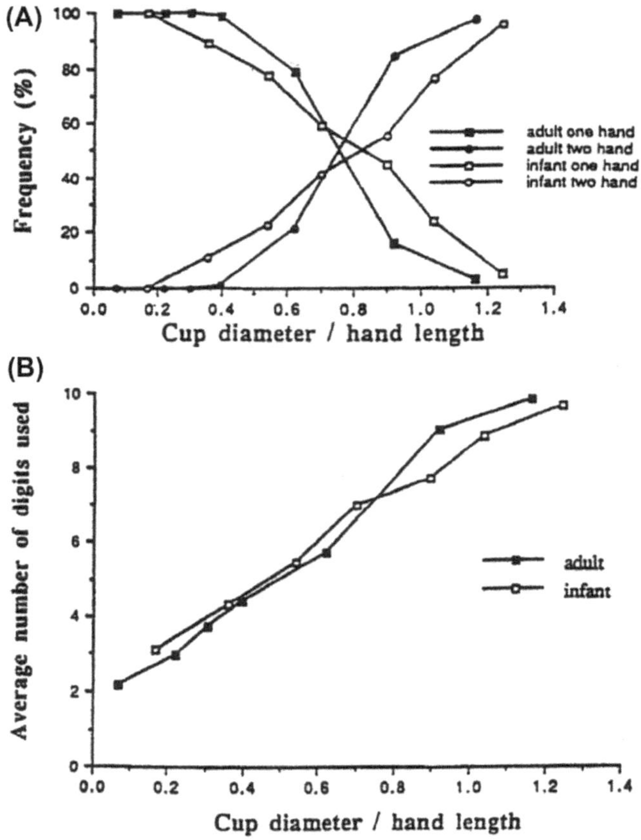

Figure 4 (A) Frequency of hand use (one vs. two hands) as a function of age group and object size. (B) Frequency of average number of digits used as a function of age group and object size. *Adapted with permission from Newell, K. M., McDonald, P. V., Baillageon, R. (1993). Body scale and infant grip configurations. Developmental Psychobiology, 26, 195–206.*

strong parallels in infant and adult grip patterns as a function of object size when the data are body scaled—that is, organized on a relative body-object scale.

In the above experiments the task goal for grasping came from either an instruction from the experimenter or was self-determined by the infant. If the grip configuration is an emergent property depending on the environment, organism, and task constraints, it should be possible to show variation in grip configuration applied to the *same* object given a different prehensile goal. Indeed, Whyte, McDonald, Baillargeon, and Newell (1994) found that infants varied their grip on the *same* object in the midrange of object size according to whether they mouthed the object as opposed to moving its base of location. This finding shows that object properties, body size, and task goal interact to determine the form of the grip configuration even in young infants. Rosenbaum and colleagues in a series of studies with adults have also shown that the task goal influences the grip configuration (underhand or overhand) to the same object (e.g., Rosenbaum, Vaughn, Barnes, Marchak, & Slotta, 1990).

In further body-scaled studies of grasping, Cesari and Newell (1999) found that including object mass in the scaling ratio added a little to the variance accounted for by limb length in predicting the grip configuration used in action. Wimmers, Savelsbergh, Beek, and Hopkins (1998) in a longitudinal study provided evidence for a phase transition in grip mode in the early development (8–24 weeks) of infant prehension. Recently, Lopresti-Goodman, Turvey, and Frank (2011) reported a general dynamical systems model of the one-to two-hand transition in grasping objects of increasing size.

Affordances in developmental context. The foregoing experimental examples show that young infants exhibit sensitivity to body-scaled properties of the environment and what they afford for action. In most of the basic perceptual-motor tasks studied, however, experience and learning typically were required in infants and young children to adapt both the robustness of the affordance and the fit of the particular coordination mode used to realize the goal. No evidence emerged for general developmental age-related effects on the perception of affordances and their mapping to movement coordinative structures. Overall, the findings reviewed here are consistent with the basic affordance construct but do not refine or extend our developmental perspective on this.

The affordance construct continues to evolve and is clearly in need of further theoretical and experimental lines of investigation. This has been the focus of work by Withagen and Chemero (2009), Withagen and van der Kamp (2010) and Franchak and Adolph (2014). All three papers extend the original Gibson (1979, p. 464) view of affordances beyond an all-or-nothing view to more of a continuum (Withagen & Chemero, 2009, p. 381). They preserve the notion that perception is sensitivity to spatiotemporal patterns in the ambient array but go beyond a fixed all-or-nothing relationship between an affordance and the information it holds for the perceiver. By way of contrast information inherent in the affordance may vary as to the precise aspects of the environmental property present.

Thus, as children develop from infancy to adolescence and beyond, Withagen and van der Kamp (2010) note "the same physical property can afford different actions to different animals and to the same animal at different points in time" (p. 601). As we have noted above the perceiver is in a constant state of developmental flux as a result of individual trajectories of growth and development. There seems to be a call for an "individual differences" view of both what information is present in the affordance and how the perceiver chooses to use such information, depending on the developmental status of that individual.

Furthermore, while Gibson (1979) sees affordances as "opportunities for action," some affordances need not specify the need for a movement. Michaels (2003) notes that a cliff, for example, may specify danger and this perception would result in avoidance. Second, affordances are present in the global array of the environment without necessarily being perceived. Thus, with essentially a separation between the existence of an affordance and the actual perception of the same, any response generated to an affordance will depend on the skill set specific to the perceiver at a particular point in time. That skill set will be a function of the timescales related to the individual's growth and development both in terms of the strength, flexibility, and perceptual-motor experiences already acquired.

Just as affordances are independent of being perceived, so perceptions and subsequent actions rely on the effectivities of the actor, which are constrained by the individual's trajectory of growth and development and the inherent constraints operating at any point in time on that trajectory. An effectivity produces an actualization of a specific affordance perceived by a particular individual, not by other individuals. Depending on where the child is located on its developmental trajectory, opportunities for action will be not only by constrained physically with respect to strength, flexibility, and coordination but also by the child's acquired perceptions, spatial cognition, social and emotional status. For example, the consequences of self-produced locomotor experience engender changes in social and emotional development, referential gestural communication, wariness of heights, the perception of self-motion, distance perception, spatial search, and spatial coding strategies (Campos et al., 2000).

All of these burgeoning abilities provide an ever-widening set of opportunities to act on the range of action possibilities present in the environment. The ability to locomote through the environment is tantamount to "crossing the Rubicon" for the developing child. Self-produced locomotion generates a greatly increased set of opportunities for action because the child now perceives and understands the influence of an ever-widening range of perceptual information and its action related consequences. It would seem that via exploration of her or his own environment the child rapidly develops both and understanding of the extrinsic constraints to action present in the environment, as well as his or her own intrinsic abilities to exploit the action possibilities present in the affordances specific to any particular context.

These developmental changes are well recognized, irrespective of the theoretical persuasion of interpretation, and illustrate the profound influence that the ability to explore has on the synergetic relationship between the overall growth and development of the individual and the environmental niche each individual inhabits. Employing an ecological analysis, we believe, will advance our understanding of the key relationship between perception and action, as well as generating important insights into not only typical development but also children who represent a range of atypical characteristics, the majority of which reflect less than optimal coordination and control abilities (Sugden & Wade, 2013).

5.4 Scaling the Environment and Equipment to Facilitate Children's Perceptual-Motor Skill Development and Safety

It is intuitive with respect to play, games, sports, and other skilled physical activities that children participate in and enjoy, that the size of the play space, apparatus, and equipment used (balls, bats etc.) must be scaled to some degree to children's bodies to derive some level of performance and skill. In the teaching of such activities this array of constraints in games and play environments can be modulated to some degree by first limiting both practice areas (smaller court or field dimensions), choosing smaller implements (ball size, racket, and bat size), and reducing the number of players in a team. There is a growing interest in the scaling of the environment in the teaching of sport skills to children (Araujo, Davids, Bennett, Button, & Chapman, 2004).

A still influential scheme for the scaling of the task constraints in motor skills with children is that developed by Bunker and Thorpe (1982) under the banner of what is now known as "teaching games for understanding" or the "small games" approach. The foundational idea was to scale down the playing space, equipment size and number of players to fit the body size, physical capacity, and skill level of children. This basic concept is now increasingly used in teaching physical education and sport and is widely implemented in particular in teaching soccer to young children, though the principles can apply to all sports, including rugby, basketball, and tennis. The demands of the playing space, equipment, number of teammates, opponents, and the complexity of the rules can gradually be enhanced to fit the evolving functional capacity of the developing child.

Despite the enthusiasm of the intuitive foundation for this approach to body scaling the niche in physical activity games, there is limited research on the dynamic principles of this body scaling and the resultant positive aspects of scaling the respective game to the child. These limitations are relevant not only for the theory of body scale and motor skill but also because there are interesting considerations for the learning and transfer of perceptual-motor skills. There are also potential short-term negative challenges of adapting to the change up of the scaling properties to the regular game conditions established for adults.

From a dynamical systems perspective, the Principle of Similitude (see for example Kugler & Turvey, 1987) operates such that children's skill acquisition is subject to changes in the growth of the child (limb length and mass). It is important that the functional system properties do not vary beyond a critical value of the scaled relationships so as to maintain "similarity." Konczak (1990) noted that the limb system involved in a coordinated action (e.g., kicking a soccer ball) is constrained by the size (mass) of the soccer ball and the physical characteristics of the actor. Beyond a critical value of size and mass, skill learning would be severely constrained by the size of the ball, the foot size of the kicker, and her or his overall limb length. These dimensions represent the coordination of what might be referred to as components of the "striking system." It is assumed that similar physical principles hold for other classes of action.

The overall scope of research on how limitations of scale act as a constraint on motor skill acquisition, especially in a sport context, is limited.

Concerning soccer balls, a ball designed and produced in South America ("Futebol de Salao" or FDS) allows manipulation of ball pressure, weight, and density. All of these changes can influence both safety aspects and also the skill acquisition of young soccer players. As reported by Araujo et al. (2004), the effects of the FDS soccer ball have to date shown mixed results as to facilitating skill learning. Likewise, Beak, Davids, and Bennett (2002) noted that variation in the size of tennis rackets was insufficient to account for the range of moments of inertia produced across the larger variation in growth and development of the children using such rackets.

In addition to such principles of scale being critical in the acquisition of motor skills, anthropometric considerations must also operate with respect to safety. If the equipment is too large or too heavy, the consequences of children interacting with such objects can lead to serious injury. The more recent concerns about concussion in sport, especially when young children are the participants, for example, inform the current debate with respect to children heading a soccer ball that may be heavy enough to cause brain injury. As a response, soccer balls are now manufactured and scaled in varying sizes, and of material that limits changes in mass by not absorbing moisture and has a lower coefficient of restitution. While not eliminating completely any incidence of a concussion, contemporary equipment design is now applying physical principles that would limit the occurrence of such incidents. Nevertheless, the American Academy of Pediatrics (2000) recommends the teaching of the proper technique for heading a soccer ball for child soccer players.

While play is an important element that allows exploration, especially for young children, the design of play areas from a scale perspective adhere primarily to the guiding principles published by the US Consumer Product Safety Commission (2015). These guidelines designate safety concerns for essentially three age groups of children; 6–23 months; 2–5 years; and 5–12 years. The recommendations speak to the nature of the equipment, fixed or stationary, height off the ground and the materials from which the equipment is constructed. There appears to be a general consideration of changes in growth and development captured in the three age groups designated for the types of play equipment installed in a play area.

The majority of the recommendations focus on safety and liability issues, both for the equipment manufacturer and the organization responsible for the administration of the play area. This is not to say that research on children's play does not exist (cf. Ellis, 1978, 2011) but merely to point out that the research emphasis is on the behavioral, cognitive, and social benefits of play behavior, and less on direct consideration of scaling the relationship between child and play apparatus, other than the design recommendations of the US Consumer Product Safety Commission.

6. CONCLUDING COMMENTS

Body scale and the timescale of its change (growth) have been shown to relate to the emergence and dissolution of the fundamental skills in infancy, the perception of what an environment affords functionally for action, together with the emerging patterns of movement coordination. A central issue for development is the mapping of the timescale of change in physical growth to the timescale of change in the acquisition of perceptual-motor skills. Here we have developed the hypothesis that an imbalance in these timescales of change can lead to performance deficits in perceptual-motor skills as exemplified in the case of clumsiness observed in the adolescent growth spurt. The developmental trajectories of these body-scaled influences in perceptual-motor skill are deserving of more systematic experimental investigation.

The individual's perceptual sensitivity to the environment has been shown to be a key consideration in perceptual-motor development in addition to the constraints that arise from changes in physical growth and the concomitant effects of body scale. The perception—action synergy and the changing ability to successfully execute a specific motor skill are directly tied to the affordance—perception relationship that is another aspect of a constraint to action. Affordances as "opportunities for action" (Gibson, 1979) are not in dispute among the ecological community, but there exists variation in interpreting how the actor might respond to an affordance.

Franchak and Adolph (2014) also draw our attention to the units of measurement, both intrinsic and extrinsic, used to describe an affordance. For example, Warren and Whang (1987) used the ratio of shoulder width and how much a person turns to successfully negotiate a doorway. Recording shoulder width is a "static" geometric unit of measurement and does not reflect any individual variation in the dynamic aspects of the task such as an individual's body sway while in motion. This lateral sway can influence the spatial requirements in addition to an overall group-derived ratio between shoulder width and how much people turn to pass through a gap. Franchak and Adolph (2014) argue that the use of dynamic (extrinsic) units produces a probabilistic range of success rather than a single binary value of how much the individual must turn to succeed. This latter "probabilistic" view suggests that a range of possible responses fits nicely with the child's changing trajectory of physical growth, body scale, strength, and flexibility. Developmental change over time produces opportunities to exploit the affordance, producing increased levels of coordination and control.

Finally, the differences between scale-based static perceptual judgments discussed above (Johnson & Wade, 2007, 2009; Warren & Whang, 1987; Wilmut et al., 2017) and the changes in those judgments when the individual is moving invoke the idea of movement or muscle sense as an important, yet often overlooked, source of perceptual information. Given the empirically reliable differences between static and dynamic perceptual judgments, a fruitful direction for future research may be a more intense focus on perception in action. In their article on muscle sense, Carello and Turvey (2004) quote Sir Charles Bell (1826) whose statement seems an appropriate end to this chapter:

> *In standing, walking, and running, every effort of the voluntary power, which gives motion to the body, is directed by a sense of the condition of the muscles, and without this sense we could not regulate their actions (p. 167).*

REFERENCES

Adolph, K. E., Eppler, M. A., & Gibson, E. J. (1993). Crawling versus walking, infants' perception of affordances for locomotion over sloping surfaces. *Child Development, 64*, 1158–1174.

Alexander, R. M. (1992). *The human machine*. New York: Columbia University Press.

American Academy of Pediatrics. (2000). Injuries in youth soccer: A subject review. *Pediatrics, 105*(3 Pt 1).

Anderson, D. I., Campos, J. J., Witherington, D. C., Dahl, A., Rivera, M., He, M., et al. (2013). The role of locomotion in psychological development. *Frontiers in Psychology, 4*, 440.

Araujo, D., Davids, K., Bennett, S., Button, C., & Chapman, G. (2004). Emergence of sport skills under constraints. In A. M. Williams, & N. J. Hodges (Eds.), *Skill acquisition in sport: Research, theory and practice* (pp. 413–430). London: Routledge.

Bayley, N. (1936). The development of motor abilities during the first three years: A study of sixty-one infants tested repeatedly. *Monographs of the Society for Research in Child Development, 1*(1), 1–26.

Beak, S., Davids, K., & Bennett, S. (2002). Child's play: Children's sensitivity to haptic information in perceiving affordances of rackets for striking a ball. In J. E. Clark, & J. Humphreys (Eds.), *Motor development: Research and reviews* (Vol. 2). Reston, VA: NASPE.

Bell, C. (1826). On the nervous circle which connects the voluntary muscles with the brain. *Philosophical Transactions of the Royal Society of London, 116*, 163–173. No. 1/3(1826).

Bernstein, N. A. (1967). *The coordination and regulation of movements*. London: Pergamon Press.

Bernstein, N. A. (1996). On dexterity and its development. In M. Latash, & M. T. Turvey (Eds.), *Dexterity and its development* (pp. 3–244). Mahwah, NJ: Lawrence Erlbaum Associates.

Brody, S. (1945). *Bioenergetics and growth*. New York: Reinhold.

Bruinincks, R. H., & Bruinincks, B. D. (2007). *Bruinincks-oseretsky test of motor performance* (2nd ed.). Minneapolis, MN: American Guidance Service.

Bunker, D., & Thorpe, R. (1982). A model for the teaching of games in secondary school. *Bulletin of Physical Education, 18*, 5–8.

Campos, J. J., Anderson, D. I., Barbu -Roth, M. A., Hubbard, E. M., Hertenstein, M. J., et al. (2000). Travel broadens the mind. *Infancy, 1*, 149–219.

Carello, C., & Turvey, M. T. (2004). Physics and psychology of the muscle sense. *Current Directions in Psychological Science, 13*, 25–28.

Carvalho, R. P., Tudella, E., Caljouw, S. R., & Savelsbergh, G. H. (2008). Early control of reaching: Effects of experience and body orientation. *Infant Behavior and Development, 31*, 23–33.

Castetbon, K., & Andreyeva, T. (2012). Obesity and motor skills among 4 to 6 year-old children in the United States: Nationally – representative surveys. *BMC Pediatrics*, 12–28.

Centers for Disease Control, Prevention. (2000). *National center for health statistics cdc growth charts: United States*. www.cdc.gov/growthcharts.htm.

Cesari, P., & Newell, K. M. (1999). The scaling of human grip configurations. *Journal of Experimental Psychology: Human Perception and Performance, 25*, 927–935.

Challis, J. H. (2018). Body size and movement. *Kinesiology Review* (in press).

Chemero, A. (2009). *Radical embodied cognitive science*. Boston, MA: MIT Press.

Clark, A. (1997). *Being there: Putting brain, body and world together again*. Cambridge, MA: MIT Press.

Cope, E. D. (1885). On the evolution of the vertebra. *The American Naturalist, 19*, 140–148.

Demetre, J. D., et al. (1992). Errors in young children's decisions about traffic gaps: Experiments with roadside simulations. *British Journal of Psychology, 83*, 189–202.

D'Hondt, E., Deforche, B., De Bourdeaudhuij, I., & Lenoir, M. (2008). Childhood obesity affects fine motor skill performance under different postural constraints. *Neuroscience Letters, 440*, 72–75.

Ellis, M. J. (1978). *Activity and play of children: International research monograph series*. Englewood Cliffs, NJ: Prentice Hall.

Ellis, M. J. (2011). *Why people play*. Englewood Cliffs, NJ: Englewood Cliffs, 1973. Japanese Edition, Prentice Hall International, via REMEI SHOBO, Tokyo, 1977. Sagamore Publishing LLC, Urbana, IL 1973 Edition re-issued 2011.

Franchak, J. M., & Adolph, K. E. (2012). What infants know and what they do: Perceiving possibilities for walking through openings. *Developmental Psychology, 48*, 1254–1261.

Franchak, J. M., & Adolph, K. E. (2013). Gut estimates: Pregnant women adapt to changing possibilities for squeezing through doorways. *Attention, Perception, & Psychophysics, 76*, 460–472.

Franchak, J. M., & Adolph, K. E. (2014). Affordances as probabilistic functions: Implications for development, perception and decisions for action. *Ecological Psychology, 26*(1–2), 109–124.

Franchak, J. M., Celano, E. C., & Adolph, K. E. (2012). Perception of passage through openings depends on the size of the body in motion. *Experimental Brain Research, 223*, 301–310.

Franchak, J. M., van der Zalm D. D., & Adolph, K. E. (2010). Learning by doing: Action performance facilitates affordance perception. *Vision Research, 50*, 2758–2765.
Galton, F. (1904). Eugenics: Its definition, scope and aims. *The American Journal of Sociology, 10*, 1–6.
Gibson, J. J. (1979). *The ecological approach to visual perception.* Boston: Houghton Mifflin.
Gibson, E. J. (1982). The concept of affordances in development; the renaissance of functionalism. In W. A. Collins (Ed.), *The concept of development. Minnesota Symposium on Child Psychology* (Vol. 15). Hillsdale, NJ: Erlbaum.
Gibson, E. J. (1988). Exploratory behavior in the development of perceiving, acting and the acquiring of knowledge. *Annual Review of Psychology, 39*, 1–41.
Gould, S. J. (1966). Allometry and size in ontogeny and phylogeny. *Biological Reviews of the Cambridge Philosophical Society, 41*, 587–640.
Hackney, A. L., Cinelli, M. E., & Frank, J. S. (2015). Does the passability of aperture change when walking through human versus pole obstacles? *Acta Psychologica, 162*, 62–68.
Haywood, K. M., & Getchell, N. (2009). *Life span motor development* (5th ed.). Champaign, IL: Human Kinetics.
Henderson, S. E., Sugden, D. A., & Barnett, A. (2007). *Movement assessment battery for children 2.Kit and manual.* London: Harcourt Assessment/Pearson.
Hills, A. P., & Parker, A. W. (1991). Gait characteristics of obese children. *Archives of Physical Medicine and Rehabilitation, 72*, 403–407.
von Hofsten, C. (1979). Development of visually directed reaching: The approach phase. *Journal of Human Movement Studies, 5*, 160–178.
von Hofsten, C., & Lindhagen, K. (1979). Observations on the development of reaching for moving objects. *Journal of Experimental Child Psychology, 28*, 158–173.
Huxley, J. S. (1932). *Problems in relative growth.* London: Methuen.
Ishak, S., Franchak, J. M., & Adolph, K. E. (2014). Perception-action development from infants to adults: Perceiving affordances for reaching through openings. *Journal of Experimental Child Psychology, 117*, 92–105.
Jensen, R. K. (1981). The effect of a 12-month growth period on the body moments of inertia of children. *Medicine & Science in Sports & Exercise, 13*, 238–242.
Jensen, R. K. (1986). The growth of children's moment of inertia. *Medicine & Science in Sports & Exercise, 18*(2), 440–445.
Johnson, D. C., & Wade, M. G. (2007). Judgment of action capabilities in children at risk for developmental coordination disorder. *Disability & Rehabilitation, 29*, 33–45.
Johnson, D. C., & Wade, M. G. (2009). Children at risk for developmental coordination disorder: Judgement of changes in action capabilities. *Developmental Medicine and Child Neurology, 51*, 397–403.
Kaplan, J. P., Liverman, C. T., & Kraak, V. I. (Eds.). (2005). *Preventing childhood obesity: Health in balance.* Washington, DC: The National Academies Press.
Keogh, J., & Sugden, D. (1985). *Movement skill development.* New York: Macmillan.
King, A. C., Challis, J. H., Bartok, C., Costigan, F. A., & Newell, K. M. (2012). Obesity mediates mechanical and strength influences on postural control in adolescents. *Gait & Posture, 35*, 261–265.
Konczak, J. E. (1990). Toward an ecological theory of motor development: The relevance of the Gibsonian approach to vision for motor development research. In J. E. Clark, & J. H. Humphreys (Eds.), *Advances in Motor development research* (Vol. 3, pp. 201–224). New York: AMS Press.
Konczak, J., Meeuwsen, H. J., & Cress, M. E. (1992). Changing affordances in stair climbing: The perception of maximum climbability in young and older adults. *Journal of Experimental Psychology: Human Perception and Performance, 18*, 691–697.

Kretch, K. S., & Adolph, K. E. (2013). No bridge too high: Infants decide whether to cross based on the probability of falling not the severity of the potential fall. *Developmental Science, 16*, 336–351.

Kugler, P. N. (1986). A morphological perspective on the origin and evolution of movement patterns. In M. G. Wade, & H. T. A. Whiting (Eds.), *Motor development in children: Aspects of coordination and control* (pp. 459–525). Boston: Martinus Nijhoff.

Kugler, P. N., Kelso, J. A. S., & Turvey, M. T. (1980). On the concept of coordinative structures as dissipative structures: I. Theoretical lines of convergence. In G. E. Stelmach, & J. Requin (Eds.), *Tutorials in motor behavior* (pp. 1–49). New York, NY: North–Holland.

Kugler, P. N., & Turvey, M. T. (1987). *Information, natural law, and the self-assembly of rhythmic movement*. Hillsdale, NJ: Erlbaum.

Lampl, M. (2009). Human growth from the cell to organism: Saltations and integrative physiology. *Annals of Human Biology, 36*, 478–495.

Lampl, M. (2012). Perspectives on modelling human growth: Mathematical models and growth biology. *Annals of Human Biology, 39*, 342–351.

Lampl, M., Veldhuis, J. D., & Johnson, M. L. (1992). Saltation and stasis: A model human growth. *Science, 258*, 801–803.

Lebiedowska, M. K., & Polisiakiewicz, A. (1997). Changes in the lower leg moment of inertia due to child's growth. *Journal of Biomechanics, 30*(7), 723–728.

Lopresti-Goodman, S. M., Turvey, M. T., & Frank, T. D. (2011). Behavioral dynamics of the affordance "graspable". *Attention, Perception, & Psychophysics, 73*, 1948–1965.

Malina, R. M., Bouchard, C., & Bar-Or, O. (2004). *Growth, maturation, and physical activity* (2nd ed.). Champaign, IL: Human Kinetics.

McMahon, T. A. (1975). Allometry and biomechanics: Limb bones in adult ungulates. *The American Naturalist, 109*, 547–563.

McMahon, T. A., & Bonner, J. T. (1983). *On size and life*. New York: Freeman.

Michaels, C. F. (2003). Affordances: Four points of debate. *Ecological Psychology, 15*, 135–148.

Michaels, C. F., & Carello, C. (1981). *Direct perception*. Englewood Cliffs, NJ: Prentice-Hall.

Michaels, C. F., & Isenhower, R. W. (2008). Direct learning in dynamic touch. *Journal of Experimental Psychology: Human Perception and Performance, 34*, 944–957.

Newell, K. M. (1984). Physical constraints to development of motor skills. In J. R. Thomas (Ed.), *Motor development during childhood and adolescence* (pp. 105–120). Minneapolis, MN: Burgess.

Newell, K. M. (1986). Constraints on the development of coordination. In M. G. Wade, & H. T. A. Whiting (Eds.), *Motor skill acquisition in children: Aspects of coordination and control* (pp. 341–360). Amsterdam, Netherlands: Martinies NIJHOS.

Newell, K. M., & Cesari, P. (1998). Body scale and the development of hand form and function in prehension. In K. J. Connolly (Ed.), *The psychobiology of the hand* (pp. 162–176). Lavenham, Suffolk: Lavenham Press.

Newell, K. M., & Jordan, K. (2007). Task constraints and movement organization: A common language. In W. E. Davis, & G. D. Broadhead (Eds.), *Ecological task analysis and movement*. Champaign, IL: Human Kinetics.

Newell, K. M., & Liu, Y.-T. (2014). Dynamics of motor learning and development across the lifespan. In P. C. M. Molenaar, R. Lerner, & K. M. Newell (Eds.), *Handbook of developmental systems theory and methodology* (pp. 316–342). New York, NY: Guilford Publications.

Newell, K. M., Liu, Y.-T., & Mayer-Kress, G. (2001). Time scales in motor learning and development. *Psychological Review, 108*, 57–82.

Newell, K. M., Liu, Y.-T., & Mayer-Kress, G. (2009). Time scales in connectionist and dynamical systems approaches to learning and development. In J. P. Spencer, M. S. C. Thomas, & J. L. McClelland (Eds.), *Toward a unified theory of development? Connectionism and dynamic systems theory re-considered* (pp. 119–138). New York: Oxford University Press.
Newell, K. M., McDonald, P. V., & Baillageon, R. (1993). Body scale and infant grip configurations. *Developmental Psychobiology, 26*, 195–206.
Newell, K. M., Scully, D. M., McDonald, P. V., & Baillargeon, R. (1989b). Task constraints and infant grip configurations. *Developmental Psychobiology, 22*, 817–832.
Newell, K. M., Scully, D. M., Tenenbaum, F., & Hardiman, S. (1989a). Body scale and the development of prehension. *Developmental Psychobiology, 22*, 1–13.
Norval, M. A. (1947). Relationship of weight and length of infants at birth to the age at which they begin to walk alone. *The Journal of Pediatrics, 30*, 676–678.
Ogden, C. L. (2016). Trends in obesity prevalence among children and adolescents in the United States, 1988-1994 through 2013-2014. *Journal of the American Medical Association, 315*, 2292–2299.
O'Neal, E. E., Jiang, Y., Franzen, L. J., Rahimian, P., Yon, J. P., Keaney, J. K., et al. (2018). Changes in perception-action tuning over long time scales: How children and adults perceive and act on dynamic affordances when crossing roads. *Journal of Experimental Psychology: Human Perception and Performance, 44*, 18–26.
O'Neal, E. E., Plumert, J. M., McClure, L. A., & Schwebel, D. C. (2016). The role of body mass index in child pedestrian injury risk. *Accident Analysis & Prevention, 90*, 29–35.
Out, L., van Soest, A. J., Savelsbergh, G. J., & Hopkins, B. (1998). The effect of posture on early reaching movements. *Journal of Motor Behavior, 30*, 260–272.
Pathare, N., Haskvitz, F. M., & Selleck, M. (2013). Comparison of measures of physical performance among young children who are healthy weight, overweight, or obese. *Pediatric Physical Therapy, 25*, 291–296.
Petersen, G. (1967). *Atlas for somatotyping children with a scheme of somatotypes in children*. Springfield, IL: Thomas.
Quetelet, A. (1842). *A treatise on man and the development of his faculties*. Edinburgh: William & Robert Chambers.
Riddiford-Harland, D. L., Steele, J. R., & Baur, L. A. (2006). Upper and lower limb functionality: Are these compromised in obese children? *International Journal of Pediatric Obesity, 1*, 42–49.
Robins, W. J., Brody, S., Hogan, A. G., Jackson, C. M., & Greene, C. W. (1928). *Growth*. New Haven, Conn: Yale University Press.
Rosenbaum, D. A., Vaughan, J., Barnes, H. J., Marchak, F., & Slotta, J. (1990). Constraints on action selection: Overhand versus underhand grips. In M. Jeannerod (Ed.), *Attention and performance XIII* (pp. 321–342). Hillsdale, NJ: Lawrence Erlbaum.
Savelsbergh, G., van der Maas, H., & van Geert, P. (Eds.). (1999). *Non-linear developmental processes*. Amsterdam, Netherlands: Royal Netherlands Academy of Arts and Sciences.
Sheldon, W. H., Stevens, S. S., & Tucker, W. B. (1940). *The varieties of human physique*. New York: Harper.
Shirley, M. M. (1931). The first two years: A study of twenty-five babies. In *Postural and locomotor development* (Vol. 1). Minneapolis: University of Minnesota Press.
Shuttleworth, F. (1939). The physical and mental growth of girls and boys age six to nineteen in relation to age at maximum growth. *Monographs of the Society of Child Development, 4*(3).
Sigmundsson, H. (2005). Disorders of motor development (clumsy child syndrome). *Journal of Neural Transmission Supplement, 69*, 51–68.

Stahl, W. R. (1962). Similarity and dimensional methods in biology. *Science, 137*, 205–212.
Sugden, D., & Wade, M. (2013). *Typical and atypical motor development*. London, UK: Mac Keith Press.
Sugovic, M., Turk, P., & Witt, J. K. (2016). Perceived distance and obesity: It's what you weigh, not what you think. *Acta Psychologica, 165*, 1–8.
Tanner, J. (1962). *Growth in adolescence* (2nd ed.). , Oxford: Blackwell.
Thelen, E., & Fisher, D. M. (1982). Newborn stepping: An explanation for a "disappearing reflex." *Developmental Psychology, 18*, 760–775.
Thelen, E., Fisher, D., & Ridley-Johnson, R. (2002). The relationship between physical growth and a newborn reflex. *Infant Behavior and Development, 25*, 72–85.
Troiano, R., Flegal, K. M., Kuczmarski, R. J., & Campbell, S. M. (1995). Overweight prevalence and trends for children and adolescents. The National health and nutritional examination surveys, 1963 to 1991. *Archives of Pediatric Adolescent Medicine, 149*, 1085–1091.
Turvey, M. T. (1990). Coordination. *American Psychologist, 45*, 938–953.
Turvey, M. T. (1992). Ecological foundations of cognition: Invariants of perception and action. In H. L. Pick, P. van den Broek, & D. C. Knill (Eds.), *Cognition: Conceptual, and methodological issues* (pp. 85–117). Washington, DC: American Psychological Association.
Turvey, M. T., & Carello, C. (1995). Dynamic touch. In W. Epstein, & S. Rogers (Eds.), *Perception of space and motion: Vol. V. Handbook of perception and cognition* (pp. 401–490). San Diego: Academic Press.
Turvey, M. T., & Carello, C. (2011). Obtaining information by dynamic (effortful) touching. *Philosophical Transactions of the Royal Society of London B Biological Sciences, 366*, 3123–3132.
Turvey, M. T., Shaw, R. E., Reed, E., & Mace, W. (1981). Ecological laws of perceiving and acting: In reply to Fodor and Pylyshyn (1981). *Cognition, 9*, 237–304.
Ulrich, B. D., Thelen, E., & Niles, D. (1990). Perceptual determinants of action: Stair-climbing choices of infants and toddlers. In J. E. Clark, & J. H. Humphrey (Eds.), *Advances in motor development research 3* (pp. 1–15). New York: AMS Press.
US Consumer Product Safety Commission.(2015).
Van der Meer, A. L., van der Weel, F. R., & Lee, D. N. (1995). The functional significance of arm movements in neonates. *Science, 267*, 693–695.
Wade, M. G., & Kazeck, M. (2018). Developmental coordination disorder and its cause: The road less travelled. *Human Movement Science, 57*, 489–500.
Warren, W. H. (1984). Perceiving affordances: Visual guidance of stair climbing. *Journal of Experimental Psychology: Human Perception and Performance, 10*, 683–703.
Warren, W. H., & Whang, S. (1987). Visual guidance of walking through apertures: Body-scaled information for guidance. *Journal of Experimental Psychology: Human Perception and Performance, 13*, 371–383.
Whyte, V., McDonald, P. V., Baillargeon, R., & Newell, K. M. (1994). Mouthing and grasping of objects by young infants. *Ecological Psychology, 6*, 205–218.
Wilmut, K., Du, W., & Barnett, A. (2017). Navigating through apertures: Perceptual judgements and actions of children with developmental coordination disorder. *Developmental Science, 20*. #6.
Wimmers, R. H., Savelsbergh, G. J., Beek, P. J., & Hopkins, B. (1998). Evidence for a phase transition in the early development of prehension. *Developmental Psychobiology, 32*, 235–248.
Withagen, R., & Chemero, A. (2009). Naturalizing perception: Developing the Gibsonian approach to perception along evolutionary lines. *Theory & Psychology, 19*, 363–389.

Withagen, R., & van der Kamp, J. (2010). Towards a new ecological conception of perceptual information: Lessons from a developmental systems perspective. *Human Movement Science, 29*, 149–163.

World Health Organization. (1995). *Physical status: The use and interpretation of anthropometry*. Geneva: World Health Organization. Technical Report series, No. 854.

Young, D. S., & Lee, D. N. (1987). Training children in road crossing skills using a roadside simulation. *Accident Analysis & Prevention, 19*, 327–341.

CHAPTER EIGHT

A Perception—Action Approach to Understanding Typical and Atypical Motor Development

Jill Whitall*,§,1 and Jane E. Clark¶
*Department of Physical Therapy & Rehabilitation Science, University of Maryland, Baltimore, MD, United States
§University of Southampton, Southampton, United Kingdom
¶Department of Kinesiology, University of Maryland, College Park, MD, United States
[1]Corresponding author: E-mail: jwhitall@som.umaryland.edu

Contents

Advances in Child Development and Behavior, Volume 55
ISSN 0065-2407
https://doi.org/10.1016/bs.acdb.2018.04.004

Abstract

In this chapter, we ask two questions. First, can the study of the perception—action system across time offer a useful model for understanding motor development? Second, can the study of the perception—action system in children with developmental coordination disorder (DCD) inform our understanding of atypical as well as typical motor development? We begin by describing the dynamical systems perspective and a control-theoretic approach that together provide the conceptual framework for our paradigms, methodology, and interpretation of our experiments. Our experimental strategy has been to perturb one or more sensory systems and observe the effect on the motor system. The majority of the chapter explains how we employed two principal perturbation strategies: (1) removing or adding a static source of sensory information believed to be salient to the task at hand and (2) enhancing a dynamic source of sensory information either implicitly or explicitly. These strategies were employed in three different action systems: posture; rhythmic interlimb coordination, and goal-directed reaching and drawing. After synthesizing our findings, we conclude by addressing the original questions and offering future directions. In brief, we consider that perception—action coupling is an underlying mechanism/foundation/constraint of motor development in the sense that the ongoing processing of sensations and the planning and execution of movements are how the brain produces goal-directed movements. Therefore, a better understanding of how this coupling changes or adapts over time has much to offer as to how motor behavior develops across the lifespan, both typically and atypically.

In a 2011 Ted talk, the neuroscientist Daniel Wolpert asked the question, "why do humans have a brain?" (Wolpert, 2011). His answer: the brain evolved to produce complex, adaptive *movement*. Indeed, Wolpert argued that our movements are our behaviors. And the development of our behavior is, therefore, the development of our movements (i.e., motor development). We start with Wolpert's assertion to underscore the argument we make here, namely, that as we look at the development of perception—action relationships, we are looking at the development of behavior. The principles we seek, then, are the principles that would inform our understanding of the development of movement behavior or motor development and, in a consummate sense, human development.

In this chapter, two questions guide our efforts. First, can the study of the perception—action system across time offer a useful model for understanding motor development? Second, can the study of the perception–action system in children with developmental coordination disorder (DCD) inform our understanding of atypical as well as typical motor development? We take the opportunity here to concentrate primarily on reviewing our own work, not because we think it is exemplary or definitive, but because it is bound together in a common framework that has informed our work and offers a conceptual framework within which to address our questions about perception–action relationships in motor development, both typical and atypical.

1. PERCEPTION–ACTION: AN INTRODUCTION AND DEFINITIONS

For decades, perception and action were considered distinct systems that were studied independently. Indeed, since the early 20th century, those studying motor development have provided detailed descriptions of how infants and children move their bodies and limbs more accurately, smoothly, and consistently, and with greater speed and force in the service of many activities of daily living and leisure, but rarely did they consider the influence of perception until around the 1970s (Clark & Whitall, 1989). The history of why this was the case and how it came to be replaced by an approach that considers the two systems as integrated has been detailed elsewhere (cf. Schmuckler, 1993; Turvey & Fitzpatrick, 1993). For our purposes here, we view perception and action as comprising a "system" in which perception and action are mutually and reciprocally related. Understanding this system and the nature of the perception–action relationship and its development is our goal and window into typical and atypical development.

As human infants come into the world, their actions are already modulated by their senses. For example, they turn their eyes toward sound (Muir & Field, 1979), extend their hands toward an object they see (Von Hofsten, 1982), and modulate their grasp to different objects placed in their palms (Molina & Jouen, 1998). Indeed, even the movements of the fetus demonstrate the coupling of intrauterine stimuli with fetal actions (Merendonk et al., 2017). These "reflexive-like" actions are not unidirectional but are modulated right from the start. While much is made of the motor "primitives" that newborns (and for that matter, fetuses) demonstrate, the reality is that these primitives are actions that emerge in unison with the sensory systems and already demonstrate an element of integration.

At this juncture, it is important that we offer a clarification. Throughout this paper, we will use the terms perception—action and sensorimotor somewhat interchangeably. We recognize, however, that perception—action relationships are built upon sensorimotor relationships. An infant can make nonspecific or spontaneous movements, but are these goal-directed actions? We would argue that they are not. So, a movement is not necessarily an action, whereas an action is, by our definition, movement with a goal. Similarly, sensation is not perception as perception arises from sensation.

2. OUR APPROACH TO STUDYING PERCEPTION–ACTION SYSTEMS

The challenge for the human is to control and coordinate a multisegmented body in the service of achieving desired goals or actions while doing so in an ever-changing environment. Born unable to manage their complex, unwieldy body, a year after birth (on average), the typically developing (TD) human infant rises, stands, and walks independently and self-feeds.

To understand how movement develops, we have studied three action systems that represent a range of functional tasks. These are posture, rhythmic interlimb coordination, and goal-directed reaching/drawing. Posture represents those actions that keep us in a positional equilibrium (e.g., quiet standing) and in a desired orientation (e.g., leaning over to pick up a toy off the floor). Rhythmic interlimb coordination is reflected in actions where repetitive movements of one limb are coordered with the actions of other limbs (e.g., walking and drumming). A reach comprises those actions where we act on and with objects and people in our environment (e.g., to draw, or pick up a spoon). While these three action groups represent separate functions and an array of specific tasks, they all result from perception and action working together. Clearly, they bring their own unique challenges to the developing infant and child, but together they cover a wide range of functions in which to investigate developing perception—action systems.

In addition to understanding how motor development is achieved in TD children, we have also investigated children who have DCD. This term first appeared in the American Psychiatric Association's *Diagnostic and Statistical Manual* (DSM Version IIIR) in 1987. Simply put, it refers to a condition where children are both late in developing motor skills and exhibit movements of poor quality that interfere with daily life and that cannot be explained by other factors. *DSM-V* (American Psychiatric Association, 2013) states the following four diagnostic criteria: A) Learning and execution of coordinated motor skills is below age level given the child's opportunity for skill learning. B) Motor difficulties significantly interfere with activities of daily living, academic productivity, prevocational and vocational activities, leisure, and play. C) Onset is in the early developmental period. D) Motor coordination difficulties are not better explained by intellectual delay, visual impairment, or other neurological conditions that affect movement. From a research perspective (Geuze, Jongmans, Schoemaker, & Smits-Engelsman, 2001), children with DCD are objectively enrolled in a study primarily by satisfying criterion A and through scoring either below the 16th percentile (possible DCD) or below the 6th percentile (probable DCD) on a standardized test for motor impairment such as the Movement Assessment Battery for Children (Henderson, Sugden, & Barnett, 2007). Other criteria are typically assessed by more subjective measures such as parent/teacher questionnaires and interviews. Since these children have no specific etiology (American Psychiatric Association, 2013), are very heterogenous (Dewey, 2002), and are noted to have sensorimotor integration problems (Wilson et al., 2017), they provide a window into atypical motor development that is not caused by a specific insult or disease but may be enlightened by probing perception–action functioning.

3. PERCEPTION–ACTION: A FRAMEWORK

As we study human motor development, our focus is, of course, first on the changes that occur across the lifespan and on the processes that underlie these changes (Clark & Whitall, 1989). While we seek to understand how perception–action systems develop, we need to situate our discussion in a defined framework that makes explicit our terms and the relevant observations and data. Our goal is to determine the relationship between the dynamics of the sensory–perceptual system and that of the musculoskeletal system so as to provide a framework for understanding the development of stable, adaptive action patterns that result in the control and coordination of our multisegmented body in an ever-changing environment. As in all science, our conceptual or theoretical framework shapes the changes described, how those changes are characterized, and finally, how the changes are explained.

Extant frameworks for the study of perception–action systems include the dynamical systems approach (Thelen, 1990; Thelen & Smith, 1996; Turvey & Fitzpatrick, 1993) and control systems approach (Wolpert, Ghahramani, & Jordan, 1995; Wolpert & Kawato, 1998). A dynamical systems approach to the development of perception–action systems seeks to describe the formation and differentiation of dynamic action patterns based on biological and physical principles. Perception and action are viewed as mutually coupled dynamical systems (Warren, 2006). On the other hand, the control systems approach assumes that there are two internal processes—the forward and inverse models—that produce, guide, and control action (Kawato, 1999). Today, these two approaches are moving closer together (Sternad, 2000), and in our work, the two together form a basis for our framework and conceptualization.

From the dynamical systems perspective, we embrace the importance of self-organizing, dynamic relationships that are constrained by the environment, the organism, and the task at hand (Kelso, 1997; Kugler, Kelso, & Turvey, 1982; Newell, 1986; Thelen & Smith, 1996; 2006). Where appropriate, we also use some of the methodological techniques of modeling limb coordination or sensorimotor coupling using concepts from oscillatory dynamics such as phasing, stability, and entrainment (Kelso, 1997). From this perspective also, sensory input is viewed as information to the motor system and thus provides one set of "constraints" that shape the action.

The control-theoretic approach provides a framework for relating the input and output features of behavior in a dynamic "internal model" (Kawato, 1999; Wolpert & Flanagan, 2009; Wolpert & Kawato, 1998). First deployed in engineering to control machines, these models and concepts have been used in human behavioral modeling to capture the dynamic and causal relationship between sensory information and action and between the action and its sensory consequences (e.g., Kawato, 1999; Wolpert & Ghahramani, 2000). One internal model, referred to as the *inverse* model, uses the initial sensory information to derive the desired action command. A second model, the *forward* model, uses a "copy" of the motor command and predicts the sensory consequences of this action (Wolpert & Ghahramani, 2000). Like all models, these are representations and, in our case, representations of how the neuromusculoskeletal system achieves goal-directed actions through dynamic relationships between the sensory and motor systems. And as with all models, we are not attempting to "prove" them right or wrong but rather to use these models to better understand the perception–action system and its development.

4. OUR EXPERIMENTAL APPROACH

To understand any system, a scientist finds ways to "poke" or perturb the system so that the system may reveal better how it works. Indeed, this has been our experimental approach to understanding the perception–action system and its development. For our work, we have used the strategy of perturbing the perceptual system and measuring the effect on the motor system. We recognize, however, that one could also perturb the motor system and study the effect on the perception of sensory information.

Together, we have perturbed four sources of sensory system information—vision, proprioception, cutaneous, and audition (both spatial and timing) across the three different action systems mentioned earlier. We employed two principal strategies across the systems: (1) removing or adding a static source of sensory information believed to be salient to the task at hand and (2) enhancing a dynamic source of sensory information either implicitly or explicitly. Within each strategy, the role of intersensory integration also was investigated. Below, we describe each strategy, separately, for the appropriate task systems and summarize what we have learned. Finally, we return to our questions of whether studying perception–action systems have informed our understanding of typical and atypical motor development.

As we probe the perception–action systems, we are interested in the developmental changes that happen both within a single sense (intramodal) and across senses (intermodal). When sensory inputs are eliminated, added, enhanced, or diminished, how does the developing perception–action system respond? One characterization of how individuals respond to changes in the sensory input is the notion that these inputs are dynamically reweighted within the perception–action mapping so as to adapt the actions to the changing sensory conditions (Nashner, Black, & Wall, 1982). This adaptation results in a new "mapping" of the sensory input to the action (Shadmehr & Wise, 2005).

5. STRATEGY 1: REMOVING OR ADDING A STATIC SOURCE OF PERCEPTUAL INFORMATION

Our first perturbation to the perception–action relationship was to remove or add one of the senses that we assumed formed the basis of the perception–action relationship of a particular task. We hypothesized that motor performance would deteriorate or improve in the short term if a salient source of perceptual information were abruptly eliminated or added. Owing to their more stable and multidimensional perception–action systems, we expected that adults would have little disruption to their actions compared with children as they could adapt their relationships to the changes. Furthermore, we reasoned that children with DCD would show a greater performance deterioration compared with age-matched TD children, since the perception–action systems of those with DCD were assumed to be delayed or different. Finally, we also hypothesized the removal of a salient sensory source for a perception–action system might result in the reweighting of an alternative source of information such that the motor performance under investigation would not necessarily be affected. This reweighting mechanism is much like what might happen when you get up in the middle of the night and it is pitch black. If you have a mature, well-functioning perception–action system, the loss of reliable visual information would immediately result in downweighting vision and upweighting the cutaneous information from your feet or perhaps your finger tips to maintain your postural stability. One might also upweight another source of information such as sound if you lived with numerous pets and wanted to avoid tripping over their moving bodies.

5.1 Development of Posture

5.1.1 Infants

Human infants take about 5 months before they sit upright without support and about 10–11 months before they stand "hands free" (i.e., not touching any surface) (Piper & Darrah, 1994). Postural control for maintaining these upright positions requires a fine-tuned relationship between the visual, vestibular, and somatosensory systems and the muscles that control the top-heavy, multisegmented body in the upright position. To probe the perception–action relationship in the developing infant's postural control, we first focused on the somatosensory input that infants employ naturalistically, namely, touching a stable surface. Pulling themselves to the upright, the infant's first upright bipedal postures rely on the coffee table, the couch, or perhaps a parent's hand to provide biomechanical support. But as we demonstrated in infants from the onset of pulling to stand, to standing alone, to walking onset, and to 1.5 months postwalking, there is a systematic developmental course in the perception–action relationship between touch and posture (Barela, Jeka, & Clark, 1999).

Using an instrumented (with force transducers) bar that was placed at hip level and to the infant's side, infants touched (but could not hold) the surface of the rounded instrumented bar. At the onset of pull to stand, infants used the bar for support as evidenced by high vertical forces applied to the touch bar. By the time they could stand alone, the infants had already reduced their vertical forces on the bar and were using the sensory input from touch to modulate their standing sway. By the time they had been walking for 1.5 months, the touch information from the bar was being used "prospectively" or in a feedforward manner to regulate postural sway. Indeed, in another study (Metcalfe and Clark, 2000), we found that the infants with varying degrees of walking experience were using touch information provided by the instrumented bar to explore their sway parameters and subsequently, we hypothesized, were developing an accurate "internal" model that would eventually be used for walking. This internal model provided a consistent, prospective relationship between perception and action.

But what happens when there is a transition from one motor skill to another such as from sitting to walking? Is the perception–action relationship disrupted or does it easily transition to the perceptual and motor demands of the new skill? Again, we used "touch" as our window into this relationship (Chen, Metcalfe, Chang, Jeka, & Clark, 2008). Nine infants were followed longitudinally (every month) from the onset of independent sitting to the time when they had been walking for 9 months. Our findings revealed that with the onset of walking, sitting (which the infants had been doing for months) was disrupted such that the infants' postural sway during sitting was greater than it had been at any other age (before and after the transition). Clearly, the infants were recalibrating the perception–action system as the new behavior was brought on line. It was not a long disruption, but it was clearly evident. Again, we argued that the internal model was expanding to include postural control for upright bipedal locomotion. In a reanalysis of the same data, we used a stabilogram-diffusion technique to measure the time-evolving properties of the effect of touch over the 9 months of walking after its onset (Metcalfe et al., 2005). The main finding was that the effect of touch in reducing sway was constant for the magnitude of the sway variability, while the rate of variability reduction decreased over time and walking experience. This differentiation between rate and magnitude, we argued, could reflect a dual role for the sensory system in both mapping with the motor commands (a basic internal model) and in adjusting to experience and growth, i.e., fine-tuning the model over time.

As we have described, this work used static and single sensory sources with infants limited to the "touch or no touch" paradigm. While this work revealed new insights into the emerging perception–action relationships and the task was highly naturalistic for infants, it was limited to the "touch" sense, salient as it may be. In a later section, we will discuss our work with dynamic and multiple senses during infancy. Next, we continue with a similar paradigm with children, where we had more opportunity to explore the richness of other sensorimotor relationships.

5.1.2 Children

If a particular perception–action coupling is not strong and multidimensional, then withdrawing a source of information would presumably result in motor difficulties. Indeed, that is exactly what happens. When children (6–9 years of age) were asked to close their eyes while standing on one foot for as long as possible, not surprisingly, they struggled to maintain a steady one-foot stand (Clark & Watkins, 1984); this was made more difficult by constraint changes in the support surface they stood on (standing cross-wise or lengthwise on a stick) or the body position they assumed (hands hanging free, hands on hips, arms folded on chest, or trunk bent over). In a later study of 4-, 6-, and 8-year-old children and adults, we combined our touch paradigm with a vision condition (eyes open, eyes closed) (Bair, Barela, Whitall, Jeka, & Clark, 2011). As with the infants, lightly touching a stationary bar had a positive effect on the postural sway of all the children and adults with or without vision. Taking away vision did not have a deleterious effect on the children's postural control regardless of whether they touched the bar. The latter finding for vision may be due to the postural task employed (i.e., parallel foot position), which differed from the earlier work by Clark and Watkins (1984) where there were more challenging postures and foot positions (one-footed and on a narrow support surface) required.

Taken together, however, these two studies would suggest that by the time children are school age or a little younger, they have a functioning perception–action system that is stable if "perturbed" by taking away a sensory input (i.e., vision) or adding one that is not usually involved in the task (i.e., touch). But what of the children who are having movement difficulties is their perception–action system stable in the face of a sensory perturbation?

5.1.3 Children With Developmental Coordination Disorder

In the same paper, Bair et al. (2011) reported a second study in which children with DCD were tested in the touch (present or absent) and vision (present or absent) conditions, although this time the participants were in a semitandem stance (one foot ahead of the other and slightly apart). Another sample of TD children was also included. The condition with vision and without light touch represent the "normal" conditions the children encounter every day. But adding the conditions in which the children were to touch lightly a stationary bar and/or to close their eyes are not typical. It was hypothesized, therefore, that the effect of light touch would improve sway in both groups as it had done previously for TD children and adults and that taking away vision would challenge the perception—action system, particularly in the children with DCD. Our findings reveal that the children with DCD have more postural sway than TD children when they are in the "typical" situation of vision and no touch and when they are in the atypical situation of no vision. However, when touch and vision are present, their sway is better than if they just had vision although their performance is still below that of TD children. Indeed, having more sensory information than normally available helped the children with DCD more than it did for the TD children and adults, suggesting their internal model was deficient compared with their TD cohorts.

5.2 Development of Rhythmic Interlimb Coordination

5.2.1 Infants

When infants have developed enough trunk postural control to stand, their next motor milestone is independent walking. This is a motor skill requiring rhythmic interlimb coordination, namely, the coordination of the two walking legs in a 180-degree phasing relationship. In an early study of newly walking babies (Clark, Whitall, & Phillips, 1988), we found that, on average, the infants were able to accomplish the same phasing pattern as adults, but with a much larger within-individual variability. However, the addition of *light* touch from a parent's or experimenter's hand had a stabilizing effect on the variability of the infant's interlimb leg coordination such that new walkers appeared as stable with touch as they were 4 weeks later without touch. This illustration of light touch modulating action in a positive manner, although not experimentally planned at the time, was the first example of a perception—action coupling with touch in walking and provides an analog to our work on the effect of touch on standing posture described above.

5.2.2 Children

Later, in children 7—8 years of age compared with adults, we employed two experimental rhythmic coordination tasks to examine perception—action coupling. One gross motor multilimb task was for participants to clap two cymbals together at the same time that they stepped in place, with the goal of timing the claps to each foot step at their own comfortable speed (Mackenzie et al., 2008). The second fine motor task was to produce bilateral antiphase finger tapping at their own comfortable speed (Roche, Wilms-Floet, Clark, & Whitall, 2011). For both experiments, we systematically manipulated vision and hearing in four conditions: normal (with vision and hearing), without vision, without hearing, and without either vision or hearing. We expected to see a deterioration of performance when sensory information was removed, with greater deterioration in the children. In both experiments, adults performed better than children, but the coordination between the clap and steps or the two fingers (relative phasing) and the consistency of each limb movement (coefficient of variation) were not affected by the differing sensory information (vision and audition) in either children or adults, thus not supporting our hypothesis. This indicates that either these two sensory sources of information were not salient for these tasks or both groups were able to equally upweight their somatosensory information to maintain the level of performance in the normal condition. The latter would indicate a well-tuned adaptive mechanism of reweighting to maintain perception—action coupling for both children and adults.

5.2.3 Children With Developmental Coordination Disorder

In the same two papers (McKenzie et al., 2008; Roche et al., 2011), we also tested age-matched children with DCD to assess whether their perception—action coupling was further impaired under the reduced sensory information conditions. To our surprise, we had the same noneffect on movement performance under the different sensory conditions despite absolute differences in motor performance between the TD children and those with DCD. In the tapping experiment (Roche et al., 2011), when we analyzed each child with DCD individually, we found that 40% performed similarly to those without DCD and that there was a subset who actually performed with less variability without vision, possibly because they could tune their internal model better without visual distraction.

That seeing one's fingers or hands/feet did not influence movement accuracy or variability is less surprising than the lack of an effect from hearing self-produced sounds. We had ensured that the fingers produced an audible click when tapping and the hands used loud cymbals when clapping so that these audible sounds could potentially be used as feedback in the conditions with hearing present. This is also surprising in that the "enhancement" of sensory information (in this case, sound or vision) did not help the children with DCD as it had done in the postural task. However, we cannot rule out that these self-produced noises might have influenced performance if we had asked the participants to pay attention to their feedback to accomplish the task. In addition, we cannot rule out that if we had specifically asked the participants to pay visual attention to their finger movements in relation to the sounds made that we might have seen an effect. Taken together with the developmental findings, we concluded that neither vision nor hearing were salient sources of perceptual information for producing these two rhythmic self-constrained coordination tasks. We doubted that any reweighting occurred because we found the same results for both sensory sources in all three groups.

5.3 Development of Goal-Directed Reaching and Drawing

5.3.1 Children

Producing accurate sensorimotor behavior depends on precise localization of the body in space that can be estimated by multiple sensory sources, especially vision and proprioception. This multisensory integration is known to change across age, but it was not known whether the development of visuomotor or proprioceptive intrasensory modulation would differentially affect the intersensory modulation. In an experiment using a two-tier apparatus with a digitizing tablet on the lower tray and a flat screen monitor on the upper tray, we tested 7- to 13-year-old children in a positional hand-matching experiment (King, Pangelinan, Kagerer, & Clark, 2010). The participants used a digitizer pen with the dominant pronated hand on the tablet of the lower tray whose position was displayed on the upper tray monitor. The participants were asked to match the position of the pen seen on the monitor with their nondominant, supinated hand underneath the digitizing tablet. By manipulating information on the top tray monitor, we were able to test the motor performance from visual, proprioceptive, and concurrent visual and proprioceptive stimuli. We then placed the concurrent visual and proprioceptive stimuli in conflicting locations to determine the relative contributions of vision and proprioception to the multisensory estimate of target positions. Results clearly revealed that the visual estimate of target position contributed more to the multisensory estimate in the younger children, whereas the proprioceptive estimate was upweighted in the older children. Additionally, regardless of age, improvement in proprioceptive, but not visual, functioning was correlated with an upweighting of proprioception in the incongruent trials suggesting that children's improvements in a unimodal sensory system may influence multisensory integration.

A subsequent study investigated the relationship between seeing a target and moving the digitizer pen to one of the multiple targets "as fast and as straight as possible" in a task known as the center-out paradigm in 5- to 12-year-old children and adults (Kagerer & Clark, 2014). The control condition, which was always first, allowed online visual feedback of the movement. In experiment 1, the perceptual perturbation was to occlude vision of the pen and target during the movement, thus forcing individuals to rely on proprioceptive feedback. In the control condition, the usual developmental trends of increasing speed, accuracy, and consistency were observed. Similarly, the proprioceptive—motor condition showed that older children and adults were much more accurate in their movement trajectory, indicating less reliance on visual feedback. Two findings were unexpected. The 7- to 12-year-olds were more variable to the ipsilateral target without vision, in contrast to being more variable to the contralateral target with vision, and accuracy to the endpoint target showed a reverse developmental trend such that adults and older children were more variable than younger children. These findings were interpreted as being consistent with the dynamic dominance hypothesis (Mutha, Haaland, & Sainburg, 2013) whereby nondominant hands are specialized for impedance control that is needed for better endpoint accuracy. Thus, the ability to form finely tuned internal models is influenced by the development of lateralization over time.

In experiment 2, the perceptual perturbation was to substitute the visual cue for an auditory cue that required spatial localization of auditory targets. Since there was no visual information available for the participant, the amplitude of the movement was not specified and only initial directional error was recorded. All groups performed relatively accurately. The lack of a developmental trend suggests that it is task experience of this specific perception—action relationship rather than other age-related factors that influence performance since auditory—motor internal models appear to be functional by 5—6 years. The two experiments together provide novel insights into both proprioceptive—motor and auditory—motor development of spatial localization. Both highlight the influence of experience in different ways.

6. STRATEGY 1: SUMMARY OF MAIN FINDINGS

The development of perception—action systems needs to be considered across varied sensory manipulations and action systems since results are both general and, in some cases, specific to tasks. Looking across the findings above, we would suggest the following summary:

1. Developmentally, adding touch (cutaneous) input stabilizes posture (and locomotion for infants) equally across all ages measured. Children with DCD are also able to use touch input.
2. Developmentally, vision is also salient for maintaining posture in infants and young adults, but less so in older children unless their stance (i.e., their base of support) is challenged. Children with DCD are affected more by loss of vision than all other groups.
3. Developmentally, vision and hearing are apparently not salient informational sources for self-produced rhythmic interlimb coordination. The same is true for children with DCD.
4. Developmentally, young children rely more on vision than proprioception in a reaching task, while older children are easily able to upweight proprioceptive information, supporting the finding of less deterioration of performance with older children when vision is removed. In addition, some aspects of reaching performance without vision are affected by the development of lateralized specialization formed by experience.

7. STRATEGY 2: ENHANCING A DYNAMIC SOURCE OF PERCEPTUAL INFORMATION

In addition to removing or adding static sensory information, we also perturbed the sensory information by enhancing its salience in a variety of situations. Removing or adding sensory information offers insights into what sources of information are well integrated and salient for the perception—action mapping, but how the information "tunes" the relationship temporally requires that we examine the dynamics of the sensory information. In these experiments, we distinguish between *implicit* sources of information where the mover is unaware that the sensory information has been changed and *explicit* sources of perceptual information where the goal is to match sensory cues that are brought to the attention of the mover. For the former, across all tasks, we hypothesized that TD infants and children would be less responsive to the dynamically enhanced cues than would adults and that children with DCD would likely be less responsive than those without DCD. For explicit cues, and specifically for auditory timing information, we hypothesized that TD children would be less able than adults to use the cues to synchronize their movements and that children with DCD would be the least able to use the explicit information.

7.1 Development of Posture

7.1.1 Infants

To examine the sensory dynamics in the perception—action relationship of postural control, we employed a "moving" rather than a stationary sensory input. In one set of experiments, we used a gently moving touch bar and in the other a moving visual display (i.e., a moving room). In both cases, we assumed that these dynamic oscillations were implicit and we did not draw attention to either set of stimuli. In our first experiment, we had infants lightly touch (but not hold) a hip-level moving bar gently oscillating medial-laterally in one of the three dynamic conditions (using touch bar oscillations at frequencies of 0.1, 0.3, and 0.5 Hz and amplitudes of 1.6, 0.59, and 0.36 cm, respectively) (Metcalfe et al., 2005). Tested longitudinally from 1 month before independent walking onset until they had been walking 9 months, infants demonstrated increasing temporal stability between the oscillating touch bar and their postural sway. That is, they increased the synchronization between the bar and their sway. Walking experience appeared to provide an opportunity for the active tuning of the perception—action relationship so as to facilitate a refinement of the temporal dynamics of this relationship.

As walking develops, sensitivity to visual surround is critical to the development of self-motion. So, would we see improved visual—postural sway coupling as infants gained more experience in walking? To test the dynamics of the visuomotor relationship, infants sat in a three-walled room with an anterior—posterior moving visual display with five varying frequency and amplitude combinations (Chen, Jeka, & Clark, 2016). Four groups of infants were tested based on the time they achieved certain postural milestones: (1) onset of independent sitting; (2) onset of independent standing; (3) onset of independent walking; and, (4) 1-year-postwalking onset. Not surprisingly, the new sitters had a highly variable relationship between the moving visual stimuli and their postural sway. Indeed, it appeared that they were not responding to the dynamic visual signal. However, after a few months of sitting exposure and from the onset of independent standing, infants were able to couple their sitting postural sway to the moving visual stimulus. And as we had observed previously with static touch (Chen, Metcalfe, Jeka, & Clark, 2007), we now observed the same with vision; namely, at the onset of walking, infants showed a transient disruption in their postural sway, suggesting a recalibration of the perception—action relationship as a new action (i.e., walking) emerged.

In addition, by varying the visual signal's amplitude, we were able to push the infants to "reweight" when the amplitude of the visual signal was so large as to be unreliable. Indeed, we found that except for new sitters, all the infants showed evidence of reweighting. This adaptive mechanism is much like what might happen visually when a train goes by very fast as you are standing on the station platform. The visual flow from the train is "downweighted" as it is perceived as too large to be meaningful to your postural stability. The ability to reweight the sensory inputs within the perception–action map is an important adaptive ability, both in real time, but also across developmental time where the "reweighting" might become a permanent change in the perception–action relationship.

7.1.2 Children

As we examine the developmental landscape for dynamic perception–action relationships in young children, how the multiple senses are related to each other and to the emerging action becomes increasingly more important. In posture, three sensory systems—vestibular, visual, and somatosensation—play critical roles in controlling and coordinating the orientation and equilibrium of the multisegmented body. Input from these three systems must be integrated and, when needed, adapted to changes within and across modalities by reweighting the sensory information. As discussed earlier, in infants we had observed within modality (vision) reweighting (Chen et al., 2016). But what happens when two modalities are presented and one is unreliable? Will the child reweight to the other sense? To answer this question, we presented children, aged 4–10 years, with simultaneously moving small-amplitude visual stimuli on a screen and an oscillating touch bar (Bair, Kiemel, Jeka, & Clark, 2007). Is the young child's perception–action mapping sufficiently robust to accommodate changes in two different sensory systems while maintaining a stable posture? Our findings suggest that the children's mapping is robust, but only first within a modality (i.e., intramodal) (present at age 4). It is not until the children are older (~10 years) that they demonstrated intermodal integration where the senses act more like a single modality rather than as separate modalities. Responses to changes in one modality (i.e., vision) are adjusted both within and across modalities. Thus, for the mature perception–action system, unreliable sensory information in one sense can be downweighted, while upweighting another more reliable sense.

7.1.3 Children With Developmental Coordination Disorder

Children with DCD are often thought to have "sensory integration" problems (Dewey, 2002). So would we find that the perception–action system of children with DCD is able to accommodate multisensory changes in a similar fashion to their TD peers? Based on their motor performance and motor learning difficulties, we hypothesized that they would not adapt well to the changing sensory stimuli or show multisensory reweighting. Secondly, if they underperform compared with their TD peers, are they merely delayed in their development or is their development qualitatively different?

To answer these questions, a sample of children with DCD, who matched the age of our TD sample described above, were tested on the same experimental protocol in which visual and touch stimuli oscillated as children were to maintain a quiet upright posture (Bair, Kiemel, Jeka, & Clark, 2012). Our findings reveal a developmental pattern that is different from their TD peers. First, the 6-year-old children with DCD were only able to reweight to touch but not to vision. It was not until they were 10 years old that they could reweight to changes in visual motion. However, even the oldest children with DCD (10-year-olds) did not demonstrate multisensory reweighting. In addition, the children with DCD had a phase lag in their response to changes in the visual and touch bar motions. Thus, the children with DCD have a different developmental trajectory for their perception–action development.

7.2 Development of Rhythmic Interlimb Coordination

In examining the development of rhythmic interlimb coordination and enhanced sensory information, we have divided the work into two sections. In Section 7.1, we report on the work we have done on providing explicit sensory cues to interlimb coordinative patterns that are familiar to participants. Then, in Section (7.2), we describe studies on how participants respond to sensory information in novel patterns of rhythmic interlimb coordination.

7.2.1 Development of Rhythmic Interlimb Coordination Using Explicit Cues

In contrast to the implicit dynamic sensory information we manipulated in the postural experiments, our first investigation of dynamic sensory information for rhythmic interlimb coordination utilized explicit auditory cues. Recall that when auditory information was self-produced in a noncue condition (Section 5.2), the information was not used by any group of participants.

7.2.1.1 Children

How adept at matching their actions to explicit auditory cues are children compared with young adults? In both the multilimb gross motor clapping and stepping task and the bilateral antiphase fine motor task described earlier, we employed auditory cueing at four frequencies with instructions to time clapping and steps (or fingers) to the beat. In the multilimb task, adults were more closely coupled to the beat than the children although even the adults were up to 15% either side of the beat (Whitall et al., 2006). Adults also demonstrated synchronized coordination between their arms and legs at all frequencies, whereas children were more likely to do so as the auditory cue frequency increased. It is not clear why children have problems with precise coordination at lower frequencies except that it may be influenced by the intersegmental joint interactions that become entrained at higher frequencies for this multilimb task.

In another study, we found that both children and adults adjusted their movements equally well to the set frequencies when tapping bilaterally (Whitall et al., 2008). Analysis of the synchronization to the beat revealed, however, that children were more variable than adults and that they tended to tap behind the beat rather than in front of the beat, which adults do, particularly at the slower frequencies. This finding suggests that children may not have yet fine-tuned their inverse internal model to produce consistent motor commands and, also, that they are not able to use information from a forward model to anticipate the beat but rely on slower feedback processing (Desmurget & Grafton, 2000).

7.2.1.2 Children With Developmental Coordination Disorder

And how would children with DCD handle the coordination between limbs and auditory signal? For the multilimb clapping and stepping task, children with DCD were similar to their age-matched controls regarding matching the beat across all frequencies (Whitall et al., 2006). However, they differed considerably in their ability to demonstrate absolute coordination between their arms and legs because, as the frequency increased, children with DCD became less coordinated between limbs rather than more coordinated. There are several related explanations for these findings. One possibility is that children with DCD are unable to access their inverse internal model quickly enough when the frequency is increased. A second explanation is that their access is quick enough, but they cannot use feedback quickly to adjust their forward model. A third is that they have not been able to build or fine-tune their inverse model to control the inertial properties of large segmental interactions of the four limbs. The last explanation would seem to have some support given our results from the study on bilateral antiphase tapping where the inertial properties (of the fingers) were minimal (Whitall et al., 2008). In the tapping study, children with DCD were equally adept as TD children at matching the frequency except for the very slowest frequency when about half the children with DCD had trouble slowing down (inhibiting their response). Being able to match the auditory cue with a tap on average, however, did not mean that children with DCD were equally as accurate and consistent. Individual tap analysis showed neither a tendency to be ahead (adultlike) or behind (childrenlike) the beat but rather an inability to synchronize consistently at all (i.e., they were extremely variable in their tap responses to the stimuli).

We interpret the findings from these two studies as suggesting that the auditory—motor coupling from explicit auditory cues is indeed impaired in children with DCD and contributes to their motor performance deficits. To examine more closely whether the children seem delayed or atypical in development, we undertook an individual analysis of their performance. We found that 20% of the children with DCD were similar to TD children, 50% were deficient in all areas (potentially developing atypically), and 30% were deficient in some areas (potentially delayed). Nevertheless, the fact that, as a group, the children with DCD were able to generally match the beat also suggests that there may be some implicit coupling with the beat, as we will see in the next section.

7.2.2 Development of Novel Rhythmic Interlimb Coordination Using Either Explicit or Implicit Cues

7.2.2.1 Children

It is well known that there are only two "stable" tapping patterns, or indeed typical forms of interlimb coordination: in-phase (0%; 0/360 degrees) and antiphase (50%; 180 degrees) (Tuller & Kelso, 1989). Can children demonstrate these tapping patterns by the age of 7 years? We designed a novel perturbation paradigm for auditory—motor coupling by asking children (7—11 years) and adults to explicitly and implicitly learn a different (new) phasing relationship between the fingers, one that was neither in-phase nor antiphase, but off-phase at 12.5% (225 degrees) (Roche, Clark, & Whitall, 2016). From preliminary work, we had established that this off-phase relationship was above the perceptual threshold of children (i.e., perceivable). That is, we knew that our participants could perceive the difference between an antiphase beat and this off-phase beat. Participants first practiced the antiphase pattern to a set audio-cued frequency that was known to be attainable from a previous experiment (Whitall et al., 2008). The new 12.5% phasing relationship was then introduced, making this an explicit perturbation. An implicit perturbation was tested by gradually increasing the phasing offset from baseline antiphase by 3.05% or 11 degrees. These changes in phasing were under the measured perceptual threshold of the children and not perceivable until 12.5% for most children. Surprisingly, children performed the new off-phase relationship in both explicit or implicit conditions as quickly as adults tested in a separate experiment (Kagerer et al., 2014). All groups reacted to the very first change in phasing relationship of 3.05% (and subsequent changes) even though this was below their own established perceptual threshold. This finding might suggest some form of implicit learning. Comparing across the studies, the adults did have a lower perceptual threshold, as well as lower levels of variability of phasing. We concluded that this "new" phasing relationship was adapted to equally by both groups, meaning that the perception–action coupling for this perturbation was not different across age groups and was in place by 7 years.

7.2.2.2 Children With Developmental Coordination Disorder

In the above experiment (Roche et al., 2016), children with DCD were no different than their age-matched peers in quickly responding to the explicit or implicit changes in phasing relationship provided by the auditory stimuli despite differences in performance for their phasing variability. To our knowledge, this specific auditory–motor paradigm was the first to demonstrate motor responses without perceptual awareness in either typically or atypically developing children. Taken together with the tapping studies in Section 7.2, we suggest that children with or without DCD and adults are able to detect and act on both explicit and implicit auditory cues that change in frequency or phasing. What distinguishes the three groups is the ability to accurately reproduce the necessary motor adjustment to the perturbed perceptual cue on every movement. Put another way, the inverse internal model appears not as finely tuned for children as adults or for children with DCD as compared with TD age-matched children.

7.3 Development of Goal-Directed Reaching and Drawing

7.3.1 Children

Using the center-out paradigm where participants draw lines between a center target and one of four (randomized) peripheral targets "as fast and straight as possible, we set out to enhance perceptual information by increasing the amount of transformation needed from viewing the visual-spatial target to the movement commands required to reach the target" (Bo, Contreras-Vidal, Kagerer, & Clark, 2006). The "normal" transformation condition consisted of being able to view the participant's hand, the pen path, and the targets throughout the condition. In this case, no transformation was needed because visual and kinesthetic guidance of the hand was present. The "aligned" condition consisted of occluding view of the hand, but seeing the pen path and targets reflected from a monitor suspended above the participant's hand (thus occluding direct vision of the hand but not excluding visual feedback). The transformation to motor commands without vision of the hand was in the same plane as the spatial map of the targets. The "vertical" transformation condition was achieved by using a computer directly in front of the individual requiring the need to transfer the vertical coordinates of the target to a movement requiring a horizontal displacement. The need for these transformations was explicit to the individual although it is unclear that individuals would use conscious processing of this fact.

In all age groups (4-, 6-, 8-year-olds and adults), movement speed, smoothness, and variability were negatively affected by the increase in the transformation; however, the rate of change among the tasks was similar in both children and adults. The young children (4 and 6 years), on the other hand, showed significantly more variability than the older children and adults. We concluded that the increased variability could be a result of imperfectly tuned parameters of the inverse kinematic model or an inability to switch between multiple models, particularly if each transformation required a different model.

In the above experiment, the task required that the nervous system estimate motor commands after transforming the visual—spatial information to accomplish the movement, a process called state estimation. In a later experiment, we looked specifically at the development of dynamic state estimation using a center-out paradigm with feedback of the movement occluded after movement initiation. In 75% of the trials (single step), there was no additional perturbation, but in 25% (double step), there was an unexpected brief (dynamic) displacement of the target (King, Oliveira, Contreras-Vidal, & Clark, 2012). Two age groups (6—8 years and 10—12 years) and adults were tested. Results of the single step condition suggested no age-related changes in speed and initial directional error. However, in the double-step condition, there were substantial age-related changes with the younger age group being more variable and consistently overshooting the displaced target. The pattern of errors suggested that they relied on delayed sensory feedback and less on feedforward processes.

8. STRATEGY 2: SUMMARY OF KEY FINDINGS

As we saw earlier, the different task paradigms again provided both similar and unique findings. As we look across our studies, we would summarize our findings as such:

1. Developmentally, all paradigms show that with increasing age and experience, there is a decrease in the variability of movement response within and/or across trials in response to the same enhanced, dynamic sensory perturbation. This is true for touch, vision, and auditory information (timing). Early longitudinal development of postural sway indicates that this variable response returns briefly as new skills are added. Children with DCD are also typically more variable than TD children in postural sway and rhythmic interlimb coordination.
2. Developmentally, all paradigms have results that indicate a reliance on feedback processing in younger children, whereas adults and older children (10 and above) are able to use feedforward processing much more effectively.
3. Developmentally, the ability to reweight touch or visual information to maintain a stable posture occurs within modality either by or before 4 years but not between these modalities until about 10 years, at which point it is adultlike. Children with DCD, however, can reweight touch by 6 years and vision by 10 years and are unable to reweight between the modalities at 10 years of age.
4. Developmentally, by age 7, children are equally adept as adults at matching the frequency of a rhythmic auditory cue, but adults can synchronize with and anticipate the beat, while children tend to be behind the beat. Surprisingly, children with DCD can also match the beat at most frequencies but are less able to actually synchronize.
5. Developmentally, children and adults respond similarly when presented with "new" visual–spatial transformations for reaching or "novel" auditory phasing relationships in tapping (either explicitly or implicitly). Children with DCD also perform similarly to TD children and adults.

9. CONCLUDING COMMENTS

We return to our original questions. How have our experiments on perception–action systems and their development contributed to our understanding of typical and atypical motor development? At one level, we can state that our summary sections list the key research findings that we consider to be relatively novel and therefore contribute to the knowledge base of motor development and that of the atypical development of children with DCD. However, we would like to make a broader comment about the usefulness of studying perception–action systems relative to motor development and human development in general.

Fundamentally, we consider that perception–action coupling is an underlying mechanism/foundation/constraint of motor development in the sense that the ongoing processing of sensations and the planning and execution of movements are how the brain produces movement behavior. Therefore, we need a good understanding of how this coupling changes or adapts over time to better understand how motor behavior develops across the lifespan. For example, the ability to adapt (or reweight) our sensory information is fundamental to actions in the real world where the sensory conditions are constantly changing induced by environmental and task constraints as well as the consequences of injury, disease, or aging processes. But as we have shown in our work, the perception–action systems of infants, children, and adults differ. Understanding these differences and how they change informs our efforts in scaffolding TD children as well as interventions for those who are developmentally delayed. As our work with children with DCD demonstrated, children who are not typically developing may not just be delayed but may be developing differently. How then might our interventions differ across the spectrum of those not developing typically?

Let us be clear, also, that our enthusiasm and efforts to understand developing perception–action systems do not mean that we believe this is the only contributing mechanism to motor development. Clearly, there are other developing systems, such as the musculoskeletal or the cognitive system, that are likely to affect how behaviors change. These and changes in other systems need to be investigated as constraints that affect the fine-tuning of "internal" models (using the control-theoretic conceptualization) or as behavioral attractor states (using a broad dynamical systems conceptualization). There is also the contribution of adaptation mechanisms on longer time scales such as consolidation, which will potentially accelerate or deaccelerate the rate of change in developing movement behaviors and will result in "learning" new perception–action mappings.

Regarding atypical development specifically, we would argue that our paradigms would be useful for other populations. They have detected differences in responding to sensory perturbations between children with and without DCD that correspond to other experiments and known characteristics of these children. In addition to our general remarks above, we have suggested that the heterogeneity of this population demands that individual analyses against a landscape of TD children are important for determining whether children are delayed or on a different trajectory (King, Kagerer, Harring, Contreras-Vidal, & Clark, 2011).

10. FUTURE DIRECTIONS

There are many potential avenues of future research including obvious ones such as extending the paradigms to older adults, carrying out further longitudinal work, or correlating each task paradigm with neurophysiological data. Here we highlight three that we think are particularly important:

1. *Perturb the sensorimotor mapping rather than the sensory information alone, which we chose to do in the above experiments.* There is an existing visual–motor adaptation paradigm that alters the existing mapping relationship (by rotating visual feedback) between seeing the target and planning the movement. This paradigm allows one to investigate: (1) how quickly and completely an individual adapts to the new relationship, as well as (2) whether this relationship is learned as evidenced by after-effects when the rotation is removed.
2. *Investigate the role of cognition in conjunction with the perception–action paradigms we already use.* For example, what role does attentional focus or intention play in whether the sensory information is salient or whether the individual is aware of the implicit enhancements of sensory information changes? In this regard, too, it would be useful to ensure that changes in sensory information are above or below a perceptual threshold for a particular sense.
3. *Investigate how to promote the learning of perception–action coupling.* Given its importance, can we promote, for example, the ability to reweight visual information in young children with DCD to potentially have them demonstrate motor behavior that is more like their peers? The suggestion here is that we already have discovered insights into the development of perception–action coupling and perhaps these insights can be utilized for interventions or methods of promoting motor development in children with and without DCD.

REFERENCES

American Psychiatric Association. (1987). *Diagnostic and statistical manual of mental disorders (DSM IIIR)*. Washington, DC: American Psychiatric Association.

American Psychiatric Association. (2013). *Diagnostic and statistical manual of mental disorders (DSM-5®)*. Washington, DC: American Psychiatric Association.

Bair, W. N., Barela, J. A., Whitall, J., Jeka, J. J., & Clark, J. E. (2011). Children with Developmental Coordination Disorder benefit from using vision in combination with touch information for quiet standing. *Gait & Posture, 34*, 183–190.

Bair, W.-N., Kiemel, T., Jeka, J. J., & Clark, J. E. (2007). Development of multisensory reweighting for posture control in children. *Experimental Brain Research, 183*, 435–446.

Bair, W.-N., Kiemel, T., Jeka, J., & Clark, J. E. (2012). Development of multisensory re-weighting is impaired for quiet stance control in children with Developmental Coordination Disorder (DCD). *PLoS One*, 7(7). e40932, 1–18.

Barela, J. A., Jeka, J. J., & Clark, J. E. (1999). The use of somatosensory information during the acquisition of independent upright stance. *Infant Behavior and Development, 22*(1), 87–102.

Bo, J., Contreras-Vidal, J. L., Kagerer, F. A., & Clark, J. E. (2006). Effects of increased complexity of visuomotor transformations on children's arm movements. *Human Movement Science, 25*, 553–567.

Chen, L.-C., Jeka, J. J., & Clark, J. E. (2016). Development of adaptive sensorimotor control in infant sitting posture. *Gait & Posture, 45*, 157–163.

Chen, L.-C., Metcalfe, J. M., Chang, T.-Y., Jeka, J. J., & Clark, J. E. (2008). The development of infant upright posture: Sway less or sway differently? *Experimental Brain Research, 186*, 293–303.

Chen, L.-C., Metcalfe, J. S., Jeka, J. J., & Clark, J. E. (2007). Two steps forward and one back: Learning to walk affects infants' sitting posture. *Infant Behavior and Development, 30*(1), 16–25.

Clark, J. E., & Watkins, D. (1984). Static balance in young children. *Child Development, 55*, 854–857.

Clark, J. E., & Whitall, J. (1989). What is motor development: The lessons of history. *Quest, 41*, 183–202.

Clark, J. E., Whitall, J., & Phillips, S. J. (1988). Human interlimb coordination: The first 6 months of independent walking. *Developmental Psychobiology, 21*, 445–456.

Desmurget, M., & Grafton, S. (2000). Forward modeling allows feedback control for fast reaching movements. *Trends in Cognitive Sciences, 4*(11), 423–431.

Dewey, D. (2002). Subtypes of developmental coordination disorder. In S. A. Cermak, & D. Larkin (Eds.), *Developmental coordination disorder* (pp. 40–53). Albany, NY: Delmar.

Geuze, R. H., Jongmans, M. J., Schoemaker, M. M., & Smits-Engelsman, B. C. (2001). Clinical and research diagnostic criteria for developmental coordination disorder: A review and discussion. *Human Movement Science, 20*(1–2), 7–47.

Henderson, S. E., Sugden, D. A., & Barnett, A. L. (2007). *Movement assessment battery for children* (2nd ed.). London, UK: Pearson Assessment.

Kagerer, F. A., & Clark, J. E. (2014). Development of interactions between sensorimotor representations in school-aged children. *Human Movement Science, 34*, 164–177.

Kagerer, F. A., Viswanathan, P., Contreras-Vidal, J. L., & Whitall, J. (2014). Auditory-motor integration of subliminal phase shifts in tapping: better than auditory discrimination would predict. *Experimental Brain Research, 232*, 1207–1218.

Kawato, M. (1999). Internal models for motor control and trajectory planning. *Current Opinion in Neurobiology, 9*(6), 718–727.

Kelso, J. A. S. (1997). *Dynamic patterns: The self-organization of brain and behavior*. Cambridge, MA: MIT Press.

King, B. R., Kagerer, F. A., Harring, J. R., Contreras-Vidal, J. L., & Clark, J. E. (2011). Multisensory adaptation of spatial-to-motor transformations in children with developmental coordination disorder. *Experimental Brain Research, 212*, 257—265.

King, B. R., Oliveira, M. A., Contreras-Vidal, J. L., & Clark, J. E. (2012). Development of state estimation explains improvements in sensorimotor performance across childhood. *Journal of Neurophysiology, 107*, 3040—3049.

King, B. R., Pangelinan, M. M., Kagerer, F. A., & Clark, J. E. (2010). Improvements in proprioceptive functioning influence multisensory-motor integration in 7- to 13-year-old children. *Neuroscience Letters, 483*(1), 36—40.

Kugler, P. N., Kelso, J. A. S., & Turvey, M. T. (1982). On the control and coordination of naturally developing systems. In J. A. S. Kelso, & J. E. Clark (Eds.), *The Development of movement control and co-ordination* (pp. 5—78). London: John Wiley & Sons.

Mackenzie, S., Getchell, N., Deutsch, K., Wilms-Floet, A., Clark, J. E., & Whitall, J. (2008). Multi-limb coordination and rhythmic variability under varying sensory availability conditions in children with DCD. *Human Movement Science, 27*(2), 256—269.

Merendonk, E. J., Brouwers, J J., De Catte, L., Hasaerts, D., Nijhuis-van der Sanden, M. W., & Kerckhofs, E. (2017). Identification of prenatal behavioral patterns of the gross motor movements within the early stages of fetal development. *Infant and Child Development, 26*(5), e2012.

Metcalfe, J. S., & Clark, J. E. (2000). Sensory information affords exploration of posture in newly walking infants and toddlers. *Infant Behavior and Development, 23*(3—4), 391—405.

Metcalfe, J. S., McDowell, K , Chang, T. Y., Chen, L.-C., Jeka, J. J., & Clark, J. E. (2005). Development of somatosensory-motor integration: An event-related analysis of infant posture in the first year of independent walking. *Developmental Psychobiology, 46*(1), 19—35.

Molina, M., & Jouen, F. (1998). Modulation of the palmar grasp behavior in neonates according to texture property. *Infant Behavior and Development, 21*(4), 659—666.

Muir, D., & Field, J. (1979). Newborn infants orient to sounds. *Child Development, 50*(2), 431—436.

Mutha, P. K., Haaland, K. Y., & Sainburg, R. L. (2013). Rethinking motor lateralization: Specialized but complementary mechanisms for motor control of each arm. *PLoS One, 8*, e58582.

Nashner, L. M., Black, F. O., & Wall, C. I. I. I. (1982). Adaptation to altered support and visual conditions during stance: Patients with vestibular deficits. *Journal of Neuroscience, 2*(5), 536—544.

Newell, K. M. (1986). Constraints on the development of coordination. In M. G. Wade, & H. T. A. Whiting (Eds.), *Motor development in children: Aspects of coordination and control* (pp. 341—360). Dordrecht, The Netherlands: Martinus Nijhoff Publishers.

Piper, M. C., & Darrah, J. (1994). *Motor assessment of the developing infant*. Philadelphia: Saunders.

Roche, R., Clark, J. E., & Whitall, J. (2016). Children with developmental coordination disorder (DCD) can adapt to perceptible and subliminal rhythm changes but are more variable. *Human Movement Science, 50*, 19—29.

Roche, R., Wilms-Floet, A. M., Clark, J. E., & Whitall, J. (2011). Auditory and visual information do not affect self-paced bilateral finger tapping in children with DCD. *Human Movement Science, 30*(3), 658—671.

Schmuckler, M. A. (1993). Perception-action coupling in infancy. In *Advances in psychology* (Vol. 97, pp. 137—173). North-Holland.

Shadmehr, R., & Wise, S. P. (2005). *The computational neurobiology of reaching and pointing. A foundation for motor learning*. Cambridge, MA: MIT Press.

Sternad, D. (2000). Debates in dynamics: A dynamical systems perspective on action and perception. *Human Movement Science, 19*, 407—423.

Thelen, E. (1990). Coupling perception and action in the development of skill: A dynamic approach. In H. Bloch, & B. I. Bertenthal (Eds.), *Sensory-motor organizations and development in infancy and early childhood* (pp. 39–56). Dordrecht: Kluwer Academic Publishers.

Thelen, E., & Smith, L. B. (1996). *A dynamic systems approach to the development of cognition and action*. MIT Press.

Thelen, E., & Smith, L. B. (2006). Dynamic systems theories. In R. M. Lerner (Ed.), *Handbook of Child Psychology. Vol.1 Theoretical models of human development* (6th ed., pp. 258–331). John Wiley & Sons.

Tuller, B., & Kelso, J. A. S. (1989). Environmentally-specified patterns of movement coordination in normal and split-brain subjects. *Experimental Brain Research, 75*(2), 306–316.

Turvey, M. T., & Fitzpatrick, P. (1993). Commentary: Development of perception-action systems and general principles of pattern formation. *Child Development, 64*(4), 1175–1190.

Von Hofsten, C. (1982). Eye–hand coordination in the newborn. *Developmental Psychology, 18*(3), 450.

Warren, W. H. (2006). The dynamics of perception and action. *Psychological Review, 113*(2), 358–389.

Whitall, J., Chang, T.-Y., Horn, C. L., Jung-Potter, J., McMenamin, S., Wilms-Floet, A., et al. (2008). Auditory-motor coupling of bilateral finger tapping in children with and without DCD compared to adults. *Human Movement Science, 27*, 914–931.

Whitall, J., Getchell, N., McMenamin, S., Horn, C., Pabreja, P., Wilms-Floet, A., et al. (2006). Perception-action coupling in children with and without DCD: Frequency locking between task relevant auditory signals and motor responses in a dual motor task. *Child, Health and Development, 32*, 679–692.

Wilson, P. H., Smits-Engelsman, B., Caeyenberghs, K., Steenbergen, B., Sugden, D., Clark, J. E., et al. (2017). Cognitive and neuroimaging findings in Developmental Coordination Disorder: New insights from a systematic review of recent research. *Developmental Medicine & Child Neurology, 59*(11), 1117–1129.

Wolpert, D. (2011). The real reason for brains. *A Ted Talk*. Retrieved from https://www.ted.com/talks/daniel_wolpert_the_real_reason_for_brains.

Wolpert, D. M., & Flanagan, J. R. (2009). Forward models. *The Oxford Companion to Consciousness*, 294–296.

Wolpert, D. M., & Ghahramani, Z. (2000). Computational principles of movement neuroscience. *Nature Neuroscience, 3*(Suppl.), 1212–1217.

Wolpert, D. M., Ghahramani, Z., & Jordan, M. I. (1995). An internal model for sensorimotor integration. *Science, 269*, 1880–1882.

Wolpert, D. M., & Kawato, M. (1998). Multiple paired forward and inverse models for motor control. *Neural Networks, 11*(7–8), 1317–1329.

Kolibri 360 GmbH
Ferdinand-Jühlke-Straße 7
99095 Erfurt, Deutschland
produktsicherheit@kolibri360.de